GOD & MONEY

GOD & MONEY

The Moral Challenge of Capitalism

CHARLES McDANIEL

ROWMAN & LITTLEFIELD PUBLISHERS, INC.
Lanham • Boulder • New York • Toronto • Plymouth, UK

ROWMAN & LITTLEFIELD PUBLISHERS, INC.

Published in the United States of America
by Rowman & Littlefield Publishers, Inc.
A wholly owned subsidiary of the Rowman & Littlefield Publishing Group, Inc.
4501 Forbes Boulevard, Suite 200, Lanham, Maryland 20706
www.rowmanlittlefield.com

Estover Road
Plymouth PL6 7PY
United Kingdom

Distributed by National Book Network

British Library Cataloging in Publication Information Available

Library of Congress Cataloging-in-Publication Data
McDaniel, Charles, 1958–
    God & money : the moral challenge of capitalism / Charles McDaniel.
        p. cm.
    Includes bibliographical references and index.
    ISBN-13: 978-0-7425-5222-7 (cloth : alk. paper)
    ISBN-10: 0-7425-5222-5 (cloth : alk. paper)
    1. Capitalism—Religious aspects—Christianity. 2. Capitalism—United States.
3. Economics—Religious aspects—Christianity. I. Title. II. Title: God and
money.

    BR115.C3M33 2007
    261.8'5—dc22   2006019039

Printed in the United States of America

∞™ The paper used in this publication meets the minimum requirements of
American National Standard for Information Sciences—Permanence of Paper for
Printed Library Materials, ANSI/NISO Z39.48-1992.

For Diane, Brian, and Austin

CONTENTS

ACKNOWLEDGMENTS

Countless conversations on the spiritual and moral consequences of economic life have inspired the contents of this book, and I am at a loss to recall all of them and their specific contributions. However, several colleagues come to mind as particularly influential. Dr. Derek Davis, my friend and mentor in the J. M. Dawson Institute of Church-State Studies at Baylor University, recommended several changes that, I believe, have enhanced the quality of the final product. Professors Barry Hankins and Daniel McGee have been an invaluable resource and guide in contributing coherence to a topic that undoubtedly is broader than most. Robert Smith and Jim McDonough also provided any number of constructive suggestions that are apparent in the finished product. Stephanie Wheatley and Amanda Napoli contributed countless hours in editing and formatting the manuscript that became *God & Money*. Special thanks are extended to Dr. James Sturgeon of the University of Missouri, Kansas City, for inspiring me as a graduate student to "follow my bliss" and to reject the conventional academic "wisdom" of specialization in pursuit of interdisciplinary education.

Finally, but most important, I would like to thank my wife, Diane, and my two sons, Brian and Austin, for their patience and support in enduring the countless inconveniences and aggravations associated with the research duties of a doctoral student and, specifically, the construction of this manuscript. Diane was supportive throughout my midlife crisis that witnessed a career change from a geek's life in information technology to the academic study of religion and politics—a Monty Pythonesque "now for something completely different." My sons inspire me to seek a Christian path to economic life that is morally redemptive and that allows capitalists of various faith traditions to engage one another with honor. My hope for their future is a world in which the quest for spiritual fulfillment and moral integrity eclipses the drive for economic prosperity.

PREFACE

This book is a radically revised version of a dissertation I completed through the J. M. Dawson Institute of Church-State Studies at Baylor University in 2002. The dissertation process was an opportunity to investigate something that had long puzzled me—the affinity of many Christian social thinkers for the Austrian economic tradition and its most prominent spokesmen, Friedrich Hayek and Ludwig Mises. My own studies of the Austrians in a graduate program under the guidance of Professor James Sturgeon at the University of Missouri, Kansas City, caused me to question how Christians can be attracted to the thought of these philosophers who fail to comprehend the transcendent essence of morality and who admit no moral guidance to civilization beyond the machinations of a "spontaneous order." While acknowledging the acumen of Hayek as a social theorist, his thought had never given me comfort as a Christian.

The puzzle of how Christians of various denominational persuasions are attracted to the thought of the Austrians led me to explore the history of American Christian economic movements and to assess how different thinkers have attempted to reconcile the moral and social teachings of their faith with economic philosophy. Reinhold Niebuhr and Christian realism stood out as something of an untapped resource for the development of uniquely "Christian" economic ideas. For all the acclaim heaped on Niebuhr as a political theorist, his economic insights have long been neglected, as demonstrated by the paucity of literature on the subject. Indeed, Niebuhr was the focus of my dissertation; G. K. Chesterton was not mentioned, and Pope John Paul II was referenced only in the context of his pronouncements on stem-cell and reproductive technologies.

Explorations of "distributism" and of John Paul's legacy as a social thinker subsequent to the dissertation led me to observe remarkable similarities in the economic views of Niebuhr, Chesterton, and the late pope. At the level of policy there are certainly differences among them and even significant alterations in the thought of each man over time regarding the market, individualism versus collectivism, and the way in which Christianity informs economic behavior. That is particularly true of Niebuhr. However, respecting core principles, what these prodigious Christian writers had to say about economic life demonstrates remarkable symmetry. Their insistence on the preservation of personalism in economic relations and on the need to structure society so as to achieve an organicism not possible in the mechanical relations of socialism or the raw interactions of industrial capitalism is consistently articulated throughout each man's career.

This book is an attempt to demonstrate these core consistencies and also to suggest that the common ideas of these three men are as close as we can get to "Christian economics." Yet it also posits that the fundamentals provided by Niebuhr, Chesterton, and John Paul often have been neglected by Christian economic theorists who instead forge dependencies on secular theories of social organization. Christians have been distracted from the economic insights of their faith not simply by Austrian philosophy but by socialism, Marxism, and other ideologies that have been influential in the development of the modern West. Christianity cannot establish unbreakable bonds with any "ism" regardless of its perceived superiority to other isms. While Christian economics comprises no system that can be implemented, it does provide a frame of reference, a philosophical attitude, and a condition of heart capable of illuminating the shortcomings of all forms of social organization. It is simply the extension of Christian virtue, morality, and compassion to economic life.

I

THE ECONOMIC THREAT
TO CHRISTIAN MORALITY

1

INTRODUCTION

One of the remarkable developments in American religious culture during the past century was the rise of Roman Catholicism as a potent institutional force in debates on social policy and public morality. Long marginalized by the perception of a "divided allegiance" between nation and pope, Catholic social thinkers are now esteemed by Evangelicals and other groups that once viewed Catholics as anathema to moral and political discourse. Catholics have become so prominent in ethical debates in the United States that one is tempted to describe contemporary religious ethics as largely an intramural struggle for the American soul. This novel attraction to Catholic thought among groups historically hostile to the tradition stems, at least in part, from what was an embarrassment of American Protestantism in the twentieth century: the decline of the once rich tradition of Protestant ethics. The legacy of the Niebuhr brothers, Paul Ramsey, Carl F. H. Henry, Walter Rauschenbusch, Francis Schaeffer, Paul Tillich, and others has dwindled to insignificance. Attempts to resuscitate the tradition today are flashes in the pan performed in obscure academic circles. This moribund state of Protestant ethics has arrived largely through assimilation—a subliminal albeit steady stream of concessions to secular theories and institutions initiated by members of mainline denominations in the nineteenth century and continued, more recently, by Evangelicals of the Christian Right. The acculturation of Protestantism has relegated to Catholic social thinkers the dominant role in sorting out the spiritual and moral consequences of the "American way of life."[1]

This transformation of American religious ethics has come at a critical time in history. Civilization is beginning to come to grips with two historical and seemingly paradoxical conclusions that were largely settled at the tail end of the twentieth century. The first, which laid the foundation for the emerging global order, is history's verdict of both the *material* and *moral* superiority of democratic capitalism to all forms of collectivism—a matter resolved dramatically in the collapse of the Soviet Union. Even among groups traditionally skeptical of capitalist institutions, there is near unanimity respecting the greater efficiency and virtue of the free market system vis-à-vis the central planning model of socialism. Reflecting on what he perceives as the classically liberal tone of John Paul II's *Centesimus Annus* (1991), social pundit Michael Novak aptly stated, "We are all capitalist now, even the Pope."[2] The second of these conclusions is gradually emanating from what Hegel described as the "universal mind," yet its implications are at least as consequential for the future world order. It is the growing realization that societies founded on principles of classical liberalism and powered by a capitalist economic system are in no fashion morally self-sustaining. Evidence from highly industrialized and technological cultures suggests that morally corrosive elements may be embedded within the intensely "subjectivist" capitalism that pervades the free world.

The latter conclusion is especially stark given the euphoria that resulted from the termination of the Cold War. Expansion of capitalist values to remote corners of the world has aided in conquering not only poverty but also human oppression in areas where such problems were particularly acute and intransigent. The development of a restricted yet vibrant market economy within the borders of the world's last remaining Communist superpower, the People's Republic of China, testifies to the finality of capitalism's triumph. Yet such miraculous accomplishments and the promise of more to come do not negate the effects of moral flux caused by the transition to what social philosopher Fred Hirsch has termed "micromorality,"[3] where the ethical burdens of human activity are systematically transferred from the foundations of institutions to the shoulders of individuals. Autonomous moral agents, acting largely independent of "traditional" institutional influences and participating in markets of high moral content, have emerged as the principal catalysts to ethical change in society.

MARKET BEHAVIOR AND MORAL CONSEQUENCES

Evidence of the phenomenon of micromorality abounds, although it is often masked by the complexity of the modern capitalist economy. William Safire, a columnist for the *New York Times*, noted the commencement of what he terms the "stem-cell gold rush" by states seeking to gain an advantage in the frenzy to harvest profits from new stem-cell medical treatments.[4] Safire observed that the "person to watch in American medical science today" is neither a doctor nor a medical ethicist but rather a California real estate developer named Robert Klein II. Klein is a "builder-financier" who heads the citizens' committee that directs the state's Institute for Regenerative Medicine, which will invest as much as $3 billion during the next decade in stem-cell research.[5] Although religious groups and medical ethicists are involved in the California initiative, the state's decision to invest in this controversial technology was decided at the polls with the passage of Proposition 71 in the 2004 general election. The structure of this emerging industry is dictating that ethical boards, religious and academic institutions, government commissions, and other institutional overseers will take a backseat to the consumer in decision making over the health, environmental, and moral implications of this new market. Moreover, the "gold rush," as Safire describes it, suggests that the decision of whether states participate is no decision at all; fear of economic loss and technical obsolescence has foreordained this "choice." The only decision that remains is that of increasingly traditionless consumers who will rely on their subjective consciences in deciding whether to partake of these new services, with little consideration as to the *aggregate* health, environmental, and moral impacts.

Another source of moral fragility in market cultures was debated within the emerging social sciences of the late nineteenth and early twentieth centuries in response to dislocations spawned by the Industrial Revolution. Those discussions centered on the existence of "cultural lags," to which Karl Marx had alluded and which became a framework for analyzing social disruptions caused by economic advance. At the very least, these debates acknowledged the true bone of contention between capitalist and Marxist theories. A common misunderstanding of history is that the central question in the global contest between capitalism and Communism has been the relative productive capacity of the two systems. However, Marx freely conceded the wealth-generating capability of bourgeois capitalism. He marveled, in fact, at its accomplishments in the opening pages of *The Communist Manifesto*, where he cites the bourgeoisie as the first social class to "show what man's activity can bring about. It has accomplished wonders far surpassing Egyptian pyramids, Roman aqueducts, and Gothic cathedrals."[6] The question for Marx concerned the *pace* of human progress and its *social* effects. Capitalism ultimately will flame out, he thought, for the reason that it conquers traditional social structures with unimaginable speed, leaving "uninterrupted disturbance of all social conditions, everlasting uncertainty and agitation."[7]

Marx underestimated capitalism's social resiliency just as history ultimately revealed Communism's defects; yet the architect of the Communist
revolution was prescient in several of his observations. The market system
does require constant *reinvention* of the modes of production, which impacts
social relations. The rapid rise of "day traders" as an economic class in the
1990s was accompanied by the decline of blue-collar workers that continues. "Creative destruction," as Marx suggested and Austrian economist
Joseph Schumpeter more fully elucidated,[8] is a reality of market economics
that points to the inevitable decline and regeneration of industries and to
the social dislocations—unemployment, class realignment, and demographic
changes—that accompany economic transformation. Webmasters appear
even as stenographers disappear, auto mechanics replaced most blacksmiths,
and many silent-movie stars could not make the transition to "talkies." Labor hangs on a technological thread that can snap overnight, making obsolete the skills of accomplished workers and replacing them with an entirely
new class of laborer that offers little more than youth and the reality of *not*
being invested in an outmoded technology. There is nothing evil in this
phenomenon; it simply stresses traditional structures in society that often
need stressing in order to maintain production at "necessary" levels.

The persistent social convulsions that Marx predicted (and that he believed would become *the* defining attribute of capitalist society) have not
been realized. Social relations within democratic capitalism have proven remarkably resilient, expanding wealth and ownership across most levels of
society and enabling individuals to traverse rungs of the socioeconomic ladder with relative ease. This fact has contributed to the discrediting of Marxist theory and our presumed arrival at "the end of history."[9] It is suggested,
however, that we may have muddled the social with the moral question to
our own confusion. Whether capitalism precipitates class conflict is an entirely different matter from whether it has qualities that contribute to the
deterioration of society's moral traditions. It seems that in answering the
former question, the latter has been muted despite a lack of congruity between them.

By any measure, the moral component to economic decision making
has escalated dramatically over the past few decades. Stem-cell technology
is a market-driven response to the scarcity of organs for transplantation and
other critical needs, yet the "creation" of transgenic pigs as laboratories for
the production of human biomaterials is unsettling to many. Bioengineer-
ing of agricultural products results from the noble human enterprise to feed
the world. In practice, it does so by employing innovations spawned by
competition, but the ethical and environmental implications of biotech-

nologies have been highly divisive throughout Europe. Even more mundane choices such as those to consume entertainment services have arguably greater moral implications than they did only a few years ago. Intense competition is spawning challenge after challenge to the tenuous ideal of an American public morality. In this regard, Janet Jackson's "accidental" exposure at the 2004 Super Bowl may not have been the singular act of an immoral individual or even an expression of values by an unusually hedonistic class; it was a market response to the "ratcheting up" of sensualism and sensationalism in the American entertainment industry as demanded by a consuming public. It was also the rational response of a worker fearing obsolescence in a profession that progressively demands more skin. Had Ms. Jackson not experienced the "wardrobe malfunction," another entertainer eventually would have. The event was a market outcome in every sense, yet the moral questions posed by this and other "transactions" in entertainment, biotechnology, and other industries are unprecedented, and they call into relief our implicit assumptions about the moral sustainability of capitalism.

Evidence of capitalism's potential to subtly reshape society's moral foundation also comes from the right side of the American political spectrum. Republican domination of the 2004 general election was hailed by many as the triumph of religious morality over the prevailing secular humanist ethos of the Democratic Party. Exit polls recorded "moral values" as the decisive issue in securing the reelection of George W. Bush and in gaining additional seats for Republicans in both houses of Congress. Yet Republican candidates demonstrated an ability to neatly partition their political campaigns and economic lives in ways that bring into question the *type* of morality that triumphed in the 2004 election. On October 10, 2004, NBC political analyst Tim Russert interviewed Colorado Republican senatorial candidate and president of the Coors Brewing Company, Peter Coors, on the network program *Meet the Press*. During the interview, Russert noted that the Coors campaign had distributed a brochure that contained the statement "Our company's values are our family's values." Yet Russert went on to quote from the *Rocky Mountain News* that the Coors Company was a sponsor of the "Black & Blue 2004 Festival in Montreal, a weeklong gay benefit" that included a "Raunch Fetish Night and a male nude revue."[10] Russert pointed out that the Coors campaign platform opposed both gay adoption and gay marriage based on its support of family values. Asked repeatedly whether he could see inconsistencies in his company's sponsorship of "male nude revues and fetish balls" and his campaigning as a "family values" candidate, Coors replied that he did not. Even better known is Vice President Dick Cheney's tenure as the head of the Halliburton Corporation at a time when the company was doing millions of dollars worth of business annually with the government of Iran, despite widespread allegations of Iranian sponsorship of terrorist activities.[11] When Cheney left the company to become George W. Bush's campaign manager and eventual vice president, he was at the forefront of those in the administration labeling Iran, North Korea, and Iraq as the "axis of evil."

This uniquely Western ability to segment our ethical lives is a trait that baffles Islamic social thinkers and some Christian ethicists as well. Americans, in particular, have achieved the ability to dissociate their economic activities from their moral consciences; there is little comprehension today that commercial behavior influences public morality. The prevailing American attitude toward conduct in the economic realm is perhaps best summarized by a popular advertising slogan for the city of Las Vegas: "What happens here, stays here." This book will demonstrate that nothing could be farther from the truth.

CHRISTIAN ECONOMIC CONSERVATISM
AND THE INFLUENCE OF AUSTRIAN LIBERALISM

Recent technological advances in combination with perceived moral decline have once again presented Christianity and other religions with a moment of decision on how (or whether) they will involve themselves in the ethical issues of our time. Many Christians, however, are turning "priestly" at the very moment in which strong "prophetic" voices are needed to deal with the increasingly complex moral issues spawned by the market. This priestly attitude is reflected in a growing economic "deferentialism" among American Christians who, like their political leaders, have become remarkably skilled in dissociating their economic lives from their religious and moral convictions.

The willingness of American Christians to defer to the moral autonomy of economic outcomes is, for the most part, mutually exclusive of their political convictions. In other words, politically liberal Christians are just as likely as their conservative counterparts to believe that Christianity, despite its unparalleled understanding of human nature and institutions, has little if anything distinctive to say about economic life. Both sides would argue vigorously against this assertion. Conservatives extol the ability of Christian values to inform "individual" economic decisions, while many liberals insist that the "preferential option for the poor" must be expressed in government programs of wealth redistribution. Yet, while Christians on opposite ends of the political spectrum engage in legal and political battles over abortion, same-sex marriage, the environment, and other issues, both sides generally have failed to investigate in any depth the religious and moral implications of the market system itself. Where they have, undue dependence on secular philosophy has subordinated uniquely Christian insights into economic behavior and caused Christian voices to "meld into" the wider economic debate. Christian critics of capitalism have often focused on the possibility of its "imminent collapse" and the prospect of replacing it with a more Christian and collective economic order. Christian proponents of the market have continued to fight the Cold War well beyond its resolution, to the detriment of their ability to offer uniquely Christian perspectives on the problems of an emerging global economy. Intransigence by both sides has contributed to the perception of dualism in Western culture that has fueled anti-Western (and specifically anti-American) sentiments.[12]

Deference to economic outcomes has, in general, contributed to a growing resignation to economic determinism among American Christians, in that most largely abdicated any uniquely Christian economic claims by the time of democratic capitalism's triumph in the Cold War. Despite its religious undertones, that "war" was fought on an almost exclusively materialistic basis—the outcome was determined by the superior industrial and technological capabilities of the United States and other Western nations over their Communist adversaries. Triumphalism in the aftermath of the Cold War led to the rise in prestige of so-called neoconservatives, converts from socialist philosophy who became stalwart defenders of liberal democracy, and many of whom were seen as prescient in their predictions of Communism's demise. Neoconservative Christians, just as Christian socialists and the Christian Marxists of liberation theology who were their adversaries, became heavily invested in secular philosophy as the foundation of their social thought. For the neoconservatives, the identification of common values and principles that mitigate tensions between capitalism and Christianity was derived, to a considerable degree, from a group of thinkers that, at least ideologically, was highly influential in the global triumph of capitalism. A clique of Austrian economists, led principally by Friedrich Hayek and Ludwig Mises, contributed significantly to the philosophical deconstruction of socialism and, consequentially, to the intellectual foundation for modern economic progress.

The "Austrian school" with which Hayek and Mises are associated advanced the idea of subjective economic actors engaging in the exchange of goods and services in markets capable of both *material* and *moral* self-correction as the only practical economic model for modern society.[13] Highly critical of all forms of "social constructivism,"[14] the Austrian economists and their theories have become increasingly popular among conservatives in the United States. Hayek's *The Road to Serfdom* was credited by U.S. Supreme Court chief justice William Rehnquist as the single most important book in molding his philosophical views, and some scholars have suggested that Hayek's philosophy was seminal to the distinctive neoconservatism that forged the economic policies of the Reagan and Thatcher administrations.[15] That influence extended to Christian social thinkers, and although socialist, democratic socialist, and even Marxist ideas are still present in particular circles, Austrian economics increasingly shapes American Christian economic thought.

Catholic neoconservatives such as Michael Novak and Robert Sirico, Reformed theologians such as Ronald Nash, and Christian reconstructionists like R. J. Rushdoony and Gary North have all expressed their admiration for Hayek and Mises, whose writings are extolled as masterful in exposing socialism's faults and revealing capitalism's virtues. Austrian economic philosophy grounds its theory of value exclusively in the subjective judgments of individuals who participate in the "extended" and "spontaneous" order of society.[16] The radical reformation brought about by the Austrian economists was to proclaim the absolute sovereignty of the consumer and to reject a central premise of classical economics—that commodities of exchange have intrinsic or "objective" value contained within. Equally significant was Austrian liberalism's insistence that a planned economy cannot function as efficiently as a capitalist one. As is now widely accepted, Austrian theory holds that the free market system is more efficient in the allocation of society's limited resources due to the greater proficiency with which private producers respond to fluctuations in consumer demand vis-à-vis the rational production choices of central planners who guide collectivist economies. Consistent with the Austrian view, libertarian and neoconservative Christians extol the ability of the market system to adjust to changes in resource constraints and consumer tastes, and they condemn government actions that interfere with the processes of self-correction ostensibly inherent in the capitalist economy.

More interesting, however, has been the increasing acceptance among Christians of the "moral" virtues of capitalism as described in Austrian economic theory. Indeed, economically conservative Christians[17] often exhibit a confidence in the moral sustainability of the free enterprise system that, in some respects, rivals even the exalted expectations of Karl Marx and his followers for the "planned society." For example, Michael Novak's admiration for the Austrian principle of *catallaxy*—the idea that the dynamics of exchange, when reinforced by certain cultural institutions, is sufficient to guide society to desired ends without need for the collective ordering of those ends[18]—has a utopian quality not unlike the belief of socialists that economic stability can be achieved through the planning and synchronization of production processes and social structures. Catallaxy greatly minimizes the need for collective determinations of the good in favor of private market exchange, with both the material and moral components of that good being determined largely as an aggregate of individual expressions. In concert with Novak, the publications of Father Sirico's Acton Institute champion Austrian economics as providing a viable alternative to the moral bankruptcy of socialism.[19]

What is striking about the attraction of Novak, Sirico, and other Christian economic thinkers to the ethical structure of Austrian economics is that the theories of Hayek and Mises are constructed upon highly naturalistic moral foundations. The evolutionary nature of morality in Austrian economic thought views all cultural institutions as gravitating intractably toward a common social value that Hayek labels "group persistence." In an essay from his seminal work, *The Fatal Conceit*, Hayek observes what he calls "perhaps the least appreciated facet of human evolution" in the spontaneous formation of the "extended order."[20] To comprehend civilization, one must first recognize that "it arose from unintentionally conforming to certain traditional and largely *moral* practices, many of which men tend to dislike, whose significance they usually fail to understand, whose validity they cannot prove, and which nonetheless have fairly rapidly spread by means of an evolutionary selection—the comparative increase of population and wealth—of those groups that happened to follow them."[21] In the Austrian model, social institutions (including religious groups) that most efficiently acquire and maintain those traits that increase their populations and collective wealth survive while other groups die out, consistent with the "organic" natural selection process of Darwinian evolution. In reinforcing his claim, Hayek observed, "*The only religions that have survived are those which support property and the family.*"[22]

THE THREAT TO TRANSCENDENT MORALITY

This book proposes that the harmonizing of Austrian liberalism and Christian virtue in the thought of economically conservative Christians is a marriage of convenience that ignores serious contradictions between the respective traditions. Further, it suggests that technology is the catalyst that has begun to expose those inconsistencies. Recent and dramatic advances in human genetics, in particular, are revealing conflicts between the increasingly individualistic form of American capitalism and elements of Christian tradition. As these new technologies encroach upon traditional Christian teachings concerning the *nature of the person*, the subjective economic actor in Austrian theory—to the extent that it accurately depicts the market participant in modern capitalism—will come into conflict with the communal and transcendent conception of the human being in Christian tradition. Conflicts will arise as members of various branches of the Christian faith participate (either voluntarily or through coercion) in markets for technological services that involve morally ambiguous outcomes.[23]

Consistent with the Austrian principle that human reason is incapable of conceptualizing the aggregate effects of subjective choices, it is suggested that Christians will be unable to foresee the cumulative effects of private decisions in human genetics and other "person-impacting" industries on their tradition. Thus, participation in markets employing technologies that have the potential to alter basic conceptions of the human person require the full weight of religious tradition to ensure that members are aware of the potential consequences of their decisions, both individually and for the institutions to which they belong. Christian morality, resting on a complex view of the person as created in the image of God, as steward over nature, and as possessing a soul that transcends the material world, is vulnerable to alteration by markets that are poorly structured to enable *collective moral voice* in economic decision making.

This book utilizes Hayek's moral system—because of his prominence in the Austrian tradition and the extensive use of Hayek's thought by Christian economic theorists—as the basis for demonstrating the inevitability of this conflict.[24] Although many Christians have been attracted to Hayek's traditionalism, it should be recognized that his respect for tradition has no transcendent mooring. Religious and other traditions are important to Hayek only in the sense that they represent the culmination of rules, values, and behaviors that have contributed most effectively to their survival in the evolution of human culture. Moreover, central to the thesis here is that *moral persistence of religious traditions in the Austrian model is possible only insofar as religious institutions have established rules to guide their adherents in market decisions and insofar as individual actors are familiar with and abide by their tradition's rules regarding those choices.* Increasingly, the proliferation of markets for new technologies is outstripping the ability of Christian and other religious institutions to deal with the theological and moral implications of that advance.

Such market-inspired challenges to religious traditions are not unique in American history. J. Albert Harrill points out that the continued bartering of human beings as slaves in the nineteenth century was decisive in shaping the hermeneutical and theological development of American Christianity, as proslavery and antislavery groups employed the Bible to reinforce their positions.[25] The slave trade split American Christianity into warring camps, leading proslavery Christians into Biblical literalism while abolitionists advanced German historical criticism in support of their cause. The slavery issue even led some groups to "the total abandonment of Biblical authority in favor of secular arguments from conscience."[26] The critical difference, however, is that the persistence of slavery in American culture was accompanied by intense Christian activism on both sides of the issue; certain groups found what they believed to be biblical validation for this immoral institution, while others used "liberal" theology to reject it. Today, by contrast, the market propulsion of morally sensitive commodities is outpacing the *ability* of religious traditions to become involved in these debates.

Evidence will be presented to demonstrate that the Hayekian moral framework is today most representative of the moral adjustment process that takes place in the American economic system. This evidence suggests that aggregate subjective choice does indeed shape religious traditions in favor of group persistence, irrespective of moral pronouncements by religious leaders or the existence of doctrine governing economic and other behavior. This vindication of Hayek implies that his theories can be highly instructive in investigating capitalism's impact on American Christianity. If Hayek is correct, then the introduction of a specific technology that, for example, enables the customization of human offspring will be adopted by religious and other cultural traditions to the extent that it is proven to enhance their competitiveness.[27] Thus, the thesis of this book does not depend upon refuting Hayek's theory of the evolutionary adjustment process that takes place in the spontaneous order of a free society. Nor does it challenge his view of the malleability of religious and other traditions as they respond to modernity's perceived demands for their survival. In fact, it will be asserted that Hayek was correct in suggesting that a society built on a predominantly subjectivist economic ethic will see group persistence emerge as the dominant social value. These concessions, along with evidence demonstrating the detachment of consumer behavior from religious morality, support the contention that the

American economy largely conforms to Austrian principles. Such observations, however, beg the question of whether this vindication of Austrian economics should comfort or concern Christians who are troubled by the moral evolution of capitalist culture.

Research uncovered only isolated references to the religious implications of Hayek's naturalism in the writings of Christian scholars who favor Austrian liberalism. This curious lack of engagement of such a critical subject implies that these writers believe either that Christians may embrace Hayek's economic principles while rejecting his naturalism or that his evolutionary concept of morality is neither a precondition nor the inevitable outcome of a system that conforms to his theories. Separation of Hayek's moral philosophy from his economic principles is analogous to the segmentation of religious and economic life practiced by many Americans. Indeed, the subtleties by which economically conservative Christians partition morality from economics is a fascinating (though ambiguous) aspect of their social thought. Michael Novak, for example, recognizes interdependencies between the political, economic, and moral-cultural sectors of his now famous tripartite system while offering little specificity as to how these sectors interrelate. In *The Spirit of Democratic Capitalism*, Novak wrote extensively of the need for Judeo-Christian and other religious and moral institutions to reinforce the capitalist system.[28] Yet Novak only lightly addresses the potential of capitalism itself to erode or undermine those institutions, despite the articulation of this hypothesis by social theorists such as Max Weber, Joseph Schumpeter, and Daniel Bell.[29] And one may include Hayek among those who predict a continual alteration of traditional morality in capitalist societies; for it will be shown that Hayek's theory of value disfavors the long-term viability of any faith tradition that clings to beliefs and ideals that lie in a source "beyond culture."

Some likely will contend that the thesis of this book is built upon a misconception of Hayek's philosophy. Christian advocates of Austrian economics might argue that Hayek accepted the possibility that belief in the transcendent and communal nature of the person could *enhance* the survivability of Christian or other religious traditions. It is conceivable that belief in the Trinity or transubstantiation or a literal six-day creation forges a critical identity that contributes to the persistence of distinctive Christian institutions. This view is tempered, however, by observing that Hayek understood cultural evolution as taking place on two levels. On one level, Hayek's writings do suggest that mythical or otherworldly beliefs help form unique identities that contribute to the continuance of religious traditions. However, Hayek also envisioned a higher level of cultural evolution that involves an intractable movement toward a common set of values among all traditions, not unlike Dewey's vision of a "common faith."[30] This understanding of a universal level of natural selection among religious groups is observed in Hayek's statement that only those religions that have emphasized family and property have survived. In fact, the bulk of Hayek's comments on religion suggest that despite the likely continuance of formal differentiation among faith traditions, he perceived the homogenization of doctrines and beliefs to common standards as determined by the participation of their adherents in the extended order. A detailed exploration of Hayek's thought on the contribution of religious institutions to cultural development will illuminate the danger posed by society's broad acceptance of subjectivism to Christianity and other transcendent religions.

The threat to religious morality presented by this exaltation of the subjective is found in the exaggerated emphasis of the individual over the community and of dynamism over teleology in economic life. The radical elevation of the individual that was reinforced by capitalism's rightful and overwhelming victory over collectivism resulted in collateral damage: denigration of the idea of collective moral guidance to the good that occurred even as the notion of a centrally and rationally planned society was eradicated from political consciousness. Having triumphed so decisively in the contest of competing economic systems, capitalism and its associated virtues have been "absolutized" by large segments of American society. Indeed, each of the Christian scholars reviewed here recognizes modernity's adverse consequences for traditional morality; yet they refuse to acknowledge the possibility that capitalism may contribute to that harm.

Christian advocates of market economics have ample basis for the pride they take in the moral (and certainly material) accomplishments of Western capitalism. They are undoubtedly right that the expansion of wealth has distributed responsibility and encouraged virtuous behavior among many who might not otherwise act virtuously. The reciprocity of capitalist institutions forges bonds of community that, in a localized venue, provide an economic incentive for the preservation of one's reputation through honorable conduct. Capitalist cultures have inspired history's greatest acts of philanthropy and have contributed to the Western cultural heritage through the development of the world's finest education systems, civic organizations, arts and science foundations, and countless other contributions. From this vantage, democratic capitalism's victory over Communism in the last century was a moral as well as material victory.

Yet these achievements have obscured some insidious ethical consequences of a phenomenally successful and increasingly pervasive market system. Depersonalizing forces within the modern mass economy have devalued the individual while the expansion of markets into virtually every area of life has helped to desacralize Western culture. The allure of capitalism's wealth-generating capability and the growth of economic life as a measure of the totality of human existence beg the question of whether Christian capitalists are systematically "transacting away" any spiritual conception of themselves. Ironically, it is Friedrich Hayek, often cited by Christians as a champion of tradition, who provides the most explanatory model to show how the transcendent values of religions are eroded in free societies.

Myriad attempts to reconcile Christian doctrine with secular philosophies have limited moral reflection on economic behavior and degraded the prophetic voice of American Christianity. Each of these attempts to meld the purposes, values, and practices of religious and economic life failed due to a common flaw in methodology. That flaw is observed in their efforts to assimilate the economic ethos of the time and dissolve tensions between secular and religious institutions. In the late nineteenth and early twentieth centuries, the *illuminati* of European socialism provided what leaders of the "left wing" of the Social Gospel movement believed was the key to the Kingdom of God on earth. In roughly the same period, Christian "progressives" were adopting the techniques of scientific management in their attempts to *corporatize* American churches. By the 1980s and after countless disappointments, "left" liberalism had been discredited, and Christian reconstructionists, libertarians, and neoconservatives turned to the "natural harmony" theorists of the Scottish Enlightenment and the Austrian liberal tradition as guides to a unified prosperity. Regardless of the specific alliances, however, the point is that various movements within American Christianity sought to harmonize religious and economic values and put definitive doctrine at risk in order to abate the cultural tension that was perceived as damaging if not evil.

Recurrent attempts by various groups of American Christians to accommodate secular theories and institutions have fully ensconced this practice in the American tradition and have instilled a self-destructive inconsistency in Christian social teaching. This history, moreover, is a powerful argument against those who contend that religion *has been removed* from the public square. While many Christians insist that they are relegated to the sidelines in debates on public policy, it may be that Christians simply "concede the field" by disregarding their faith's incomparable understanding of human nature and institutions in favor of the transitory theories of secular philosophy.[31]

THE POSSIBILITY OF A REDEMPTIVE ECONOMY

Recognition of this persistent failure in methodology may offer a unique opportunity for American Christianity. Having observed the disappointments of various "synthetic" approaches to a morally sustainable prosperity through the resolution of religious and economic conflict, Christians must recognize the need to review their fundamental approach to the problem. It may be that Christians are in a unique position to make a meaningful contribution to economic life if they can return to and develop their own distinctive resources without yielding to the "embarrassment of particularity." Yet this requires the development of Christian perspectives on economic life that are not simply restatements of secular philosophy in Christian language.

Three prolific Christian social thinkers, in particular, understood the dangers of aligning Christian ideals with secular philosophy. Reinhold Niebuhr, G. K. Chesterton, and Pope John Paul II collectively have produced a body of work in "Christian economics" that offers an alternative to compromise and assimilation. Although they come at the challenge of reconciling Christian teaching and the necessities of a modern economy from different perspectives, Niebuhr, Chesterton, and John Paul arrive at similar conclusions because of their common teleology: the superordinate desires to (a) preserve the humanity of the person and (b) foster economic relationships that replenish religious and moral traditions. Distilling the essence of each man's economic thought yields remarkably similar results— one can envision attributes of what may be described as a "redemptive economy." Use of this term is not intended to exalt economics above its rightful station; nor does it seek to intrude upon St. Paul's soteriological use of the term in II Corinthians 3:17. Rather, the term "redemptive economy" is intended to describe and preserve the Christian idealism of these three men with an affirmation of Niebuhr's dictum: "there is no 'Christian' economic or political system. But there is a Christian attitude toward all systems and schemes of justice."[32] It seeks to revive the idea that a capitalist economy can embrace Christian values in elevating human dignity over output, morality over mass production, and community over individualism. "Redemptive" is used here not in a salvific sense but rather to suggest the possibility of a morally regenerative economic system. Each transaction that takes place in a redemptive economy works to replenish those moral stores that serve as the foundation of Christian economic life, while promoting cultural prosperity and the dignity of the individual.

Niebuhr's association with the philosophy called "Christian realism" makes him somewhat suspect as a contributor to this admittedly idealistic concept of a redemptive economy. It is true that Niebuhr came to recognize the omnipresent force of self-interest in economic affairs; yet he always understood the need to maintain the "ideal" as a critical norm for determination of what realistically can be accomplished in the political and economic order. Maintaining a status as a political theorist unparalleled for a religious leader during much of the twentieth century, Niebuhr also demonstrated a profound interest in and knowledge of economic theory. His critiques of both Marxism and capitalism in *The Children of Light and the Children of Darkness, The Irony of American History, Moral Man and Immoral Society, Christian Realism and Political Problems,* and other books and essays constitute more than insightful criticism. Niebuhr's economic thought offers a foundation for the development of uniquely Christian economic ideas that blend elements of neoorthodox theology with a pragmatism honed by his "torturous" journey from the "original Protestant heritage of individualism and perfectionism through a world depression and two world wars to the . . . realities of a highly technical and collective culture."[33] It was Niebuhr's intellectual development, beginning at the tail end of the Industrial Revolution, continuing through the Depression era and the rise of Christian socialism, and culminating in the euphoria of the 1960s that makes him so fascinating and potentially valuable as an economic theorist. Although Niebuhr's economic thought shifted significantly at various times in his life, his foundational principles demonstrate remarkable consistency for someone so economically malleable at the surface.

Niebuhr's complex dialectic of idealism and realism occupies a unique place in American Christian social thought, for no social philosopher of the twentieth century was more convinced of the benefits of a stable and enduring tension to the orderly progression of society. And no theologian of that same period recognized so clearly that Christianity's unique conception of the person could only be maintained by its suspension above competing secular views. He recognized the foundational materialism of both capitalist and Communist philosophies: "their common effort to understand man without considering the final dimension of his spirit; his transcendent freedom over both the natural and the historical process in which he is involved. This freedom accounts for both the creative and destructive possibilities in human history."[34] Thus, a healthy Christian idealism was, for Niebuhr, essential in staving off the reductionism of social systems and in preserving the uniquely human capacity for "self-transcendence."

Similarly, Chesterton's "distributism" emphasizes a return to organic forms of community through expansive distributions of property and a more holistic concept of ownership than that employed in modern capitalism. Society in the distributist paradigm is to be constructed from the bottom up, employing guildlike structures that promote the active involvement of all citizens in the determination of the good. Essential to this model of economic cooperation advanced not only by Chesterton but also Hilaire Belloc, Arthur Penty, Harold Robbins, and the founders of the Catholic Worker Movement is the downscaling of manufacturing and other business functions such that workers can participate in the ownership of society's physical capital while being able to observe the fruits of their labor. It was also the conviction of Chesterton and other distributists that the modern ideal of "progress" had lost all sense of proportion. Those who champion progress as the answer to social problems mean only that we have become, through technological development and mass production, capable of producing "more" while remaining unable to answer the crucial question, "More of what?" In *The Outline of Sanity*, Chesterton exposes this simplistic notion of progress and the social damage it incurs. Disproportion in progress is fueled by consumerism, monopoly, government regulation, the fragmentation of Christianity, and other ills that prevent realization of a common teleology.[35]

Chesterton was convinced that the displacement of artisans, craftsmen, and agricultural laborers by merchants and assembly workers has exacted a cultural and moral cost. Its principal results are detachment—from land, democracy, and even society itself—and a quality that he describes as "indirection." Indirection leads to inhumanity, by which Chesterton means

> the condition in which the courtier or pander of the rich man, instead of excitedly mixing a rare, original poison for the Borgias, or carving exquisite ornamental poignard for the political purposes of the Medici, works monotonously in a factory turning out a small type of screw, which will fit into a plate he will never see; to form part of a gun he will never see; to be used in a battle he will never see, and about the merits of which he knows far less than the Renaissance rascal knew about the purposes of the poison and the dagger.[36]

Although certain objects in Chesterton's criticisms of industrial capitalism have moderated—concentration of ownership and labor hours worked in unsafe factories are examples—indirectness and detachment have only increased in postindustrial society. We invest in unknown companies, transact across the Internet with anonymous persons, donate our money to misunderstood or misrepresented causes, and engage a mass bureaucracy in even the simplest of economic functions. Thus, Chesterton's observation that "humanitarianism has been the mark of an inhuman time"[37] is as relevant to the Information Age as it was to the Industrial Revolution.

Karol Wojtyla was elected as Pope John Paul II in 1978, a critical time in the history of Catholicism. The promotion of ecumenism, the effects of the Second Vatican Council, and the Catholic Church's self-conscious rethinking of its role in society all contributed to the elevation of Catholic social thought as preeminent among Christian traditions. John Paul continued the tradition of Pope Leo XIII in *Rerum Novarum* (1891), contributing encyclicals such as *Laborem Exercens* (1981) and *Centesimus Annus* (1991) that present distinctively Catholic positions on economic issues. Although some have suggested that the church has taken a decidedly capitalist turn in economic philosophy in recent years, examination of these encyclicals reveals consistency in the articulation of certain core principles. The concept of "subsidiarity," for example, was developed in *Rerum Novarum* and given modern salience in a definition by Pius XI in 1931: "It is injustice and at the same time a grave evil and disturbance of right order to assign to a greater and higher association what lesser and subordinate organizations can do."[38] Subsidiarity's priority for bottom-up social organization and decision making is consistent with distributism's emphasis on familial and other "lower-order" associations and Niebuhr's recognition that institutions become increasingly self-interested as they grow in size and complexity. In *Centesimus Annus*, John Paul balances subsidiarity with the notion of social solidarity, articulating the state's obligation to create conditions for a humane economy,

> indirectly and according to the principle of subsidiarity, by creating favorable conditions for the free exercise of economic activity, which will lead to abundant opportunities for employment and sources of wealth. Directly and according to the principle of solidarity, by defending the weakest, by placing certain limits on the autonomy of the parties who determine working conditions, and by ensuring in every case the necessary minimum support for the unemployed worker.[39]

Complementing subsidiarity in the social encyclicals of John Paul II is an approach to economic issues commonly described as "Christian personalism"—the idea that Christian attitudes toward commercial structures should consistently focus on enabling concrete relationships between persons and lead to the fullest development of human personality. The personalist approach was championed by philosophers like Gabriel

Marcel and Jaques Maritain early in the twentieth century; however, John Paul's contribution has been to blend rather seamlessly these concepts of personalism and subsidiarity in ways relevant to a modern economy and to solidify their place in the Catholic tradition. His concern for the primacy of lower-order associations in economic affairs is analogous to Chesterton's spirited defense of small-scale production and distributed ownership during the Industrial Revolution and Niebuhr's advocacy on behalf of assembly workers as a young Detroit pastor in his debates with Henry Ford. All three men recognize the tendency of modern economic systems to invert the *appropriate* relationship between labor and capital that Christians must be vigilant in defending. John Paul articulates this principle in *Laborem Exercens*, insisting that, for Christians, "labor is always a primary efficient cause, while capital, the whole collection of means of production, remains a mere instrument or instrumental cause."[40] Personal responsibility is extinguished "in a system of excessive bureaucratic centralization, which makes the worker feel that he is just a cog in a huge machine moved from above."[41] Constructing and maintaining the appropriate priority in working relationships establishes a "gospel of work" in which the value of human labor is not focused primarily on the work itself but on the personhood of those engaged in its performance.[42] Thus, John Paul, just as Niebuhr and Chesterton, perceives a critical role for Christianity in the preservation of human dignity, not only in work environments but in all social relations, to counter the depersonalizing forces of a mass, global economy.

This book suggests that distilling core values and principles from the work of Niebuhr, Chesterton, and Pope John Paul provides the foundation for a consistently prophetic Christian voice on economic issues. That voice describes an economy that enables the flowering of human personality while contributing to the moral regeneration of cultural traditions. Niebuhr's concept of social balance, not merely between political and economic structures but also among goals and values, outlines a system in which the balance of power between economic actors is critical to socially harmonious and morally sustainable growth. Chesterton's distributism accents an aesthetic and pastoral quality to economic life that conforms to the Christian imperative to maintain personal dignity in economic relations. Moreover, his writings on the inseparably private and social natures of property insist that we must locate and employ *collective moral voice* in economic decisions while avoiding the strictures and morally deteriorative effects of *collectivism*. Similarly, for John Paul II, the philosophies of Christian personalism and subsidiarity are necessary counterweights to impersonal forces in those bureaucratic institutions that make up much of the capital-ist infrastructure. In addition, his insistence on the need to reinterpret the person, "which will at the same time allow us to reproduce *in the right pro-portions* the subjectiveness of man,"[43] offers an alternative to the bottomless subjectivism of Friedrich Hayek that is remarkably popular today among Christian social thinkers.

American Christians, in particular, must *relearn* the ability to envision a market-based society that is morally regenerative. The pace of economic and technological change is pressing moral questions that require our im-mediate and collective attention. Christianity, both Protestant and Catholic, has a rich tradition of engaging the moral and ethical consequences of eco-nomic behavior and developing theology, ethics, and social philosophy that address the challenges of modernity. Spanning an increasingly narrow Protestant-Catholic divide, one can envision an emerging consensus, a "Christian attitude" toward economic systems that elevates the status of the human person, recognizes the inherent injustice in extreme concentrations of economic power, and values the contribution of moral-cultural institu-tions to the attainment of the social good.[44] This conception of a redemp-tive economy envisions an economic system capable of preserving critical individual and collective freedoms while enabling a holistic approach to progress. It can accept neither the panacea of government planning and in-tervention advanced by Christians of the political left nor the absolute sov-ereignty of the market professed by libertarians. Rather, the redemptive economy's *via media* observes the inescapable shortcomings of both govern-ment action and the market system and suggests a balanced approach to the attainment of economic goals that diffuses injustice through the dispersion of political and economic power.

Aspirations to a redemptive economy encounter an immediate obsta-cle, however. The dominance of individualism in Western culture has ren-dered anachronistic most teleological views, whether religious or secular. Contrary to the idea popularized by Daniel Bell and others in the mid-twentieth century that we have reached the "end of ideology,"[45] one might suggest that it is "teleology" that is endangered. The vitriol and political dogmatism displayed in the 2004 election, despite the inability of either Republicans or Democrats to articulate a clear vision of America's future, suggest that ideology is rampant; teleology is dead. An economic reflection of this phenomenon is found in the inability of Americans to conceptual-ize an economy that is morally regenerative, despite the presence of that idea in the nation's religious and Enlightenment traditions. Harvard scholar Michael Sandel, for example, chronicles the Founders' concern for development of economic arrangements that promote self-government and a virtuous citizenry in his book *Democracy's Discontent.* He notes Thomas Jefferson's fear of the impact of large-scale manufacturing on ethics and virtue and George Mason's criticisms of the moral influence of "port cities" as commercial centers.[46] Jefferson, Mason, and other American Founders consciously sought to craft an economic system that would make a positive contribution to private virtue and collective self-government. According to Sandel, these concerns were prominent in American discourse until the end of the nineteenth century, when American political debate began to focus "less on what economic conditions were necessary for the formation of virtuous citizens, and more on what economic conditions were necessary for the exercise of genuinely free choice."[47]

"Choice" has indeed won the day. Such teleological questions as those of the Founders are out of vogue. Moral "neutrality" has become the goal of modern capitalism not only among secular philosophers but also among religious thinkers, as will be shown. Yet the ubiquity of markets and their rising moral content insists that neutrality is itself unrealistic. The values associated with economic behavior bleed into many traditions in the spontaneous orders of free societies in ways that, as Hayek observed, are thoroughly unpredictable.

Transition to a redemptive economy will entail some risk. To achieve an economy that is morally as well as materially sustainable, Christians must transact in ways that will encourage a redefinition of "progress." In the short run, that discipline may be detrimental to competitiveness in certain markets. Yet "risk" has forever been associated with the Christian tradition: from the first-century martyrs of the Roman Empire to the sixteenth-century "Protestants" of Europe to the evangelical advocates for religious liberty of the American founding era. Persecutions are no longer common in the West. The notion of risk taking for the Christian has evolved from the threat of suffering a torturous death for expressing one's beliefs to that of jeopardizing a middle-class existence for living by one's values. Fear of religious warfare, the Black Death, or being overrun by pagan hordes has been replaced by fear of a fractional percentage-point dip in gross domestic product. This book suggests that Christian values can provide a critical throttling mechanism necessary to decelerate materialism and avoid a technologically deterministic existence. We are arriving at a point in history where we may be required to deny ourselves some of the benefits of our economic and technological prowess for the sake of our moral survival.

The inability of Christian social theorists to develop consistent and enduring prophetic voices concerning economic life has contributed to the marginalization of Christian social thought and an unhealthy deference to the moral outcomes of market decisions. Isolation of the Catholic Church in American history likely shielded it from this process to some extent and contributed to its now favored status in ethics and social thought. However, the prominence of Catholic priests such as Richard John Neuhaus and Robert Sirico among leaders of American neoconservatism suggests that Catholic social thinkers may be at risk of repeating the mistake that devalued Protestant ethics in the second half of the twentieth century. Historically, the eagerness to locate and incorporate the "most Christian" systems of political economy has often attenuated those theological and moral tenets of the faith that have potential to prevent abuses by the very systems targeted for assimilation. This desire to synchronize religious and economic life has been a persistent force in Western history and is arguably one of the most defining aspects of American culture. Pursuit of the American way of life has been dependent upon some form of religious–economic assimilation in attaining the "easy conscience," and it has contributed to the flux in Christian social thought and the moral drift in American culture that are described in this book. The cost of that contentment has been considerable, and it has risen in parallel with advances in modernity. A significant part of that cost has been the loss of esteem for religious traditions as guides to the moral good in American society.

Two principal paths to the easy conscience have been developing in American history and have threatened its realization. One path is through the persistent erosion of the sacred by forces of modernity such that the synthesis of religious and secular values becomes increasingly effortless. The second path is via the radical triumph of one ideology over all others such that religious traditions are compelled to conform to that victorious philosophy as sanctified by history. Although both forces are ever present, it is the second path to the easy conscience that appears closer to realization and that is offered as the principal threat to Christian and other religious traditions. Reflection on various movements in American history that have sought to harmonize religious and economic ideals, and their evolution to a dominant view of near seamless compatibility between Christian and capitalist values, will demonstrate the immediacy of the threat and the entrenchment of the problem.

NOTES

1. Will Herberg explored the religious significance of the "American way of life," stating that it is not a synthetic but an "organic structure of ideas, values, and beliefs that

constitutes a faith common to Americans and [that is] genuinely operative in their lives." It is "individualistic, dynamic, pragmatic" as much as it is spiritual, reverential, or theological. In the American way of life, "'deeds, not creeds, are what count." See Will Herberg, *Protestant-Catholic-Jew: An Essay in American Religious Sociology* (Garden City, NY: Anchor Books, 1960), 77, 79, 254.

2. Michael Novak, *The Catholic Ethic and the Spirit of Capitalism* (New York: The Free Press, 1993), 101.

3. Fred Hirsch, *Social Limits to Growth* (Cambridge, MA: Harvard University Press, 1976), 132–34. Hirsch's concept of "micromorality" was explored briefly in Charles McDaniel, "Friedrich Hayek and Reinhold Niebuhr on the Moral Persistence of Liberal Society," *Journal of Interdisciplinary Studies* 16, nos. 1–2 (2004): 150–51.

4. William Safire, "California's Stem-Cell Gold Rush," *New York Times*, December 16, 2004, A33.

5. Safire, "California's Stem-Cell Gold Rush." See also Kelly Rayburn, "States Grapple with Stem-Cell Research; Some Governors Fear Job Losses and Follow California's Lead, while Others Support Limits," *Wall Street Journal*, December 24, 2004, A4.

6. Karl Marx, *The Communist Manifesto*, in *Karl Marx Selected Writings*, ed. Lawrence H. Simon (Indianapolis: Hackett Publishing, 1994), 161.

7. Marx, *The Communist Manifesto*, 161. Moreover, Marx noted how "the bourgeoisie has stripped of its halo every occupation hitherto honored and looked up to with reverent awe," including "the lawyer, the priest, the poet, the man of science" and reduced them to the status of mere "wage-labourers." In this regard perhaps the atheist Marx should be acknowledged as a "defender of the faith," joining Henry VIII and other ironic figures in the annals of Christian history.

8. Schumpeter calls creative destruction "the essential fact about capitalism" in which there exists a continual "revolutionizing" from within. See Joseph A. Schumpeter, *Capitalism, Socialism and Democracy*, 3rd ed. (New York: Harper & Brothers, 1950), 83–88.

9. Social theorist Francis Fukuyama famously posited that "modern liberal democracy and technologically driven capitalism" may, as he put it, "constitute the 'end point of mankind's ideological evolution.'" See *The End of History and the Last Man* (New York: The Free Press, 1992), xi–xii, 88–89.

10. NBC News, *Meet the Press*, October 10, 2004. A transcript of this show is available at www.msnbc.com/id/6200928.

11. Jane Mayer, "Contract Sport: What Did the Vice-President Do for Halliburton?" *New Yorker*, "Fact: Letter from Washington," November 23, 2004, at www.newyorker .com/fact/content/?040216fa_fact (accessed December 16, 2004).

12. Timur Kuran describes the fear of Western dualism infecting Islamic culture among notable Muslim thinkers such as Pakistan's Sayyid Abu'l-A'la Mawdudi. Economics was considered a particular purveyor of an emerging "cognitive and moral dualism" due to the fact that, in Mawdudi's words, "there is such a plethora of discussion and scientific research about economic problems that . . . the other problems of mankind seem to have paled into insignificance." Mawdudi, Sayyid Abu'l-A'la, *The Economic Problem of Man and Its Islamic Solution* (Orig. Urdu ed., 1941; Lahore: Islamic Publications, 1978), 1; quoted in Kuran, "The Genesis of Islamic Economics: A Chapter in the Politics of Muslim Identity," *Social Research* 64 (Summer 1997), at www.mtholyoke.edu/ acad/intrel/kuran.htm (accessed June 5, 2005).

13. It is recognized that the theories of Hayek and Mises do not exhaust the full range of economic thought within the "school" known as Austrian economics. Joseph Schumpeter and Wilhelm Röpke were theorists who made significant contributions to this tradition and whose economic ideas were more critical of capitalism. However, the term "Austrian economics" has come to be associated with subjective valuation, spontaneous order, and other conceptions of a free market system; therefore, that connotation will be employed here.

14. Hayek used the term "constructivism" to describe the common philosophy that underlay collectivist systems and the "progressive" programs of democratic societies (e.g., Franklin Roosevelt's "New Deal") that were based on the necessity for the rational and planned development of social institutions. Hayek stated that the principle flaw of constructivism resulted from the belief "that human institutions will serve human purposes only if they have been deliberately designed for those purposes." See F. A. Hayek, *Law, Legislation and Liberty*, vol. 1, *Rules and Order* (Chicago: University of Chicago Press, 1973), 8, 13.

15. Rehnquist's comment was in response to an interview question on the Public Broadcasting System's Charlie Rose program. See Charlie Rose, "Interview with William Rehnquist," *The Charlie Rose Show*, Public Broadcasting System (February 16, 2001). For a summary on Hayek's influence on the Reagan and Thatcher administrations, see Ralph Harris, "The Plan to End Planning," *National Review* 49 (June 16, 1997): 23–24.

16. Friedrich Hayek, "Was Socialism a Mistake?" in *The Collected Works of F. A. Hayek*, vol. 1, *The Fatal Conceit: The Errors of Socialism*, ed. W. W. Bartley III (Chicago: University of Chicago Press, 1988), 7; and *The Constitution of Liberty* (Chicago: University of Chicago Press, 1960), 31. See also McDaniel, "Friedrich Hayek and Reinhold Niebuhr," 135.

17. The term "economically conservative Christians" is used throughout this book to collectively identify Christian libertarians, neoconservatives, and other groups that advocate market economics and are generally critical of government intervention in the private sector of market economies.

18. Novak, *The Catholic Ethic and the Spirit of Capitalism*, 81–82.

19. See Michael Novak, "Economics as Humanism," *First Things* 76 (October 1997): 18–19; and Robert A. Sirico, "The Late-Scholastic and Austrian Link to Modern Catholic Economic Thought," *Journal of Markets and Morality* 1 (October 1998), available from the Acton Institute website at www.acton.org/publicat/m_and_m/1998_Oct/sirico.html (accessed October 3, 2001).

20. Hayek, "Was Socialism a Mistake?" 7. See also McDaniel, "Friedrich Hayek and Reinhold Niebuhr," 135.

21. Hayek, "Was Socialism a Mistake?" 6 (emphasis Hayek's). Hayek further compares the natural selection process for social groups with that of organisms by stating that group selection is "incomparably faster than biological evolution." See F. A. Hayek, "Between Instinct and Reason," in *The Collected Works of F. A. Hayek*, vol. 1, *The Fatal Conceit: The Errors of Socialism*, ed. W. W. Bartley III, 11–28 (Chicago: University of Chicago Press, 1988), 25.

22. Hayek, "Religion and the Guardians of Tradition," in *The Collected Works of F. A. Hayek*, vol. 1, *The Fatal Conceit: The Errors of Socialism*, ed. W. W. Bartley III, 135–42 (Chicago: University of Chicago Press, 1988), 137 (emphasis Hayek's).

23. Evidence will be presented to show how certain cultural establishments coerce participation in biomedical and other technologies that may conflict with Christian ethics or for which no doctrinal principles have been established to support the individual Christian's decision making in these markets.

24. Association of a "moral system" with Friedrich Hayek is admittedly an inexact exercise. No one more clearly recognized the limitations of "systematic" social science than Hayek himself. However, he did understand its value in the derivation of principles not so much for prediction but rather for describing "patterns" of human behavior. It is suggested that these recognizable patterns with respect to moral evolution and social value transformation constitute a moral system, albeit a nonteleological one in which "good" has little meaning beyond "persistence." John Gray, "F. A. Hayck and the Rebirth of Classical Liberalism," *Literature of Liberty* 5 (Winter 1982), explores Hayek's moral theories and cites especially his *Studies in Philosophy, Politics and Economics* (London: Routledge and Kegan Paul, 1967), 30–38 as a helpful source for Hayek's views on both the limits of social science and his understanding of the purpose of moral traditions.

25. J. Albert Harrill, "The Use of the New Testament in the American Slave Controversy: A Case History in the Hermeneutical Tension between Biblical Criticism and Christian Moral Debate," *Religion and American Culture* 10 (Summer 2000): 149–86.

26. Harrill, "The Use of the New Testament in the American Slave Controversy," 174.

27. Certain exceptions are acknowledged here. The Pennsylvania Shakers, with their doctrinal requirement of sexual abstinence, have chosen a precarious institutional existence over cultural assimilation and doctrinal compromise. However, such groups exist outside the religious mainstream, and evidence will be presented in chapter 2 to show that a far greater number of religious organizations have been willing to adopt cultural beliefs and practices that are perceived as essential to their survival.

28. Novak states that the democratic capitalist order "calls forth not only a new theology but a new type of religion. The institutional force of religion is dramatically altered under it: strengthened in some respects, weakened in others. Ways of life, beliefs, and styles compete. Each shares an equal lack of social enforcement." See Michael Novak, *The Spirit of Democratic Capitalism* (New York: Simon & Schuster, 1982), 69.

29. Bell sees the process of modernism as undermining social, to include religious, traditions by "insisting on the autonomy of the aesthetic from moral norms; by valuing more highly the new and experimental; and by taking the self (in its quest for originality and uniqueness) as the touchstone of cultural judgment." Modern capitalism also spawned a social structure such that "for the advanced social groups, the *intelligentsia* and the educated classes, and later for the middle class itself—*the legitimation of social behavior passed from religion to modernist culture*." See Daniel Bell, *The Cultural Contradictions of Capitalism*, Twentieth Anniversary Edition (New York: Basic Books, 1976), xxi, xxiv (emphasis Bell's). See also Schumpeter, *Capitalism, Socialism and Democracy*, 417–18, 424; and Max Weber, *The Protestant Ethic and the Spirit of Capitalism*, trans. Talcott Parsons (Gloucester, MA: Peter Smith, 1988 [orig. pub. 1904–1905]), 170, 182.

30. Dewey predicted that scientific advance would steadily erode the anachronisms and superstitions of religious myth and ultimately realize a "common faith," the tenets of which would be synchronized with the "truths" of science and reason. See John Dewey, *A Common Faith* (New Haven, CT: Yale University Press, 1934), 30–32.

31. Roman Catholic priest and social thinker Richard John Neuhaus wrote about the marginalization of Christianity in the American public square in his widely discussed book *The Naked Public Square: Religion and Democracy in America* (Grand Rapids, MI: W. B. Eerdmans, 1984). This idea that Christians often subordinate their faith's social insights to secular philosophy is discussed in McDaniel, "Friedrich Hayek and Reinhold Niebuhr," 134.

32. Reinhold Niebuhr, "Theology and Political Thought in the Western World," in *Faith and Politics: A Commentary on Religious, Social and Political Thought in a Technological Age*, ed. Ronald H. Stone (New York: George Braziller, 1968), 56.

33. Reinhold Niebuhr, *Man's Nature and His Communities: Essays on the Dynamics and Enigmas of Man's Personal and Social Existence* (New York: Charles Scribner's Sons, 1965), 16.

34. Reinhold Niebuhr, *Man's Nature and His Communities*, 59.

35. G. K. Chesterton, *The Outline of Sanity*, in *The Collected Works of G. K. Chesterton*, vol. 5, ed. George J. Marlin et al. (San Francisco: Ignatius Press, 1986).

36. Chesterton continues by noting, "In short, what is the matter with industrialism is indirection; the fact that nothing is straightforward; that all its ways are crooked even when they are meant to be straight." G. K. Chesterton, "Democracy and Industrialism," available from the American Chesterton Society website at www.chesterton.org/gkc/Distributist/industrial.htm (accessed December 21, 2004).

37. Chesterton, "Democracy and Industrialism."

38. Pius XI, *Quadragesimo Anno*, May 15, 1931, no. 79, in *Contemporary Catholic Social Teaching* (Washington, DC: United States Catholic Conference, 1991), 71.

39. John Paul II, *Centesimus Annus: On the Hundredth Anniversary of Rerum Novarum*, May 1, 1991, no. 15. At the end of this passage, the pope cites another of his encyclicals, *Encyclical Letter Laborem Exercens* (September 14, 1981): AAS 73 (1981), 594–98.

40. John Paul II, *Laborem Exercens* [On Human Work]: *On the Ninetieth Anniversary of Rerum Novarum*, 1981 (Washington, DC: United States Catholic Conference Office of Publishing Services, 1981), nos. 12, 25.

41. John Paul II, *Laborem Exercens*, nos. 15, 34. Personalization of the workplace has cultural benefits, as the pope observes that through work the individual contributes "to the continual advance of science and technology and, above all, to elevating unceasingly the cultural and moral level of society within which he lives in community with those who belong to the same family." John Paul II, *Laborem Exercens*, "Salutation," 1.

42. John Paul II, *Laborem Exercens*, nos. 6, 14.

43. Karol Wojtyla [John Paul II], *The Acting Person*, trans. Andrzej Potocki (Boston: D. Reidel Publishing Company, 1979), 19 (emphasis added).

44. Limiting the scope of this "Christian attitude" to members of the Roman Catholic and Protestant traditions admittedly excludes some brilliant social thinkers in the Christian tradition. Alexei Khomiakov, a member of the Russian Orthodox Church, was an original and inspiring social philosopher who contributed substantially to Christian thought through development of the concept of *sobornost*, which offers a holistic Christian vision of society that counters the rationalism and ethical fragmentation of modern life. Khomiakov addresses many of the same problems of modernity noted by Niebuhr, Chesterton, and John Paul II; unfortunately, for purely practical considerations, his contribution is beyond this scope of this book. Khomiakov's classic work, *The*

Church Is One (Seattle, WA: St. Nectarios Press, 1979), contains the essence of his theological and social ideas.

45. Daniel Bell, *The End of Ideology: On the Exhaustion of Political Ideas in the Fifties* (Glencoe, IL: The Free Press, 1960).

46. Michael Sandel, *Democracy's Discontent: America in Search of a Public Philosophy* (Cambridge, MA: The Belknap Press of Harvard University Press, 1996), 125–26.

47. Sandel, *Democracy's Discontent*, 189.

2

THE LESS DIVIDED ECONOMIC
MIND OF AMERICAN CHRISTIANITY

Perhaps the least explored and thus most undervalued dynamic in the formation of American culture has been the drive to synthesize religious and economic life. Despite the primacy of both faith and commerce in the development of a distinctly American ethos, scholars generally have overlooked the cultural significance of recurrent attempts to fuse spiritual values and economic principles.[1] This persistent impulse has been manifested in many forms in the nation's history, from basic social attitudes to philosophical movements to utopian social experiments. Factions from across the ideological spectrum of Christianity, in particular, have employed diverse methods in their attempts to harmonize the ideals of the American economic system with their religious values and beliefs. A few obscure groups, most notably Christian reconstructionists and the utopian "Bible communists" of the early nineteenth century, determined that scripture alone contains sufficient resources to guide the economic construction of harmonious Christian communities. The majority of American practitioners of "theological economics," however, including Christian libertarians and neoconservatives, late nineteenth- and early twentieth-century Christian socialists, Christian Marxists, and the Social Gospelers, have incorporated secular theories in the hope that their ideas will resonate with the wider society.[2]

This historic dependence on secular philosophy has intensified divisions within American Christianity and contributed to a pronounced dialectical progression of its social thought. Increasingly, the terms of that dialectic have been dictated by the philosophical and institutional products of Enlightenment utopianism. Economically engaged American Christians traditionally have aligned themselves with the two distinct camps of economic philosophy that are built respectively upon the principles of "social constructivism" and "subjectivist liberalism" described in the introduction. When one school of Christian economic thought that advocates a system built on constructivist principles, as for example Christian socialism, gains the upper hand in this debate, another faction championing a subjectivist economic philosophy (i.e., Christian neoconservativism) inevitably emerges to challenge the perceived structural flaws and utopian expectations of the former. The vision of harmony between spiritual and material life has spurred advocates of both philosophies to champion their respective systems as the "most Christian."

Yet utopianism commonly has been associated with communism or other collectivist and constructivist social philosophies, whether inspired by scripture or science. Indeed, the very meaning of the term has evolved so as to be associated with the *planned* construction of institutions designed to achieve a particular manifestation of social justice. Consequently, rejection of the viability of social planning in subjectivist economic theory has led Americans who are convinced of the profound Christianness of capitalism to reject the label "utopian." In their view, liberalism is the ideal system for an inherently sinful society, and any shortcomings of this philosophy correspond to the natural flaws observed in individuals and social groups.[3]

One of the profound insights of Reinhold Niebuhr, however, was to observe that the utopianism that emerged from the Enlightenment and that has so heavily influenced Christian social thought took two distinct forms that developed along distinctly different channels. The first branch of Enlightenment philosophy observed by Niebuhr is characterized by socially positivistic ideas and roughly follows a lineage of René Descartes, Auguste Comte, Karl Marx, and John Dewey. Its utopian outlook results from a glorification of human reason and a belief that the collective good results from the purposeful manipulation of social institutions in concert with humankind's mastery of nature. The second thread of the Enlightenment traversed a quite different course. Its origins are found in the natural law theories of Thomas Aquinas and the Scholastics. Roman Catholic conceptions of the natural order influenced a similar albeit less unified development within Protestantism after the Reformation, and this Protestant natural law tradition became a cornerstone of the Scottish Enlightenment, which included social theorists such as Frances Hutcheson, Adam Smith, and Adam Ferguson.[4] It was the belief of these philosophers that nature rather than reason held the key to harmonious progress and that the principles observed in natural phenomena could be applied, virtually verbatim, to human societies. For Niebuhr, such optimism in the symmetries of nature and culture contributed to what his biographer Ronald Stone characterized as the "illusion of moral progress"—the idea that naturally ordered systems such as the market, when unencumbered by outside interference, will contribute to a near linear progression in the moral as well as material well-being of society.[5] Such notions, to Niebuhr, were as utopian as the pretensions of socialists concerning the power of collective reason.

To make his case, Niebuhr articulated a critical error that was common to both the "natural harmony" and "rational constructivist" subtraditions of the Enlightenment by observing the "confidence of both bourgeois and proletarian idealists in the possibility of achieving an easy resolution of the tension and conflict between the general interest and self-interest."[6] For the constructivist proletarians, resolution of this tension is through the rational planning and manipulation of society such that human reason becomes *the* vital force of social organization. Conflict is eliminated through the application of collective reason to myriad problems resulting from the asynchronous processes of cultural advance. By contrast, the bourgeois tradition maintains that cultural discord can be abated by preventing the state from intervening in economic life, thereby enabling the natural harmonies of the market order to synchronize the common good with self-interest "rightly understood." Both distinctly utopian traditions of the Enlightenment identified by Niebuhr have greatly influenced Christian social thought. Moreover, the historical reliance of American Christianity on secular philosophy *in general* has had fateful consequences: first, it has relegated the Christian economic debate largely to mimicry of the wider secular debate; second, it has enabled philosophy to challenge theology as the prime differentiator between liberal and conservative Christianity; and, finally, it has narrowly subjected Christian social theory to the fortunes of history.

Given the recent and overwhelming triumph of the market system, this chapter chronicles the resolution of the dialectic that traditionally has guided American Christian economic thought. It will be shown that at no point in American history has there been a greater consensus on the path to the common good. That consensus is founded upon a pervasive belief in the market as a moral instrument that achieves the highest degree of social and economic justice possible in modern society. Yet Niebuhr understood that maintenance of the tension between the two dominant traditions of Enlightenment philosophy is critical to prevent the spiritual devaluation of Christianity resulting from a too-easy synthesis of Christian values with either capitalist or socialist ideals. He insisted that the unopposed dominance of either capitalism or collectivism would reshape our collective understanding of social morality and the human person by orienting attitudes in favor of the naturalism that exists at the core of both systems. This chapter traces the elimination of that philosophical tension at a time when emerging genetic and other technologies are raising serious questions about the nature of the person. It also posits an emerging consensus among American Christians in the essential truth of the natural harmony tradition as founded upon a belief in the congruity of values between capitalist and Christian institutions.

THE AMERICAN MARCH TO
RELIGIOUS-ECONOMIC SYNTHESIS

American Christianity has exhibited a remarkable malleability in its social thought throughout its history. Especially in the field of economics, one may discover Christian devotees of classical, neoclassical, socialist, Marxist, Keynesian, and institutional economic philosophies as well as various amalgamations and misrepresentations thereof. A cynic might be tempted to characterize American Christianity's wanderings through economic ideas in the same way that William Lee Miller described the unpredictability in William O. Douglas's decisions in the Supreme Court's church-state cases as resembling the "homeward journey of a New Year's eve reveler."[7] But perhaps the Christian tradition may be forgiven for its lack of uniformity in this area with the observation that the secular world has struggled equally with competing philosophies of economic organization. Changes in Christian ideas about economic life commonly have resulted from the efforts of Christian theorists to blend theology and doctrine with secular economic principles that rise and fall with the fortunes of history.

Recurrent attempts to accommodate secular philosophy have resulted in significant shifts in Christian economic ideas and in divisions among American Christians over issues such as wealth and poverty, consumption and morality, and the social and ethical consequences of technological change. One source of these divisions has stemmed from what religious historian George Marsden identifies as the "preeminent theoretical issue inherited from the Middle Ages"—that being the "question of how to relate Christian truths to pagan learning."[8] In its efforts to grasp the mechanics and dynamics of *modern* economic systems, early American society and its dominant Christian subculture struggled through periods of economic expansion, recession, and depression. Social dislocations brought about by the natural cycle of the market economy greatly impacted the nation's moral and spiritual foundations. Christianity, as the central moral pillar of American culture, was greatly stressed by the urgency to absorb, synthesize, refine, or reject the evolving principles of the new economics. The formation of divisions within and between American Christian institutions was inevitable.

Evidence of these divisions was seen late in the eighteenth century as Christian factions aligned themselves in a multifaceted debate over the desired economic structure of the new nation. Both republican virtue and Christian ethics were discussed as to whether they were likely to become beneficiaries or casualties of burgeoning capitalism.[9] The expansion of Wesleyan theology and its perfectionist doctrine in the nation's churches likely exacerbated divisions, for, as scholars have noted, both individualist and collectivist themes are found in John Wesley's writings. Liberation theologian Jose Miguez Bonino has described Wesley's theology as "incurably individualistic," stating that for Wesley, "society is not an anthropological concept, but simply a convenient arrangement for the growth of the individual."[10] Others scholars observe collectivist and constructivist themes in Wesley's economic ideas. Theodore Runyon states that Wesley's "conservatism caused him to oppose the new *laissez-faire* economic policies" and advocate the use of government to "assure more just distribution."[11] Wesley was concerned with both the material inequities of capitalist society and the *spiritual* consequences of wealth in industrious and resourceful nations like the United States:

> I fear, wherever riches have increased, the essence of religion has decreased in the same proportion. Therefore, I do not see how it is possible, in the nature of things, for any revival of true religion to continue long. For religion must necessarily produce industry and frugality, and these cannot but produce riches. But as riches increase, so will pride, anger, and love of the world in all its branches.[12]

Despite Wesley's angst, many American Christians came to accept the notion of a unique affinity between the individual responsibility demanded by their faith and the personal freedom enabled by the market economy. The continuing presence of Calvinist alongside Wesleyan theology among the nation's early churches undoubtedly was decisive in affirming the moral virtues of capitalism and in the development of an industrial mentality. The contribution of the country's Puritan heritage to its industrialization may be inferred from Max Weber's observation that the Puritan calling was not fatalistic—a mere station to be held with apocalyptic resoluteness as in Lutheran theology—but rather it embodied a "thankfulness for one's own perfection by the grace of God" that contributed to the "formalistic, hard, correct character which was peculiar to the men of that heroic age of capitalism."[13] This Puritan spirit, with its ennoblement of the Christian "vocation," provided an "ethical justification of the modern specialized division of labor" essential to the rise of mass production.[14]

The Emergence of Christian Capitalism and Collectivism

In the United States as perhaps nowhere else, Christian asceticism "strode into the market-place of life, slammed the door of the monastery behind it, and undertook to penetrate . . . the daily routine of life with its methodicalness, to fashion it into a life in this world, but neither of nor for this world."[15] The religious zeal with which American economic life was pursued precipitated an industrial miracle—the transition from an economically dependent British colony to a global economic force—within the span of a single century. But that miracle also prompted responses from the American Christian community. Recognition that the "artisan republicanism" on which the nation was founded was of questionable viability[16] in a rapidly globalizing and "modern" economy stimulated American leaders, both Christian and non-Christian, to explore emerging secular philosophies as possible sources of virtue and prosperity.

Sean Wilentz observes that the specialization of labor required in the new economy contributed to a situation where duties became simpler; men stopped learning "true crafts"; apprentices were often substituted for journeymen; and new types of workers, "foremen and contractors," were put in the places formerly occupied by master craftsmen.[17] The rising intensity of competition resulting from the termination of embargoes after the War of 1812 resulted in a great push to reduce costs by producers. The traditional artisan lifestyle was poorly suited to adapt to the changes required, both economically and socially.[18] Gradual displacement of artisanship by wage labor in the industrial age favored the philosophies developed by the rationalistic (and often deistic) thinkers of the Scottish Enlightenment as a principal source for public morality in the United States.[19] Scottish philosophy, with its emphasis on free enterprise and the self-regulating capabilities of markets, retained enough "moral sentiment" to Christianize self-interest and thus attracted many Christian adherents throughout the Occident. The American faithful were enamored with its modest and organic principles of social organization that seemed to reconcile cultural tensions; moreover, the American frontier was opportune territory for social experimentation. The capitalist ethic espoused by Scottish social theorists filled the philosophical void and supported westward expansion.

The Second Great Awakening begun at Cane Ridge, Kentucky, in 1801 was what literary critic Harold Bloom has described as an event of "orgiastic individualism"[20] that conditioned the American climate for the acceptance of Scottish moral philosophy. Frontier revivalists brought more than messages of salvation; economic liberation was conceived in the spread of the gospel in a land of limitless possibilities. That sermon was preached with vigor throughout the West whether or not its messengers were aware of the double entendre. The individualistic themes of Wesleyan theology bubbled to the surface in a region unencumbered by political and industrial institutions. R. Laurence Moore points out the cultural change that accompanied the highly impassioned, even salacious, revival meetings that took place on the American frontier:

> If the emotionalism generated by theatrical and revivalistic performance had been merely ephemeral, critics might have comforted themselves by saying that at least no permanent damage had been done. But they viewed the demand for spectacle as an addiction. Having tasted novelty, [Americans who participated in the revivals] wanted more of it. Revivals thus fed the psychology of consumption.[21]

George Marsden, referring to the great nineteenth-century revivalist Charles Grandison Finney, observes, "He and the many lesser-known evangelists of the day were promoting the American emphasis on the free individual. Conversion was becoming more and more a question of individual choice."[22] The revivalism begun at Cane Ridge precipitated an explosion of individualism that splintered American religion and, at the same time, charted a course for economic expansion. Commercial and religious ideas multiplied at a rate far beyond the capability of individuals and institutions to grasp their social and moral consequences.

Perhaps influenced by the cultural transformation that was taking place on the American frontier, leaders of the eastern Protestant establishment began attempts to blend principles of Scottish moral philosophy with Christian theology. The extent to which clergymen like the Reverend John McVickar, a patriarch of "academic economics" from Columbia University,[23] assimilated economic theories into theology led the historian Henry F. May to suggest that the second quarter of the nineteenth century in American history experienced the rise of "a school of political economy which might well be labeled clerical *laissez-faire*."[24] McVickar no doubt belonged to the natural harmony tradition, believing that the economic advance of the United States was due to compatibilities between American religious traditions and the country's economic system in their mutual appreciation of the values of private property, individual responsibility, and limited government.[25] In his *Outlines of Political Economy*, McVickar stated, "That science and religion eventually teach the same lesson, is a necessary consequence of the unity of truth, but it is seldom that this union is so early and satisfactorily displayed as in the researches of Political Economy."[26]

Another convert to the group of nineteenth-century Christian intellectuals who observed an essential harmony between Scottish philosophy and Christian moral theology was Francis Wayland, the irrepressible Baptist who served as president of Brown University from 1827 to 1855. Wayland, an eager student of the Scottish Enlightenment, took his message of the material and moral benefits of the free market system directly to American Christians. Paul Heyne detects the influence of Adam Smith on Wayland in his "use of Smithian classifications, premises, and analyses as well as what might be called a Smithian 'tone' on particular topics."[27] Indeed, Wayland followed a Smithian formula by laying the moral groundwork for his economic philosophy in *The Elements of Moral Science* (1835), much as Smith constructed an ethical framework for his economic ideas in *A Theory of Moral Sentiments* (1753). Wayland's moral system, just as Smith's, depended on a natural confluence of individual and collective interests, and on the potency of reputation in limiting human greed and other vices.[28] His belief that "the truths of revealed religion *harmonize* perfectly with those of natural religion" greatly influenced his economic philosophy, as did his understanding that the *system of natural religion* "rests upon as sure and certain a basis as any system of laws whatever."[29] Wayland's *The Elements of Political Economy* (1837) was the most widely read textbook of its kind in the Civil War era.[30]

The French prodigy of social science Alexis de Tocqueville provides confirmation of the success of Wayland and McVickar, as well as the frontier revivalists, in assimilating Scottish philosophy and disseminating a theology of economic self-reliance during this period. In his classic work, *Democracy in America*, Tocqueville observed that self-interest is "at the root of all actions" of Americans and that it "is the chief means used by religions themselves to guide man." He described the behavior of Americans that "in the very midst of their zeal [for religion] one generally sees something so quiet, so methodical, so calculated that it would seem the head rather than the heart leads them to the foot of the altar."[31] This penchant for rational religion helps to confirm the influence of the Scottish Enlightenment on nineteenth-century American culture. As historian Mark Noll has observed, "Scottish philosophy proved immensely useful as an intellectually respectable way for political leaders to reestablish public virtue and for religious leaders to defend Christian truth on the basis of a science unencumbered by tradition."[32]

The principles of Scottish moral philosophy were not the only tools employed by Christians in attempting to bridge the divide between religious and economic life at this time in American history, however. Countering the rise of individualism on the American frontier, utopian Christian communities began to form early in the nineteenth century based on collectivist ideals derived from the unique exegetical formulations and socioreligious imaginations of self-styled religious leaders. John Humphrey Noyes' Oneida, the Rappite townships of "Harmony" and "Economy," Joseph Bimeler's Zoar Separatists, and the Amana communities formed by German pietists all testify to the fertility of the American experience to "collective" forms of community. Each of these societies adopted an ethic of communal sharing that their members believed was prescribed by the teachings of Jesus Christ as revealed in the scriptures. The philosophy and organization of each community was heavily influenced by the past economic experience of its membership. The same confluence of religious oppression and economic hardship that precipitated mass immigration from Europe to the New World often fostered these utopian attitudes among the immigrants. For many, religious repression and economic privation were intellectually inseparable; therefore, any solution to one of these conditions must necessarily address the other.

Most of these radical social experiments attempted to reproduce the "Christian communism" that members (or at least leaders) of these communities believed was outlined clearly in the second chapter of the Acts of the Apostles. Fawn Brodie, biographer of one of the most influential American religious utopians, Joseph Smith, eloquently captures the spirit of the age:

> Never in American history was [the second chapter of Acts] so influential as in the second quarter of the nineteenth century. Scores of communal societies sprang up over the country, religious, non-religious, celibate, and free-love. The Shakers were communists, as were the followers of Jemima Wilkinson. When Joseph Smith first rode into the Susquehanna Valley to find the silver mine for Josiah Stowel, he went into the province where Coleridge, Southey, and Wordsworth had planned to found Pantisocracy and where the German Harmonists, led by George Rapp, were building Economy on the banks of the Ohio.[33]

The unique cultural practices of these largely separatist societies testify to the ambiguity inherent in attempts at the absolute integration of

religious and economic values. The system of "complex marriage" practiced by Noyes' Oneida community, for example, where every man was
the husband of every woman and vice versa, extended Christian commu-
nalism to the sexual realm. Noyes attempted an explanation of complex
marriage, stating, "The marriage supper of the Lamb is a feast at which
every dish is free to every guest. In a holy community there is no more
reason why sexual intercourse should be restrained by law, than why eat-
ing and drinking should be."[34] The purity of Oneida's egalitarianism and
its rejection of the "evil" of private property converged in an ethic of sexual liberation. Yet Mother Ann Lee's Shaker communities, though similarly communistic as Oneida regarding material possessions, required sexual abstinence and prohibited marriage among their members. These
values and practices, plus those of countless other groups, have been more
or less ascetic, communistic, pietistic, promiscuous, and separatist, and yet
they all have something in common: the nourishment they received in
scripture and in the liberating climate of American culture.

Mainstream American society, however, did not participate in the
primitive Christian communism of the "cults." The majority of Americans
in the nineteenth century sought more traditional methods of synthesizing
religious and economic ideas. Christian intellectuals such as Washington
Gladden and the prominent Protestant economist Richard T. Ely became
convinced like Wayland of the need for an economically literate population, although they were more wary of the potential for injustice in the
rapidly industrializing American economy. Ely, the Presbyterian turned
Episcopalian who gained prominence as an economist at the University of
Wisconsin, was appalled by the social Darwinist William Graham Sumner's
defense of unbridled free enterprise. Fear of what were perceived to be the
anti-Christian values of laissez-faire capitalism prompted men like Ely and
Gladden to import socialist philosophy—principally from German and
English universities[35]—and to explore its potential as *the* genuinely Chris-
tian economic system. These early efforts to synthesize socialism and
Christianity culminated in the formation of the Society of Christian Socialists in 1889.

Some American religious leaders became quite zealous in promoting
the ideals of Christian socialism. The Reverend Edward Ellis Carr, who re-
nounced Methodism to form a "People's Church," founded a journal called
The Christian Socialist in 1903.[36] The momentum generated by the journal,
which was to reach more than 300,000 American subscribers by 1909, led
to the formation of the Christian Socialist Fellowship in 1906.[37] Episcopalians and Methodists were the most heavily represented denominations in

the organizations that formed under the umbrella of American Christian socialism. Some prominent Christian socialists in the United States included Bernard Iddings Bell, W. D. P. Bliss, and Frances Willard. George Herron, a leader of the radical left wing of the Social Gospel, also became an enthusiastic advocate of Christian socialism, although he ultimately tarnished the movement through scandals in his personal life.[38]

Much of the drift toward socialism among American Christians late in the nineteenth century resulted from rising class divisions in American society that were perceived to be a natural consequence of the capitalist system. H. Richard Niebuhr's book *The Social Sources of Denominationalism* charted the stratification of American Christianity, which Niebuhr attributed largely to economic forces. The book was written in 1929, the initial year of the Great Depression and a time during which Niebuhr (as other prominent American theologians) was intrigued by the ideals of Marxism; thus, its observations must be considered in that context. Still, his comment that the "divisions of the church have been occasioned more frequently by the direct and indirect operation of economic factors than by the influence of any other major interest of man"[39] offers insight into the perceived intrusion of commercial values on religious culture in the first quarter of the twentieth century. Historian of religion Winthrop Hudson notes that the segregation of American Christianity along economic lines was occurring in the early antebellum period when, for example, Boston's upper-crust Unitarians separated themselves from its theologically similar though generally lowbrow and low-income Universalists.[40] Recognition of the economic causes of such social divisions was disconcerting to American ministers, who, while not fully convinced that the Bible was consonant with the principles of European socialism, did perceive a strongly egalitarian attitude in the gospels.

This shift in the direction of socialist philosophy by American Christians reflected more than rebellion against rising class divisions in the United States. It also illustrated the extent to which conceptions of "social salvation" had penetrated the American consciousness. More importantly, the reliance of Christian socialists on academic theory differentiated this movement from the "Bible communism" of the earlier Christian cooperatives. This distinction suggests that by the dawn of the twentieth century, the two major factions—socialist and capitalist—in the American Christian economic debate were fully invested in secular philosophy. American Christians of the left aligned themselves with constructivist and collectivist ideas of social organization developed in the German and British academies, while more socially conservative Christians continued to rely on the "natural harmony" principles derived from Scottish moral philosophy. Major victories by either of these philosophical schools from this time forward necessarily would affect the content and direction of Christian social thought and would possibly even impact Christian theology itself.

A Gospel of Wealth and the Social Gospel

The prevailing dialectic in American Christian economic thought necessitated a response to the rise of Christian socialism from the opposite end of the philosophical continuum. Socialism's excessive reliance on government as the arbiter of justice and its perceived detrimental effects on individual initiative stimulated a reaction from certain Americans who envisioned their country to be founded upon an ethos of individual resilience and self-determination. In 1889, the famous industrialist Andrew Carnegie wrote an essay, the title of which came to symbolize the unique American compulsion to synthesize religious and economic life. "The Gospel of Wealth" championed the virtues of capitalism over the naive and ultimately unattainable ideals that were commonly attributed to socialism. As Carnegie put it, "We might as well urge the destruction of the highest existing type of man because he failed to reach our ideal as to favor the destruction of Individualism, Private Property, the Law of Accumulation of Wealth, and the Law of Competition; for these are the highest result of human experience, the soil in which society, so far, has produced the best fruit."[41]

The impact of the "Gospel of Wealth" was remarkably pervasive in the United States. George Marsden notes that the man often cited as the "father of American religious liberalism," Horace Bushnell, "maintained unabashedly that prosperity was one of the Christian's major goals."[42] Yet Carnegie's book did not intend to sacralize American capitalism. It contained candid admissions of what Carnegie considered to be the rough edges of the free market system. Even in its imperfection, however, Carnegie believed that *his* gospel, with an emphasis upon *his* understanding of the Christian call to philanthropy, was but a restatement of the principles articulated by Jesus Christ. According to Carnegie, the "gospel of wealth but echoes Christ's words. It calls upon the millionaire to sell all that he hath and give it in the highest and best form to the poor by administering his estate himself for the good of his fellows, before he is called upon to lie down and rest upon the bosom of Mother Earth."[43] Carnegie's "gospel" was a countervailing force that tempered the voices of Christian socialism in an era of rising labor unrest. Its defense of wealth and emphasis on Christian philanthropy also demonstrated the continued presence of the individualist strain of Wesleyan theology, exemplified by his famous dictum: "Gain all you can, save all you can, give all you can."

The gospel of wealth's emphasis on munificence did not extend to the traditional American church as a beneficiary, however. Carnegie encouraged the rich to live modestly and to give generously to institutions of many types, but he believed that giving surplus wealth to the churches should be last on the list of priorities for persons of his economic class. Such giving inevitably put private interests above the interests of society, and because of its sectarian character, "gifts to churches . . . are not, in one sense, gifts to the community at large, but to special classes."[44] Carnegie was not the only philanthropist to limit charitable donations to religious organizations in this period. Various trusts, corporations, and other institutional overseers of the nation's wealth restricted their philanthropy due to what was perceived as the divisive effects of American sectarianism. The Rockefeller Foundation dropped sectarian groups as beneficiaries of its patronage in favor of the exclusive funding of "ecumenical" organizations several years after Carnegie's decision.[45] Moreover, churches were not the only religious institutions toward which such pressure was applied. In 1906, the Carnegie Foundation began providing financial incentives to religiously affiliated colleges in the United States to drop their denominational identities.[46] The emergence of economic forces favoring individualism within American religious institutions and coercing ecumenism between them undoubtedly contributed to the diversity and service orientation of the Christian churches. These market forces compelled religious organizations to reconceive their very identities in order accommodate secular ideals.

Perhaps no era of American Christianity better illustrates the bipolarity of its economic thinking than the often-misunderstood period of the Social Gospel. The casualness with which it has been mischaracterized as one among many attempts at Christian socialism does an injustice to this ideologically formative period of American Christian social thought. Susan Curtis's exceptional book, *A Consuming Faith*, shatters such oversimplifications with powerful evidence that the Social Gospel achieved the philosophical breadth to incorporate ideas from both ends of the dialectic by which religious-economic synthesis has traditionally progressed in the United States. Yet Curtis's conclusion is that on the whole, American religion, or at least American Protestantism, found sufficient justification in contemporary ideas to modernize its own institutions, to promote the virtues and techniques of mass production, and to encourage increased consumption among its membership as the gift of God's bounty. Curtis observes that the "alacrity with which the Social Gospelers embraced the slogans and tools of advertising, financial growth, and efficient scientific management assumed almost apocalyptic significance."[47] The Gospelers were eager to adopt the *best practices* from such diverse sources as capitalism, socialism, and even European nationalism,[48] all in the effort to advance their vision for the Kingdom of God on earth.

University of Chicago theologian Shailer Mathews was one Gospeler who borrowed heavily from modern organizational and economic theory. Mathews adopted from management science the "language of self-realization," which was incorporated into his sermons with the intended result of shifting "the basis of salvation from productive work and future reward to personal development and immediate gratification."[49] Mathews was one of many prominent American religious leaders of the early twentieth century who rejected the ideals of Christian socialism advanced by their colleagues and instead championed the virtues of technological innovation spawned by the free market system. William H. P. Faunce, renowned theologian and president of Brown University (1899–1929), envisioned in the development of wireless telegraphy, the airplane, the submarine, and the telephone a "transformation of the social order" in which "every inventor is an unconscious worker in the field of ethics and society."[50]

Certain institutions associated with the Social Gospel reflected the market's influence in reshaping American religious culture early in the twentieth century. At a meeting in 1912, the Federal Council of Churches talked openly of "cutthroat competition" and suggested denominational consolidations as a possible means of easing competitive pressures.[51] American religious leaders' "unacknowledged source of concern about the wasteful ecclesiastical economy was that 'respectable' denominations were not faring well in competition against the 'emotional sects,'" particularly in rural America.[52] Churches began to view adoption of the corporate model as essential to their survival in an age of unparalleled denominational competition. In *Twilight of the Saints*, historians Robert Linder and Richard Pierard contend that from 1890 to 1914, "the Protestant Establishment cohabited with corporate capitalism and began to procreate. Their miscegenetic offspring were materialism, militant nationalism and a much more broadly-based, much less evangelically-influenced civil religion."[53]

Other scholars have perceived spiritually detrimental consequences associated with the growing synthesis between capitalism and Christianity in the United States around the turn of the century. R. Laurence Moore believes this was a period of intense commodification of American religion as religious groups, deprived of legal privilege, were forced to sell themselves to increasingly empowered "consumers" with rather fickle values. Significant in the evolution of American culture, according to Moore, was the growing acceptance of leisure that forced religious leaders

> into the marketplace of culture where they found themselves steadily revising their standards. They did so, however, in line with experience. Everyone changed—religious leaders, promoters of commercial culture, and audiences. A lot of the expanding options of commercial culture were not morally safe by anyone's standards. At the same time, the number of options that serious and sensible men and women could construe as moral choices did multiply.[54]

This cultural reformation brought about by the sheer pervasiveness of American markets extended beyond religious tradition to influence other moral institutions that established the foundation of American society. Renowned sociologist of religion Robert Wuthnow observes the transformation of American culture to the point where the "corporate body," including that of religion, "became subtly transposed into a service agency for the fulfillment of its individual members."[55] Just as in past movements, the euphoria of capitalist expansion combined with religious zeal inspired a countermovement when economic fortunes declined.

The Great Depression and Christian Marxism

The Great Depression cast a pervasive and lingering pall that tempered American euphoria over the rather effortless convergence of capitalist and Christian (especially Protestant) values that had been achieved in the early twentieth century. Skepticism by religious leaders over perceived inequities in the distribution of the nation's income and fear of the social and moral consequences of a system founded on self-interest turned to questions about the very viability of capitalism in the face of unprecedented economic hardship. Robert Handy suggests that the strong association of religious and economic well-being in American society contributed to a "religious depression" (particularly in American Protestantism) that roughly coincided with the economic depression of the 1930s.[56] To support this conclusion, Handy produces statistics that demonstrate significant declines in church attendance, missions, tithing, and religious education in the period.[57] The dual effects of affluence, which crippled Christian spirituality in the economically expansive decade of the 1920s, followed by the Great

Depression's fiscal pummeling of religious institutions, limited the ability of American churches to respond to the myriad social crises of the 1930s.

The stark economic realities of the time contributed to philosophical and political moves to the left by clergymen and theologians, and to their association with what were considered "communist-front" organizations. To the amazement of many Americans, this clerical radicalism eventually culminated in congressional investigations. Harry Ward, the "Red Dean" of Union Theological Seminary, was the poster boy of Protestantism's so-called pink fringe—clergymen who found a convergence between Christian theology and Marxist philosophy. Ward, a member of the "left-leaning" Methodist Federation for Social Service and one of the early leaders of the American Civil Liberties Union, had explored Christian-Marxist connections from his days as a student of economics at Northwestern University and his graduate work in philosophy at Harvard in the late 1890s.[58] His Methodist upbringing was highly influential in his studies of theology and social philosophy as, according to Robert Craig, Ward "detached Wesley's stress upon human perfectibility from its dependence upon God's grace and redirected the course of piety from the individual to the social group."[59] For Ward, the Great Depression demonstrated the instability of the capitalist system. In the wake of the economic calamity brought on by the perceived errors of capitalism, he stressed the urgency for Christians to embrace collectivism. Moreover, Ward believed that Marxist philosophy *extended democracy to economic life* in much the same way that Christianity elevated all persons to the same status in the eyes of God.[60]

Ward's conviction that science and theology ultimately are derived from the same source and proceed in the same direction was central to his acceptance of the historicism in Marxist philosophy. There was remarkable similarity between Ward's use of science and Francis Wayland's employment of "natural religion." Ward believed in the consistency of science with "the religious ideal" in much the same way that Wayland perceived uniformity between "natural" and "revealed" religion. Despite differing economic philosophies, Wayland and Ward both depended upon an essential harmony—between nature and religion in the former case and science and religion in the latter—to achieve synthesis in their respective systems.

Paul Tillich was another prominent theologian who achieved notoriety for attempting to blend Christian theology and communist philosophy, although Tillich was more academic and less activist than Ward. In *Communism and the Theologians*, Charles C. West describes the three "structural analogies" that Tillich used to connect Christianity and Marxism. First, both traditions view "truth" as being revealed through an essential "unity of theory and practice."[61] Truth for the Christian as well as the Marxist must be, to some extent, ideologically grounded in a particular social and historical situation. Second, Christian tradition and Marxist philosophy have a common teleological view of history as having "a beginning, a middle, and an end," in which history "has a meaning of its own, toward which it develops and which becomes visible in its centre."[62] Finally, Tillich suggests a structural analogy in their respective anthropologies. Both view man as living below his true potential; in the case of Marxism, this results from class conflict and alienation, while Christianity perceives man's sinful state as a limiting condition. West notes that for Tillich, "The Marxist expectation reflects the Christian hope, in not being merely an abstract demand placed upon the social situation . . . but a promise inherent in the movement of Being in history itself."[63] Tillich reinforced the Christian-Marxist connection by blending together metaphors and ideals, as illustrated, for example, in his observation that man's "true being and his real existence contradict each other. Man is fallen. . . . He is estranged from himself and his true humanity."[64] Tillich achieved considerable fame for a theologian; yet, like other notable Christians of the era, he drew criticism for his willingness to explore connections between the ethical systems of Christianity and communism.

The crescendo of Christian (largely Protestant) association with the Communist movement in the United States was signaled in a statement by J. B. Matthews, an aide to Senator Joseph McCarthy, in his 1953 article, "Reds and Our Churches." His provocative opening comment, "The largest single group supporting the Communist apparatus in the United States today is composed of Protestant clergymen,"[65] drew praise for its candor from the right wing of American Christianity and criticism from the left wing for its defamatory and hate-inspiring consequences. Matthews' accusation illustrated the deep political divide that separated American Christians, and his comment reflected the nation's fear that communist philosophy had penetrated to the heart of American culture and threatened to undermine its sacred democracy.

What in truth was happening was less subversive than what Matthews imagined. There was growing recognition by Ward, Tillich, and other clergymen and theologians of the rising importance of economic philosophy to the orderly progression of human culture. Economics held a potential key to the eradication of intractable social pathologies such as war and poverty, and Christians persisted in their beliefs of the inadequacy and, in some instances, irrelevancy of Christian ethics to modern problems. Ward, in particular, believed that if Christian tradition could be preserved, it must find its moorings within one of the secular philosophies over which nations warred; yet capitalism often seemed an inhospitable host to Christianity, and the experience of the Great Depression only heightened such anxieties. Spiritual despair often accompanied economic hardship. And it was not only economic "bad times" that contributed to spiritual malaise. Most Protestants, including radical leftists like Ward, observed that both capitalism and collectivism had moral limitations even in the best of times:

> It is the vision of ends that Western life lacks. It has no sense of direction. It is all motion—at unequaled speed—but what is its goal? It is atomic, chaotic—not yet corporate. Why do its millions work and fight and breed and die? Do even their leaders know? For what shall man live? For all, says Communism. For each, says Individualism. For both, says the ethic of Jesus. Having in the course of its development rescued the individual from both the early communal society of the East and the aristocratic society of the West that he may find himself in a voluntary brotherhood, this religious morality is not to be deceived by the suicidal separatism of individualistic democracy nor the equally fatal subordination which dogmatic Communism imposes upon personality.[66]

In the minds of Ward and other economically engaged American religious leaders, the fate of the church and of industrial society had somewhere along the line become conjoined, and the contradictions between the two were beginning to fester. According to Ward, "industrial society cannot continue in its present divided, inconsistent, increasingly futile state—partly humane and partly callous, now democratic and now imperialistic. Nor can a religion whose function it is to develop the ethic of Jesus remain half bound to, and half free from, the living death of this acquisitive society."[67] For many American clergymen of the early twentieth century, religious–economic tension was not durable but debilitating.

Christian Progressivism

The era of Christian progressivism is more difficult to define chronologically, and to some extent philosophically, than any other American movement that has sought to harmonize religious and economic ideals. One reason for this ambiguity is that the movement has at times been associated more narrowly with the Social Gospel, while at other times it has been seen as part of the larger secular movement called American progressivism. While there are parallels among these movements, there are also differences. The era of American progressivism commonly is associated with the trust-busting programs of the Theodore Roosevelt and Woodrow Wilson administrations and their efforts to counter the monopolistic practices of American industrial giants while preserving the nation's newfound economic dominance. In a general sense, progressivism embraced the "rise of scientific professionalism in all areas of endeavor" along with broadsweeping campaigns of moral reform.[68] Yet, while it emphasized the attainment of a just society through the techniques of social constructivism, it is not commonly associated with "collectivist" economic philosophy. Progressivists recognized the importance of private property to American economic success but understood equally that the gross distributions of income that had resulted from American industrialization were not socially just, healthy, or even tenable. They also believed that government had a significant economic role to play in maintaining a level playing field between various interests that engaged one another in the American economy. Seen in this light, Christian progressivism incorporated the "right wing" of the Social Gospel movement and its most prominent thinkers such as Harry Emerson Fosdick and Shailer Mathews, but it excluded the left-wing socialists like George Herron. In addition, Ferenc Szasz and Gary Scott Smith offer evidence to suggest that Christian progressivism also incorporated elements of American evangelicalism that are often overlooked.[69]

Despite the efforts of Szasz and other scholars to bind Christian progressivism within a narrow chronology, the underlying philosophy that advocated a strong governmental commitment to social justice continued through the eras of the New Deal and Great Society and, though muted, exists today. Martin Marty states that for the fifty-year period running roughly from 1925 to 1975, "most Catholic and Protestant theological economists and economic theologians were devotees of some form of welfare-minded, liberal, New-Deal progressivism."[70] Yet it is not the chronological but the philosophical breadth of Christian progressivism that is of interest here, for it welcomed the participation of new voices to the religious-economic debate in the United States.

Of those groups that helped to expand and energize Christian economic thought in the progressive era, Roman Catholic clergymen, theologians, and social ethicists made perhaps the most significant contributions, although much of that endowment has only recently been recognized. American Catholic leaders had greater obstacles to overcome in their efforts to accommodate new ideas of politics and economics than their Protestant counterparts. Not the least of these impediments was the enormity of their own tradition and the resistance of the Vatican to the perceived Americanism that was infecting U.S. Catholics. One of the most prominent of the economically engaged Catholic leaders was Father John A. Ryan, a nationally renowned social ethicist who was a major contributor to the American Bishops' "Program of Social Reconstruction" (1919). Ryan was a progressive Catholic who was sympathetic to the Americanism of the period, a supporter of Franklin Roosevelt's New Deal, and an avid student of three famous economists who viewed "aggregate demand" as the "key to economic health": Jean Sismondi, Thomas Malthus, and John Maynard Keynes.[71] Richard C. Bayer states that Ryan's book *Distributive Justice* "represents an interesting combination of market economics and a natural law theory applied to the problem of income distribution in the United States."[72]

Also significant was Jesuit theologian Bernard Dempsey's conception of the "functional economy," which caused a stir upon the publication of a book by that title in 1958. Recent scholarly efforts to resurrect Dempsey's ideas have contributed to a rekindling of interest in this influential social thinker. Dempsey, who received his PhD from Harvard in 1940, insisted that a truly functional economy does more than simply contribute to the material advance of society; it also serves to orient each person toward the "true end" of his or her existence. Dempsey's affinity for more organic forms of social organization vis-à-vis Enlightenment rationalism, according to D. Stephen Long, dictated that he "could not find palatable Keynes's appropriation of the Jesuitical theological tradition for the Keynesian revolution."[73] Dempsey was an interdisciplinarian by nature who believed, like Reinhold Niebuhr, that capitalism must be reconstructed around a "*telos* of the perfection of human personality"; moreover, he was convinced that Keynes and other secular economists misrepresented Scholastic ideas on usury and other economic principles for the crass purpose of advancing their own positions.[74]

The addition of Roman Catholic progressives to the Christian economic debate served to counterbalance some of the conservatism that appeared among evangelical and fundamentalist Protestants during the Eisenhower administration. The 1950s were in many ways one of the most formative periods in the confluence of religious and economic thought in American history. Challenging the stereotype of a staid and conservative decade, Robert Ellwood provides evidence that the 1950s "were a potent spiritual marketplace in which traditional denominations were highly competitive, the nostalgia for normalcy working in their favor"; yet, concurrently, there was an emerging underground market for New Age spirituality and the religious eclecticism of "monks and professors."[75] The 1950s exhibited the "paradox of a boom in conventional religion running alongside an upsurge of interest in exoticism."[76] Its religious diversity was a "supply-side phenomenon" that demonstrated the spiritual aspects of Austrian economist Joseph Schumpeter's theory of "creative destruction." Baptists and Methodists displaced traditional American religious groups (Episcopalians, Presbyterians, and Congregationalists) even as evangelicals and charismatics made inroads into the Baptist and Methodist denominations. Rather than religious traditionalism, for the first time the nation was forced to confront the phenomenon of "religious obsolescence."[77]

The following decade, the 1960s, witnessed the rise of two radical yet antithetical attempts to synthesize religious and economic ideas in the movements known as liberation theology and Christian reconstructionism. The former, a blend of "liberal" theological doctrine with socialist (often Marxist) economic principles, was born in Central and South America, but its influence quickly spread to the Northern Hemisphere. However, lingering fear of communism in the aftermath of the Cold War, in combination with the enormous economic prosperity of the United States, has limited liberation theology's influence on American social philosophy. In fact, the connection between liberation theology and communism has been downplayed in the United States in favor of using its theological precepts as a platform from which to criticize the perceived injustices of modern capitalism. As Long observes, American exponents of liberation theology such as James Cone and Rosemary Radford Ruether are more reticent than their southern contemporaries to directly link Christianity and Marxism; rather, "what binds these theologians together is their rejection of capitalism as an appropriate practice for Christians."[78] Cone's theology, articulated forcefully in *A Black Theology of Liberation*, "is implicitly suspicious of sociological analyses as are found in Hayek. Capitalism did not provide some inevitable road out of serfdom for African Americans. Capitalism was the problem not the solution."[79] Similarly, Long notes that the Catholic "eco-feminist" Ruether finds capitalism "wicked because it has arisen out of imperialism and because it is marked by male aggressiveness, dominance and ecological destructiveness."[80]

At the opposite end from liberation theology on the continuum of Christian economic thought is Christian reconstructionism, a philosophy that views a theologically restructured capitalism as a tool for achieving a Christian theocracy in the United States. Gary North of the Institute for Christian Economics (ICE) promotes *disciplined* participation in the capitalist economy through the application of biblical (primarily Old Testament) values and principles as a means for Christians to differentiate themselves from unbelievers and ultimately usher in a Christianized social order. The triumph of Christian society will be determined through the more sound economic behavior of a select Christian community, an economic discipline that the secular world has abandoned. The fragility of the fractional reserve banking system in combination with the nation's dependence on unbacked currency will precipitate a world financial crisis in which winners will be separated from losers as determined by their adherence to biblical principles.[81] Reconstructionists believe that even some nonbelievers will come to realize the truth of "Christian economics," and a theocratic order will emerge.

North follows the monetary prescriptions of the famed Austrian economist Ludwig Mises in arguing for radical reform of the American banking system. His affinity for Mises' monetary principles is justified through the logic of Cornelius Van Til's concept of "borrowed premises"—that is, secular thinkers (i.e., Mises) sometimes unwittingly borrow their ideas and principles from scripture without realizing or acknowledging their biblical debt.[82] North agrees with Mises and Murray Rothbard that the government's unchecked authority in the creation of currency constitutes an inflationary bomb that ultimately will detonate, leading to financial chaos. He insists that the only way to avoid destruction is by deregulating the banking industry and developing a system of "private coinage."[83] God has revealed his opposition in the scriptures to the inflationary system of exchange that government now imposes upon society. Although less economically instructional than the Old Testament, even the gospels are revelatory of God's economic plan for mankind. North states that "any systematic teaching by Jesus on economic matters is limited almost exclusively to the economic framework of his spiritual parables. These are generally conservative in outline: first, private property is affirmed in them; second, men are encouraged to add to their wealth."[84]

Almost every form of economic planning is demonized within the ICE as contrary to biblical teaching. A page from the ICE website entitled "What Is the ICE?" demonstrates the depth of North's revulsion (and that of members of his organization) for those who contend that collective decision making has any role within the modern capitalist economy. North references a statement issued by the National Council of Churches General Board in 1967 as especially egregious:

> Accompanying this growing diversity in the structures of national life has been a growing recognition of the importance of competent planning within and among all resource sectors of the society: education, economic development, land use, social health services, the family system and congregational life. It is not generally recognized that an effective

approach to problem solving requires a comprehensive planning process and coordination in the development of all those resource areas.[85]

North is appalled that Christians have not condemned such proclamations that he considers the equivalent of heresy for their inherently antibiblical economic ideas. The relative innocuousness of this statement by the National Council above and North's response to it provide an indication of the degree to which social and economic planning are anathemas for many Christian economic conservatives.

North and the ICE are representative of an extreme form of religious-economic fundamentalism in the United States that has a limited following. The ICE and other fringe groups of economically activist Christians often undermine their own popular appeal by employing Gnostic theologies that require persistent and intensive instruction by their leaders and cultlike devotion by their followers to maintain cohesion. And the policies they advocate (i.e., "private coinage") are so extreme as to preclude the allegiance of socially moderate Christians. More mainstream movements that have sought to blend Christian theology and economic philosophy are perhaps less exotic but have been highly influential in the development of American culture over the past few decades.

The Rise of a "New" Conservatism

Far more significant than the fringe groups of Christian economic activism is the rising influence of Christian "neoconservatives" and their more subtle fusion of Christian and capitalist values. In 1979, Peter Steinfels described the larger American neoconservative movement as "the serious and intelligent conservatism America has lacked."[86] Constructing a list of prominent Christian neoconservatives adds credibility to Steinfels' claim: Richard John Neuhaus, Michael Novak, George Weigel, and Robert Benne, to name a few. Although some scholars have suggested that the movement has lost momentum in recent years, neoconservatives remain perhaps the most influential group of contemporary Christian economic theorists, buoyed by the demise of socialism (as some neoconservatives predicted)[87] and the rising dominance of capitalism worldwide. In a tongue-in-cheek piece entitled "Neoconservatism: A Eulogy," Norman Podhoretz, a Jewish patriarch of the larger faction of American neoconservatives, suggests that the movement is dead only in the sense that it is no longer "new"; many of its ideas have been assimilated into more traditional American conservatism. Podhoretz insists that neoconservatism has accomplished its objective: "The defense neoconservatives mounted of American society and its traditional values against the frontal assault of the counterculture ended with a victory that in its own modest way resembled the victory of the West over Communism in the cold war. Who today shies away from the word capitalism?"[88]

Indeed, it is appropriate that the successful defense of capitalism is the first and most decisive neoconservative victory cited by Podhoretz (he goes on to list others), for it was the unrelenting criticism of American capitalism in the 1960s that spawned the movement. Michael Novak notes that the failure of the liberal agenda and the marked anticapitalist bias of America's "elite" in this period caused him and many fellow Christians to reject the Great Society idealism of their political upbringings. Especially instrumental for Novak in his conversion to neoconservatism was the fact that despite extensive explorations of socialism for much of the twentieth century, "no theologian, Christian or Jewish, has yet assessed the theological significance of democratic capitalism."[89] In his own Catholic tradition, Novak detects a preoccupation with "distributive ethics" and a lack of understanding of money and other instruments necessary to the proper function of a modern economy.[90] Also significant in Novak's philosophical transformation was his discovery of the economic ideas of Friedrich Hayek. Gary Dorrien notes that in Hayek, Novak discovered "an instructive theorist for Catholic social doctrine" who blended a respect for nature's harmonies with a rejection of collective ideas of social justice, favoring instead a subjective path to the common good.[91] The reliance of contemporary Christian neoconservatives on Austrian economic philosophy is explored in greater detail in the following chapter; for now, it is sufficient to recognize that Christian neoconservativism, just as countless efforts at religious-economic synthesis that came before it, has enlisted secular economic theory in an effort to substantiate its claims.

Significantly, the subjectivist economic ethic with which Christian neoconservativism has aligned itself has emerged victorious, within both American Christianity and the global society. The collapse of Soviet Communism triggered a series of events that spelled the end for collectivist and constructivist ideas of social organization. The fact that the world's last remaining Communist superpower, the People's Republic of China, has a thriving market economy within its borders that produces much of the world's consumer goods is a testament to the overwhelming triumph of capitalism. Moreover, it is unmistakable evidence that the "market" as an instrument essential to modern technological civilization has been conceded. Much of this has to do with Robert Wuthnow's observation that people believe the market to be an essentially moral institution.[92] Reinforcing Wuthnow's conclusion, Martin Marty recognizes that the perceived moral supremacy of the market has marked the end for ideas of Christian progressivism and has led to the reemergence of "a generation of qualified advocates of 'clerical laissez-faire.'"[93] Novak *globalizes* the victory of the free enterprise system, noting, "Both the traditionalist (Third World) and socialist methods have failed; for the whole world there is now only one form of economics."[94] And Stephen Long argues convincingly that a procapitalist economic conservatism has emerged as the "dominant tradition" among American Christians, although he includes both the free market foundation of neoconservatism and the "mixed-economy" stance of more liberal thinkers in that tradition.[95] Still, the mood of American Christianity, as with the secular world with which it has so often aligned itself, is decidedly procapitalist, and neoconservative influence has contributed to the vigor of market-based economic philosophy and to the pervasive enthusiasm for capitalist institutions.

Yet the reality is not so much that economic conservatism has achieved victory within American Christianity but rather that the constructivist liberalism of the opposition has faded from view. The dialectic that has served to balance American Christian economic thought has crumbled under the weight of historical determinism. In 1992, Francis Fukuyama wrote *The End of History and the Last Man*, in which he posits that "modern liberal democracy and technologically driven capitalism" may, as he put it, "constitute the 'end point of mankind's ideological evolution.'"[96] Although Fukuyama was roundly criticized for conjectures that the ideological end of history might concurrently bring about an end to war and other social pathologies (criticisms that Fukuyama believes were unfounded), his recognition of this milestone stated clearly what many had begun to recognize— that the victory of democratic capitalism over socialism was seemingly total and final. It also signaled that the common constructivist foundation of the left wing of the Social Gospel, Christian socialism, Christian progressivism, and the Christian Marxism of liberation theology has been mortally wounded. Each of these movements has depended upon secular theories that viewed government or other secular institutions as the final arbiters of social justice and the sources of a positively constructed social vision, which the triumph of subjectivist capitalism will no longer permit. It is the death of social constructivism that, for all its pretensions, underpinned the visions of the Christian left and served to temper the ambitions of the natural harmony tradition, which today ensures the destruction of the long-standing dialectic of religious-economic synthesis in American society. And it was the dependence of both sides on secular economic philosophy that sub-jected their debate to the arbitration of history, which obligingly has deter-mined the victor.

THE TRANSFORMATION OF
AMERICAN CHRISTIAN ETHICS

One might characterize as remarkable the rise in prestige of Roman Catholicism in American culture over the past several decades. For much of its history, the United States and its predominantly Protestant traditions fos-tered an intense anti-Catholic bias that witnessed violence such as that por-trayed in books and movies like Martin Scorsese's *Gangs of New York*. While the entertainment industry may well have sensationalized this rivalry for profit, a legitimate historical record of this hostility exists.[97] There was a time not so long ago when Catholics were reviled by many Protestants for their allegiance to Rome and their apocryphal beliefs. At a meeting of the Evangelical Alliance in New York City in 1873, a Canadian evangelical spokesman rose to proclaim, "The most formidable foe among us is not Deism or Atheism, or any form of infidelity, but the nominally Christian Church of Rome."[98] Hostility continued well into the twentieth century. Presbyterian fundamentalist Carl McIntyre stated in 1945 that "one would be much better off in a communistic society than in a Roman Catholic fas-cist set-up. . . . America has to face the Roman Catholic terror."[99] While the basis for such long-standing antagonism was primarily theological, the divisions extended to politics, morality, and even economic ideology.

American Protestantism considered itself to be constructed on dis-tinctly different values and principles than the "Church of Rome." Ac-cording to Thomas C. Reeves, nineteenth-century Protestantism "en-dorsed stern public and private morality, free-enterprise capitalism, individualism, and a generally optimistic view of human nature."[100] Its ethic conformed perfectly to an emerging liberal democracy on a still vir-gin continent. Liberal Protestant theologians and pastors, having "ab-sorbed much that was fashionable, especially in academic circles," were generally moving to the left and "choosing increasingly to shun the su-pernatural and flirt with pragmatism, empiricism, and science."[101] Al-though mainline denominations were already in decline vis-à-vis evangel-ical and fundamentalist denominations in this period, "liberal" Protestant theologians and ethicists like the Niebuhr brothers, John C. Bennett, Paul

Tillich, and Paul Ramsey enjoyed continuing prestige. They took their place alongside conservatives like Francis Schaeffer and Carl Henry in constituting the Golden Age of Protestant ethics. Even those associated with Protestantism's "pink fringe" and targeted by McCarthy's Committee on Un-American Activities, such as Methodist Bishop G. Bromley Oxnam, were highly regarded in many circles. They were considered to be experts in politics, ethics, economics, and other disciplines, in addition to being pastors, theologians, and church historians. These public theologians were multifaceted, writing works of philosophy and theology while simultaneously maintaining pastoral ministries or academic positions. The absence of widespread media like television prevented mass promotion of their messages and encouraged reflection on the critical issues of the time. These were giants by the standard of today's televangelists.

Public theologians like those of the early to mid-twentieth century have disappeared from the radar screen. Presidents today rarely consult men of the cloth for reasons other than personal confession or, more crassly, promotional opportunities in appealing to various constituencies, and for good reason. Protestant theologians in the United States lost their reputation as learned and religious men who can offer insight into perplexing problems of politics and culture. Reading the ethical and theological works of the "Golden Age" in light of the feel-good theology of today reveals the extent of decline. Books like Reinhold Niebuhr's *The Nature and Destiny of Man* or Henry's *The Uneasy Conscience of Modern Fundamentalism* offer profound theological insights in the context of unique social, historical, and anthropological views. The decline of Protestant ethics in the last half of the twentieth century, and general conservatism of Catholic social thought in the same period, opened the door to what is today a remarkable cultural alliance between traditional Catholics and conservative Protestants (principally Evangelicals).

Because the underlying reasons for the traditional hostility between Catholics and Protestants in the United States are myriad and complex, it is unsurprising that the newfound conviviality between Evangelicals and Catholics is equally complicated. A microcosm of this attitudinal makeover is found in the personal transformation of American Evangelical leader Billy Graham. In 1962, Graham's associate Robert Ferm penned a letter to a Kansas minister in which he said, "Certainly Catholic priests do not attend [crusade services]. [They] have not been invited to participate in any way."[102] Yet Mark Noll and Carolyn Nystrom note that by the 1980s, "Catholic leaders appeared on crusade planning committees, crusade platforms, and counselor training classes—with growing mutual respect from both sides."[103]

It was the Catholic approach to governance and civil order, long perceived as inimical to liberty, that, as much as sacraments, doctrines like papal infallibility, and other theological issues, precipitated the immense divide between Protestants and Catholics in the United States. Many detected anti-American sentiments in the social commentary of American priests and bishops. Noll and Nystrom characterize the attitude of nineteenth-century New York Bishop John Hughes as believing "Americans were dangerously mad about acquiring wealth, which resulted from the excessive individualism of American political and social principles, which were a direct manifestation of Protestantism."[104] Those Catholic attitudes were perceived to have changed dramatically, however, during the period of the Cold War. Catholic leaders became champions of the American way. Thus, the perceived socialist leanings of mainline Protestant leadership in the mid-twentieth century combined with the zealous anticommunist attitudes of the Catholic hierarchy in prompting a change of attitude among conservative Protestants who increasingly parted ways with the "elitist" stances of their own clergy. As far back as 1923, J. Gresham Machen's book *Christianity and Liberalism* hinted at the transformation, conceding a "gulf" between Catholic and Evangelical thought on various issues. "'But profound as it is,' Machen continued, 'it seems almost trifling compared to the abyss which stands between us and many ministers of our own church.'"[105]

The new alliance was forged largely by what Timothy George described as "ecumenism of the trenches"—an emerging coalescence on "support for parental choice in education, advocacy of the traditional values of chastity, family, and community, opposition to abortion on demand, and repudiation of pornography."[106] The point here is that while theological issues still divide Catholics and Evangelicals in significant ways, the two groups have grown together in their respective views of social ethics and moral theology. Not the least of the issues of convergence has been in the area of economics. Reconciliation of the two groups has been a two-way street, as Noll and Nystrom observed: "American Catholics have come to accept some aspects of the liberal tradition about which they had earlier been ambiguous, and American evangelicals have begun to modify their once wholehearted embrace of political liberalism."[107] Evangelical leader Charles Colson and Lutheran turned Catholic priest Richard John Neuhaus (among others) combined to forge the Evangelicals and Catholics Together movement that has been highly influential in bridging the gaps between the groups by emphasizing social and moral thought in lieu of theology. While acknowledging the theological differences that remain, Colson and Neuhaus find a bridge that unites:

> The lines of conflict are variously drawn and the combatants are variously defined, but the undeniable contention is between a militantly secular naturalism, on the one side, and, on the other, a biblical understanding of reality as the object of God's creating and redeeming work. Those who deny or ignore that understanding have met with considerable success in eliminating the influence and even the memory of Christianity from more and more aspects of our public life.[108]

The Second Vatican Council and the pontificate of Pope John Paul II were instrumental in reshaping Evangelical attitudes toward Catholicism and in giving a "new face" to the Catholic Church in America. The pope's ecumenism was instrumental in this transformation. In December of 2003, John Paul hosted Thomas Oden and other editors of the evangelically oriented InterVarsity Press. What was unusual about the meeting was that such Evangelical colloquiums at the Vatican were, by this time, not uncommon.[109] John Paul's ostensibly rising appreciation for the virtues of democratic capitalism, observed in the writings of Novak, George Weigel, Richard John Neuhaus, and others, was critical in bridging this gap between Evangelicals and Catholics. Evangelical acceptance and even admiration of Catholic social teaching was radically heightened by the impression that the supposed "socialist leanings" of Catholic clergy were at an end. Papal condemnation of liberation theology and its Marxist economic philosophy provided additional evidence of the Catholic Church's acceptance of capitalist values. Subsequently, Catholic economic ideas like "personalism" and "subsidiarity" began to be embraced by conservative American Protestants in growing numbers.

The importance of political and economic philosophy in American religious culture is no better illustrated than by this narrowing of the longstanding divide between Protestants and Catholics. Capitalism and a conservative political agenda have achieved unification around common principles capable of overcoming the theological gulf formed by doctrines like papal infallibility and justification by faith. Theological issues have retreated to the background even as politics, economics, and ethics have taken center stage. This novel alliance of politically and economically conservative Protestants and Catholics has formed principally around common political objectives and a natural theology of the market that combines Christian and capitalist values and is capable of healing old and noxious wounds. The power of religious and economic synthesis in American culture lives on.

CONCLUDING REMARKS

A resounding majority of the world's population now recognizes that society has become too complex to enable centralized planning or other forms of institutional coordination that were once considered essential to peaceful and equitable progress. Philosophically, "Real Socialism" is maintained as a patient on life support—ironically kept alive by conservatives to periodically resurrect for the purposes of warning society of the perils of government interventionism. There are still those who question the justice of the market, to be sure. However, their focus is no longer "constructivist" but rather "activist," targeting causes like the environment, human rights, nuclear power, and globalization.

If Fukuyama's thesis is accurate that we have arrived at the endpoint of political and economic ideology, the question becomes, what does this resolution of history mean for American Christianity? Does it also resolve the dialectic that has tempered religious-economic utopianism by preventing the triumph of either constructivist or subjectivist philosophies in American Christian social thought? To posit our arrival at the ideological end of history as "good" for Christianity would be to suggest that the maintenance of tension between opposing theories of social organization has no benefit. Yet do these implications not defy the lessons of history? For, while there have been periods in the American Christian tradition when one side gained the upper hand in the social debate, such periods inevitably were followed by countervailing forces that prevented total ideological conquest. The evangelical free market theology of the frontier was subsequently offset by the late nineteenth-century development of Christian socialism. The "gospel of wealth" was countered by the left wing of the Social Gospel movement. The dominance of Christian progressives in the mid-twentieth century gave way to the rise of the Christian Right in the seventies and eighties, just as liberation theology was opposed by Christian reconstructionism and, more recently, by Christian libertarianism and neoconservatism. Each attempt to blend Christian theology and economic philosophy was responded to by a complementary movement that helped neutralize its pretensions to "Truth" while reenabling Christianity's prophetic voice. Fukuyama's thesis implies that no foundational response is forthcoming to contemporary Christian conservatism and its allegiance to capitalism.

But what problem does this pose for Christianity? If history, through its exhaustive process of trial and error, has determined that the aggregation of individual expressions in a market context is the only feasible means to the collective good, why should this be of concern? The rise of Third World economies and the relative affluence of so many countries at this period in history would seem to validate this conclusion. However, Reinhold Niebuhr believed that the radical triumph of either side in the economic debate posed a grave threat to Christian conceptions of transcendence and human "personality." Niebuhr insisted that both the liberal and collectivist traditions of the Enlightenment diminish the religious dimension of personality by defining the individual exclusively in rational and behavioral terms.[110] Collectivism does this by suppressing man's need and ability to rise above the historical situation and by forcing him into planned institutional arrangements as dictated by a central authority. Ironically, the individualism of "bourgeois civilization" accomplishes the same end by damaging the organic quality of human culture and promoting development of the "discrete individual who makes himself the final end of his own existence."[111] Deluded into believing that the freedom exercised through involvement in the capitalist order is sufficient to preserve a transcendent self-awareness, Niebuhr's "bourgeois individual" denies the need for institutional supports and believes himself to be impervious to materialist influences on his self-understanding.

Niebuhr insists that the depth of the religious dimension of human personality can only be preserved by its suspension above competing secular philosophies. He stated that the "controversy between those who would 'plan' justice and order and those who trust in freedom to establish both is, therefore, an irresolvable one. Every healthy society will live in the tension of that controversy until the *end of history*, and will prove its health by preventing either side from gaining complete victory."[112] Niebuhr's words are ominous when read in the context of Fukuyama's pronouncement, and their foreboding tone is only heightened by the triumphalism of conservative American Christians like George Gilder, who states, "Capitalism is simply the essential mode of human life that corresponds to religious truth."[113]

An unfortunate consequence of the persistent efforts by Christians to synthesize their religious and economic lives has been to eliminate the tension among competing social systems that has helped to *preserve* the religious dimension of human personality. Moreover, the church's voice on social issues has been attenuated through its vacillation through a minefield of economic theory. Disagreements over the "Christian way" in economic life are healthy; too close alignments with secular theories that change with vicissitudes of history are not. As American culture approaches the possible realization of this vast project through resolution of the dialectic, its prospective benefits and potential dangers come more fully into view. The triumph of capitalism and the belief by Christians that the market is a moral instrument implies less of a need for Christian reflection on market outcomes and causes us to drift farther away from the concept of a morally redemptive economy. Yet, as more markets and their associated technologies begin to infringe upon the most sacred aspects of our lives, the need is greater than ever to assess the moral persistence of democratic capitalism.

NOTES

1. This statement is not intended to devalue the exceptional work of Roger Finke, Rodney Stark, Robert Handy, R. Laurence Moore, Susan Curtis, Robert Ellwood, and other scholars who will be referenced in this chapter. It only suggests that given the importance of this dynamic to the development of American culture, relatively few have investigated its structure, methods, and consequences.

2. As John Howard Yoder observed of the early church, American Christians of the nineteenth and twentieth centuries (as today) believed that "Jesus did not provide a social ethic relevant to the continuing life of human communities" and found themselves "obliged to borrow one from somewhere else." See John Howard Yoder, *The Politics of Jesus: Vicit Agnus Noster*, 2nd ed. (Grand Rapids, MI: William B. Eerdmans, 1994), 162.

3. Michael Novak, in fact, attempts to forestall possible charges of utopianism in liberal philosophy by stating, "Utopian theories of liberty are out of place in the real world. No perfectly free, just, or rational society has ever existed or ever will exist. This fact and this expectation are wholly consistent both with Christian conceptions of original sin and with the nonutopian liberal political philosophies of the West." See Michael Novak, *Toward a Theology of the Corporation*, rev. ed. (Washington, DC: The American Enterprise Institute Press, 1990), 32–33.

4. Niebuhr included Darwin in this line of Enlightenment thinkers because of his belief that Darwinism embraced a mood of historical optimism in which "the law of survival in nature is thought of as a force of harmony and progress which will transmute even the most tragic conflicts of history into means of historical advance." See Reinhold Niebuhr, *The Nature and Destiny of Man: A Christian Interpretation*, vol. 2, *Human Destiny* (New York: Charles Scribner's Sons, 1941), 165.

5. Stone observes that the "liberalism against which Niebuhr directed his polemics consisted of the illusion of moral progress, which he found in very diverse forms in Leibniz, Herder, Kant, Hegel, Mill, Spencer, Darwin, Marx, Comte, Condorcet, McConnell, and Dewey. Liberalism for Niebuhr necessarily included an illusion of optimism, and the illusion became the central theme in Niebuhr's attacks on it." See Ronald H. Stone, *Reinhold Niebuhr: Prophet to Politicians* (Nashville: Abingdon Press, 1972), 61, 38–39.

6. Reinhold Niebuhr, *The Children of Light and the Children of Darkness: A Vindication of Democracy and a Critique of Its Traditional Defense* (New York: Charles Scribner's Sons, 1944), 7.

7. William Lee Miller, *The First Liberty: Religion and the American Republic* (New York: Paragon House Publishers, 1985), 303.

8. George Marsden, *The Soul of the American University: From Protestant Establishment to Established Nonbelief* (New York: Oxford University Press, 1994), 34.

9. Michael Sandel observes that the public philosophy of the early American nation was largely republican in that the organization of society was not neutral respecting values and ends. Economic debates focused more on the contribution of economic structures to self-government and the preservation of virtue among the citizenry than on measures of economic growth. See Michael J. Sandel, *Democracy's Discontent: America in Search of Public Philosophy* (Cambridge, MA: The Belknap Press of Harvard University Press, 1996), 5–6, 125–26, 136.

10. Jose Miguez Bonino, "Wesley's Doctrine of Sanctification from a Liberationist Perspective," in *Sanctification & Liberation: Liberation Theologies in Light of the Wesleyan Tradition*, ed. Theodore Runyan (Nashville: Abingdon Press, 1981), 55.

11. Theodore Runyon, "Introduction: Wesley and the Theologies of Liberation," in *Sanctification & Liberation: Liberation Theologies in Light of the Wesleyan Tradition*, edited by Theodore Runyon, 9–48 (Nashville: Abingdon Press, 1981), 17.

12. Quoted in Robert Southey, *The Life of Wesley* (London: Hutchison & Co., 1820), in Max Weber, *The Protestant Ethic and the Spirit of Capitalism*, trans. Talcott Parsons (Gloucester, MA: Peter Smith, 1988 [orig. pub. 1904–1905]), 175.

13. Weber, *The Protestant Ethic and the Spirit of Capitalism*, 166.

14. Weber, *The Protestant Ethic and the Spirit of Capitalism*, 163. Perhaps just as significant was a demonstrable split within American Puritanism over economic issues as affluence spawned by the "Protestant ethic" led some to question restrictions on consumption and other kinds of economic behavior. Governor John Winthrop's own son, John Winthrop Jr., was instrumental in acquiring state-of-the-art milling and foundry equipment and bringing in non-Puritan ironworkers who had a "reputation for drunkenness and brawling." These economically expansionist activities plus the rise of a merchant class within Puritanism that adhered to a set of more "worldly" values doomed the distinctly Puritan economy of the Massachusetts Bay Colony. See Stephen Innes, *Creating the Commonwealth: The Economic Culture of Puritan New England* (New York: W. W. Norton, 1995), 248–49, 254–55, 302.

15. Innes, *Creating the Commonwealth*, 154.

16. Robert Babcock marked the beginning of the end of this American institution, stating "by the late 1820s, . . . if not before, industrial capitalism had undermined artisan republicanism in the larger seaports." See Robert H. Babcock, "The Decline of Artisan Republicanism in Portland, Maine, 1825–1850," *The New England Quarterly* 63 (March 1990): 9.

17. Wilentz further notes the abandonment of "just price-book arrangements" in favor of hiring the "least expensive hands available." See Sean Wilentz, *Chants Democratic: New York City & the Rise of the American Working Class, 1788–1850* (New York: Oxford University Press, 1984), 33–34.

18. Wilentz, *Chants Democratic*, 24–26.

19. For an assessment of Scottish influence on the philosophy of James Madison, see Roy Branson, "James Madison and the Scottish Enlightenment," *Journal of the History of Ideas* 40 (April–June, 1979): 235–50.

20. Harold Bloom, *The American Religion: The Emergence of the Post-Christian Nation* (New York: Simon & Schuster, 1992), 63.

21. R. Laurence Moore, *Selling God: American Religion in the Marketplace of Culture* (Oxford: Oxford University Press, 1994), 48–49.

22. George M. Marsden, *Religion and American Culture* (New York: Harcourt Brace College Publishers, 1990), 53.

23. Paul Heyne, "Clerical Laissez-Faire: A Study in Theological Economics," in *Religion, Economics and Social Thought*, ed. Walter Block and Irving Hexham (Vancouver, BC: The Fraser Institute, 1986), 126. McVickar was one of many "theologian-economists" of the early nineteenth century. His designation as one of the first academic economists in the United States is attributed to Edwin Seligman. See Edwin R. A. Seligman, "Economics in the United States: An Historical Sketch," reprinted in his *Essays in Economics* (1925), 137; cited in Heyne, "Clerical Laissez-Faire."

24. Henry F. May, *Protestant Churches and Industrial America* (1949), 14; quoted in Heyne, "Clerical Laissez-Faire," 126. Describing American life between 1812 and the Civil War, H. Richard Niebuhr observed, "The church seemed to accept a religious version of the doctrine of *laissez faire* and the belief that enlightened self-interest was the agent of divine providence." See H. Richard Niebuhr, *The Social Sources of Denominationalism* (Hamden, CT: The Shoestring Press, 1929), 234.

25. Heyne, "Clerical Laissez-Faire," 126.

26. John McVickar, *Outlines of Political Economy: Being a Republication of the Article upon That Subject [by J. R. McCulloch] Contained in the Edinburgh Supplement to the Encyclopedia Britannica, Together with Notes Explanatory and Critical, and a Summary of the Science* (1825), 69; quoted in Heyne, "Clerical Laissez-Faire," 148n3.

27. Heyne, "Clerical Laissez-Faire," 130. Heyne uses extracts from Wayland's texts to confirm the penetration of Adam Smith's belief in the existence of natural harmonies into Wayland's thought. For example, Wayland said, "As all relations, whether moral or physical, are the result of this enactment, an order of sequence once discovered in morals, is just as invariable as an order of sequence in physics." Francis Wayland, *The Elements of Moral Science* (Boston: Gould & Lincoln, 1854), 25; quoted in Heyne, "Clerical Laissez-Faire," 129.

28. Wayland's "Chapter Fourth" of *The Elements of Moral Science*, entitled "Justice as It Respects Reputation," describes the means by which individual reputation limits human vice. See Wayland, *The Elements of Moral Science*, 264–74.

29. Wayland, *The Elements of Moral Science*, 135, 22 (emphasis author's).

30. See Heyne, "Clerical Laissez-Faire," 131, 149n21.

31. According to Tocqueville, "Americans cleave to the things of this world as if assured that they will never die," and further, "They clutch everything but hold nothing fast." See Alexis de Tocqueville, *Democracy in America*, trans. George Lawrence, ed. J. P. Mayer (Garden City, NY: Doubleday & Company, 1969), 526, 529, 536.

32. Noll cites Morton White, *The Philosophy of the American Revolution* (New York: Oxford University Press, 1978); and Garry Wills, *Inventing America: Jefferson's Declaration of Independence* (New York: Doubleday, 1978) as "providing alternative explanations for the intellectual contexts in which Scottish Common Sense came to prominence in America. Still, we do not yet have a convincing explanation of the processes lying behind this occurrence." See Mark A. Noll, "Common Sense Traditions and American Evangelical Thought," *American Quarterly* 37 (Summer 1985): 218, 218n5.

33. Fawn M. Brodie, *No Man Knows My History: The Life of Joseph Smith the Mormon Prophet* (New York: Alfred A. Knopf, 1966), 104–5.

34. Quoted in W. Hepworth Dixon, *Spiritual Wives* (Philadelphia, 1868), 237, 262ff; cited in Brodie, 186. Kenneth Ludmerer also notes the extension of Noyes' perfection-

ism to an early form of eugenics, stating that Noyes "was the first in modern times to suggest the possibility of improving the human race specifically by selective breeding." See Kenneth M. Ludmerer, *Genetics and American Society: A Historical Appraisal* (Baltimore: Johns Hopkins University Press, 1972), 10.

35. German influences on Ely and other Protestants were critical in the intellectual formation of American Christian socialism. William Hutchison specifically references Frederick Schleiermacher, who "explicated as well as embodied the argument for religious-cultural accommodation" and who embraced the new concepts of social science. See William R. Hutchison, *The Modernist Impulse in American Protestantism* (Cambridge, MA: Harvard University Press, 1976), 5.

36. Robert T. Handy, "Christianity and Socialism in America, 1900–1920," in *Modern American Protestantism and Its World: Historical Articles on Protestantism in American Religious Life*, vol. 6, *Protestantism and Social Christianity*, ed. Martin E. Marty (Munich: K. G. Saur, 1992), 87.

37. Handy, "Christianity and Socialism in America, 1900–1920," 87–88. A goal of the Christian Socialist Fellowship was "to show that Socialism is the necessary economic expression of the Christian life." See *The Christian Socialist*, May 15, 1909, 1; quoted in Handy, "Christianity and Socialism in America, 1900–1920."

38. Unheard of for a Christian minister of his time, Herron divorced his wife and quickly remarried. Later he would renounce his Christian faith for which he was publicly shamed. See Handy, "Christianity and Socialism in America, 1900–1920," 88–89, 91.

39. Niebuhr observed that "denominational Christianity, that is a Christianity that surrenders its leadership to the social forces of national and economic life, offers no hope to the divided world. . . . From it the world can expect none of the prophetic guidance it requires in its search for synthesis." See Niebuhr, *The Social Sources of Denominationalism*, 26–27, 275.

40. Winthrop S. Hudson, *Religion in America: An Historical Account of the Development of American Religious Life*, 4th ed. (New York: Macmillan Publishing Company, 1987), 154.

41. What came to be titled "The Gospel of Wealth" initially was published in two parts as "Wealth" and "The Best Fields for Philanthropy" in *North American Review*, June and December 1889. See Andrew Carnegie, "The Gospel of Wealth," in *The Responsibilities of Wealth*, ed. Dwight F. Burlingame (Bloomington, IN: Indiana University Press, 1992), 5.

42. Marsden notes Charles Cole's comment that "the justification of prosperity" is "no better illustrated than in Horace Bushnell's sermon, *Prosperity Our Duty* (1847)." See Charles C. Cole Jr., *The Social Ideas of Northern Evangelists 1826–1860* (New York, 1954), 169; cited in George Marsden, "The Gospel of Wealth, the Social Gospel, and the Salvation of Souls in Nineteenth-Century America," in *Modern American Protestantism and its World*, 5n7.

43. Carnegie, "The Gospel of Wealth," 27.

44. Carnegie, "The Gospel of Wealth," 25.

45. John D. Rockefeller Jr. founded the Institute for Social and Religious Research in order to promote his own brand of liberal, ecumenical Protestantism. To further the cause, he ceased all denominational philanthropy in 1934, providing only "general" funding of religious institutions and projects thereafter. Albert Schenkel observes that for

Rockefeller, "liberal Protestantism provided both the perfect framework for an affirmation of modern technological society and the idealism with which to keep the technology working for the benefit of mankind." See Albert F. Schenkel, *The Rich Man and the Kingdom: John D. Rockefeller, Jr., and the Protestant Establishment* (Minneapolis: Fortress Press, 1995), 94, 148, 174.

46. Marsden, *The Soul of the American University*, 257.

47. Curtis notes that while the Gospelers "did not abandon their commitment to social justice, as the decade [the 1920s] wore on they came to believe that business strength, governmental oversight, and an ethos of consumption could deliver abundance, justice and meaning to Americans." See Susan Curtis, *A Consuming Faith: The Social Gospel and Modern American Culture* (Baltimore: Johns Hopkins University Press, 1991), xiii.

48. The reference to the *best practices* of European nationalism is derisive. It refers to the fact that there was some support within the Social Gospel for ideas of ethnic purity associated with European nationalism. Social Darwinism and its leading proponent Herbert Spencer had a major influence on American intellectuals during this period to include Josiah Strong and other adherents of the Social Gospel.

49. According to Curtis, "many social gospelers by the 1920s advised their audiences to find fulfillment by 'consuming' Protestant values and services just as they would the goods of the marketplace." The blending of religious, political, and commercial themes began to appear in the nation's unique civil religion as well. Curtis notes particularly Woodrow Wilson's famous "Message to the American People" (1917) that "fused social gospel ideas, a benevolent and protective state, and the corporate ethos into a national creed. Like the church advertisers, he left unclear whether religious, political, or economic forces held the key to that faith." See Curtis, *A Consuming Faith*, 50, 12, 191–92.

50. William H. P. Faunce, *The New Horizon of State and Church* (New York: Macmillan, 1918), 14; quoted in Curtis, *A Consuming Faith*, 193.

51. Roger Finke and Rodney Stark, *The Churching of America, 1776–1990: Winners and Losers in Our Religious Economy* (New Brunswick, NJ: Rutgers University Press, 1992), 210–12.

52. Finke and Stark refer to Edward Brunner's *Village Communities* (New York: George H. Doran Company, 1927) as providing evidence of the friction between traditional and charismatic religions and the heightened competition between them in rural America. See Finke and Stark, *The Churching of America, 1776–1990*, 209.

53. Robert D. Linder and Richard V. Pierard, *Twilight of the Saints: Biblical Christianity and Civil Religion in America* (Downers Grove, IL: InterVarsity Press, 1978), 73.

54. R. Laurence Moore, *Selling God*, 117.

55. Robert Wuthnow, *The Restructuring of American Religion: Society and Faith Since World War II* (Princeton, NJ: Princeton University Press, 1988), 55.

56. Robert T. Handy, *The American Religious Depression, 1925–1935*, Facet Books Historical Series, no. 9, ed. Richard C. Wolf (Philadelphia: Fortress Press, 1968).

57. Handy observes that twenty of the thirty-five largest denominations reduced total expenditures from between 30 to 50 percent in 1934. See Handy, *The American Religious Depression, 1925–1935*, 7, 13–14.

58. Robert H. Craig, "An Introduction to the Life and Thought of Harry F. Ward," in *Modern American Protestantism and Its World: Historical Articles on Protestantism in Ameri-*

can Religious Life, vol. 6, *Protestantism and Social Christianity*, ed. Martin E. Marty, 258–83 (Munich: K. G. Saur, 1992), 260–61.

59. Craig sees evidence of Ward's application of Wesleyan perfectibility to the social group in works such as *The Gospel for a Working World* (New York, 1918); *The New Social Order* (New York, 1919); and *In Place of Profit* (New York, 1933). See Craig, "An Introduction to the Life and Thought of Harry F. Ward," 259n3.

60. Craig, "An Introduction to the Life and Thought of Harry F. Ward," 265.

61. Charles C. West, *Communism and the Theologians: Study of an Encounter* (Philadelphia: The Westminster Press, 1958), 91. According to West, Tillich rationalizes the Marxist rejection of religion as "basically a class reaction to the actual alliances which the Church has made with feudal or bourgeois structures of power." See West, *Communism and the Theologians*, 92.

62. West, *Communism and the Theologians*, 93.

63. West, *Communism and the Theologians*, 94.

64. Paul Tillich, *The Protestant Era* (London, 1951), 279; quoted in West, *Communism and the Theologians*, 95.

65. J. B. Matthews, "Reds and Our Churches," *American Mercury*, July 1953, 3.

66. Harry F. Ward, *Our Economic Morality & the Ethic of Jesus* (New York: The Macmillan Company, 1929), 318–19.

67. In the absence of a common telos in American society, Ward became convinced that "our economic machine is giving the average man the modern equivalent of bread and circuses, but when its final defense is reduced to these terms it is an ominous sign." See Ward, *Our Economic Morality & the Ethic of Jesus*, 9, 68.

68. Szasz differentiates between the "head" of progressivism that emphasized scientific professionalism and its "heart" that promoted social and moral reform. See Ferenc M. Szasz, "The Progressive Clergy and the Kingdom of God," *Mid-America* 55 (January 1973): 4, 5.

69. Szasz, "The Progressive Clergy and the Kingdom of God," 10–20; and Gary Scott Smith, "The Men and Religion Forward Movement of 1911–12: New Perspectives on Evangelical Social Concern and the Relationship between Christianity and Progressivism," in *Modern American Protestantism and Its World*, vol. 6, *Protestantism and Social Christianity*, ed. Martin E. Marty, 166–93 (Munich: K. G. Saur, 1992).

70. Martin E. Marty, "Comment," in *Religion, Economics and Social Thought*, ed. Walter Block and Irving Hexham, 153–59 (Vancouver, BC: Fraser Institute, 1986), 158.

71. Richard C. Bayer, *Capitalism and Christianity: The Possibility of Christian Personalism* (Washington, DC: Georgetown University Press, 1999), 38.

72. Bayer, *Capitalism and Christianity*, 39.

73. D. Stephen Long, *Divine Economy: Theology and the Market* (New York: Routledge, 2000), 201. For a more complete analysis of the Dempsey's theological economics, see Bernard Dempsey, *The Functional Economy: The Bases of Economic Organization* (Englewood Cliffs, NJ: Prentice-Hall, 1958) and Long, *Divine Economy*, 195–205.

74. Long, *Divine Economy*, 201–2, 207.

75. Robert S. Ellwood, *The Fifties Spiritual Marketplace: American Religion in a Decade of Conflict* (New Brunswick, NJ: Rutgers University Press, 1997), 6–10, 215–17.

76. Ellwood, *The Fifties Spiritual Marketplace*, 160.

77. Ellwood, *The Fifties Spiritual Marketplace*, 8.

78. However, Long states, "Liberation theologians have not adequately dealt with the fact that capitalism itself developed as a tradition of liberation—liberation from the ancient regime, from the church and from interference by the state." See Long, *Divine Economy*, 89.

79. Long's reference to Cone's suspicion of "sociological analyses as are found in Hayek" and his mention of "serfdom" refer explicitly to Friedrich Hayek's *The Road to Serfdom* in which capitalism and socialism are presented respectively as inherently liberating and inherently enslaving economic systems. Long obviously interprets Cone as rejecting capitalism as a source of liberation for black Americans. See Long, *Divine Economy*, 106.

80. Long, *Divine Economy*, 108.

81. Gary North, *An Introduction to Christian Economics* (n.p.: The Craig Press, 1976), 8–9, 29–52.

82. North maintains that Mises and another Austrian economist, Murray Rothbard, are correct "because the presuppositions concerning the proper 'givens' of economic analysis are in fact the same 'givens' set forth by the Scriptures" irrespective of whether the two scholars are aware of this dependency. See North, *An Introduction to Christian Economics*, xiii. In this belief North is following closely the principle articulated by Cornelius Van Til that "natural man has valid knowledge only as a thief possesses goods." See Cornelius Van Til, *By What Standard?* (Philadelphia: Presbyterian and Reformed Publishing Company, 1958), 24; quoted in North, *An Introduction to Christian Economics*.

83. North states that "either we destroy the fraud of unbacked paper currency and unbacked bank credit, or the fraud will destroy us—morally, economically, politically and spiritually." See North, *An Introduction to Christian Economics*, 43.

84. North, *An Introduction to Christian Economics*, 219.

85. Quote from the National Council of Churches General Board (1967); available from the Institute for Christian Economics website at http://freebooks.commentary.net/freebooks/whatsice.htm (accessed on 15 May 2001).

86. Peter Steinfels, *The Neoconservatives: The Men Who Are Changing America's Politics* (New York: Simon & Schuster, 1979), 15.

87. Neoconservatism can be viewed as defining itself over and against the socialism that its devotees came to reject. Robert Benne has been lauded for his recognition of the moral superiority of capitalism and "his critique of the socialist presuppositions behind liberation theology" that "was early, acute and compelling." See Max Stackhouse and Dennis McCann, "Max Stackhouse and Dennis McCann Reply," *Christian Century* 108 (January 23, 1991): 83.

88. Podhoretz states that the neoconservative legacy "has wrought a profound change in the scope and the character and the ethos of American conservatism." See Norman Podhoretz, "Neoconservatism: A Eulogy," *Commentary* 101 (March 1996): 19–27.

89. Michael Novak, *The Spirit of Democratic Capitalism* (New York: Simon & Schuster, 1982), 13.

90. Novak, *The Spirit of Democratic Capitalism*, 25.

91. Gary Dorrien, *The Neoconservative Mind: Politics, Culture and the War of Ideology* (Philadelphia: Temple University Press, 1993), 255–56.

92. Wuthnow also notes that Americans respond favorably to the claim that capitalism is a prerequisite of political liberty. See Wuthnow, *The Restructuring of American Religion*, 263, 261.

93. Marty, "Comment," 158.

94. Michael Novak, *The Catholic Ethic and the Spirit of Capitalism* (New York: The Free Press, 1993), 101.

95. Long, *Divine Economy*, 78.

96. Fukuyama suggested that because modern natural science is "irreversible," so too are the "economic, social, and political consequences that flow from it." This implies directional rather than cyclical history and "certain uniform social changes across different nations and cultures," namely, the evolution toward democratic capitalism. See Francis Fukuyama, *The End of History and the Last Man* (New York: The Free Press, 1992), xi–xii, 88–89.

97. For example, in 1843–1844 a ruling by the Philadelphia School Board that Catholic students in the public schools could read from their own Bibles and opt out of religious instruction led to riots in which many citizens were killed or injured.

98. Robert Murray, "The British Provinces of North America," in *History, Essays, Orations, and Other Documents of the Sixth General Conference of the Evangelical Alliance* (New York: Harper & Brothers, 1874), 130; cited in Mark A. Noll and Carolyn Nystrom, *Is the Reformation Over? An Evangelical Assessment of Contemporary Roman Catholicism* (Grand Rapids, MI: Baker Academic, 2005), 11.

99. Quoted in James Morris, *The Preachers* (New York: St. Martin's, 1973), 199; cited in Noll and Nystrom, *Is the Reformation Over?* 38.

100. Thomas C. Reeves, *The Empty Church: The Suicide of Liberal Christianity* (New York: The Free Press, 1996), 91.

101. Reeves, *The Empty Church*, 105.

102. Ferm to E. Loren Pugsley, Newton, Kansas, July 31, 1962, CN 19 (Ferm papers), box 4, folder 21 (general correspondence), Billy Graham Center Archives, as quoted in Donald W. Sweeting, "From Conflict to Cooperation? Changing American Attitudes towards Roman Catholics: 1960–1998" (PhD diss., Trinity Evangelical Divinity School, 1998), 114–15; cited in Noll and Nystrom, *Is the Reformation Over?* 18.

103. Noll and Nystrom, *Is the Reformation Over?* 18.

104. Noll and Nystrom, *Is the Reformation Over?* 219.

105. Quoted in Richard J. Mouw, foreword to *Catholics and Evangelicals: Do They Share a Common Future?* (New York: Paulist Press, 2000), 3.

106. Timothy George, "Catholics and Evangelicals in the Trenches," *Christianity Today*, May 16, 1994, 16.

107. Noll and Nystrom, *Is the Reformation Over?* 210.

108. Charles Colson and Richard John Neuhaus, introduction to *Your Word Is Truth: A Project of Evangelicals and Catholics Working Together*, ed. Charles Colson and Richard John Neuhaus (Grand Rapids, MI: William B. Eerdmans, 2002), ix.

109. Noll and Nystrom, *Is the Reformation Over?* 21.

110. Reinhold Niebuhr, *The Nature and Destiny of Man: A Christian Interpretation*, vol. 1, *Human Nature*, one-volume ed. (New York: Charles Scribner's Sons, 1949 [orig. pub. 1941]), 61–92.

111. Reinhold Niebuhr, *The Irony of American History* (New York: Charles Scribner's Sons, 1952), 13.

112. Niebuhr, *The Irony of American History*, 108 (emphasis added).

113. Quoted in an interview with Rodney Clapp, "Where Capitalism and Christianity Meet," *Christianity Today* 27 (February 4, 1983): 27.

3

THE AUSTRIAN FOUNDATIONS
OF CHRISTIAN
ECONOMIC CONSERVATISM

The affinity of some Christians for Austrian social philosophy and their attempts to assimilate elements of Austrian thought with the Christian worldview are consistent with the American tradition of religious-economic synthesis. Christians have sought to incorporate the economic principles of Hayek and other Austrian social thinkers in ways not unlike the efforts of Wayland and McVickar to integrate ideas from the Scottish Enlightenment or the attempts of Ward and Tillich to assimilate the philosophy of Karl Marx into their respective moral theologies. So one might logically ask, regarding the thesis of this book, what *unique* danger is posed to Christian tradition by what is only the most recent of attempts to synthesize religious ideas with secular economic thought?

One answer already has been put forth in the unique historical context in which the modern synthesis is taking place. The emergence of genetic and other technologies pose unprecedented challenges to the Christian view of the person at a time when the dialectic that traditionally has guided Christian social thought is being dismantled. The rise of global capitalism and the concurrent delegitimization of collectivist social philosophy have had the broad effect of devaluing the contribution of corporate entities to the common good. As an institution advancing a *shared view* of human spirituality, the church has been caught up in this pervasive devaluation of collectives. The westward expansion of the American frontier contributed to this phenomenon, as did waves of economic and technological development. R. Laurence Moore observes the significance of the Industrial Revolution to the privatization of American religion, as various denominational groups "commodified" their offerings to satisfy the fickle values of "consumers."[1] In a more contemporary and generally Westernized context, philosopher S. S. Acquaviva perceives the intensification of this process brought about by technological and social forces to the point where the individual has become what he calls the "final receptacle" of spirituality.[2] Thus, the institutional voice of religion increasingly has been displaced by the privatization of Western culture as propelled by, among other factors, the forces of the market.

Hayek's view of the boundless potential for moral and institutional evolution in free societies suggests that not only the historical context but also the "content" of the relationship between American Christianity and Austrian liberalism is critical to understanding the threat to Christian tradition. The Austrian Nobel laureate's keen insight into cultural evolution makes his views on "institutional" Christianity potentially invaluable. At the very least, it can be stated that given Hayek's evolutionary and naturalistic view of religious and moral traditions, the connection between Austrian economics and Christian social philosophy is not self-evident. This chapter explores that connection and the means by which Christians attempt to assimilate Hayek's ideas. Although Christian economic thinkers such as Michael Novak, Robert Sirico, and Ronald Nash[3] use Hayek in various ways and to varying degrees, there are sufficient similarities to establish—in concert with Tillich's observations of structural analogies between Christianity and Marxism—similar analogies between Christian economic conservatism and Austrian liberalism.[4]

The first analogy is found in Austrian liberalism's emphasis on the vital role of human liberty in capitalist cultures, and a similar emphasis on individual initiative and responsibility, which Christian libertarians and neoconservatives perceive as central to their religious tradition.[5] The prominence of liberty in both Christian and Austrian thought contributes to a commonly held "subjective theory of value" that is the cornerstone not only of economic development but also of social order and even public morality. Neoconservatives observe in Christian history the importance of personal choice to the integrity and prosperity of the faith, just as the Austrians recognize subjective decision making as the fuel that fires the spontaneous order that is the engine of social progress.

A second analogy may be observed in that Austrian liberalism and the economic conservatism of Nash, Novak, and Sirico commonly emphasize the subjective creativity of the individual as the source of what is essentially human. "Human action" defines the human being in Austrian tradition, as demonstrated most clearly in Ludwig Mises' famous treatise by that title. In a passage that is chilling when viewed from the perspective of modern technological developments, Mises stated, "Beings of human descent who either from birth or from acquired defects are unchangeably unfit for any action . . . are practically not human."[6] While most Christian devotees of Austrian liberalism do not extend the human-action dependency to this extreme, some like Michael Novak do present creative activity as a divine obligation for the Christian and as the essence of what separates humankind from the rest of creation. This emphasis on human creativity and action contributes to a highly functional definition of the person.

The third structural analogy is that the Austrian and Christian economic theorists reviewed here are virulently opposed to anything that smells remotely "collectivist." Because many Christians today accept the Austrian view that the subjective decisions of individuals are the only "true" expressions of value, government and other collectives impede attainment of the good as it is expressed by individuals in a dynamic (primarily market) context. For Hayek and Mises, just as for Novak and Nash, the state with its coercive authority often denies or corrupts personal values in attempting to enforce a particular teleology or ideology that is frequently at odds with the true values of the citizenry.

Lastly, "tradition" plays a significant role in the philosophies of the Austrian philosophers and their Christian admirers. Both groups recognize the need for moral-cultural traditions to underpin the operations of a capitalist economy. More significant, however, is their shared belief that the values of religious and other traditions exist in a reciprocal relationship with the values derived from subjective decision making in a market context. Many Christian conservatives believe they have found in Austrian economics an exception to economist Albert Hirschmann's observation that "modern social science arose to a considerable extent in the process of emancipating itself from traditional moral teachings."[7] Hayek and other Austrian theorists are indeed respectful of the contribution of traditional religious morality to progress. However, it is Hayek's understanding of the *purpose* of tradition as determined by its evolutionary development, along with the consequences of that view, that, assuming its veracity, will be challenged as undermining Christian tradition and its conception of the person.

LINKS BETWEEN CHRISTIAN SOCIAL THOUGHT AND AUSTRIAN LIBERALISM

Before exploring these analogies, it should be noted that some Catholic conservatives posit a *historical* connection between Christian economic thought and Austrian liberalism, stressing what they view as philosophical consistency between the traditions. Moreover, they emphasize Catholic influence on various groups within classical liberalism, including the Austrian philosophers, as much as the reverse case. Sirico, for example, explores the impact of the Scholastic tradition on the development of Austrian economic ideas in many of his writings. The Scholastics of Salamanca such as the Dominicans Francisco de Vitoria (1485–1546) and Domingo de Soto (1494–1560) are portrayed as influential in the development of modern economic philosophy through their articulations of the subjective nature of economic value and their observations of the natural harmonies found in market structures.[8] Sirico and Novak both note the tribute paid by the Austrians Hayek and Schumpeter to the Salamancan Scholastics for their insights into the process of economic decision making.[9] In *Rules and Order*, Hayek speaks directly of the contribution of the "Spanish schoolmen" to our understanding of the evolutionary nature of the natural law that was not *invented* but rather was *discovered* in its evolved state. Hayek views the theories of the Salamancans as the basis for his notion of "evolutionary natural reason" that underpins his economic philosophy.[10]

Other scholars have verified this historical connection between Christian and Austrian liberal traditions; moreover, they observe that the influence was bidirectional. Philosopher Barry Smith locates a link between Austrian economics and Catholic social thought in the person of Franz Brentano (1838–1917), a one-time priest turned professor who rejected the German idealism popular in the late nineteenth century in favor of the Austrian conception of value.[11] Echoing Smith's conclusion, Sirico describes Brentano as the champion of Austrian economics during his faculty appointment at the University of Vienna and as a major transitional figure in the preservation of Austrian ideas within the Roman Catholic tradition.[12] These historical links are used by Catholic proponents of Austrian theory to trace common philosophical elements from the economic ideas of Thomas Aquinas through the "Late Scholastics" of Salamanca to the Austrian economists and, finally, to the social encyclicals of Pope John Paul II.

This historical linkage contributes to what many Christian economic conservatives view as philosophical consistency between the traditions, which in turn becomes critical in their unique syntheses of Christian and capitalist values. The Acton Institute, a bastion of neoconservative philosophy headed by Father Sirico, has produced countless articles lauding what contributors deem as commonalities between Austrian economics and Christian moral theology and social thought.[13] Many of these articles are complimentary of Hayek and especially his articulation of the means by which capitalism supports and is supported by society's religious-moral framework. A survey of their contents and that of various other sources will shed light on the relationship between Austrian liberalism and contemporary Christian economic conservatism.

The Exaltation of Human Liberty

A chief means by which many American Christians arrive at the "truth" of Austrian economics is by conflating the freedom of the subjective actor in Austrian economic theory with "Christian liberty." The essential identity of the Christian for many conservatives is grounded in the freedom of the will and the ability to choose truth and the good. Christianity and freedom forge a critical and defining dependency: neither one survives without the existence of the other. For Michael Novak, it is the "natural system of liberty," commonly articulated in the thought of Hayek, Mises, Adam Smith, and other philosophers in the liberal tradition, that is key to the orderly progression of society.[14] Yet Novak notes that its true origins precede the rise of liberalism. Thomas Aquinas, to whom the British nobleman Lord Acton assigned the moniker "the First Whig," is considered by Novak and Hayek alike to have been instrumental in providing religious legitimacy to the concept of human liberty.[15] Indeed, Aquinas's book, *On the Governance of Rulers*, exhibits nascent elements of modern liberalism, including the idea that individuals acting virtuously will, of necessity, contribute to the collective good:

> Therefore, since man, by living virtuously is ordained to a higher end, which consists of the enjoyment of God . . . then human society must have the same end as individual man. Therefore, it is not the ultimate end of an assembled multitude to live virtuously, but through virtuous living to attain the possession of God.[16]

Thus, evidence supports the claims of Novak and Hayek that Thomas Aquinas was an early champion of human liberty. In addition, Aquinas's ideas on the relationships between the individual and society reflect a subtle devaluation of corporate life and an elevation of individual action in responding to the divine imperative of virtuous living.

Novak notes a similar exaltation of freedom in the works of Dante Alighieri such as *The Divine Comedy*:

> Dante had wholeheartedly accepted the fact that every story in the Bible, Jewish and Christian, gathers its suspense from the free choices that confront every human being. How humans use their liberty determines

their destiny; how we use our freedom is the essential human drama. Liberty is the axial point of the universe, the point of its creation. That is the premise of *The Divine Comedy* and the ground of human dignity.[17]

Establishing a Christian basis for human liberty thus creates a critical synergy with Austrian liberalism and its emphasis on the individual. In the Austrian tradition, however, the human freedom that enables subjective expressions of value in the spontaneous order of a free society does not necessitate that such choices will conform to any predetermined conception of the good. Quite the contrary, as Hayek noted, "Freedom necessarily means that many things will be done which we do not like. Our faith in freedom does not rest on the foreseeable results in particular circumstances but on the belief that it will, on balance, release more forces for the good than for the bad."[18] Liberty is thus bounded by the limitations of human reason and morality in subjective decision making, yet destined, in aggregate and as an *article of faith*, to move society in the direction of the good.

The economically conservative Christians considered here are fully attuned to Hayek's conception of liberty and its contribution to the material and moral progression of society; moreover, they perceive the unique potential of their faith to broaden this conception. Some have attempted to apply a Christian face to liberty in the specific context of market economics through the development of "Christian personalism." As described by Catholic neoconservative Richard Bayer, Christian personalism is a synthesis of Catholic social thought and "orthodox economics" that is "informed by philosophical liberalism and by theological sources, so it can and does take the market system and liberal economics as acceptable starting points by which to build a more just economy."[19] Christian personalism's emergence within Catholic social thought is significant because of the historical inability of Christian institutions to attain the appropriate "starting points" in working toward a more just economy. This has long been considered by conservatives to be a major source of dissonance within the tradition and of economic backwardness in the Christian churches. In criticizing his own Roman Catholic tradition, Novak speculates that a lack of reflection on liberty by past pontiffs has contributed to a persistent anticapitalist bias within Catholicism.[20] Sirico, too, has detected this bias, and he speculates that it results from the tendency of Catholic social theorists to equate "economic liberalism with moral libertinism."[21]

Both Novak and Sirico perceive hope, however, in the encyclicals of John Paul II, which adopt a Christian personalist view of society that breaks rank with the church's collectivist (and thus outmoded) conceptions of social justice. Past expressions of the collective good invariably tilted Catholic political and economic thought toward socialism. Sirico observes positive signs in John Paul's acceptance of more enlightened (and thus more Austrian) views on human liberty, as expressed in his 1991 encyclical *Centesimus Annus*. Sirico agrees with those who believe the encyclical has prompted "a springtime in Christian social teaching because it makes it easier to see freedom, specifically economic freedom, as a moral mandate."[22] He is keen to point out John Paul's philosophical consistency with the Salamancan Fathers on whom the Austrian economists relied for much of their insight into economic behavior. Sirico explains that just as "John Paul II's Christian Personalism utilizes a 'bottom-up' anthropology—beginning with concrete human experience and culminating with reflection on the persons of the Trinity—so, too, does Scholastic economics employ a 'bottom-up' methodology that begins with an understanding of human need and desire."[23] The liberty that enables action based on "human need and desire" thus becomes both an anthropological and theological construct for some Christian economic conservatives, in some ways matching its preeminent status in Austrian economic philosophy.

Evangelical Christian George Gilder provides confirmation that some of the more zealous Christian advocates of capitalism rival (or perhaps even surpass) the Austrians in their exaltation of human freedom. In a passage from *Wealth and Poverty*, Gilder states that economists from both the Austrian and Monetary schools do not go far enough in their mere "celebrations" of human liberty:

> The great Austrian political economists Friedrich von Hayek and Ludwig von Mises, like Milton Friedman in *Capitalism and Freedom*, are all eloquent in their critique of collectivism and their celebration of liberty, but they are uncertain of what it is for: their argument tends to be technical and pragmatic. Freedom is good in itself and also makes us rich; collectivism compounds bondage with poverty. None of these writers sees reason to give capitalism a theology or even assign to its results any assurance of justice.[24]

Gilder's suggestion that human liberty and the capitalist system it inspires should be crafted into a theology demonstrates the extent to which some Christian social theorists are willing to go in synthesizing their religious and economic ideas. Consistent with its foundational position in Austrian liberalism, human liberty serves as the ground of that synthesis. Yet Gilder is correct in observing the reticence of Hayek and Mises to grant metaphysical properties of any kind to capitalism. Hayek made no theological or moral claims for systems that emerge from cultural evolution based on the decisions of individuals in the context of liberty, other than that the evolutionary course would sustain those groups whose members best determined the means of survival.

While not all Christian libertarians and neoconservatives would, like Gilder, elevate liberty above the "technical and pragmatic" to the transcendent, most of them espouse beliefs that are highly consistent with Hayek's ideas on freedom. The views of Novak, Nash, and Sirico are consonant with Hayek's observation that freedom "to order our own conduct in the sphere where material circumstances force a choice upon us . . . is the air in which alone moral sense grows and in which moral values are daily re-created in the free decision of the individual."[25] Indeed, Hayek's view of liberty might be seen as the inspiration for Sirico's belief in freedom as a "moral mandate," and Hayek's positioning of the free individual at the center of the daily transformations of morals in the extended order is consistent with Novak's location of human liberty as the "axial point of the universe."

Critics, however, have charged that the radical elevation of individual freedom in Austrian economic philosophy has the commensurate effect of denigrating collective contributions to the social good. Christian economic scholar Daniel Rush Finn contends that Hayek and other Austrian philosophers make a "foundational claim" for "methodological individualism" that devalues all social claims and ideals.[26] Finn states, "What [Hayek] intends by methodological individualism is that there is nothing to social reality other than the individual realities that make it up. Thus, when people speak about 'the market' or 'war' or 'society,' they are simply using linguistic shorthand for the interaction of individuals in particular settings."[27] According to Finn, Hayek's methodological individualism relegates terms such as "social justice" and the "common good" not to the status of mere obscurity but rather to the more ignominious category of "inherent deception" because they "pretend to indicate a reality larger than the meanings and values of the individuals who make up society."[28]

The relegation of all social institutions to flux if not fiction by Hayek's methodological individualism goes beyond the emphasis on the individual found in the economic personalism of John Paul II, despite attempts by some scholars to harmonize these views. Finn, in fact, suggests that "Hayek's rejection of social justice and [Milton] Friedman's restriction of the social responsibility of the business firm to making a profit are exactly the sort of 'radical' capitalist ideology John Paul intends to criticize."[29] Economically conservative Catholics tend to exaggerate John Paul's procapitalist comments, often excerpted from larger bodies of text that soften their individualistic tone, in order to portray him as a good student of Austrian economics. Yet there is much in John Paul's encyclicals that contradicts the highly subjectivist philosophies of Hayek and Mises, as will be seen. For now, it is sufficient to recognize his cautions against the "idolatry of the market" and to heed his observation of "needs and common goods that cannot be satisfied by the market system."[30] For John Paul, it is the duty of the State and civil society to join forces in meeting social needs that evade satisfaction by capitalist institutions, which also means that "to overcome today's individualistic mentality, a concrete commitment to solidarity and charity is needed, beginning in the family."[31]

Scholars have suggested that the extreme emphasis of Christian libertarians and neoconservatives on liberty leads to more than undue accentuation of the individual and the market. Long observes that Novak's preoccupation with human liberty becomes foundational even to man's unique transcendent connection to the Creator, suggesting that there may be theological as well as social consequences to such immoderation:

> Novak's ability to find "analogies" to Christ based solely on the formal principles of liberty and creativity threatens the heart of theology. The identification of human liberty with God's liberty actually breaks from analogy altogether and becomes an identity by which God's actions are now appended to a formal human freedom. What is certain is human freedom, and that certainty makes God credible.[32]

Novak indeed connects *human liberty* and *human dignity* in such a way that might be problematic for some Christians. In an essay that describes the development of the concept of liberty in the Judeo-Christian tradition, Novak states that "Jews and Christians explain human dignity by pointing to human liberty" and, further, that for Christianity and Judaism, "human liberty is an absolutely fundamental datum of God's revelation to humanity—or, if you prefer, an absolutely central datum of Jewish and Christian philosophy."[33] On first inspection, Novak's standard appears to greatly lessen the possibility of dignity for persons who find themselves outside the bounds of human liberty. One might infer that Novak's comments tarnish the moral dignity of the Christian martyrs or the Jews of the Holocaust and Babylonian exile. However, Novak attempts to dissuade such criticism by drawing on Aquinas's acknowledgment of "two moments of liberty": the interior and the exterior. He states, "Because the teaching of the Gospels is intended for Christians in every sort of culture, political system, and time, Christian philosophers are first of all concerned with an understanding of the interior act of liberty, only in the second place with liberty as a political and economic act."[34] Yet Novak's attempt to soften the fusion of political and economic liberty with human dignity comes across as "too little, too late"; it is unable to compensate for the intensity of association established between these concepts in the bulk of his writings. Sirico and other neoconservatives are subject to similar criticism for their acceptance of Hayek's contention that the condition of liberty, especially that which exists in a market context, is fundamental to the development of human morality.[35]

The synergy between Austrian liberal theory and the economic ideas of Christian libertarians and neoconservatives in their mutual exaltation of human liberty is unmistakable. Liberty exists as a foundational value from which virtually all others emanate. And that liberty serves as the basis for human action that ultimately shapes the development of religious and moral traditions, just as Hayek insisted. But there is no argument here that these Christian social theorists are out of step with American mores in their extreme elevation of liberty. As Robert Bellah and the other authors of *Habits of the Heart* observed, "Freedom is perhaps the most resonant, deeply held American value."[36] In this as in many other ways, Nash, Novak, Sirico, and other economically conservative Christians are consonant with the values of the American people, offering credibility to Norman Podhoretz's claim that neoconservatism is "dead" only in the sense that its values have been assimilated by the wider society.

Creative Subjectivity and Its Contribution to the Spontaneous Order

Human liberty and the subjectivist economic philosophy it inspires can only be expressed through human action. Thus, it is unsurprising that a second analogy may be drawn between Austrian liberalism and Christian economic conservatism in their common view of the importance of human creativity and action in providing a critical, if not definitional, identity for the person. The scholars reviewed here see definite parallels between the Austrian and Christian traditions in their respective elevations of the individual to statuses of unparalleled importance vis-à-vis other religious and economic traditions. However, this heightened esteem for the subjective individual is contingent upon his or her ability to take purposeful action toward desired ends. Thus both the Austrian philosophers and their Christian admirers arrive at rather functional definitions of the human person. The problem is that one might even infer from the prominence of human action in these traditions that the greater the capacity for effective action, the greater the level of personhood that may be achieved.

There is unquestionably a more robust conception of the person with his unique preferences and subjective valuations in Austrian thought vis-à-vis the simplistic "utility maximizer" of Benthamite utilitarianism or the machinelike, rational agent of neoclassical economics.[37] Austrian economic theory views the individual as a complex entity, shaped by heterogeneous traditions and possessing unique talents that may be channeled to the achievement of diverse, and at times competing, ends. The subjective agent of Austrian economics is capable of spontaneously devising and executing imaginative plans for the satisfaction of those desires. These individual plans of action, some effective and others ineffective, shape institutions in their interaction with each other and contribute to a natural order that guides the development of society through a process of trial and error.[38] Thus, Austrian theory views the person as similarly complex to the individual in Christian theology, who is ascribed certain freedoms for the pursuit of desired ends that may or may not conform to God's plan. Just as the subjective agent of Austrian economics, the Christian "person," too, achieved a dramatic elevation in autonomy and responsibility over the pawnlike individual in the polytheistic and pantheistic religions of ancient societies.

Even many secular philosophers view the Austrian school as having resurrected economics from its status as the "dismal science" through its positioning of the individual, with his or her unique preferences and subjective motivations, as the source of economic value. Wolfgang Grassl observes that for Austrian economists, "man and his actions stand at the center of economic theory." Therefore, markets are not merely mechanisms "that lead to equilibrium given an efficient allocation of resources. They are rather conceived as a *spontaneous order* that emerges as people, attempting to pursue their own interests, adjust and readjust their own actions to the actions of others."[39] The attraction of Christians to Austrian economic ideas is thus more easily understood when viewed in relation either to more atomistic economic philosophies such as neoclassical economics or to the simplistic bourgeois/proletarian distinction of Marxism. Austrian thought allows for the interplay of various influences on individual behavior and retains a sense of the importance of religious and other traditions on that behavior. Yet it is still individual initiative and responsibility that fire the engine of the economic system in Austrian theory, consistent with the biblical directive to human dominion over creation. Austrian economics also stresses the institutional effects of human action through emphasis on the dynamics of human enterprise and cultural evolution. Significantly, this dynamism extends beyond the economic realm to religion, which is, as Peter Berger has described, the "*human enterprise* by which a sacred cosmos is established."[40]

Maintenance of religious tradition requires persistent creative activity for sustenance, just as in the industries of a modern capitalist economy.

This subjective economic activity that accompanies human liberty and serves to direct the development of society operates through its contribution to the spontaneous order, an evolved system of norms and rules that exists beyond the comprehension of any of its participants. The individual economic actor, engaging a market economy with limited knowledge and rationality, contributes to society even in his ignorance. As Hayek stated, "most of the rules of conduct which govern our actions, and most of the institutions which arise out of this regularity, are adaptations to the impossibility of anyone taking conscious account of all the particular facts which enter into the order of society."[41] The harmony achieved in a free market economy is established via the system's "evolutionary rationalism," developed as the distillate of free choices by individuals who adjust to changing conditions. Through an endless process of trial and error, "successful" behaviors are rewarded and others rejected, enabling the system to overcome the limits of individual and institutional reason.

Sirico's interpretation of the Austrian school and its "accurate" view of the market economy lead to his agreement that the subjective individual is *the* source of value in capitalist society. Moreover, he perceives significant parallels between Hayek's economic philosophy and the natural law tradition of the Roman Catholic Church. Sirico voices obvious agreement in describing Hayek's philosophy, stating, "Cause and effect in the market is no different from that in society at large; there are no overarching and anonymous social forces that propel evolution apart from individual valuation. Social evolution is brought about by millions of individual calculations, decisions, and actions that create the appearance of an overarching order."[42] But are there transcendent moral forces that shape and transform culture in ways distinct from natural processes? The obvious question for a Roman Catholic priest is whether his own religious tradition is simply the product of millions of individual decisions that span two millennia.

Nash concurs on the subjective nature of value, noting that the Austrians properly elevated the human propensity for "entrepreneurial discovery" to its rightful position of importance through recognition of its contribution to the spontaneous order.[43] And, consistent with Hayek's view, Nash states that the exact contribution of inventive and industrious activity to this natural order cannot be predicted, for "uncertainty and lack of knowledge are inherent features of a market process in which individuals are constantly making economic choices that reflect the changing subjective valuations they make with regard to their options."[44] Both Nash and

Sirico are in agreement with Hayek that the spontaneous order exists beyond the comprehension of individual or collective participants and therefore defies accurate prediction. Hence, the attempts by institutions to employ collective reason in guiding the system are worse than ineffectual; they are absurd.

The elevation of subjective and self-interested action by individuals to such an exalted state in Austrian philosophy raises the question of whether it conflicts with the Christian's communal responsibility to "love thy neighbor." Nash addresses this frequently asked question with the insight that "every person in a market economy has to be other-directed"[45] through his or her active contribution to the market order. A major attribute of the market economy as conceived in Austrian philosophy and in the thought of its Christian proponents is the market's ability to channel the efforts of each individual, irrespective of his or her self-serving intentions, to the greater benefit of society. Creative human action that enriches a particular individual necessarily must benefit others in order to stimulate other equally self-interested actors to enter into market exchange. Novak contends that "since market exchanges are voluntary, and since the objects the purchaser might acquire are many, entry into the market obliges sellers to become to an important degree other-regarding."[46] Thus, the system is inherently reciprocating and, thereby, "other-directed."

Also important in the philosophy of Christian libertarians and neoconservatives is the idea of human creativity both as a gift of God and, coequally, a responsibility for human involvement in creation. Novak's understanding of the *imago Dei* leads to a unique obligation on the part of human beings to be "creative, inventive, and intellectually alert in a practical way, in order 'to build up the kingdom of God.'"[47] It is not so much the asceticism of biblical teaching but rather its call to creativity and inventiveness that accounts for the dynamism of Jewish and Christian civilization, including economic dynamism."[48] For Novak, the exercise of God's gift of human creativity enables man to assume his responsibility in the order of an unfulfilled creation. Novak states, "Creation left to itself is incomplete, and humans are called to be co-creators with God, bringing forth the potentialities the Creator has hidden."[49]

This analogy between divine and human creativity, according to George Weigel, provides an "important theological foundation" for an ethic of wealth creation.[50] However, wealth and the virtues that accompany it have been much maligned among clerics and academics. Novak particularly dislikes the negativity associated with the term "acquisitiveness" as a motive for human action in capitalist society. Novak contends that the negative

connotation applied to acquisitiveness by economist R. H. Tawney deni-
grates the noble ambitions of those who seek to acquire goods in a market
economy, and he argues for a more positive spin on the virtues of acquisition, as derived from the fact that it "is not *having* that characterizes the capitalist spirit, but *venturing* and *creating*."[51]

Novak is able to discern creativity and its contribution to Hayek's
spontaneous order in the most unlikely of places, stating, "Even the mine
owners who played such an unsavory role at Lattimer Mines must, in all justice, be given credit for the inventive genius which opened new worlds to
those they 'exploited.'"[52] Lattimer was one of the most infamous labor-
management conflicts in the U.S. mining industry's rather sordid history. In
1897, sheriff's deputies and strike-breaking mercenaries fired on a crowd of
striking coal miners, killing nineteen and injuring forty-nine.[53] The mine
owners' restriction of other industries from entering the region to prevent
the increase in wages that would have resulted from expanded producer
competition is considered to have been a major factor in the labor rebellion. Yet Novak is able to find "genius" in the owners' actions that created
harsh conditions for their workers and enforced those conditions with the
backing of civil authority. Novak suggests that the creative brilliance of the
mine owners was to force a decision upon workers; they could accept the
conditions presented to them or exercise their own "genius" in the effort to
seek out new sources of income.[54]

Novak's interpretation of the Lattimer Mines incident demonstrates
another link between Christian economic conservatism and Austrian liberalism. Both are reticent to consider economics an appropriate discipline
from which to make moral judgments concerning the economizing behavior of individuals. Mises declined to assign to economics the responsibility
for judging the morality of action by free individuals in the market. In describing economic behavior, he stated, "Action on the part of the economizing individual is neither correct nor incorrect. Modern economics is
not and cannot be concerned with whether someone prefers healthful food
or narcotic poisons, no matter how perverted may be the ethical or other
ideas that govern his conduct, its 'correctness' is not a matter to be judged
by economics."[55] While Christian admirers of Austrian economics pull
back from such extremes, they too are often reluctant to apply moral judgments to market behavior in the trust that subjective action, in aggregate,
will produce desired material and moral outcomes.

Father Sirico believes that creative subjectivity is a critical conduit
linking together different eras of Catholic social thought:

The reliance of the modern Catholic view of economics on Late-Scholastic thought has been more pronounced than ever. Both place human enterprise, human initiative, the price system, exchange, private property, the division of labor, and the liberty of contract at the center of economic life. Unlike more positivist schools of economic thought, the modern Catholic approach never loses sight of the centrality of the acting person; the subjective will, and all that this implies, is the driving force behind economic life.[56]

Sirico claims as the "modern Catholic view of economics" the common confidence of Austrian liberalism and Salamancan Scholasticism in the subjective guidance of a society founded on human liberty.[57] This "enlightened" view of the modern Catholic centers on a belief in the moral sustainability of the market system and the understanding that value "resides not in the objective qualities of the good itself but, rather, in how people personally regard the good. That is, economic value derives from individual impressions and intentions and is, ultimately, subjective."[58] Sirico gives credit where credit is due, explaining his intent to "expand on the embryonic thesis given to us by Michael Novak; namely, that the Austrian School of economics, with its emphasis on subjectivity and choice, offers the transmission of a body of thought that makes the link between old and new Catholic economics coherent, notable, and strong."[59] The "old" Catholic economics of the Late Scholastics was prescient in recognizing that the collective good of an increasingly pluralistic society could not be divined by detached monarchs or by appeals to the virtues of classical philosophy. Rather, it could only be discerned in myriad subjective valuations of individuals as revealed in their personal decisions, a view later reinforced by Austrian social theorists.[60]

Gregory Gronbacher, in an article posted on the Acton Institute's website, draws directly the connection between Austrian economic philosophy and what he collapses under the neatly constructed category "Catholic social thought." After reviewing the essentials of Austrian theory (i.e., value subjectivism, rejection of positivism) and its historical dependencies on Catholic tradition in the philosophies of Aquinas and the Salamancan Scholastics, Gronbacher brings together the two traditions in full embrace:

These same methodological tenets [of Austrian economics] are shared by Catholic social thought. In its analysis of the social and moral concerns of humanity the Church relies on [sic] heavily on an Aristotelian

essentialism in its view of the social sciences, a methodological individualism in its treatment of social morality, and accepts the legitimacy of
value subjectivism for economic analysis.[61]

Gronbacher's attempt to minimize the rich body of Catholic social thought
is common among Catholic neoconservatives. They talk of their religious
tradition as having broken completely with its naive constructivist and collectivist economic ideas, and they view it today as standing solidly in their
corner. John Paul II is often cast as a transitional figure in this perceived reformation in Catholic economic philosophy.

For many Catholic economic conservatives, subjective decision making
in the context of liberty is capable of sustaining social, economic, and even
moral harmony when left undisturbed by the conceit of collective reason
most often embodied by the state. This leads to their unwavering rejection
of collectivism as utopian. However, the view that a natural order built on
subjective valuation and individual choice is largely self-sustaining given a
supportive complement of political and moral institutions might itself be
considered somewhat utopian. More troubling in the modern context is the
close connection in neoconservative thought of human creativity and action
with the identity of the human being that could contribute to a highly
"functional" understanding of the person. Novak, for example, discusses the
"historical genesis of the concept of person" in the description of the two
natures of Jesus Christ. Yet he goes further to state that the modern "utility"
of this idea of the person "lies in designating what exactly it is in humans
that is the ground of their dignity and the source of their free acts of insight
and choice. A person is a substance with a capacity for insight and choice
and an independent existence as a locus of responsibility."[62] If one reworks
Novak's definition in the negative to identify what a person "is not," one
comes precariously close to Mises' view that an individual who is incapable
of independent insight and action is "practically not human." To soften this
stance, Novak attempts to draw a distinction between the "individual" and
the "person" in his book *Free Persons and the Common Good.*[63] However, emphasis on function and utility in the greater part of Novak's writing causes
one to fear the adoption of such a view in the context of modern technological developments. If, as Hayek believes, group persistence is the central
cultural value, then such a functional definition of the person has ominous
implications for the future of Christian views such as that advanced by ethicist Helmut Thielicke and his concept of "alien dignity," which grounds the
value of the human person exclusively in God's grace.[64] Creative subjectivity is a gift of God; it can never be the defining attribute of man.

Opposition to State Control

Rejection of both the wisdom and necessity of state control over the private lives of its citizens serves as another important structural analogy between Austrian liberalism and Christian tradition in neoconservative thought. The state, in seeking to carry out its principal duty of securing order, imposes its will on the citizenry and thereby displaces the subjective will of individual citizens—a violation of both Christian and Austrian principles. Thus coercion is an inherent impulse built into the institution of state due to its unique role as the guarantor of social order and its unique possession of a monopoly on violence. The state's ability to coerce extends beyond its authoritarian and policing structures to the more insidious imposition of values and ideals that often conflicts with society's religious and moral traditions. Mises offered a view of the state that, though perhaps exaggerated, is largely representative of the Austrian position: "Government means always coercion and compulsion and is by necessity the opposite of liberty."[65]

Hayek, too, was distrusting of the institutions of state, although he certainly favored democratic-capitalist governments to those inspired by collectivism. And Hayek seemed to recognize more so than Mises the willingness of citizens to subjugate themselves to state authority, especially during periods of social strife. In his most influential work, *The Road to Serfdom*, Hayek described not only the coercive nature of government but also the inclination of human beings to seek refuge from life's hazards by enslaving themselves in the warm fuzziness of the state. He even conceded a strange attractiveness to totalitarian government in its "unselfish devotion to an ideal."[66] In describing the predictable and monistic nature of National Socialism, Hayek stated, "Every activity must derive its justification from a conscious social purpose. There must be no spontaneous, unguided activity, because it might produce results which cannot be foreseen and for which the plan does not provide."[67] To Hayek, oppressive government establishes the ultimate obstacle to the formation of the spontaneous order within which efficient resource allocations are determined and moral choices are enabled.

This is not to suggest that Hayek perceived no role for the state. It performs a vital function in providing for the basic safety and security needs of its citizens, which serves to underwrite the smooth operation of a market economy. Hayek conceded that there is "no incompatibility in principle between the state providing greater security in [social insurance programs] and the preservation of individual freedom."[68] The limit, however, in defining the appropriate role of government is where its actions result in altering the nation's income structure, even when the intent is to advance "security." Hayek noted that the type of planning for security that has an "insidious effect on liberty" is that which is "designed to protect individuals or groups against diminutions of their income which although in no way deserved yet in a competitive society occur daily."[69] In other words, government action to assist citizens in times of crisis or economic hardship is generally acceptable; what it must not do is fundamentally alter the distribution of national income.

Many libertarians and neoconservatives heartily agree, and some would go even further than Hayek in disavowing the desirability of government largesse. For them, even the "benevolent" acts of government deserve assignment to the category of coercion. Novak states, "The effort to impose 'humane' and 'organic' values upon the whole of society is inevitably authoritarian and, when extended to the life of the spirit, totalitarian. It is so because individuals do not all share the same values or desire the same things."[70] Such government actions are authoritarian because they defy subjective expressions of value by private citizens. In its most extreme form, the authoritarianism of collectivist government saps the very spirit from the society it purports to aid. Nash has stated in classic Misesean hyperbole that socialist systems are the "economic equivalent of the Black Death."[71] Even the lesser "interventionism" of nontotalitarian governments is viewed by Nash and other conservative Christian economic thinkers as producing tragic consequences for society, from initiating the Great Depression to imposing values associated with the welfare state.[72]

The intrinsic nature of state coercion dictates two principal remedies to negate its effects: the reduction of the state's size and functions wherever possible, and the promotion of private "mediating institutions" to offset state power. For Novak, this call to eradicate or at least to minimize state authority is fundamental to Christian tradition. The state seeks to interject itself between the Christian person and his definitive teleology that is communion with the Creator. In *Free Persons and the Common Good*, Novak describes a famous debate between Charles DeKoninck of Laval and Jacques Maritain over the meaning of the social good in attempting to arrive at a "Christian" conception of that term.[73] Novak derives from that dialogue and from his own Christian experience a definition of the common good, explaining it as the desire "for every human person 'to come home to' God—to be one with God in an everlasting communion of insight and love. God is the universal common good not only of humans but of all created things."[74]

Christianizing the common good has not only individual but also sociopolitical consequences. As Novak explains, "The implications of this insight for political philosophy . . . are profound. No state and no society can legitimately frustrate the drive of each person for his true destination [communion with God]. In this respect, all powers of the state are radically limited."[75] Yet Novak offers little discussion of whether other institutions such as the market or even religious institutions can frustrate the *individual's* attainment of his or her "true destination"; moreover, he reveals the foundational status of liberalism in his own philosophy. The leaders of medieval Christendom (as those of most "traditional societies") likely would have viewed the myriad choices of modern liberal culture as "frustrating" the individual's pursuit of his or her true destination by depriving the individual of a more clearly focused earthly communion. Novak must establish liberal society a priori as the ground on which to make his claim that the state or other authoritarian institutions necessarily inhibit the attainment of the individual's true end, which is communion with the Creator. Otherwise, he risks implying that even the church itself may have, at times in history, served as an obstacle to individual salvation.

Again, it is the "inherently" coercive and constructivist nature of government in seeking to plan and control social arrangements that defines the "problem of the state" for Christian conservatives. Referring to *The Fatal Conceit*, Sirico notes its sweeping rejection of constructivist social philosophy, stating, "The conceit [Hayek] wanted us to recognize is the idea that human reason is capable of designing a social order without taking into account the evolved patterns of human law, relationships, economy, and traditions." This attitude causes societies to empower government and other institutions that "override the natural order of liberty in an attempt to impose a plan on society."[76]

Sirico finds in *The Fatal Conceit* more than an eloquent warning against the omnipresent threat of state power. He also locates a common principle between Austrian-style classical liberalism and contemporary Catholic social thought on which to base their common resistance to governmental control:

> We find here in Hayek the potential for complementarity between an indispensable principle of Christian social teaching—namely, subsidiarity—and the classical liberal tradition. And if we are looking for the extent of this complementarity, we need look no further than Pope John Paul's 1991 encyclical *Centesimus Annus*, which accomplished the great task of repairing the damage done by centuries of unnecessary separation between these two great traditions. Because of the courage of John Paul II

and his case in favor of the free society now that socialism is being discredited worldwide, we have entered into a new era of intellectual and social history. No longer do we feel compelled to speak of classical liberalism and religious orthodoxy as belonging to two separate intellectual worlds. We have begun to speak of them as one and to repair the split that was unnecessary and proved so dangerous to the cause of human liberty.[77]

The principle of *subsidiarity* thus emerges as a conduit between Roman Catholic and liberal traditions and as a cornerstone of neoconservatism's resistance to what is perceived as government's uncontrollable compulsion to acquire and wield power.

Subsidiarity was given salience and firmly ensconced in Catholic social thought in Pope Pius XI's encyclical *Quadragesimo Anno*, which sought to rebuke excessive concentrations of authority and control in society:

> Just as it is wrong to take from individuals what they can accomplish by their own initiative and industry and give it to the community, so it is an injustice and at the same time a grave evil and disturbance of right order to assign to a greater and higher association what lesser and subordinate organizations can do.[78]

Here, Pius articulates a model by which the functions of society should be distributed. The lowest-level entities within an institution that are most affected by particular activities should be empowered to perform those duties, thus minimizing the tendency to coercion by larger and more powerful groups.

While one can interpret Pius XI's statement as critical of the centralizing tendencies of big government, his rather general term "higher association" implies a commensurate criticism of the often top-heavy, bureaucratic structures of large business, academic, and other institutions (perhaps even religious ones). The economically conservative Christians addressed here, however, utilize subsidiarity primarily as a platform for criticism of the state. Part of the reason for this bias undoubtedly has to do with the prominent view among conservatives that corporate structures often serve as mediating institutions in tempering the ambitions of big government. In concert with the Austrian economic theorists, they observe in the nature of capitalist competition an inherent tendency toward the distribution of political and economic power. As Father Sirico has stated, "What competition does is diffuse power across the whole of a society. It has a tendency to decentralize power where government has the exact opposite tendency."[79]

Even the growing power of large multinational corporations plays a critical role in neutralizing the hegemony of a concurrently expansive and ambitious state. Novak goes so far as to posit a common history between the Roman Catholic Church and modern corporate structures, stating, "The lineage of the modern multinational corporation may likewise be traced in legal and economic history to the internationalism of the Benedictines and other general congregations of religious men and women."[80] The extent to which Novak aligns religious and corporate structures in their respective cultural roles is seen in his contention that "even the largest corporations are significant defenses against the power of the state. In an extended but real sense, General Motors is a mediating structure (it is smaller than the Lutheran Church), and its individual units are as much mediating structures as parishes are."[81]

But this decentralizing power of the market is susceptible to even slight impositions by government authority according to conservatives. Just as Hayek and Mises, they fear the "slippery slope" of the mixed economy that leads inexorably to the expansion of government control. And both traditions view this drift toward socialism as being powered by the intelligentsia. Novak describes "an intellectual environment driven by the left, in which the 'mixed economy' merely moves more slowly than the left but in the same general direction."[82] Similarly, Hayek observes that the "strongest support of the trend towards socialism comes today from those who claim that they want neither capitalism nor socialism but a 'middle way' or a 'third world.'" Hayek is convinced that to follow the middle path is certain to lead to socialism, since once politicians are allowed "to interfere in the spontaneous order of the market for the benefit of particular groups, they cannot deny such concessions to any group on which their support depends."[83]

Ironically, libertarians and neoconservatives may be overlooking another slippery slope leading from their emphasis on the market to *greater* concentrations of political and economic power in government. Nicholas Boyle, a scholar at the University of Cambridge, has written an interesting critique of "Thatcherism" that has relevance here. Applying Boyle's assessment of Thatcherism to neoconservative and Austrian views of the state seems reasonable, given Thatcher's reliance on Austrian principles to guide development of her government's economic policies. As David Glasner has recognized, both Ronald Reagan and Margaret Thatcher were "proud to list Hayek among their intellectual mentors."[84]

Boyle believes that Thatcherism's myopic focus on the market contributed to a "proletarianization" of British society in which the status of all intermediary institutions was greatly diminished. In effect, a significant but largely unnoticed consequence of Thatcherism was to ensconce the market as the sole mediating institution of British society. As Boyle observes, the Thatcher government used the term "public" pejoratively to refer to "anything other than the supposed desires of the individual (usually called a 'consumer'). Freedom is the freedom to satisfy those desires and anything other than the market is a restriction of that freedom. Thatcherism is thus able to present its assault on the social fabric as a reduction in public control, as an increase in freedom for the individual, and as an act of self sacrifice."[85] In fact, what has happened in British society, according to Boyle, is that it no longer has an organic and collective identity but has been reduced to a "system of needs" by the erosion of those elements from the domain of the state that the market considers insignificant—"things such as nationhood, political liberties, a collective purpose, a sense of morality, tradition, or responsibility."[86]

This proletarianization has been accomplished by homogenizing and commodifying British labor and by disempowering labor unions and other intermediary institutions. Moreover, it has reduced the once diverse and organically interdependent British culture to a single identity—that being a collection of individually marketable commodities. According to Boyle, the net and quite ironic result of Thatcherism is that the "proletarianization of the population makes the state, as regulator of the economic mechanism, more necessary, and more omnipresent, not less."[87] Thus, the state elevates its own position in society via its declaration of the unworthiness of any institution to stand in judgment of the individual in a market context. Because some social structure must provide the measure of security necessary to underwrite the operations of the market (as Hayek recognized) and to offer a legal framework for contracts and other instruments of capitalism, the state itself thrives in a market culture littered with moribund institutions.

Boyle's critique is insightful and sheds considerable light on the nature of change in all societies caught up in the frenzy of globalization. By focusing narrowly on the market as the central and ubiquitous institution for resource distribution in British society, Thatcherite conservatives (just as American neoconservatives) believe that their disdain for the state and their calls for its reduction are sufficient to make it go away, without understanding the institutional effects of their policies. Similarly, they believe that pleas to reinvigorate intermediary institutions will realize that goal without recognizing that their own political and economic philosophies, when translated into public policy, actually hamper its attainment. Boyle's thesis helps to explain the alienation felt by many individuals in a modern society that celebrates the individual. And it provides insight into the paradox of enormous and ever-growing state institutions that are reviled by many of the same citizens who demand their services.

Emphasis on Moral Tradition

A fourth and, for purposes of this book, highly important structural analogy derived from the writings of the economically conservative Christians addressed here is the importance of religious and moral traditions to "progress" in both Austrian and Christian thought. Christian emphasis on moral standards and their importance to social stability and cultural prosperity are easily demonstrated by the prominence of the Old Testament's Ten Commandments and its larger body of Mosaic law, and, equivalently, in the New Testament through the Sermon on the Mount and the ethically instructive letters of St. Paul. Christian history demonstrates that God often deprives his people of prosperity in periods when they have strayed from his law. Similarly, the Austrian tradition recognizes the essential role of religion as a source of morality that stabilizes cultural advance, and it acknowledges that periods of moral decay often lead to political and economic turmoil. Hayek, in particular, perceived the need for religious and moral guidance in the advancement of culture, as demonstrated most clearly in his essay "Religion and the Guardians of Tradition."[88] Hayek's views on the role and ultimate disposition of religion are quite controversial and will be discussed in more detail in chapter 4. A few comments are appropriate here, however.

Both Austrian and neoconservative philosophy insist that the inherent freedom of the market economy places a greater, not lesser, emphasis on religious and other traditions as a guide for human behavior than do the static relations of socialism. Novak notes that Max Weber "is quite right in discerning that without a certain moral ethos . . . the objective institutions of capitalism would be hollow sepulchers."[89] Capitalism is dependent upon society's moral-cultural traditions, for "its practice imposes certain moral and cultural attitudes, requirements and demands. Cultures that fail to develop the required habits cannot expect to eat broadly of capitalism's fruits."[90] Moreover, Novak perceives the Judeo-Christian tradition as uniquely capable of supplying the necessary moral foundation to modern capitalism due to its emphasis on the subjective creativity of the human being, its rejection of the need for an omnipresent state, and its preestablished set of moral codes and instructions.[91]

The Austrian or, more specifically, the Hayekian understanding of the religious foundation of moral tradition is quite different from the traditional Christian understanding, however. In Austrian thought, moral codes and norms of behavior observed in religious traditions were not revealed but rather have evolved over time to a state that, although incomprehensible to any particular individual, is a superior guide to social order than the rational pretensions of constructivism. Perhaps Hayek was referring to Christian revelation in a passage from "Religion and the Guardians of Tradition" that describes the importance of religious morality to human progress:

> The religious view that morals were determined by processes incomprehensible to us may at any rate be truer (even if not exactly the way intended) than the rationalist delusion that man, by exercising his intelligence, invented morals that gave him the power to achieve more than he could ever foresee. If we bear these things in mind, we can better understand and appreciate those clerics who are said to have become somewhat skeptical of the validity of some of their teachings and who yet continued to teach them because they feared that a loss of faith would lead to a decline of morals.[92]

Hayek continued in the same essay by disavowing a transcendent basis for morality, stating, "Perhaps what many people mean in speaking of God is just a personification of that tradition of morals or values that keeps their community alive. The source of order that religion ascribes to a human-like divinity . . . we now learn to see to be not outside the physical world but one of its characteristics."[93] This immanentist aspect of Hayek's thought serves as a red flag calling attention to possible conflicts between Christian and Austrian thought. A brief biography of Hayek on the Acton Institute website illustrates through its omissions the difficulty of reconciling Hayek's agnosticism and his evolutionary view of human morality with the moral structure derived from the teleological and apocalyptic paradigm of Christian tradition:

> Like [Lord] Acton, Hayek emphasized the central importance of morality in the development of an advanced civilization, although unlike Acton, Hayek was a professed agnostic. He showed that a prosperous and advancing economy required a sound moral order. Parallel to his understanding of the development of law as an evolutionary process, he viewed morality also as the result of an evolutionary process. Civilizations acknowledge the moral principles which experience shows lead to a healthy society of prosperity and liberty.[94]

What this bio does not address is whether the evolutionary moral principles that lead to a "healthy society of prosperity and liberty" necessarily sustain a transcendent conception of the human person. And does Hayek's description of the dynamic nature of morality, if accurate, portend dire consequences for Christian tradition? More importantly, is the shifting moral structure of liberal society that Hayek perceived to be essential to cultural advance compatible with the transcendent foundation of Christian morality?

Even those traditions within Christianity that adhere to natural law and other sources of general revelation see them as supplemental to the revealed law of God. Yet Hayek made no claim that the course of social and moral evolution will tend toward the Judeo-Christian or even a deistic worldview. He, in fact, implied quite the opposite as will be shown. And it should be noted that the Acton Institute bio subtly overstates Hayek's position in its suggestion that the evolutionary course of morality leads to "a healthy society of prosperity and liberty." While Hayek strongly suggested that a culture constructed so as to enable the full flowering of the spontaneous order would emerge more prosperous than a planned society, his more modest claim for cultural evolution was that it operated in such a way as to promote the persistence of groups that adopt values and practices that best ensure their survival.[95]

CONCLUDING REMARKS

Differences between Austrian and traditional Christian understandings concerning the nature of the person and the sources of social morality are key to the thesis of this book and necessitate a more comprehensive treatment in chapter 4. Similarities and differences in respective views of the state and of the contribution of creative subjectivity to the spontaneous order, while important to understanding the basic relationship, are not seen as threatening to Christian tradition. However, the following chapters will argue that acceptance by Christians of Hayek's views respecting the evolutionary course of religious and moral traditions in capitalist society does pose a danger by inspiring an unwarranted confidence in the moral sustainability of modern capitalism. In supporting this contention, it will be argued that Hayek was a highly systematic thinker whose theories exhibit a great degree of interdependence. The implications of Novak and others that one may simply pick and choose among Hayek's theories "cafeteria style" are dubious and seem to treat Hayek too conventionally, in the same way that Christian thinkers traditionally have absorbed philosophical elements from other secular theorists.[96] Hayek stands apart from many other philosophers, however, in his insistence that he discovered nothing but merely described the causations and consequences of human behavior in various social contexts.

Hayek was perhaps the greatest theoretician of the processes by which norms and values are transformed in a free society. However, acknowledgment of Hayek's brilliance begs the question of whether it should comfort or concern Christians and people of other faiths, for it simultaneously suggests that to dismiss the implications of Hayek's theories for religious traditions would be a serious mistake. Chapter 4 offers evidence that Hayek surmised a similar outcome for religion in liberal society as that predicted by the American philosophical pragmatist John Dewey. Hayek's comments suggest an erosion of the sacred necessitated by the dominant goal of group persistence among all cultural institutions. Although Dewey's prophecy of a "common faith" built on the foundations of reason seems less plausible today given the proliferation of religious groups, Christian admirers of Hayek should not ignore the possibility that the Austrian was correct in hinting at the development of a religious culture that retains institutional differentiation and yet arrives at a common set of largely naturalistic and rational values. A more extensive analysis of the similarities and differences between Austrian and Christian views on the development of religious tradition will lay the groundwork for exploring the implications of the Hayekian moral system for American Christianity.

NOTES

1. R. Laurence Moore, *Selling God: American Religion in the Marketplace of Culture* (Oxford: Oxford University Press, 1994), 11, 255.

2. S. S. Acquaviva, *The Decline of the Sacred in Industrial Society*, trans. Patricia Lipscomb (New York: Harper & Row, 1979), 190. Acquaviva emphasizes the contribution of technology to the erosion of the sacred in society, a process by which religious language and symbolism are crowded out by the "desacralizing rationality" of technology. But he also notes the concurrent privatization of religion that has contributed its own unique harm, to include a decline in the sacredness of the human person. Acquaviva asks, "Does anything vital survive once religious reality becomes detached from institutionalized religion?" See Acquaviva, *The Decline of the Sacred in Industrial Society*, 137, 155–56, 169–79, 188.

3. Of the principal scholars reviewed in this chapter, Novak and Sirico are the ones appropriately labeled "neoconservative" in the sense that their embrace of capitalism involved the rejection of their early socialist or democratic socialist ideals. Ronald Nash is a theologian-philosopher of the Reformed Christian tradition whose economic thought is also highly consistent with the theories of Hayek and Mises. Nash, George Gilder

(who has been described as a Christian "techno-libertarian" for his emphasis on free markets and the good of technology), and other Christian scholars are included in this analysis to demonstrate that the influence of Austrian economic ideas extends beyond libertarians and neoconservatives to a wider group that will be classified simply as "economically conservative Christians."

4. Some Christians directly acknowledge their dependence on Austrian economic theory and are defensive toward critics' misidentification of that philosophical debt. Ronald Nash states, "My approach to economics is grounded on the work of the Austrian school of economics, a movement that some careless economists fail to distinguish adequately from the Chicago School of Milton Friedman." See Ronald H. Nash, "A Reply to Eric Beversluis," in *Economic Justice and the State: A Debate between Ronald H. Nash and Eric H. Beversluis*, ed. John A. Bernbaum (Grand Rapids: Baker Book House, 1986), 54.

5. These structural analogies between Christian and Austrian philosophy are discussed briefly in Charles McDaniel, "Friedrich Hayek and Reinhold Niebuhr on the Moral Persistence of Liberal Society," *Journal of Interdisciplinary Studies* 16, nos. 1–2 (2004): 137.

6. Ludwig von Mises, *Human Action: A Treatise on Economics*, 3rd rev. ed. (Chicago: Henry Regnery Company, 1949), 14.

7. Albert O. Hirschmann, *Morality and the Social Sciences: A Durable Tension* (Memphis: P. K. Seidman Foundation, 1980), 1. This book was developed from Hirschmann's acceptance paper for the Frank E. Seidman Distinguished Award in Political Economy.

8. Sirico credits de Vitoria, de Soto, and other Salamancan scholars with the development of basic ideas of property rights, the determination of "just price" as "market price," and the formation of fundamental monetary theories. See Robert A. Sirico, "The Late-Scholastic and Austrian Link to Modern Catholic Economic Thought," *Journal of Markets and Morality* 1 (October 1998), available from the Acton Institute website at www.acton.org/publicat/m_and_m/1998_Oct/sirico.html (accessed October 3, 2001).

9. Novak cites Joseph Schumpeter's *History of Economic Analysis*, ed. E. B. Schumpeter (New York: Oxford University Press, 1954), 165; and Friedrich A. Hayek's *New Studies in Philosophy, Economics and the History of Ideas* (Chicago: University of Chicago Press, 1978), 123 as pointing out the indebtedness of Austrian economic theorists to the Scholastics of Salamanca. See Michael Novak, "The Judeo-Christian Foundation of Human Dignity, Personal Liberty, and the Concept of the Person," *Journal of Markets and Morality* 1 (October 1998), available from the Acton Institute website at www.acton.org/publicat/m_and_m/1998_Oct/novak.html, note 17.

10. Friedrich A. Hayek, *Law, Legislation and Liberty*, vol. 1, *Rules and Order* (Chicago: University of Chicago Press, 1973), 84; and Sirico, "The Late-Scholastic and Austrian Link."

11. Barry Smith, *Austrian Philosophy* (Chicago: Open Court Publishing, 1994), 17; cited in Hayek, *Rules and Order*.

12. Sirico, "The Late-Scholastic and Austrian Link."

13. Many articles found in Acton's *Journal of Markets and Morality* attempt to establish the complementarity between Christian and Austrian traditions, including Robin Klay and John Lunn, "The Relationship of God's Providence to Market Economics and Economic Theory," 6 (Fall 2003); and Gabriel Zanotti's "Misesian Praxeology and Christian Philosophy," 1 (March 1998). Another Acton journal, *Religion & Liberty*, has published

articles such as Sirico's "Toward a New Liberty," 7 (September–October 1997), which also advance common themes between Christian and Austrian traditions.

14. Michael Novak, *The Spirit of Democratic Capitalism* (New York: Simon & Schuster, 1982), 78.

15. Novak cites Hayek's *The Constitution of Liberty* (Chicago: University of Chicago Press, 1978), 457n4, stating, "Hayek notes: 'In some respects Lord Acton was not being altogether paradoxical when he described Aquinas as the First Whig.' Acton defined the Whigs as 'defenders of liberty who defended it for the sake of religion.'" See *Selected Writings of Lord Acton*, vol. 3, ed. J. Rufus Fears (Indianapolis: *Liberty Classics*, 1988), 536; cited in Novak, "The Judeo-Christian Foundation of Human Dignity," note 5.

16. Thomas Aquinas, *On the Governance of Rulers*, trans. Gerald Phelan (New York: Sheed & Ward, 1938), 97–98; quoted in James Wiser, "The Assertion of the Self," in *Political Theory: A Thematic Inquiry* (Chicago: Nelson-Hall, 1986), 112.

17. Novak, "The Judeo-Christian Foundation of Human Dignity." Gary Dorrien notes an epiphany for Novak in his reading of Hayek's essay "Why I Am Not a Conservative" in which Hayek identified himself with the Whig tradition. According to Dorrien, it was at this point in Novak's intellectual development that he became a "convert to Whiggery." See Gary Dorrien, *The Neoconservative Mind: Politics, Culture, and the War of Ideology* (Philadelphia: Temple University Press, 1993), 229.

18. Hayek, *The Constitution of Liberty* (Chicago: University of Chicago Press, 1960), 31.

19. Richard C. Bayer, *Capitalism and Christianity: The Possibility of Christian Personalism* (Washington, DC: Georgetown University Press, 1999), xvi.

20. Novak, *The Spirit of Democratic Capitalism*, 248.

21. Sirico, "Toward a New Liberty," *Religion & Liberty* 7 (September and October, 1997), available from the Acton Institute website at www.acton.org/publicat/randl/97sep_oct/sirico.html (accessed August 22, 2001).

22. Sirico, "Toward a New Liberty." Sirico further contends, "It is only in freedom that man can direct himself toward goodness. So I would add that freedom is necessary for goodness." See John G. West and Sonja E. West, eds., *The Theology of Welfare: Protestants, Catholics, and Jews in Conversation about Welfare* (Lanham, MD: University Press of America, 2000), 33.

23. Sirico, "The Late-Scholastic and Austrian Link." Sirico observed earlier signs of this transformation in Catholic social thought in Pope John XXIII's encyclical *Mater et Magistra*. He particularly notes the pope's comment, "The cardinal point of [*Mater et Magistra*] is that individual men are necessarily the foundation, cause and end of all social institutions." See Sirico, "Mater et Magistra (1961)," in *A Century of Catholic Social Thought*, ed. George Weigel and Robert Royal (Washington, DC: Ethics and Public Policy Center, 1991), 54.

24. George Gilder, *Wealth and Poverty* (New York: Basic Books, 1981), 6.

25. F. A. Hayek, *The Road to Serfdom* (London: George Routledge & Sons, 1944), 157.

26. Daniel Rush Finn, "The Economic Personalism of John Paul II: Neither Right Nor Left," *Journal of Markets and Morality* 2 (Spring 1999), available from the Acton Institute website at www.acton.org/publicat/m_and_m/1999_spr/finn.html (accessed August 22, 2001).

27. Finn quotes Hayek that it is "an erroneous anthropomorphic interpretation" to understand society as "an organization rather than as a spontaneous order." Hayek,

"Principles of a Liberal Social Order," in *Studies in Philosophy, Politics and Economics* (London: Routledge and Kegan Paul, 1967), 171; quoted in Finn, "The Economic Personalism of John Paul II."

28. Finn notes Hayek's statement that there "is only a justice of individual conduct but not a separate 'social justice.'" Hayek, "Principles of a Liberal Social Order," 175; quoted in Finn, "The Economic Personalism of John Paul II."

29. Finn, "The Economic Personalism of John Paul II." Michael Novak has echoed a similar view of the business firm to that of Milton Friedman, although he qualifies his position somewhat. Novak largely agrees with a statement from Friedman's *Capitalism and Freedom* that the essential responsibility of the business firm is "to use its resources and engage in activities designed to increase its profits so long as it stays within the rules of the game." Yet Novak adds a caveat. He says Friedman is correct "in stressing how basic [corporate responsibility] is," but Novak would also place it in the "context of other responsibilities." Further, "it turns out that even a narrow conception of the purposes of business includes a high level of moral performance found in only a few existing cultures." See Novak, *Business as a Calling: Work and the Examined Life* (New York: The Free Press, 1996), 140–41.

30. Pope John Paul II, *Centesimus Annus* (Washington, DC: Office for Publishing and Promotion Services, United States Catholic Conference, 1991), no. 40.

31. Pope John Paul II, *Centesimus Annus*, no. 49.

32. D. Stephen Long, *Divine Economy: Theology and the Market* (New York: Routledge, 2000), 266.

33. Novak, "The Judeo-Christian Foundation of Human Dignity."

34. See Novak, "The Judeo-Christian Foundation of Human Dignity."

35. Sirico has stated, "Humans are moral beings and the only context in which morality can occur is the context of the human liberty." Quoted in *The Theology of Welfare*, 6. Other neoconservatives tend to absolutize the market as the ground for democratic and other principles. For example, Robert Benne states that there is a "certain sense in which the economic liberty encouraged by market economics is constitutive of freedom itself." See Robert Benne, "Capitalism with Fewer Tears," in *Christianity and Capitalism: Perspectives in Religion, Liberalism and the Economy*, ed. Bruce Grelle and David A. Krueger (Chicago: Center for the Scientific Study of Religion, 1986), 73.

36. Robert Bellah et al., *Habits of the Heart: Individualism and Commitment in American Life* (New York: Harper & Row, 1985), 23.

37. The utilitarian school of economics is most closely associated with the theories of Jeremy Bentham and John Stuart Mill. Wolfgang Grassl states, "Where Bentham had viewed man as a pleasure machine, neoclassical economists see him as a maximizer of his own utility, motivated by a stable set of preferences." See Wolfgang Grassl, "Markets and Morality: Austrian Perspectives on the Economic Approach to Human Behaviour," in *Austrian Economics: Historical and Philosophical Background*, ed. Wolfgang Grassl and Barry Smith (New York: New York University Press, 1986), 170.

38. Hayek, *Rules and Order*, 38–39, 51.

39. Grassl notes that in the Austrian conception of the market (as opposed to the neoclassical idea), "human beings do not merely react to a given situation; they can and do act purposefully and they are capable of learning from experience, revising their plans accordingly." See Grassl, "Markets and Morality," 171.

40. Berger says that religion "is the audacious attempt to conceive of the entire universe as humanly significant." See Peter Berger, *The Sacred Canopy: Elements of a Sociological Theory of Religion* (Garden City, NY: Doubleday & Company, 1967), 26, 28 (emphasis added).

41. Hayek, *Rules and Order*, 13.

42. Attributing this understanding of social evolution to Pope John Paul II in the sentence following this quotation, Sirico states, "Much of this same method of analysis can be found in Wojtyla." See Sirico, "The Late-Scholastic and Austrian Link."

43. Nash cites Israel Kirzner's "The Open-Endedness of Knowledge," *The Freeman* 36 (1986) as an essay that expertly explains this aspect of Austrian economic thought. See Ronald H. Nash, *Poverty and Wealth: The Christian Debate over Capitalism* (Westchester, IL: Crossway Books, 1986), 45.

44. Nash, *Poverty and Wealth*, 56.

45. Nash, *Poverty and Wealth*, 73.

46. Michael Novak, *Free Persons and the Common Good* (Lanham, MD: Madison Books, 1989), 106.

47. Michael Novak, *The Catholic Ethic and the Spirit of Capitalism* (New York: The Free Press, 1993), 1–14, 222–37; *Business as a Calling* (New York: The Free Press, 1996), 18–40, 117–59; and *The Spirit of Democratic Capitalism* (Lanham, MD: Madison Books, 1991), 36–48.

48. Novak, "The Judeo-Christian Foundation of Human Dignity." Novak also states, "The most distinctive contribution of Judaism and Christianity to social theory is the identification of the individual conscience as a major source of social energy." See Novak, *Toward a Theology of the Corporation* (Washington, DC: The American Enterprise Institute Press, 1990), 29.

49. In the economic sphere, this is accomplished through what Novak calls the "human imitation of the Creator." See Novak, *The Spirit of Democratic Capitalism*, 39, 356.

50. George Weigel, "Camels and Needles, Talents and Treasure: American Catholicism and the Capitalist Ethic," in *The Capitalist Spirit: Toward a Religious Ethic of Wealth Creation*, ed. Peter Berger, 81–105 (San Francisco: ICS Press, 1990), 104.

51. Michael Novak, "Overview," in *Morality of the Market: Religious and Economic Perspectives*, ed. Walter Bloch, Geoffrey Brennan, and Kenneth Elzinga (Vancouver, BC: Fraser Institute, 1985), 569–70 (emphasis author's). Tawney made his views on acquisitiveness well known in his famous book, *The Acquisitive Society* (New York: Harcourt, Brace and Howe, 1920).

52. Novak, *The Spirit of Democratic Capitalism*, 27.

53. The Lattimer mine owners referred to themselves as "Christian men to whom God in his infinite wisdom had give [*sic*] control of the property interests in this country." See "Anthracite Coal Mining in the Scranton Steamtown Pocono Wilkes Barre Region," available from www.microserve.com/magicusa/coalmine.html (accessed October 22, 2001) [Copyright 1993–2002 by the Houdini Museum].

54. Novak, *The Spirit of Democratic Capitalism*, 27.

55. Concerning "the science of exchange," Mises stated, "Catallactics does not ask whether or not the consumers are right, noble, generous, wise, moral, patriotic, or church-going. It is concerned not with why they act, but only with how they act." See

Ludwig von Mises, *Epistemological Problems of Economics*, trans. George Reisman (Princeton, NJ: D. Van Nostrand Company, 1960), 93–94.

56. Sirico, "The Late-Scholastic and Austrian Link."

57. See Sirico, "The Late-Scholastic and Austrian Link."

58. The term "good" is used here in the context of a commodity or service, and not as in common or social good. See Sirico, "The Late-Scholastic and Austrian Link."

59. Sirico states simply, "The link between the Late Scholastics and the late-nineteenth century Austrian School is the [subjective] theory of economic value." See Sirico, "The Late-Scholastic and Austrian Link."

60. The Late Scholastics of the sixteenth century and their "proto-personalist" approach are portrayed as the economic culmination of the project begun by Thomas Aquinas and the successive refinement of liberal ideas built upon Thomist economic thought. See Sirico, "The Late-Scholastic and Austrian Link."

61. Gronbacher describes his project as one "that seeks to establish a meaningful dialogue between the Austrian school of economics and Catholic social thought. The purpose of this dialogue is to synthesize elements from both intellectual traditions to generate a revised economic model, one that could help to construct a more humane economy." See Gregory M. A. Gronbacher, "Ethics and Economics: The Philosophical Foundations of the Austrian School of Economics," paper prepared for McGill University, Faculty of Education, November 1995, available from the Center for Economic Personalism of the Acton Institute, accessed at the Acton Institute website at www.acton.org on August 22, 2001.

62. Novak, "The Judeo-Christian Foundation of Human Dignity."

63. Novak relies on the distinction articulated by Jacques Maritain that "man will be fully a person, a *per se subsistens* and a *per se operans*, only in so far as the life of reason and liberty dominates that of the senses and passions in him; otherwise he will remain like the animal, a simple individual, the slave of events and circumstances, always led by something else, incapable of guiding himself; he will be only a part, without being able to aspire to the whole." From *Three Reformers* (1925), 24; quoted in Novak, *Free Persons and the Common Good*, 32–33.

64. Thielicke stated that alien dignity becomes paramount when a person's "functional value is no longer listed on society's stock market and he is perhaps declared to be 'unfit to live.'" For more on Thielicke's concept of alien dignity see Helmut Thielicke, *Theological Ethics*, vol. 1, *Foundations*, ed. William H. Lazareth (Philadelphia: Fortress Press, 1966), 1, 21, 151, 170, 242.

65. Mises, *Human Action*, 285. Mises is even against the imposition of narcotic laws, stating, "Opium and morphine are certainly dangerous, habit-forming drugs. But once the principle is admitted that it is the duty of government to protect the individual against his own foolishness, no serious objections can be advanced against further encroachments." See Mises, *Human Action*, 733. However, Mises toned down the antistate rhetoric in *Liberalism in the Classical Tradition*, where he stated, "It is incorrect to represent the attitude of liberalism toward the state by saying that it wishes to restrict the latter's sphere of possible activity or that it abhors, in principle, all activity on the part of the state in relation to economic life." See Mises, *Liberalism in the Classical Tradition*, trans. Ralph Raico (Irvington-on-Hudson, NY: Foundation for Economic Education, 1985), n.p.; quoted in Novak, *Free Persons and the Common Good*, 165.

66. Hayek, *The Road to Serfdom*, 111.

67. Hayek, *The Road to Serfdom*, 120.

68. Hayek includes as appropriate certain programs of government assistance as, for example, those of the "state rendering assistance to the victims of such 'acts of God' as earthquakes and floods." See Hayek, *The Road to Serfdom*, 90. Interestingly, Hayek's mentor Mises offered a rebuke of his prodigy over the role of government, citing Hayek's "rather disappointing" acceptance of some aspects of the welfare state and his belief that it is, "under certain conditions, compatible with liberty." See Mises, "Liberty and Its Antithesis," in *Economic Freedom and Interventionism: An Anthology of Articles and Essays by Ludwig von Mises*, ed. Bettina Bien Greaves (Irving-on-Hudson, NY: The Foundation for Economic Education, 1990), 151.

69. Hayek, *The Road to Serfdom*, 91.

70. Novak, introduction to *The Denigration of Capitalism: Six Points of View*, ed. Michael Novak (Washington, DC: American Enterprise Institute for Public Policy Research, 1980), 3.

71. Nash believes that socialist governments incite conflict within their societies, stating, "Collectivism pits man against man." See Nash, *Poverty and Wealth*, 67.

72. Nash, *Poverty and Wealth*, 130–35.

73. For a synopsis of this debate, see Novak, *Free Persons and the Common Good*, 4, 30–31.

74. Consistent with the Christian's call to creativity and action, Novak states, "God is imagined to be more like insight and choice than like anything else known to humans." See Novak, *Free Persons and the Common Good*, 30.

75. Novak, *Free Persons and the Common Good*, 31.

76. Sirico, "Toward a New Liberty." Mises in his famous treatise *Human Action* stated, "Every step a government takes beyond the fulfillment of its essential function of protecting the smooth operation of the market economy against aggression . . . is a step forward on a road that directly leads into the totalitarian system where there is no freedom at all." See Mises, *Human Action*, 282.

77. Sirico, "Toward a New Liberty."

78. Pius XI, *Quadragesimo Anno* (Washington, DC: United States Catholic Conference, 1991. Originally issued on May 15, 1931. Published by the Catholic Truth Society in 1939), no. 79.

79. Quoted in West and West, *The Theology of Welfare*, 107.

80. Novak, *Toward a Theology of the Corporation*, 8.

81. Novak, *Toward a Theology of the Corporation*, 11n9. Novak observes that among clergymen, "to argue in favor of corporations large enough to check, at least in part, the immense power of the central administrative state is not common." Novak does not address a possible explanation in that, not being religious or moral institutions, large corporations with their own bureaucracies of central administration are likely seen by many clergymen and theologians as not being sufficiently different from the state to be worthy of the "mediating" status Novak grants to them. See Novak, "New Questions for Humanists," in *The Denigration of Capitalism*, ed. Michael Novak, 54–62 (Washington, DC: American Enterprise Institute for Public Policy Research, 1980), 57–58.

82. Novak, *The Catholic Ethic and the Spirit of Capitalism*, 48.

83. Hayek, *Law, Legislation and Liberty*, vol. 3, *The Political Order of a Free People*, 2nd ed. (Chicago: University of Chicago Press, 1981), 150–51.

84. Glasner believes that it was Hayek's thought that helped to coalesce a "fragmented and discredited" American conservatism. See David Glasner, "Hayek and the Conservatives," *Commentary* (October 1992): 48–49.

85. Nicholas Boyle, "Understanding Thatcherism (1988)," in *Who Are We Now? Christian Humanism and the Global Market from Hegel to Heaney* (Notre Dame, IN: University of Notre Dame Press, 1998), 19.

86. Boyle, "Understanding Thatcherism (1988)," 30–31. The process has greatly reduced the sense of collective purpose in Great Britain as well as other nations caught up in the juggernaut of the global economy because, "From the point of view of the market, any act of national government is a restrictive practice, an unwelcome act of protectionism, and national central government itself, the raiser of taxes, the spender of other people's money, the originator of regulations, the fixer of bank rates and would be fixer of exchange rates, is just another vested interest, another unjustified obstacle to the free flow of capital." See Boyle, "After Thatcherism: Who Are We Now?" in *Who Are We Now?* 37.

87. Boyle, "After Thatcherism," 43.

88. Hayek stated, "Mythical beliefs of some sort may be needed to [ensure the continuation of traditions], especially where rules of conduct conflicting with instinct are concerned. A merely utilitarian or even functionalist explanation of the different rites or ceremonies will be insufficient, and even implausible." See Hayek, "Religion and the Guardians of Tradition," in *The Fatal Conceit: The Errors of Socialism* in *The Collected Works of F. A. Hayek*, vol. 1, ed. W. W. Bartley III (Chicago: University of Chicago Press, 1988), 136.

89. Novak, *The Catholic Ethic and the Spirit of Capitalism,* 108.

90. Novak, *The Catholic Ethic and the Spirit of Capitalism,* 8.

91. Novak, *Toward a Theology of the Corporation,* 29–31; and "The Judeo-Christian Foundation of Human Dignity."

92. Hayek's observation of the superiority of religious to constructivist morality in supporting social and economic development reveals the adoption of a theory somewhat akin to Van Til's "borrowed premises," though perhaps operating in reverse. In this case religious writers have observed and chronicled evolutionary moral principles that most closely approximate "truth," as opposed to secular theorists unconsciously adopting the truth found in religious doctrine as Van Til theorized. See Hayek, "Religion and the Guardians of Tradition," 137.

93. Hayek, "Religion and the Guardians of Tradition," 140.

94. "Friedrich August von Hayek (1899–1992)," Acton Institute, available from the Acton Institute website at www.acton.org/research/libtrad/text/hayek.html (accessed August 22, 2001).

95. Hayek believed that the "groups which happen to have adopted rules conducive to a more effective order of actions will tend to prevail over other groups with a less effective order." Here, Hayek adds a footnote that the notion of prevailing groups does not mean conflict between groups in which a victor emerges for obvious reasons; rather, members of a thriving institution often will not know "to which peculiarity they owe their success." See Hayek, *Rules and Order,* 99, 99n7. However, Hayek also understood that the historical context and institutional complexity of a particular society conditioned its cultural evolution. He recognized that "it is the state of civilization at any given moment that determines the scope and possibilities of human ends and values."

Hayek suggested that bureaucratic intransigence might stall society's path to prosperity, stating, "As organizations grow larger and more complex, the task of ascertaining the individual's contribution will become more difficult; and it will become increasingly necessary that, for many, merit in the eyes of managers rather than the ascertainable value of the contribution should determine the rewards." See Hayek, *The Constitution of Liberty*, 24, 99.

96. Novak does part company with Hayek on certain issues; however, he believes that on the whole the Austrian's theories have great potential to enrich Christian ideas. Novak states, "Hayek's work, both in its genius and its errors, has been sorely neglected by Catholic social thinkers." See Novak, *Free Persons and the Common Good*, 86. Novak also stated, "This humanistic turn in economics, first made by the great Austrian economists of our century, seems to have gone largely unobserved outside of the field of economics, even by humanists. But if economics is not only a science, if it is also a way of looking at reality and a way of thinking, . . . , then modern economics offers enormous resources for future generations of thinkers—and the possibilities for a new synthesis are immense." See Novak, "Economics as Humanism," *First Things* 76 (October 1997): 19.

4

HAYEK'S MORAL SYSTEM
AND THE THREAT
TO CHRISTIAN TRADITION

Christian devotees of Friedrich Hayek's social philosophy have written extensively on what they perceive as parallels between Christian tradition and Austrian liberalism, yet they have been more reticent to explore potential conflicts.[1] The most obvious of these seeming contradictions is Hayek's assertion of the limitless malleability of religious traditions in the spontaneous orders of free societies. Hayek's social model implies that the evolutionary development of Christianity, by the very nature of its theological and moral structure, will witness conflicts between the faith's desire to uphold its sacred ideals and moral principles and its more base desire to survive as an institution. If Hayek is correct, then the former may be sacrificed without intention or even the cognition of Christians as they respond to the perceived dictates of group survival.

The reasons for the pliability of religious tradition in Hayek's description of "free societies" is obvious when one considers the implications of the Austrian economic principles previously examined. The central project of Austrian economics—to demonstrate the superiority of individual to collective valuation as the driving force to human progress—necessarily diminishes the role for institutions in seeking the common good for society. Moreover, Hayek's philosophical triumph in demonstrating that social orders cannot be separated into distinct spheres; that values cannot be assigned to categories as purely political, economic, religious, and so on; and that borders between social institutions are porous in the context of liberty, insists that this devaluation of collectives will loosen the doctrinal moorings of religious traditions. One recalls Hayek's statement that freedom "is the air in which alone moral sense grows and in which *moral values are daily re-created* in the free decision of the individual."[2] The moral dynamism embedded in Hayek's theory of the spontaneous order extends to even the most sacred institutions.

Another of the philosophical triumphs of Austrian economics was to account for the limited knowledge of the actor in market exchange, contrary to more traditional strains of classical economic theory, which assume that market participants have adequate knowledge to make utility-maximizing decisions. Ronald Nash states that recognizing the limits to human knowledge in economic decision making is "one of the most important contributions that members of the Austrian school of economics have made to economic theory."[3] This admission of human limitations is not simply a descriptive statement about the parties involved in exchange, however. It is rather a foundational proposition that serves as the basis for the superiority of the market system to central planning, and as an essential component of the evolutionary dynamic that forges the spontaneous order. Nash quotes economist Karen Vaughn that the "very subjectivist ignorance, error and uncertainty confronting man . . . helps to explain the development and persistence of markets as corrective and coordinating institutions" in the sense that "markets enable individuals to compare their subjective judgment with the evaluations of others in a continual process of giving and receiving information relevant to economic decision-making."[4] However, complexity combined with the "drive to survive" and the fact that the knowledge of market participants is limited suggests that the outcomes of exchange will not always conform to their original intentions. These conditions establish the basis for the "unintended consequences" to human action that Hayek believed to be an inevitable by-product of the spontaneous order.

The principle of unintended consequences might be seen as equally applicable to the moral as to the material outcomes of economic decision making. While religious and other cultural traditions influence the subjective judgments of market participants, human ignorance of the ultimate effects of economic decisions in combination with the overriding and unyielding goal of group persistence ensures moral flux. According to Hayek, even if individuals could foresee the consequences of their actions (which they cannot), they would still be pressured into making decisions that contribute to the survival of their institutions, which requires continuous adaptation and even eradication of values, beliefs, and practices. The imperfect knowledge applied in market and other decisions has moral consequences; moreover, the proliferation of technologies that have the potential to reshape our conceptions of the natural world ensures that the moral content of market participation is growing. Human ignorance only compounds the unpredictable results of the spontaneous order for religious morality and for society's broader moral foundation given the instinctual predisposition to *survive*.

Christianity, however, even in its myriad forms, assumes that certain truths exist beyond the uncertainty and moral dynamism of Hayek's social model. In Christian tradition, the individual possesses knowledge of certain "fixed principles" that theoretically impact his economic behavior. Christians are certain, for example, that the existence of sin has consequences not only for individual salvation but for society as well.[5] Belief in the final judgment and in divine redemption necessarily impacts human actions, including economic activities. Therefore, while Christians may accept some malleability to religious tradition inspired by human progress, there ostensibly are limits found in the eternal truths of the Christian faith—limits that Hayek does not recognize.

Moreover, there is irony in the acceptance by some Christians of Hayek's subjectivist model of society, especially when it is accompanied by intense criticism of government. For, if one views the church as an institution that seeks to instill certain values and coerce particular behaviors in its membership, then the church becomes much like the state in the Hayekian view of society, differing largely in its inability to coerce conformity of the wider culture. One can infer that to the extent the church is able to impose its values on society (an extreme case being the Roman Catholic Church of the Middle Ages), then it too would seem subject to Austrian censure for its role as an impediment to the evolution of social institutions necessary for the efficient operation of the spontaneous order. Indeed, Hayek stated this directly in *The Political Order of a Free People*, where he observed that civilization advances only by overcoming defenses of the "old principles" by those "indignant moralists" of religious traditions.[6] The only means by which religious institutions escape the reproach heaped on the state by the Austrian economists is through their more limited sphere of influence and their accommodation of progress through internal adaptation. And the latter they have accomplished in Hayek's view as he notes that only those religions that value property and the family have survived.[7]

This chapter explores in greater depth the writings of Friedrich Hayek respecting religion and its role and ultimate disposition in societies that adopt a predominantly subjectivist ethic. The attempt here is to gain a better understanding of the apparent comfort that some Christians find in Hayek's description of the evolutionary process of value transformation that occurs in the highly individualistic order of modern capitalism. Although Hayek was complimentary toward the past contributions of religious traditions to the development of civilization, it will be shown that he also surmised the persistent erosion of those doctrines and beliefs that serve to inhibit the proper function of the spontaneous order. For Hayek, religions are no different from other social institutions in their instinctual predispositions to *evolve*.

HAYEK ON RELIGION

The role of religion in the thought of Friedrich Hayek has been a matter of considerable speculation. Given the growing number of Hayek's Christian admirers in the United States and in the West more generally, one might surmise that he held religion, or at least Christianity, in high esteem. Indeed, some of his writings reflect appreciation for religious tradition as an essential stabilizer for the orderly progression of society. In his essay "Religion and the Guardians of Tradition," he notes that mythical beliefs of various religions have helped to throttle progress to levels that are socially and morally sustainable. Moreover, certain religious tenets are superior to human reason for the attainment of progress because they represent the result of countless human decisions that have been verified over centuries by the prosperity of those institutions that adhere to them. In other words, Hayek judged religion from a distinctly utilitarian perspective, assessing the contribution of religious traditions to the overall progression of society.

While he insisted that religions evolve just as other institutions, Hayek did not envision the rise of a "new religion" built on reason but rather the evolution of the moral systems of traditional faiths to states more compatible with the requirements of the extended order. He also observed that the contest of institutional survival among religious groups resulted in the extinction of certain faiths.[8] This process occurs naturally through interreligious competition as ecclesial organizations adjust their beliefs and values to the demands of the extended order and its principal mediating institution—the market.

But what did Hayek say specifically regarding the nature and purpose of religion in society? The simple answer is, surprisingly little, yet Hayek did make certain observations and generalizations that leave little doubt as to his view of religion's role in cultural evolution. First, he insisted that "mythical beliefs" may be necessary to guide human behavior, "especially where rules of conduct conflicting with instinct are concerned."[9] Appeals to the transcendent or other religious values have utility in encouraging human action that may appear to conflict with self-preservation and other individual instincts even though they have proven benefits to institutional preservation. Second, while he was insistent that such "myths" were evolutionary in nature and that their benefits were beyond human discernment, he also recognized that "choice among many particular versions of basic religious beliefs was often decided by the expedient decisions of secular rulers."[10] Despite apparent arbitrariness in the course of religious development, characteristics of contemporary religious groups have "proven" utilitarian value by their very persistence, as Marlo Lewis observes:

> Hayek's comments on religion are unusually blunt. Faith, he contends, cannot be a source of our moral heritage, since faith has been used to support all kinds of moral beliefs. True, when faith aligns itself with the rules of property and family, it makes them easier to accept. Indeed, Hayek argues, because the social function of those rules was for a long time not understood at all, they would have been discarded without the support given them by "supernatural sanctions." However, he goes on to say, the "mystical beliefs" that helped preserve traditional morality owe their preservation, in turn, to it. "I believe," says Hayek, "that you will find about every ten years some new creator of a religion that is against property and the family. *But the only religions that have survived are those which support property and family.*"[11]

Hayek's use of the term "traditional morality" must be understood in the context of his infinitely pliant moral system. Culture has the *potential* to evolve such that even the values of property and family—no less than that of human spirituality—become unnecessary baggage to the furtherance of progress.

Scholars have debated the extent to which Hayek applied a "Darwinian" understanding to his unique conception of social evolution. While Hayek expressly criticized Social Darwinism, John Gray notes the progressively Darwinian aspects of Hayek's later philosophy that "accorded increasing prominence to the Darwinian mechanism itself. Social institutions and structures—such as religions and modes of production—come to prevail insofar as they enhance the reproductive fitness of the groups which practice them." Moreover, those religions that "emphasize the importance of private or several property and which support the institution of the family will enhance the life prospects of their practitioners by creating conditions of high productivity in which there will be relatively more numerous infant survivals."[12]

Enforcement of theological doctrine has a limited effect on a particular religious organization's survival chances. Far more important in Hayek's understanding is the arrival of group members at a set of values that are consistent with those that enhance their survival chances, irrespective of doctrinal pronouncements or long-established tenets. Ultimately, the values of religious associations are changed from the "outside in" rather than from the "inside out" for those institutions that survive.

Progress as First Principle

Such extreme emphasis on the competitive selection process in social evolution has led some scholars to conclude that *progress* was the object of faith in the philosophy of Friedrich Hayek. David Koyzis suggests that Hayek was the exemplar of that class of liberal intellectual for whom progress had become a first principle. Koyzis notes the "widespread acceptance of progress presupposes a general secularization in which the Christian faith in a provident God has yielded to an alternative faith in an impersonal surrogate deity. This is true of classical liberalism as a whole and is especially apparent in the thought of Hayek."[13] But the impersonal surrogate is a poor substitute for the personal and loving God of Christianity. Something must supplement the void formed by the decline of belief in a transcendent connection between God and man. Koyzis insists that that object of faith *is* human progress, and who better than Friedrich Hayek to make the case for its canonization?

> For Hayek progress is a faith-object in two senses. First, it is something which he believes to be utterly certain and trustworthy. Second, it constitutes a presupposition *from* which he reasons rather than a conclusion *to* which he reasons. In other words, faith in progress is the basis upon which the other elements of Hayek's thought fall into place.[14]

Hayek emphasized the subliminal processes of the market order in systematically displacing traditional religious and moral values. Graham Walker detects this subtlety in Hayek's philosophy—a process of continual value transformation facilitated by market exchange in contrast to the episodic destruction of traditional values resulting from scientific and technological achievement. Walker notes that for Hayek, the "historical transition to this 'abstract' order of the free market entailed the modification of 'instinctual' morals and the growth of 'commercial' morals, rules of conduct suited to the complex division of labor that ensures the success of modern, free civilization."[15] Walker also notes a paradox in Hayek's belief that religious (as other) traditions must be continuously remade in responding to the imperatives of progress. He states, "Hayek's own philosophical presuppositions—

especially as epitomized in his own rejection of 'the accounts which religion gave' of the source and validity of ethics—indebt him, in a significant and foundational way, to some of the very 'constructivists' whom he so eagerly refutes in other realms."[16] One of those constructivists to whom Hayek no doubt was indebted was the great American philosopher John Dewey.

Hayek and Dewey Revisited

In his book *A Common Faith*, Dewey attempted to demonstrate that "faith in the continued disclosing of truth through directed cooperative human endeavor is more religious in quality than is any faith in a completed revelation."[17] Dewey's faith was also the faith in human progress delivered through the liberating force of democracy and the revelatory power of the scientific method to unravel the mysteries of the universe. The religious fabrications of so-called divine revelation or inspiration professed by historic religions were largely vestigial superstitions of primitive societies that serve to inhibit social, political, and economic advance, although Dewey, just as Hayek, valued religion as a stabilizing institution.[18] Dewey's intellectualization not only of religion but also of the process of social value transformation admittedly differs with Hayek's notion of "cultural spontaneity."[19] To emphasize this difference, Hayek often referred to the particular understanding of human reason held by Dewey and other progressivists as "scientific" or "constructivist" rationalism, to contrast it with his own "evolutionary" view.[20] However, Hayek's use of these modifiers implies that it was principally the means rather than the ends of the respective systems that differed. Indeed, evidence seems to confirm that inference.

Although Dewey never achieved an appreciation of the individual to approach that of the Austrian school, he nevertheless came to a greater awareness of the person as a principal source of material and moral change in society. Over time, Dewey lowered his estimate of the "formality" by which science and technology act on social institutions, and he gained an appreciation of the subtleties by which individual decisions are aggregated into social values. For Dewey, it was the concessions of "liberal theologians" that served as testaments to the power of modernity to eliminate myth and untruth from religious tradition. He stated, "Whenever a particular [religious] outpost is surrendered it is usually met by the remark from a liberal theologian that the particular doctrine or supposed historic or literary tenet surrendered was never, after all, an intrinsic part of religious belief, and that without it the true nature of religion stands out more clearly than before."[21] Moreover, the resistance of some groups to this "emancipation" of religion by progress was considered by Dewey to have been a cause of the religious malaise enveloping American society in the early twentieth century.[22]

Despite such characterizations, Dewey was not so coldly scientific respecting the process by which religious and other values are transformed as some have implied. Rather, his descriptions at times reveal comprehension of the very subtleties that Hayek described and reflect distinctly Hayekian themes regarding the advance of progress:

> Inventor and technology, in alliance with industry and commerce, have, needless to say, profoundly affected these underlying conditions of association. Every political and social problem of the present day reflects the indirect influence, from unemployment to banking, from municipal administration to the great migration of peoples made possible by new modes of transportation, from birth control to foreign commerce and war. The social changes that have come about through the application of new knowledge affect everyone, whether or not he is aware of the forces that play upon him. The effect is deeper, indeed, because so largely unconscious.[23]

Hayek himself could not have articulated a better description of the dynamics of evolutionary rationalism, with the exception that Dewey emphasizes more the "problems" involved in working toward ultimate solutions and he neglects to mention the learning process by which individuals adjust and readjust their behavior based on prior experience. Still, such a staunch advocate of the scientific method as John Dewey likely agreed with Hayek's explanation of the adjustment process as well. And Dewey's stated awareness of the "unconscious" forces that play upon the individual reveals an obvious similarity to Hayek's perspective on the nature of social value change.

In *John Dewey: Religious Faith and Democratic Humanism*, Steven Rockefeller chronicles this shift in Dewey's understanding of cultural evolution and the increasing importance of individual valuation and action to diverse elements of his philosophical system. Rockefeller captures a seminal statement in Dewey's ideological conversion to the importance of the individual in an essay with the confessional and intriguing title, "What I Believe, Revised":

> It has been shown in the last few years that democratic institutions are no guarantee for the existence of democratic individuals. The alternative is that individuals who prize their own liberties and who prize the liberties of other individuals, individuals who are democratic in thought

and action, are the sole final warrant for the existence and endurance of democratic institutions.[24]

Rockefeller traces the origins of this metamorphosis in Dewey's thought to his revulsion at the rise of European nationalism in the late 1920s.[25] It was the disintegration of European society that brought home for Dewey a rather stark realization of the injurious potential of human reason in combination with institutional power.

Although Dewey never abandoned his view of the primacy of the scientific method or its relevance as an instrument of social change, he ultimately arrived at a more subjectivist view of society. The experimental intelligence that forms the "general mind" retained its importance along with a greater appreciation of human liberty's contribution to cultural development in Dewey's later thought. Dewey stated, "The ability of individuals to develop genuine individuality is intimately connected with the social conditions under which they associate with one another," yet he conceded, "I should now wish to emphasize more than I formerly did that *individuals* are the finally decisive factors of the nature and movement of associated life."[26] According to Rockefeller, Dewey came to recognize that "experimentalism cannot guarantee a wholesale solution to the problem of unifying the ideal and the actual, but it may be instrumental to freedom, individual growth, and social progress."[27]

Just as Dewey in his later works seemed to approach a Hayekian understanding of the means by which norms and values are transformed in "associated life," Crowley suggests that Hayek's views were more "scientific" (and thus more Deweyan) than has been recognized. According to Crowley, for Hayek the "process of evolutionary competition is like that of scientific experimentation: one judges the results not by what one thinks desirable, but by the method used to arrive at the results. And since the development of morals and principles is not in any way different, one must be free to reject principles in which one has always believed when the operation of the abstract social order proves them not to be conducive to long-term social survival."[28] The use of "trial and error" to describe the dynamic selection process of institutions hints at Hayek's experimentalist view of the spontaneous order. His statement that the system's regularity "rests on purposive action of its elements" and the adjustment and readjustment of those actions to changing conditions[29] implies that the philosophical gap separating these two eminent social theorists may not be as great as many have concluded. Further binding the philosophies of Dewey and Hayek is the absence of any teleological foundation in their epistemologies. Their respective systems are bounded only by the limits of scientific rationalism in the one case and evolutionary rationalism in the other.

The absence of any metaphysical ground for their respective systems of ethics has caused scholars to speculate on the religious implications of Dewey's and Hayek's social philosophies. Walker contends that the concept of "ethical transcendence becomes a little-noticed casualty in Hayek's war against 'constructivism.'"[30] One reason for this "casualty" might be observed in Berger's recognition of religion as "human enterprise." Development and maintenance of religious tradition requires deliberative human action toward the creation of doctrine and theology designed to preserve the sacred core of religious belief. The transcendent foundation of Christianity, although a sacrosanct element of the tradition, is not self-sustaining. Even those Christian theologians who stress the centrality of divine revelation understand that its interpretation and preservation require the involvement of the human intellect, the potential for human error, and the influence of human values.[31] The persistence of religious values and beliefs cannot be accomplished entirely through an unguided dynamic of human interaction. Therefore, the rise of the subjectivist order of modern capitalism that has contributed to increasing disregard for planned and collective human activities at the level of government may signal the coequal demise of *the* human enterprise that *is* institutional religion.

The philosophies of Hayek and Dewey converged not only over the idea of progress as the object of faith but also in their recognition of the means of institutional adjustment necessary to sustain it. As noted, Dewey came to perceive many of the same subtle sociological influences at work on religious and other social institutions. His suggestion that the action of the "general mind"—a term Hayek likely detested for its collectivization of the inherently dynamic process of human interaction—is the ultimate source both of collective reason and human values moderates his earlier emphasis on the scientific method. Regardless of the source of change, however, the implications of Dewey's system for religious tradition are much the same as that of Hayek's—an erosion of elements from the sacred core of religious traditions resulting from the advance of human progress. Dewey stated, "The hold of the supernatural upon the general mind has become more and more disassociated from the power of ecclesiastical organization. Thus the very idea that was central in religions has more and more oozed away, so to speak, from the guardianship and care of any particular social institution."[32]

Both men came to recognize a downside to the erosion of faith from the guardianship of tradition and its replacement by the new faith in progress that accompanies modernity. Dewey stated, "The direct pursuit of happiness always ends in looking for happiness in possessions," an inevitably frustrating journey because we "do not tend the roots of life from which a lasting happiness springs."[33] Hayek was even more fatalistic than Dewey in addressing the enslavement to materialism that results from an all-consuming faith in human progress:

> The aspirations of the great mass of the world's population can today be satisfied only by rapid material progress. There can be little doubt that in their present mood a serious disappointment of their expectations would lead to grave international friction—indeed, it would probably lead to war. The peace of the world and, with it, civilization itself thus depend on continued progress at a fast rate. At this juncture we are therefore not only the creatures but the captives of progress; even if we wished to, we could not sit back and enjoy at leisure what we have achieved.[34]

Who can doubt that the continual push to accelerate material progress can only mean a coequal imperative for moral adjustment in Hayek's evolutionary system? And that moral adjustment must be accomplished in relative harmony with the material progress that it seeks to accommodate. As productivity increases in capitalist society, so too must the attendant moral structure evolve at a faster rate in order to keep pace. This is accomplished seamlessly in Hayek's system because the human action that leads to material improvement has moral consequences, one of which is altering the value systems of those institutions to which market participants belong.

Because Hayek emphasized the indeterminacy of moral evolution, however, some might question whether he believed that the evolutionary course of religious tradition necessarily leads to the displacement of the sacred by commercial and other secular values. Yet, despite Hayek's articulation of the good of religious and moral traditions in underpinning capitalism, there can be little doubt of his view on the ultimate disposition of faith traditions in their competition with political and economic institutions:

> Religious prophets and ethical philosophers have of course at all times been mostly reactionaries, defending the old principles against the new principles. Indeed, in most parts of the world the development of an open market economy has long been prevented by those very morals preached by prophets and philosophers, even before governmental measures did the same. *We must admit that modern civilization has become largely possible by the disregard of those indignant moralists.*[35]

First, one might note support for a contention made previously that Hayek viewed the institutions of religion and government, to the extent that they attempt to *enforce* values on society, as similar impediments to the proper function of the spontaneous order. Religion can, in some cases, stabilize change to levels that are more culturally harmonious, yet it can also impede progress through dogmatic conservatism, in which case the obstacle must be removed. Second, this quotation along with Hayek's comments from "Religion and the Guardians of Tradition" make it clear that Hayek discerned an evolution away from sacred or transcendent values for those religious "survivors" to a collection of largely commercial and utilitarian values more conducive to market processes and group persistence.

Ludwig Mises reinforces the Austrian position on the purpose of religious tradition in the evolution of human culture where he states, "The drop in infant mortality, the successful fight against plagues and famines, the general improvement of the standard of living—are to be highly valued from the point of view of the teachings of any religious creed and of any system of ethical doctrines. No religious or ethical tenet can justify a policy that aims at the substitution of a social system under which output per unit of input is lower for a system in which it is higher."[36] Mises' statement demonstrates the preeminent position of physical survival in the Austrian conception of social morality. He cannot countenance the possibility that in an environment where the value of human life is being eroded by technological and material expansion into formerly sacred aspects of life, religious leaders might be justified in calling for a "lowering of output" or a deceleration of technological development.

Ultimately, the systems of Hayek and Dewey are linked by a pervasive and deterministic *rationalism* that, over the course of time and through the value changes associated with economic development, becomes the core of all social traditions, including the religious. Although these seemingly antithetical philosophers made certain concessions to the "other side" in the debate over progress, it was Dewey's growing recognition of the importance of subjective behavior in transforming institutions that was most important in narrowing the philosophical gap between them. Dewey illustrated this point in a religious context, stating, "Although there is much that is non-Christian and anti-Christian in existing economic and political institutions, it is better that change be accomplished by the sum total of efforts of men and women who are imbued with personal faith, than that they be effected by any wholesale institutional effort that subordinates the individual to an external and ultimately worldly authority."[37] His description suggests growing appreciation for the subjective valuations and actions of individuals in recomposing social values. For both Dewey and Hayek, this process necessarily includes the alteration or even elimination of religious values and beliefs that impede the procession of modernity. The question is whether these two eminent social philosophers were correct in their assessments of the mutability of religious tradition and in their confidence of faith in progress.

HYPOTHETICALITY AND REVITALIZATION OF THE CULTURAL LAG QUESTION

In his 1982 book *Forced Options: Social Decisions for the 21st Century*, Roger Shinn, the Reinhold Niebuhr professor of social ethics emeritus at Union Theological Seminary, explores the relevance to modern culture of German physicist Wolf Häfele's concept of "hypotheticality." Häfele coined the term to characterize a modern world in which the number and magnitude of potential consequences to natural events and human action have grown so great that we are simply unable to conceive the possible outcomes; thus, we proceed into increasing uncertainty.[38] Shinn applies Häfele's concept to society in suggesting that human beings are making "far-reaching decisions" based on knowledge that will "necessarily and ultimately remain inconclusive."[39] The result of hypotheticality for human culture is that we are increasingly unable to predict the future. It is conceivable that science and technology will enable long, fulfilled, and happy lives for future generations, but this is uncertain. Ambiguity toward the future caused by the complexity of modern society and its ability to overwhelm both individual and collective reason causes human beings, in Shinn's view, to "act in a frightening ambience of mingled urgency and ignorance."[40]

While the hypotheticality of human action has always been present, it is the magnitude of consequences that has grown exponentially due to the level of technological achievement and the impossibility of knowing how various technologies will interact.[41] The dynamic trial-and-error method that has proven so beneficial to human progress (and over which Hayek was so ebullient) today realizes potentially cataclysmic possibilities, though the exact nature of those cataclysms is unknown. Shinn uses examples of genetic experimentation, modern weaponry, and environmental pollution to make his point. His fear is that "an unintended self-destruct apparatus [has been] put into the system by eager, groping, blundering people who are doing things for the first time and don't know entirely what they are doing."[42]

Shinn's somber acquiescence to Häfele's principle offers evidence that little disagreement exists today over the course of cultural development. The often errant groping and blundering of human beings that Shinn acknowledges but of which he is fearful is the very behavior by which society progresses according to Hayek. Despite their agreement on the mechanics of change, Shinn and Hayek represent opposing views of the material and moral sustainability of liberal society. Differences exist today not so much between capitalists and socialists (the latter for all intents and purposes having been eradicated) but rather between those who are confident in the nature of progress that will result from modern capitalism and those who are not. Even social constructivists such as Shinn and institutional economist John Kenneth Galbraith have conceded the triumph of subjectivist liberalism. And, though some might challenge aspects of Hayek's system, few today refute his description of the principles by which civilization advances. Galbraith, in fact, was one of the first "American liberals" to concede victory to the classical liberals in his book *The Affluent Society* published in 1976:

> In the advanced countries, the facts are inescapable. It is the increase in output in recent decades, not the redistribution of income, which has brought the great material increase in the well-being of the average man. And, however suspiciously, the liberal has come to accept the fact. As a result, the goal of an expanding economy has also become deeply embedded in the conventional wisdom of the American left. The beneficent effects of such an economy, moreover, are held to be comprehensive.[43]

Shinn attempted to resuscitate the constructivist ideal in *Forced Options*, stating, "The uses of technology are not given necessity, like the orbit of the earth around the sun. They are a human decision."[44] In the overall context of the book, however, one gets the impression that, deep down, even Shinn acknowledges that technological determinism[45] and the subjective economic ethic that powers it have triumphed and are today the unstoppable engines of change.

The "age of hypotheticality" has considerable relevance to the subject here, for, not only the material outcomes but also the potential moral consequences of human action have grown dramatically through the technical advances of recent decades. Burgeoning markets for human body parts, the prospects of human clones and custom-designed offspring, and an emerging industry based on xenotransplantation (cross-species organ and tissue transfer technologies) all testify that the moral content of economic behavior is on the rise.[46] Shinn blends together the potential technological and moral consequences of hypotheticality in such a way that one perceives civilization to be engaged in a race between ecological calamity and moral collapse.

Importantly, Shinn's social application of Häfele's hypothesis revivifies the cultural lag question that was presented earlier as central to the debate over human progress in the first half of the twentieth century. Häfele's belief that the outcomes of human decisions are outpacing society's ability to intellectually digest and respond to their consequences is only a more contemporary restatement of the cultural lag problem. This phenomenon was described in the introduction as the divide that exists between society's technical-economic establishments and its moral traditions. However, a more general definition of cultural lag was offered by one of its chief protagonists, the sociologist William F. Ogburn, who stated, "A cultural lag occurs when one of two parts of culture which are correlated, changes before or in greater degree than the other part does, thereby causing less adjustment between the two parts than existed previously."[47] Thus, Ogburn described not *a* cultural lag but potentially *myriad* lags resulting from the inherently asynchronous processes of cultural development. His definition also refers to the phenomenon of lag expansion as one part of culture fails to change proportionately with alterations in another. Ogburn's definition is particularly appropriate to the lag of interest here—that between the moral consequences of economic decisions and the values of religious traditions—yet few social scientists today consider the cultural lag question fertile ground for sociological study.

The paucity of current literature on the cultural lag phenomenon demonstrates that it has fallen into disfavor as an object of scientific investigation. Sociologists Richard and June Brinkman are among the few who have attempted to revive academic exploration of this paradigm for research, yet they are isolated voices in a sea of rational choice and other theories of human behavior that dominate contemporary scholarship.[48] At the very least, it can be said that cultural lag theory no longer occupies the position of prominence it held early in the twentieth century when virtually every major social theorist was embroiled in the debate.[49] How is one to explain the fall of cultural lag theory from the academic heights considering the ever-increasing pace of technology and the relative backwardness, so often noted by Christian libertarians and neoconservatives, of religious institutions and their leadership respecting technical and economic development?[50]

The question of what happened to the cultural lag model for social analysis is worthy of more significant study than can be afforded here; however, two possible explanations are offered for its demise, both of which factor into the subject at hand. First, the idea of cultural lag was associated with the theories of Dewey, Ogburn, Veblen, and others who trusted in the power of human reason to correct the social inequities and dislocations associated most directly with industrial capitalism. These theorists, who are aptly categorized by the term "social constructivists" that has been used throughout this book, were prominent during the formative period of social science—the late nineteenth and early twentieth centuries. As their behavioral theories and interventionist solutions to social problems became discredited, so too were the presuppositions on which those theories were based. One of the assumptions that led to their advocacy of institutional remedies for the correction of social problems was the existence of cultural lags. Second, increasing acceptance of subjectivist capitalism as the sole path to the good for modern societies necessarily employs a process of moral adjustment that conforms to Hayek's conception of evolutionary rationalism. In other words, the triumph of the subjectivist ethic has enabled a dynamic institutional adjustment process, just as Hayek described, that is perceived as superior to the more static relations of socialism, interventionist liberalism, or traditional societies[51] in minimizing value differences between social groups. Thus, the absence of contemporary dialogue on the cultural lag problem may signify a tacit consensus that lags are minimized to the extent possible in societies where subjective valuation and the freedom to act are the principal determinants of the good.

This explanation for the decline of cultural lag theory has significant implications for religious morality. In a formal sense, there is little to suggest that Christian or other religious traditions are today better able to respond to the moral questions arising from economic and technological advance than they were in the early decades of the twentieth century. As will be shown, the evidence implies that religious leadership increasingly is unable to identify, evaluate, and respond to the moral questions arising from the rapid expansion of markets and deployment of new technologies. In the previous statement alone, four distinct "minilags" might be inferred that contribute to the problem facing Christianity[52] and other religions: the time required to ascertain the moral consequences of participation in markets offering advanced technological services, the effort involved in relating possible moral outcomes to a religious group's doctrinal positions and moral theology, the time necessary for the group's leaders to develop and articulate new doctrine on unique technologies, and the difficulty and time involved in disseminating information on these changes to their respective memberships. And it should be recognized that this process must be repeated for each new technology that prompts moral questions for which previous doctrinal and moral statements are inadequate. The problem of cultural lags has never been resolved but rather has been deferred to the dynamic and evolutionary process of value transformation that takes place in the modern capitalist economy as best described by Friedrich Hayek's value theory. Thus, the moral reflection and action of religious communities, as other collectives, increasingly has been subjugated to the aggregate moral outcomes resulting from the market decisions of their members, just as he described.

THE TRUTH OF HAYEK'S THEORY OF VALUE EVOLUTION

In 1989, bioethicist Robert Veatch's book *Death, Dying, and the Biological Revolution* startled many persons interested in moral aspects of medical science by finding no significant opposition from the "major Western religious traditions" to controversial experiments centering on the emerging science of xenotransplantation.[53] This technology enables the transplant of cells, tissues, and organs between species, including transfer between humans and other species, which is thought to offer potential for the eradication of certain diseases and a solution to the chronic shortage of human organs available for transplantation. A burgeoning industry is emerging around this technology as biotech companies scramble to reap the profits from what is considered a revolutionary scientific achievement. Already, special transgenic pigs have been engineered that carry human DNA, which enables the production of organs for transplant into human beings, and experiments are being conducted on a widening basis despite public health concerns.[54]

Xenotransplantation has obvious implications for religious conceptions of the human person in its potential to biologically alter human beings. Beyond the uncertainty involved in the manipulation of an unfathomably complex biological equation are the ethical questions: principally, does scripture or the various Christian traditions speak to the transference of tissues and organs from nonhuman species into human beings? And should theologians have anything to say about the transplantation of organic material between *any* species, plant or animal? Yet despite the enormity of these questions, Veatch discovered in an admittedly limited study that few religious groups responded to this technological development with statements of any kind during the first few years after the innovation. Even religions that are traditionally skeptical of technical advances, such as Roman Catholicism and Orthodox Judaism, were largely silent on the issue, while some ethicists within these traditions were even positive concerning the potential future benefits of this new technology.[55] Veatch's study is admittedly dated; however, even given its limitations, it suggests that religious traditions have difficulty in responding to moral questions brought about by technological developments. It also suggests a lack of urgency by religious leaders and institutions in dealing with these issues.

The larger contention here that Hayek's theory of social value transformation in free societies is accurate does not depend on any "presumed" prohibitions of religious traditions respecting the transplantation of tissue between species. This example merely points out the magnitude of what is at stake. Rather, the failure of religious groups to deal with such a critical issue demonstrates that they often lag behind in examining the implications of new technologies even for their most sacred beliefs. It also provides additional evidence to the previous contention that the problem of cultural lags was never resolved but rather was deferred by the de facto acceptance of a Hayekian-like system of evolutionary morality that enables the subjective decisions of individuals to shape and reshape the moral content of their respective institutions. The anticipated argument that religious leaders simply cannot keep up with the pace of technological change and respond to each new development is a valid one, yet it only reinforces Hayek's dynamic view of social morality. Absent doctrinal or other guidelines to participation, members of traditions are likely to employ those biomedical services that they believe offer the greatest possibilities for long-term survival, irrespective of the potential cumulative effects on their religious traditions.[56]

This is not to suggest that religious groups have been silent in debates concerning the moral consequences of technological and other developments that may clash with their traditional beliefs. Some churches have been highly involved in past controversies that centered on the definition of life in the context of emerging technologies. The Roman Catholic Church, for example, has been quite active in the abortion debate (most recently concerning the "abortion pill" RU-486)[57] and in questions concerning euthanasia, contraception, and human fertility technologies. Evangelical Protestants, too, have found outlets for their views on these issues that involve the most basic conceptions of the human person.[58] Yet the results of controversies over abortion and contraception within the Roman Catholic Church, in particular, provide additional evidence that Hayek's theory of moral adjustment is accurate. The Catholic Church is referenced here for its traditionally rigid opposition to both abortion and contraception. Modernism's influence has fomented dissension within Catholicism around these issues as abortions became more commonplace following the Supreme Court's *Roe v. Wade* decision in 1973, and as contraception became more widely accepted within American society to include much of American Protestantism.

Pope Paul VI's 1968 encyclical *Humanae Vitae*[59] was a tendentious and touchstone document within the Catholic Church. The very process by which the encyclical was developed illustrates the moral tension between the subjective valuations of individual Catholics and long-held institutional values and practices. Paul VI's predecessor, Pope John XXIII, had actually begun the process of reassessing the church's position with regard to contraception by appointing a special commission to study the issue in 1963.[60] Following Pope John's death, Paul VI expanded the commission through the addition of married couples and population experts.[61] The commission completed its study in 1966 and voted 52 to 4 to recommend an end to the church's traditional ban on artificial contraception. A special panel of bishops also voted to support many of the commission's recommendations.[62] Going against the findings of both the commission and the bishops, however, Pope Paul's encyclical, calling on the teachings of natural law, insisted, "In any use of marriage whatever there must be no impairment of its natural capacity to procreate human life."[63] Thus, the Catholic Church's prohibition of contraception for its members has remained in force.

Considerable evidence exists, however, to show that *Humanae Vitae* today is neither definitive nor authoritative within the Catholic Church as a guideline to member behavior. In a recent book, Randall Balmer chronicles the initial fallout resulting from Pope Paul VI's encyclical, specifically within the American Catholic Church, noting a significant drop in calls to the priesthood, falling attendance at weekly mass, a decline in tithing, and a reduction in parochial school enrollments "from 5.6 million in 1965 to 3.5 million a decade later."[64] Balmer suggests that the immediate response of individual Catholics to *Humanae Vitae* was one of rejection and defection. Yet evidence also demonstrates that the American Catholic Church has greatly stabilized its member population over the past decade and actually has increased membership over the past few years.[65] The obvious question becomes whether the stabilization of membership in American Catholicism reflects greater acceptance of the principles articulated in Paul VI's controversial encyclical.

Studies suggest that Roman Catholic attitudes toward abortion, contraception, and other practices prohibited by *Humanae Vitae* are quite consistent with those of Americans generally. In *The Restructuring of American Religion*, Princeton sociologist Robert Wuthnow reported that by the late 1970s (approximately ten years after *Humanae Vitae*), statistical differences among religious groups even over questions as controversial as abortion, contraception, and premarital sex showed little variation across religious and denominational lines. Wuthnow discovered, for example, that on the question of whether a respondent approved of abortion "for someone who simply did not want more children," the percentages who responded affirmatively "ranged only between 44 percent among Lutherans, Catholics, and members of the Protestant sects, and 50 percent among Episcopalians." Baptists, Methodists, Presbyterians, and Jews scored in the middle range between these figures.[66]

More contemporarily and specific to the Roman Catholic Church, a poll conducted by the Roper organization indicates the willingness of individual Catholics to go against their church's teachings even on foundational and controversial issues. The poll, commissioned in 1997 by *Catholic World Report*, found that 70 percent of Catholics who *disagree* with the statement "women cannot be ordained in the priesthood" also believe that abortion can be justified.[67] An even greater number, 85 percent, "deny that artificial contraception is morally wrong, while only 12 percent uphold the Church's teaching."[68] One might infer that limiting the population only to those Catholics who disagree with the church's prohibition on the ordination of women may skew the statistics; however, the poll recorded that "despite the recent, clear, emphatic, and repeated magisterial pronouncements that women cannot be ordained, a solid majority of the [total] respondents to the Roper poll—58 percent—disagreed with that statement and 42 percent disagreed strongly."[69]

The willingness of laypersons and even some parish priests to go against their Catholic leadership provides evidence of Thorstein Veblen's theory of the more rapid adjustment of the "outer relations" (in this case, lay Catholics and priests) vis-à-vis the "inner relations" (the papacy, curia, and bishops) in responding to cultural changes. Moreover, the divide between the two groups substantiates the existence of cultural lags. Catholic lay theologian Christine Gudorf describes the transformations that have taken place within Catholicism in recent years, noting, "The Roman Catholic Church (and Christianity in general) has in the last century drastically rethought the meaning of marriage, the dignity and worth of women, the relationship between the body and the soul, and the role of bodily pleasure in Christian life, all of which together have revolutionary implications for church teaching on sexuality and reproduction. In effect, the foundations of the old bans have been razed and their replacements will not support the walls of the traditional bans."[70] Reinforcing Hayek's view of the evolutionary nature of social change, Gudorf recognizes that it is the "foundations" of the "old bans" and not the bans themselves that have been razed. The term "foundations" as used in this context indicates not only the attitudes of the Catholic membership toward these practices but also their respect for church teaching as authoritative regarding these issues. Indeed, the evidence suggests that individual Catholics have simply applied their own subjective value judgments (even those that conflict with church doctrine) while retaining their membership within the church. Gudorf observes this sardonically by noting the dramatic drop in birthrates in predominantly Catholic countries in Europe and South America and stating that "it is difficult to believe that fertility was cut in half through voluntary abstinence from sex."[71] Although the bans on artificial contraception remain in place, individual Catholic behavior has radically changed, even in those countries considered most devout.[72]

Confirming the value changes within American Catholicism in another context are two ABC News polls taken in June and July 2001 to assess public attitudes toward stem-cell research and that reveal additional evidence to support Hayek's value theory. One particular subgroup observed in each poll was white American Catholics. What is interesting about the timing of these polls is that they were conducted both prior to and subsequent to a rather forceful and widely publicized statement by Pope John Paul II in which he warned President Bush that this technology would contribute to a "tragic coarsening of consciences" and urged the president to reject research using stem cells.[73] In the first poll taken June 24, 2001, 54 percent of white Catholics said that they supported stem-cell research. The second poll, taken July 30, 2001, revealed that support among white Catholics had actually risen to 65 percent despite the pope's critical statement.[74] A journalist described these results as "a fresh example of American Catholics' independence from church leaders."[75] For purposes here, the polls also serve as evidence of the veracity of Hayek's theory of social value transformation and his insistence that the values of institutions are most affected by the interactions of their members in the spontaneous order. American Catholics apparently are convinced that stem-cell treatments are or will become necessary for future survival, and the polls would suggest that this attitude is sufficiently strong such that Catholics are willing to contravene the directives of perhaps the most popular pope of the twentieth century.

Evidence that the subjectivism of modern society increasingly impinges upon the moral voice of religious institutions offers considerable weight to Hayek's value theory. The evidence suggests that moral traditions are largely those distillations of individual decision making that have best contributed to group success, just as Hayek suggested. In his evolutionary moral system, such a conclusion is neither nihilistic nor tragic—it simply *is*.

Thus, for Hayek, no transcendent moral principles are jeopardized by cultural evolution because no transcendent moral principles exist. Although we may be unable to discern the exact contributions of particular norms or practices to group survival, those benefits nevertheless must exist to enable persistence. Brian Crowley neatly summarizes this aspect of Hayek's moral theory:

> While not denying the existence of values, [Hayek] denies that their source is knowable or can ever be satisfactorily articulated by anyone. Men hold the values they do, not because these values are intrinsically worthwhile, but because they have proven their worth in the struggle for social survival; they have proven utility. Since no one can know why they have this utility, to deliberate on the values men should have is to be guilty of a particularly dangerous hubris.[76]

Mises was even more extreme in grounding morality fully within the natural world, or, more specifically, within the evolutionary and naturalistic context of human civilization, stating, "Everything that serves to preserve the social order is moral; everything that is detrimental to it is immoral."[77]

Other scholars have espoused theories that tend to support Hayek's understanding of the means by which human progress is accomplished. Regarding the "mechanics" of cultural development, few would challenge Alfred North Whitehead's observation that "civilization advances by extending the number of important operations which we can perform without thinking about them."[78] Yet Whitehead's theorem may be seen as applying equally to the moral consequences of human action as to the activities themselves. It is not enough to relegate important operations to the background; their social and moral implications must also be made subliminal in order to lessen contentious issues that accompany development. Society, for example, accepts certain "social costs" associated with economic growth, such as increased levels of environmental pollution and traffic congestion, viewing them as necessary though undesired consequences of economic development.[79] Although certain activist groups address these problems, the social costs of development are generally subordinated to larger imperatives such as maintaining adequate production and employment levels and other macroeconomic measures considered indispensable to economic health.

Similarly, many of the moral consequences of economic behavior are placed beyond societal reflection in order to eliminate potential obstacles to future progress. Legendary heart surgeon Christian Barnard, for example, once commented that people largely have forgotten the collective sigh that was uttered over the initial efforts at heart transplantation.[80] The fact that many Christian groups had long considered the heart to hold special significance for the uniqueness of the human person (for some it remains the very location of the soul) meant that science, through the advent of this technique, was dabbling with the very identity of the human person. Would the heart recipient retain his own soul, receive that of another, or exist as some hybrid freak of nature—a human being with a muddled transcendent identity? The disappearance of such debates along with the statistical evidence presented previously suggest that the moral costs of economic development are, in some respects, equally tangible to its social costs.

That the techniques spawned by economic development have unintended consequences and that, as Whitehead observed, those techniques and their consequences largely are placed beyond human reflection as a requisite of progress adds to the moral flux inherent in cultural advance. The arrival of the "age of hypotheticality" suggests that we ignore, or at least defer, ultimate questions in our procession into the future. The reasons for such deference are the rising complexity that overwhelms reason and the pressures of institutional competition noted by Hayek. In a sense, this concession to progress is affirmation of Häfele's belief that the consequences of human progress have grown beyond either individual or collective comprehension. Thus, proponents of Austrian economic theory, having rejected the adequacy of human reason to manage change, *must contend* that the natural harmonies of the free market system are sufficient to remedy problems resulting from economic advance, for the absence of an alternative.

However, some challenge the notion that natural harmonies will prevent society from self-destructing, either materially or morally. Economic philosopher Fred Hirsch, in concert with Hayek's observations, has detected the unintended consequences of human action, in that "major changes in social patterns or social norms can take place without being willed by any individual and without being consistent with any summation of individual wishes."[81] Yet Hirsch is less sanguine about this dynamic process that is both the glory and the mystery of Hayek's spontaneous order. For Hayek, it enables a rate of human progress unimaginable under socialism or other attempts at social construction, while Hirsch seems to conceive from this social "fact" that modern man has become dislodged from the mother ship and is drifting into an uncharted cosmos filled with previously unexperienced strains and stresses on the human person.

For one, Hirsch notes how the arrival of the "modern mixed economy" absent adequate collective moral structures has placed a tremendous strain on individual morality.[82] He defines the resultant moral order as "micromorality,"[83] in which the collective weight of the market's moral consequences falls almost exclusively on the shoulders of isolated individuals who are forced to internalize the norms and values of the myriad institutions to which they belong. The result of this increasing complexity is that the aggregation of subjective decision making has "become a less sure guide to promoting the objectives of individuals taken together."[84] Hirsch's thesis offers another explanation for the decline of cultural lag theory: moral dilemmas that were once addressed principally by institutions have shifted to the individual in modern capitalism. Cultural lags are no longer significant because institutions are no longer presumed to carry the lion's share of society's moral burdens. Thus, cultural lags among institutions cannot exist because they have, to a considerable extent, been absolved of moral responsibility.

One might speculate that a consequence of Häfele's hypotheticality and Hirsch's micromorality, if both are accurate, is a quite dynamic form of moral relativism. One could also speculate that such a moral system would be consonant with that described by Friedrich Hayek. In fact, Hayek stated, "However much we dislike it, we are again and again forced to recognize that there are no truly absolute values whatever. Not even human life itself. This again and again we are prepared to sacrifice, and must sacrifice, for some other higher values, even if it be one life to save a large number of other lives."[85] Graham Walker concluded upon his reading of *Rules and Order* that, in Hayek's mind, "no conscious or teleological force, no supra-natural deity autonomous from the natural order either set evolution in motion or guided its progress."[86] Indeed, it is the lack of mooring for Hayek's moral system which, if truly the most accurate description of contemporary social morality, should greatly concern Christian admirers of Austrian economics.

Ultimately, the danger to the Christian "person" posed by modern society's overwhelming complexity and the existence of a moral system that approaches the Hayekian model is best described in economic terms. S. S. Acquaviva utilizes a concept similar to the "crowding out" phenomenon of economic theory to articulate the threat posed by technological advance to the "religious" generally, but in particular to the concept of transcendence:

> If, at bottom, it is the chain of the wholly other that securely binds together the various manifestations of the religious through space and time, and if, in society, taken as a unified whole, it is transcendence which most specifically characterizes the religious in industrial society, we are confronted with the following problem: do industrial and post-industrial societies leave any space within themselves, and within the process of rationalization to which they are committed, for the transcendent as a conscious, objective dimension of the wholly other?[87]

The "crowding out" concept has long been used by economists in other contexts—for example, to explain how public expenditures often displace private contributions to public goods. In this case, Acquaviva uses an analogous concept to ask whether transcendent values are systematically crowded out by the rationalizing forces of industrial societies.[88] Perhaps Galbraith anticipated Acquaviva's question in *The Affluent Society*, where he stated, "So all embracing, indeed, is our sense of the importance of production as a goal that the first reaction to any questioning of this attitude will be, 'What else is there?' So large does production bulk in our thoughts that we can only suppose that a vacuum must remain if it should be relegated to a smaller role."[89] The "vacuum" that Galbraith theorized can also be applied to the crowding out of the sacred and transcendent to the point that all that remains is the material and the immanent.

Another social theorist who became preoccupied with the value displacement processes of modern society was the eminent economist Frank Knight. Professor Knight observed the erosion of the sacred in the specific context of the Sabbath-day observance in his classic essay "The Ethics of Competition":

> The striking fact in modern life is the virtually complete separation between the spiritual ethics which constitutes its accepted theory of conduct and the unethical, uncriticized notion of efficiency which forms its substitute for a practical working ideal. . . . For "spirituality" is preserved in practice for a smaller and smaller fraction of the seventh day, by a smaller and smaller fraction of the population; and even that is more and more transformed by organizations into a mere contest in membership and display, with a larger or smaller admixture of the element of the aesthetic diversion and a smaller or larger admixture of pure commercialism.[90]

Who can deny that spirituality, at least in the context of Sabbath observance, has eroded considerably even from the time of Knight's observation? He was also convinced that the values expressed in a capitalist economy via the price mechanism do not accurately correspond to "ethical value or human significance."[91] It is an acknowledged limitation of our system: human spirituality and morality cannot be adequately expressed in a market context. Rather, "the final results diverge notoriously from the ethical standards actually held. No one contends that a bottle of old wine is ethically worth as much as a barrel of flour, or a fantastic evening wrap for some potentate's mistress as much as a substantial dwelling-house, though such relative prices are not unusual."[92]

In the end, it is the rationalization process of economic exchange that works to commodify previously uncommodified elements in order to facilitate the transaction, which results in crowding out those elements that defy commodification. This process systematically carves away at the spiritual aspects of human culture. Max Weber applied the term "rationalization of the cosmos" to describe this phenomenon of industrial capitalism.[93] Weber's observation is consistent with Hayek's view of religion and its evolutionary course in capitalist societies, a process in which the sacred is eroded not by the force of collectively applied reason but by the incessant, miniscule, and ubiquitous calculation of subjective decision making.[94]

Hirsch detects a cause of the crowding out of sacred by commercial values in that modern capitalist cultures possess what he describes as a "commodity bias," where "market institutions are inefficient at any collective provision and may fail completely at collective provision of social norms. Correspondingly, they have a tendency to overproduce specific commodities or services at which they are efficient."[95] Therefore, because markets are unable to accomplish the provision of collective norms, they are unable to preserve the collective ideal of the sacred. This market failure, resulting from the inability of the pricing mechanism to account for the sacred value of things, is not simply a benign shortcoming. Rather, it leads to overproduction of those products and services to which prices can more easily be applied. Hirsch pairs the commodity bias on the production side of the market economy with a complimentary and resultant "commodity fetishism" on the part of consumers. According to Hirsch, the combination of commodity bias and commodity fetishism in society "implies that an excessive proportion of individual activity is channeled through the market so that the commercialized sector of our lives is unduly large."[96]

Hirsch's thesis might be extended in this context to suggest that commodity bias also works to pull in sacred elements of life not traditionally considered commodifiable. One could conjecture that the pervasiveness of markets and the widespread belief in the market as a "moral instrument" noted by Wuthnow, especially if that belief is growing, leads to the absorption of more social and moral "goods" as the demand for efficiency increases. Such a contention is supported by the recent growth in markets for human organs and body parts and emerging industries that require a system for the patenting of human genetic code.[97] Price tags are today being applied to "commodities" that only a few years ago would have seemed absurd or immoral.

Hirsch's view of the displacement of sacred by commercial values and of the shifting of moral responsibility from institutions to individuals is consistent with Hayek's view of moral evolution in a subjective, capitalist order. So, too, is Häfele's hypotheticality essentially a restatement of Hayek's principle of the impossibility of human reason to grasp the complexities of mass society and its inability to predict the outcomes of capitalism's myriad processes. Thus, all are agreed but not equally sanguine. Hayek's view of the ultimate disposition of religious tradition in society is largely consistent with that of Dewey, Schumpeter, Weber, Bell, Hirsch, and many other social philosophers who have theorized that capitalism has a corrosive effect on the religious and moral traditions of society. However, Dewey and Hayek believed that the systematic erosion of the sacred core of religious faith is *good* for society. Dewey in particular saw the benefit in this transformation of values:

> The crisis today as to the intellectual content of religious belief has been caused by the change in the intellectual climate due to the increase of knowledge and our means of understanding. I have tried to show that the change is not fatal to religious values in our common experience, however adverse its impact may be upon historic religions. Rather, provided that the models and results of intelligence at work are frankly adopted, the change is liberating.[98]

Dewey's view is consistent with Hayek's presentation of religious tradition—stripped of its supernatural pretensions but clinging to superior moral principles—as necessary to the sustainability of capitalism. Religion, perhaps more so for Hayek than for Dewey, has served as a throttling mechanism in moderating economic growth to levels consistent with the pace of institutional change.[99] However, continued progress in the views of both men requires the persistent erosion of elements that do not conform with the rising commercial and technocratic nature of modern society. Thus, commercial and technical values must displace religious ones for progress to continue. The question is whether there are limits to this crowding out of the sacred that both men perceived.

CONCLUDING REMARKS

Christians should be concerned with the "unconscious" nature of cultural evolution that Hayek described. He noted that what is commonly overlooked "is that the facts which result from certain values being held are not those to which the values which guide the actions of several individuals are attached, but a pattern comprising the actions of many individuals, a pattern of which the acting individuals may not even be aware and which was certainly not the aim of their actions."[100] He suggests that the spontaneous order is a dynamic universe filled with unintended consequences. If Hayek is correct, then Christians who believe they are engaging that order in a "Christian way" may in fact be contributing to the emergence of values that are unchristian or anti-Christian—it is simply impossible to tell due to the complexity and opaqueness of modern civilization. Importantly, Hayek's theories suggest that the market can be classified as a "moral instrument" only in the context of *his* moral system as values emerge based on their contribution to victorious social groups in the evolution of human culture.

In the context of this chapter, two questions emerge. First, can Christians participating in a capitalist order that is constructed upon a thoroughly subjectivist ethos and that performs most efficiently in a "transcendently ungrounded" state retain their sacred beliefs? Second, is it possible that Christians will come to accept values over time that conflict with those of their religious tradition without consciously willing them or acting in such a way as to support them? Hayek suggests that such are possible if not probable outcomes of a truly free system of exchange via the dynamics imposed by evolutionary rationalism. If Mises was correct that despite communal mores and the constraints of religious tradition, human beings seek to live their lives in the "most favorable physiological conditions possible," then the Austrian model of social morality is likely most accurate as well. If it can be proven that the *ultimate value* is to escape our mortality and live the longest possible lives in the greatest physical comfort, then it should be no surprise that Hayek's moral model is reflective of actual experience and the rules by which humankind exists. But this also suggests that the "seat at the table" granted religion by the Austrians is no more desirable than that assigned by Dewey and the constructivists who predicted the eventual demise of "historic" religions.

Christians who accept Hayek's view of the process by which values are transformed in human culture must engage the possibility that society will experience a profound moral alteration as stimulated by the rise of markets for new technologies, some of which will touch upon our very understanding of the human person. For those Christians who express an appreciation of Hayek's thought and are knowledgeable of his philosophy, the obvious question is, what do they believe are the implications of Hayek's moral theory for Christianity? One assumes that Christian admirers of Hayek do not believe that the system he describes is destructive of Christian tradition or they would be more critical either of Hayek's theories or of the subjectivist ethos of modern capitalism. Thus, one may speculate that they do not interpret Hayek as portending negative consequences for Christian tradition, or that they perceive limits or inaccuracies in his theories regarding the role and disposition of religion in society. Michael Novak implies as much in his recognition both of Hayek's "genius" and his "errors." Chapter 5 explores the ideas of Michael Novak, Robert Sirico, Ronald Nash, and other Christian social thinkers on the implications of Austrian economic philosophy for tradition, and, more generally, it examines their views on the influence of the market on social morality.

NOTES

1. As an example, Michael Novak's reference to Catholic social thinkers' neglect of Hayek's work "both in its genius and its errors" in *Free Persons and the Common Good* provides little clue as to where Hayek erred. Novak does state that Hayek's emphasis (in concert with the classical liberal philosophers) on unleashing the individual misses "the comparable philosophical power of the medieval thinkers who gave 'common good' and 'social justice' their modern salience." However, he fails to delve deeper into this line of criticism. See Michael Novak, *Free Persons and the Common Good* (Lanham, MD: Madison Books, 1989), 86, 79.

2. F. A. Hayek, *The Road to Serfdom* (London: George Routledge & Sons, 1944), 157 (emphasis added). This idea that the aggregate effects of participation in the spontaneous order reconstitutes traditional religious values is discussed briefly in Charles McDaniel, "Friedrich Hayek and Reinhold Niebuhr on the Moral Persistence of Liberal Society," *Journal of Interdisciplinary Studies* 16, nos. 1–2 (2004): 140–41.

3. Ronald Nash, "The Subjective Theory of Economic Value," in *Biblical Principles and Economics: The Foundations*, ed. Richard C. Chewning (Colorado Springs, CO: NavPress, 1989), 93.

4. Karen Vaughn, "Does It Matter That Costs Are Subjective?" *Southern Economic Journal* 46 (1980): 708–9; quoted in Nash, "The Subjective Theory of Economic Value," 87.

5. This is not to imply consistency in Christian tradition on the personal and social consequences of sin. In the Reformation period, for example, Martin Luther and his "two kingdoms" theory differed dramatically from the Roman Catholic view and its system of penance, and both of these conflicted with the Anabaptist notion of Christian perfectionism. Yet all three recognized both individual and social consequences to the sinful human condition. For more on Luther's views on the "two kingdoms," see Martin Luther, "On Secular Authority," in *Luther and Calvin on Secular Authority*, ed. Harro Höpfl, Cambridge Text in the History of Political Thought Series (New York: Cambridge University Press, 1991): 8–9, 12, 22, 23, 33–34.

6. Friedrich Hayek, *Law, Legislation and Liberty*, vol. 3, *The Political Order of a Free People*, 2nd ed. (Chicago: University of Chicago Press, 1981), 165–66.

7. Brian Crowley seems to agree that simply targeting the state as the villain in Hayek's model is too limiting; rather, any institution that has the power to restrict individual choice works against the proper moral evolution of society. Crowley states that

for Hayek, "To restrict the individual's range of choice (either by coercing him, or by reducing the universe of potential consummations) is to restrict his moral development, whose untrammeled unfolding is the only possible justification of society." Here, Crowley describes the positive spin generally applied by economic conservatives to Hayek's individualism—that restriction of choice limits the development of personal and, ultimately, social morality. See Brian Lee Crowley, *The Self, the Individual, and the Community: Liberalism in the Political Thought of F. A. Hayek and Sidney and Beatrice Webb* (Oxford: Clarendon Press, 1987), 53.

8. To Hayek, the quickest route to extinction for a religious tradition was to reject the values of property and family. However, he still appreciated the value of myth in religious belief, and regarding the moral systems of faith traditions, he observed, "Morals that took the form of rigid rules may sometimes have been more effective than more flexible rules whose adherents attempted to steer their practice." See Hayek, "Religion and the Guardians of Tradition," in *The Collected Works of F. A. Hayek*, vol. 1, *The Fatal Conceit: The Errors of Socialism*, ed. W. W. Bartley III (Chicago: University of Chicago Press, 1988), 136, 137, 139.

9. Hayek, "Religion and the Guardians of Tradition," 136.

10. Hayek, "Religion and the Guardians of Tradition," 138.

11. Hayek said of Communism that it is "one of those religions which is anti-property, anti-family, which had its time, and which is now declining rapidly. We are watching one instance where the process of natural selection of religious beliefs disposes of yet another mistaken one and restores the basic beliefs in property and the family." Quoted in Marlo Lewis Jr., "The Achilles Heel of F. A. Hayek," *National Review* 37 (May 17, 1985): 33, 36 (emphasis author's).

12. See John Gray, *Hayek on Liberty* (Oxford: Basil Blackwell Publishers, 1984), 32. Interestingly, Hayek disliked the association of his economic philosophy with Social Darwinism. He stated, "The error of 'Social Darwinism' was that it concentrated on the selection of individuals rather than on that of institutions and practices." See Hayek, *Law, Legislation and Liberty*, vol. 1, *Rules and Order* (Chicago: University of Chicago Press, 1973), 23.

13. David T. Koyzis, "Progress as an Object of Faith in the Thought of Friedrich A. von Hayek," *Christian Scholars Review* 12 (1983): 139.

14. Koyzis, "Progress as an Object of Faith," 139 (emphasis author's).

15. Walker notes that "Hayek's ethical position is marked by a striking juxtaposition of agnosticism and reverence [for traditional morals]." See Graham Walker, *The Ethics of F. A. Hayek* (Lanham, MD: University Press of America, 1986), 23–24.

16. Walker describes Hayek as a "thoroughgoing naturalist" who "rejects any notion of transcendence" and whose "ethics are fully immanent, fully of this world, fully the result of the process of evolution." See Walker, *The Ethics of F. A. Hayek*, 34–35.

17. Dewey says there "is one sure road of access to truth—the road of patient, cooperative inquiry operating by means of observation, experiment, record and controlled reflections." See Dewey, *A Common Faith* (New Haven, CT: Yale University Press, 1934), 26, 32.

18. Dewey, *A Common Faith*, 28–30, 40–49.

19. Significantly, Dewey identifies in *A Common Faith* that which ultimately distinguishes his philosophy from that of the natural harmony tradition and its representatives

such as Friedrich Hayek. Dewey stated, "The fundamental root of the *laissez faire* idea is denial . . . of the possibility of radical intervention of intelligence in the conduct of human life." See Dewey, *A Common Faith*, 78.

20. Walker, *The Ethics of F. A. Hayek*, 95.

21. Dewey, *A Common Faith*, 32.

22. Dewey observed, "It is conceivable that the present depression in religion is closely connected with the fact that religions now prevent, because of their weight of historic encumbrances, the religious quality of experience from coming to consciousness and finding the expression that is appropriate to present conditions, intellectual and moral." See Dewey, *A Common Faith*, 9.

23. Dewey, *A Common Faith*, 62.

24. Dewey, "What I Believe, Revised," in *Later Works* in *The Works of John Dewey: 1925–1953*, 14:91–92; quoted in Steven C. Rockefeller, *John Dewey: Religious Faith and Democratic Humanism* (New York: Columbia University Press, 1991), 440.

25. Rockefeller references an article written in 1928 in which Dewey made the surprisingly Hayekian comment that "our faith is ultimately in individuals and their potentialities." The atrocities of war only reinforced his newfound commitment to the individual as the engine of social change. See Dewey, "A Critique of American Civilization," in *The Later Works of John Dewey: 1925–1953*, 3:144, first published in *World Tomorrow* 2 (1928): 394–95, cited in Rockefeller, *John Dewey: Religious Faith and Democratic Humanism*, 439–40.

26. Quoted in Rockefeller, *John Dewey: Religious Faith and Democratic Humanism*, 440 (emphasis added).

27. Rockefeller, *John Dewey: Religious Faith and Democratic Humanism*, 441.

28. Crowley, *The Self, the Individual, and the Community*, 215n59. Crowley also questions the normative structure of Hayekian morality, stating, "Nowhere is Hayek's rather instrumental view of the nature of the terms 'good' and 'bad' brought out more clearly than in *Constitution* [*of Liberty*], page 36. In the passage concerned Hayek first appears to deny that values are to be implied by the mere fact of social selection, but this hardly seems to fit in with the rest of his argument, the burden of which is that if we do not accept that what works is for all intents and purposes what is right, that we shall perish in the evolutionary struggle." See Crowley, *The Self, the Individual, and the Community*, 56n60.

29. Friedrich A. Hayek, *Rules and Order*, 39, 51.

30. Walker, *The Ethics of F. A. Hayek*, 97.

31. Swiss theologian Karl Barth, whose theology focused intensely on the revelation of Jesus Christ, recognized the necessity of purposeful human activity to the preservation of the Christian tradition. Barth stated, "Dogmatics will always be able to fulfill its task only in accordance with the state of the Church at different times. It is because the Church is conscious of its limitations that it owes a reckoning and a responsibility to the good it has to administer and to cherish, and to the good One who has entrusted this good to it. It will never be able to do this perfectly; Christian dogmatics will always be a thinking, an investigation, and an exposition which are relative and liable to error." See Karl Barth, "The Task," in *Dogmatics in Outline* (New York: Harper & Row, 1959), 11.

32. Dewey, *A Common Faith*, 65.

33. Dewey, "In Response," in *The Later Works of John Dewey*, ed. Jo Ann Boydston (Carbondale, IL: Southern Illinois University Press, 1981), 422–23.

34. Oddly, Hayek, the defender of liberty, perceived the erosion of freedom brought about by the very system he championed. He stated, "The changes to which such people must submit are part of the cost of progress, an illustration of the fact that not only the mass of men but, strictly speaking, every human being is led by the growth of civilization into a path that is not of his own choosing." See Hayek, *The Constitution of Liberty* (London: Routledge and Kegan Paul, 1960), 52, 50; quoted in Koyzis, "Progress as an Object of Faith," 147, 146.

35. Hayek, *The Political Order of a Free People*, 165–66; quoted in Gray, *Hayek on Liberty*, 133 (emphasis author's). One should also remember Hayek's disclaimer on the process of moral evolution, where he stated, "I do not claim that the results of group selection of traditions are necessarily 'good'—any more than I claim that other things that have long survived in the course of evolution, such as cockroaches, have moral value." See Hayek, "Between Instinct and Reason," in *The Fatal Conceit*, 27.

36. Ludwig von Mises, "Economic Freedom in the Present-Day World," in *Economic Freedom and Interventionism: An Anthology of Articles and Essays by Ludwig von Mises*, ed. Bettina Bien Greaves (Irvington-on-Hudson, NY: The Foundation for Economic Education, 1990), 238. Despite Hayek's frequent denials of the biological basis of evolution, Mises asserted, "No matter how much their wishes, desires, and valuations may differ in details, men aim, for biological reasons, at the same basic ends. Regardless of their worldview, religion, nationality, race, class, position, education, personal abilities, age, health, or sex, they aspire above all to be able to pass their lives under the most favorable physiological conditions possible." See Mises, *Epistemological Problems of Economics*, trans. George Reisman (Princeton, NJ: D. Van Nostrand Company, 1960), 38.

37. Dewey, *A Common Faith*, 68.

38. Roger Lincoln Shinn, *Forced Options: Social Decisions for the 21st Century* (San Francisco: Harper & Row, 1982), 9–12, 201–22.

39. Wolf Häfele, "Hypotheticality and the New Challenges: The Pathfinder Role of Nuclear Energy," *Anticipation* (World Council of Churches) 20 (May 1975); reprinted from *Minerva*, July 1974; cited in Shinn, *Forced Options*, 9.

40. Shinn, *Forced Options*, 25.

41. Shinn emphasizes the enormity and complexity of human culture as contributing to the "age of hypotheticality." Interestingly, a member of the Austrian economic tradition, Wilhelm Röpke, has concerns similar to Shinn's and observes consequences for the individual and society of *Vermassung*, or "enmassment," the growth of the modern society into a mass of undefinable, unpredictable, and depersonalizing forces. Röpke states, "Our conception of the mass society is this: The individual is, in our time, losing his own features, soul, intrinsic worth, and personality because and in so far as he is immersed in the 'mass,' and the latter is 'mass' because and in so far as it consists of such depersonalized individuals. To the extent of this shift of the center of gravity, the essential element which the individual needs in order to be a complete human being and spiritual and moral personality seems to be missing. At the same time, one of the basic conditions of sound social life is destroyed." See Wilhelm Röpke, *A Humane Economy: The Social Framework of the Free Market* (Chicago: Henry Regnery Company, 1960), 53. For a comprehensive discussion of "enmassment," see chapter 2, "Modern Mass Society," in *A Humane Economy*, 36–89.

42. Shinn, *Forced Options*, 26.

43. John Kenneth Galbraith, *The Affluent Society* (Boston: Houghton Mifflin, 1976), 80.

44. Shinn, *Forced Options*, 129.

45. Technological determinism is a concept advanced by a number of philosophers, theologians, and scientists that technology is no longer simply a tool but has become *the* autonomous and driving force of cultural change. For a discussion of the technologically deterministic aspects of modern society, see Ian Barbour, *Ethics in an Age of Technology: The Gifford Lectures* (San Francisco: Harper, 1992).

46. Christian ethicist Gilbert Meilaender, for example, observes in human embryo research the very "question of membership within our community," one question among many raised by developing technologies on which Americans hold varying views. As markets for biotechnological and genetic services expand, the social and moral questions generated by the technologies they spawn are strewn behind in the advance of progress. David Hopper notes, "Technological innovation proceeds at an ever more rapid pace with little regard for the long-term social impact of any given innovation or the political purposes and values a particular nation or people may embrace." See Gilbert C. Meilaender, *Body, Soul, and Bioethics* (Notre Dame, IN: University of Notre Dame Press, 1995), 99.

47. William F. Ogburn, "Cultural Lag as Theory," *Sociology and Social Research* 41 (1957): 167; quoted in Richard L. Brinkman and June E. Brinkman, "Cultural Lag: Conception and Theory," *International Journal of Social Economics* 24 (1997); available from alidoro.emeraldinsight.com/v.../cw/mcb/03068293/v24n6/s2/p609.html (accessed November 27, 2001). Ogburn originally employed the term in 1914 as a professor of economics and sociology at Reed College. See Ogburn, "Cultural Lag as Theory."

48. The Brinkmans concede that "relative to its importance, there is little current discussion pointedly directed to a specific statement of cultural lag theory and its relevance to current problem identification and resolution." Their expressed attempt is to "clarify and update the concept and theory of cultural lag." See Richard L. Brinkman and June E. Brinkman, "Cultural Lag."

49. In addition to Dewey and Ogburn, the brilliant though eccentric economist Thorstein Veblen is more closely associated with cultural lag theory, which he crafted into his exploration of class structure in his famous work *The Theory of the Leisure Class*. Veblen's attempt was to articulate a theory by which "inner relations," those institutional relationships most sheltered from the impact of changes in the economic environment, adjust to "outer relations," or institutions more directly affected by economic change. Veblen stated, "A readjustment of men's habits of thought to conform with the exigencies of an altered situation is in any case made only tardily and reluctantly, and only under the coercion exercised by a situation which has made the accredited views untenable." See Thorstein Veblen, *The Theory of the Leisure Class: An Economic Study of Institutions* (New York: B. W. Huebsch, 1912): 192–93.

50. One recalls Michael Novak's assertion that prior to the arrival of John Paul II, virtually every papal reference to liberalism was pejorative. See Novak, *Freedom with Justice: Catholic Social Thought and Liberal Institutions* (San Francisco: Harper & Row, 1984), 29, 33–35.

51. "Traditional" is used here in the context of Islamic, Hindu, or other societies or tribal cultures that ground social relations in a particular religious tradition or an established social caste that has been reinforced through generations of custom and practice.

52. Reference to Christianity here is not intended to suggest that the Christian faith is solely or even uniquely challenged by these developments vis-à-vis other traditions. If

one accepts Hayek's view of the adaptable nature of religious and other institutions, then it might be inferred that the degree to which the values of a particular religious group are "threatened" by new economic and technological developments depends on the extent to which its values are grounded in "culture" (as opposed to, say, sacred writings or the doctrinal pronouncements of a clerical class) and, more importantly, the adaptability of its membership to the changing values of the wider culture. Given this view, the extent of threats to denominations within Christianity itself will vary according to the theological foundations of these groups and differences in their respective memberships.

53. Robert M. Veatch, *Death, Dying and the Biological Revolution: Our Last Quest for Responsibility* (New Haven, CT: Yale University Press, 1989), 202–3.

54. The Public Broadcasting System's acclaimed series *Frontline* produced a documentary entitled "Organ Farm" that chronicled the rise of this technology. The *Frontline* episode attempted to capture both the promise and the risks of this technology. Participants in the xenotransplantation program were required to sign waivers absolving researchers and their sponsors of liability for negative consequences resulting from this highly experimental program. More frightening were the comments of specialists interviewed for "Organ Farm" that it is conceivable that interspecies transplantation could spawn the development of viruses that are resistant to present scientific methods of containment. Again, Häfele's hypotheticality is in evidence. The researchers consistently answered questions as to the possibility of a xenotransplant-induced epidemic by stating, "We just don't know." Public Broadcast System, *Frontline*: "Organ Farm"; part 1 aired on March 27, 2001 and part 2 on April 3, 2001.

55. As noted in the introduction, Veatch uses the rather liberal Catholic ethicist Richard McCormick as his source for Roman Catholicism, but he also cites Fred Rosner, "a Talmudic scholar and physician," who is highly supportive of this emerging technology as the representative for Orthodox Judaism. See Veatch, *Death, Dying and the Biological Revolution*, 202–3.

56. One might extend this postulate by stating that the greater the perceived threat to survival, the more willing an individual will be to "push the envelope" by engaging in practices that "may" conflict with the religious values or beliefs of her religious community.

57. Despite critical pronouncements of Roman Catholic leadership on recent trials of the abortion pill RU-486 in the United States, most of the media coverage has been of the controversy between the church and European governments. See John L. Allen Jr., "Abortion Debates Rock Germany," *National Catholic Reporter* 35 (February 12, 1999): 5.

58. Michael R. Welch and David C. Leege explore the convergence of Roman Catholic and evangelical Protestant attitudes and activism on various issues, especially in the fight against abortion in the United States in "Dual Reference Groups and Political Orientations: An Examination of Evangelically Oriented Catholics," in *American Journal of Political Science* 35 (February 1991): 28–56.

59. *Humanae Vitae* was developed by Pope Paul VI to clarify the Roman Catholic Church's teachings on marriage, conjugal love, responsible parenthood, and most particularly contraception. See Pope Paul VI, *Humanae Vitae: Encyclical Letter of His Holiness Pope Paul VI on the Regulation of Births* (San Francisco: Ignatius Press, 1978 [orig. pub. 1968]).

60. James T. Fisher, *Catholics in America* (Oxford: Oxford University Press, 2000), 144.

61. Fisher, *Catholics in America*, 145.

62. Fisher, *Catholics in America*, 145.

63. Quoted in *Catholics in America*.

64. Randall Balmer, *Religion in Twentieth Century America* (Oxford: Oxford University Press, 2001), 69–70.

65. Gallup polling data indicate that the percentage of Americans describing their religious preference as Roman Catholic has been largely stable over the past ten years, fluctuating between 25 and 28 percent of respondents. See "Gallup Polling Data over the Last Ten Years," available from the adherents.com website at www.adherents.com/rel_USA.html#gallup (accessed December 19, 2001).

66. Similarly, the percentages of those who believe that premarital sex is "wrong" varied between 43 and 50 percent for the same religious groups. See Robert Wuthnow, *The Restructuring of American Religion: Society and Faith since World War II* (Princeton, NJ: Princeton University Press, 1988), 86–87. See also McDaniel, "Friedrich Hayek and Reinhold Niebuhr on the Moral Persistence of Liberal Society," 143–44.

67. Only 17 percent of respondents "take an uncompromising pro-life position." See Phillip F. Lawler, "Special Report: Issues That Divide"; available from www.catholic.net/RCC/Periodicals/Igpress/CWR/CWR0497/specialreport.html (accessed September 10, 2001).

68. Lawler, "Special Report: Issues That Divide."

69. Lawler, "Special Report: Issues That Divide."

70. Gudorf insists that the Catholic position on contraception and even on abortion "is not set in stone and is rather in development." Quoted in Daniel C. Maguire, *Sacred Choices: The Right to Contraception and Abortion in Ten World Religions* (Minneapolis: Fortress Press, 2001), 39.

71. Maguire, *Sacred Choices*, 40.

72. Daniel Maguire offers an explanation, stating, "This means that the consciences and experiences of good people are guideposts to truth that even the [Catholic] hierarchy must consult." Maguire, *Sacred Choices*.

73. Pope John Paul warned President Bush on July 23, 2001, of developments contributing to the assault on innocent life to include "most recently, proposals for the creation for research purposes of human embryos destined to destruction in the process." See "Pope Warns Bush on Stem Cells," *BBC News*, July 23, 2001; available from the *BBC News* website at news.bbc.co.uk/hi/english/world/europe/newsid_1452000/1452314.stm (accessed December 14, 2001).

74. Jesse F. Derris, "Life Support? Stem-Cell Backing Holds at Six in 10," n.d.; available from the ABC News website at abcnews.go.com/sections/politics/DailyNews/poll01080.html (accessed October 15, 2001).

75. Derris, "Life Support? Stem-Cell Backing Holds at Six in 10."

76. Crowley, *The Self, the Individual, and the Community*, 14.

77. The social nature of morality in Mises' thought is illustrated in a quotation from *Liberalism in the Classical Tradition*. Mises stated, "A man living in isolation has no moral rules to follow. He need have no qualms about doing anything he finds it to his advantage to do, for he does not have to consider whether he is not thereby injuring others. But as a member of society, a man must take into consideration, in everything he does, not only his own immediate advantage, but also the necessity, in every action, of affirming society as such. For the life of the individual in society is possible only by virtue

of social cooperation, and every individual would be most seriously harmed if the social organization of life and of production were to break down." See Ludwig von Mises, *Liberalism in the Classical Tradition*, trans. Ralph Raico (Irvington-on-Hudson, NY: Foundation for Economic Education, 1985), 7–8, 33–34; quoted in Michael Novak, *Free Persons and the Common Good* (Lanham, MD: Madison Books, 1989), 162, 156.

78. Alfred North Whitehead, *Introduction to Mathematics* (London, 1911), 61; quoted in Hayek, *The Constitution of Liberty* (Chicago: University of Chicago Press, 1960), 22.

79. For an excellent summary of terms and ideas associated with the social costs of environmental pollution, see "Externalities," available from dspace.dial.pipex.com/geoff .riley/pollutio.htm (accessed December 19, 2001).

80. For an excellent discussion of the evolution of Christian views on organ transplantation, see Robert G. Clouse and Rodney Clapp, "A Little Victory over Death," *Christianity Today* 32 (March 18, 1988): 17–23.

81. Fred Hirsch, *Social Limits to Growth* (Cambridge, MA: Harvard University Press, 1976), 92.

82. Hirsch, *Social Limits to Growth*, 120.

83. Hirsch observes the near subliminal process of moral transformation that satisfies the requirements of the market. He states, "Morality of the minimum order necessary for the functioning of the market system was assumed, nearly always implicitly, to be a kind of permanent free good, a natural resource of the nondepleting kind." This moral reductionism was realized as "the utilitarian-consumerist view of man banished from the social plane the explicit moral content that was embodied in Christian philosophy and sought after in Marxist and other social thought." See Hirsch, *Social Limits to Growth*, 132, 124, 134.

84. Hirsch, *Social Limits to Growth*, 132, 118. Hirsch recognizes that the "specialized moral obligations" of individuals are growing rapidly in concert with the rise in economic complexity. See Hirsch, *Social Limits to Growth*, 157. See also McDaniel, "Friedrich Hayek and Reinhold Niebuhr on the Moral Persistence of Liberal Society," 150–51.

85. Friedrich A. Hayek, *New Studies in Philosophy, Politics, Economics and the History of Ideas* (London: Routledge and Kegan Paul, 1979), 298; quoted in Walker, *The Ethics of F. A. Hayek*, 58n78. Walker notes Hayek's observation "that the gravest error of 'the older prophets,' including Moses and St. Augustine, 'was their belief that the intuitively perceived ethical values, divined out of the depth of man's breast, were immutable and eternal. This prevented them from recognizing that all rules of conduct served a particular kind of order to society.'" Internal quotation taken from Hayek, *The Political Order of a Free People*, 166; quoted in Walker, *The Ethics of F. A. Hayek*, 56–57.

86. Walker, *The Ethics of F. A. Hayek*, 10.

87. Acquaviva tips his hand as to his own answer to this question when he states, "Modern society tends . . . to translate everything into 'one dimension,' which in and of itself excludes the religious, even extra-ecclesial religion." See S. S. Acquaviva, *The Decline of the Sacred in Industrial Society*, trans. Patricia Lipscomb (New York: Harper & Row, 1979), 191, 196.

88. Just as Wuthnow, Acquaviva utilizes polling statistics to back up his claim. He cites a Haverford College poll that evidenced changes in transcendent beliefs between 1948 and 1968, where the percentage of respondents affirming belief in God dropped from 79 percent to 58 percent and those professing belief in life after death declined

from 46 percent to 34 percent. See Acquaviva, *The Decline of the Sacred in Industrial Society*, 54.

89. Galbraith, *The Affluent Society*, 102.

90. Knight believed that the Christian nations have gotten "away from the spiritual attitude toward life, and do not know how to get back." See Frank Hyneman Knight, "The Ethics of Competition," in *The Ethics of Competition* (New Brunswick, NJ: Transaction Publishers, 1997), 65–66.

91. Knight, "The Ethics of Competition," 47.

92. Knight, "The Ethics of Competition," 47.

93. Weber recognized the foundations of "economic rationalization" in the "extension of the productivity of labor which has, through the subordination of the process of production to scientific points of view, relieved it from the natural organic limitations of the human individual." Weber recognized that "with the dying out of the religious root, the utilitarian interpretation crept in unnoticed." Thus has evolved the potential for a society of "specialists without spirit, sensualists without heart; this nullity imagines that it has attained a level of civilization never before achieved." See Max Weber, *The Protestant Ethic and the Spirit of Capitalism*, trans. Talcott Parsons (Gloucester, MA: Peter Smith, 1988), 75, 177, 182.

94. Hayek does, however, imply some form of collective and evolutionary reason. He stated, "*Our* reason is as much the result of an evolutionary selection process as is our morality." See Hayek, "Between Instinct and Reason," 21 (emphasis added).

95. Hirsch, *Social Limits to Growth*, 89.

96. Hirsch notes that products and services are "produced more efficiently when property rights are strictly delineated"; thus, there is a market bias in favor of products and services that are "amenable to commercialization." This is part of what Hirsch perceives as capitalism's corrosive influence on the moral-cultural sector of society. He states, "The social morality that has served as an understructure for economic individualism has been a legacy of the precapitalist and preindustrial past. This legacy has diminished with time and with the corrosive contact of the active capitalist values—and more generally with the greater anonymity and mobility of industrial society." See Hirsch, *Social Limits to Growth*, 84, 91, 117.

97. For an analysis of recent legal and moral controversies in genetic patenting, see Thomas D. Mays, "Biotech Incites Outcry: Public Policy Debates Arise over Human-Animal Hybrid Patents and Germline Gene Therapy," *The National Law Journal* 20 (June 22, 1998).

98. Dewey, *A Common Faith*, 56.

99. Hayek stated that by "following the spontaneously generated moral traditions underlying the competitive market order . . . we generate and garner greater knowledge and wealth than could ever be obtained or utilized in a centrally-directed economy." See Hayek, "Was Socialism a Mistake?" in *The Collected Works of F. A. Hayek*, vol. 1, *The Fatal Conceit: The Errors of Socialism*, ed. W. W. Bartley, 6–10 (Chicago: University of Chicago Press, 1988), 7.

100. Hayek, "Rules and Order," 110.

5

A QUESTION OF
MORAL SUSTAINABILITY

Taken collectively, the conclusions of the preceding chapters admittedly compose a rather pessimistic view of the future for American religion. It has been shown that both Friedrich Hayek and John Dewey, who respectively have served as exemplars for the subjectivist and constructivist threads of the Enlightenment tradition, predicted dire consequences for "traditional" religion given the encroachments of modernity. The subjectivist ethos at the core of modern capitalism has contributed to that harm through its devaluation of collectives as guides to the good and its reduction of the human person to the status of "autonomous economic agent." But it was conceded that this reductionist phenomenon is more insidious under collective forms of social organization for the reason that planning and coercion rather than market forces are the engine of reduction. Reinforcing this assertion, history has evidenced the disastrous consequences of communism for faith traditions, and it demonstrates that the application of collective reason in efforts to manipulate progress has the coterminous effects of overrationalizing the human being, depressing the human spirit, and eroding society's moral foundation.

At the same time, capitalism's consummate victory and the material miracle that it has precipitated have taken away much of the impetus to hope for something better. The elevation of human liberty to a sacred status in free societies has solidified a capitalist-socialist dualism in modern social philosophy that has served as an impediment to open dialogue over the good and bad that inhere in all systems of political economy. Christian defenders of capitalism often contribute to this attenuation of discourse through a too-casual belief that the virtues of the free market system—creativity, thrift, and industriousness—overwhelm any moral and spiritual deficiencies. However, chapter 4 demonstrated that if Hayek was indeed as prescient in his view of the evolving role and future disposition of religion in capitalist society as he was in observing the general process of social value transformation, then the destruction of sacred elements of Christianity and other faiths is virtually assured. If Hayek was correct and if Francis Fukuyama, too, is accurate that civilization has arrived at the "end of history," then humanity has been relegated to a philosophical monopoly with respect to economic systems that bodes poorly for faith traditions. But it should be recognized that it is these *dichotomous views of society*—capitalist-collectivist, individualist-communitarian, subjectivist-constructivist—in social theory that have realized this historical and philosophical climax and have inspired this pessimism.

The economically conservative Christians addressed here, however, admit to no such pessimism. In fact, they are rather ebullient over the prospects for the flourishing of religion in capitalist society and see no *inherent* tendency toward the deterioration of religious tradition or social morality in the free market milieu. Their views concerning the moral sustainability of the capitalist economy must be addressed, for, if nothing else, they reflect a disjuncture on key issues with the thought of their philosophical guide, Friedrich Hayek. Certainly, these Christian scholars do not view a steady displacement of religious by commercial values, as Hayek articulated in *The Political Order of a Free People*, or the erosion of belief in transcendence through the maturation of evolutionary rationalism, implied in his essay "Religion and the Guardians of Tradition."[1] Yet they often point to the genius of Hayek and insist, as does the present author, that he was one of the greatest economic theorists of the classical tradition.

A skeptic might speculate that the apparent confidence of many economically conservative Christians in the moral sustainability of capitalist societies emerges through a process of elimination. Recognition of the historical failures of socialist revolutions, communitarian experiments, and republican empires leaves the presumed natural harmonies of liberal society as the last gasp of philosophical hope. Liberalism is the logical and historically proven conclusion of the long, tragic social experiment. And it is capitalism, one of the central pillars of liberal society, and its greater consistency with both the natural and spiritual essence of the human person, which leads to this conclusion. But another reason for the attraction of these Christian scholars to capitalism and Austrian liberal philosophy undoubtedly results from the overwhelming complexity of modern society. Perhaps philosopher Alasdair MacIntyre, in his seminal book *After Virtue*, inadvertently offers an explanation for liberalism's appeal in his comment that "our social order is in a very literal sense out of our, and indeed anyone's, control. No one is or could be in charge."[2] In such an environment, liberalism emerges victorious by default for those who reject the feasibility of localized, communitarian solutions. It is tailor-made to a society that exists beyond the control of individuals, institutions, or traditions. MacIntyre's comment defrocks socialism and subtly scoffs at the pretensions of the interventionist liberals. Ironically, it would seem that even republicanism's grand vision of virtuous community would be ineffectual in taming such a society. But a thoroughly subjectivist liberalism envelops comfortably a culture that careens its way into the future.

This chapter explores the views of Michael Novak, Ronald Nash, and Robert Sirico on the moral sustainability of capitalist society and attempts to reconcile those views with the dynamic and evolutionary moral system outlined by their philosophical mentor Friedrich Hayek. An assumption is made that three possibilities exhaust the potential moral outcomes in the relationship between capitalism and Christianity: first, that capitalism reinforces Christian tradition and its accompanying moral system; second, that it undermines Christian values either by corrupting them in some way or by displacing those values with its own; and, finally, that it is largely "neutral" respecting Christian morality. In the first view, capitalism has been portrayed to be so consistent with Christian tradition through its inculcation of virtue that it actually buttresses the moral systems of Christianity, Judaism, and other religions. George Gilder's statement that "capitalism is simply the essential mode of human life that corresponds to religious truth"[3] is representative of this view. The second possibility is consistent with theories articulated by social thinkers like Max Weber, Joseph Schumpeter, and Daniel Bell that capitalism actually undermines its own moral-cultural framework. Finally, one might observe the possibility that capitalism and Christian tradition coexist in a morally neutral relationship. In other words, either the moral consequences of a market economy are negligible for religious tradition, or any negative moral and spiritual consequences of capitalism are offset by its positive moral outcomes. Because the first and third views are dominant among economically conservative Christians, this chapter will focus on their attempts to substantiate either a morally positive or a morally neutral relationship between Christianity and capitalism in American society.

MORAL DIMENSIONS OF THE FREE MARKET

Christian libertarians and neoconservatives have contributed tomes on the virtues of the free market system, and often they have enlisted the Austrian economists—most notably Hayek and Mises, but also Wilhelm Röepke, Henry Hazlitt, and others—to provide theoretical foundations for their defenses of capitalism. Ironically, many Christians may be seen as using Austrian economics in much the same way that the Austrian economists have made use of religion: the moral "truths" at the core of the respective systems are unimportant so long as the principles derived lead to greater social stability and material sustainability. Hayek, Mises, and others have often taken this utilitarian stance toward the tenets of religious traditions, while conservative Christians seem to extract from the Austrian philosophy those principles (catallaxy, subjective value, spontaneous order) that presumably lead to greater prosperity and social stability while largely ignoring (or claiming either as error or whimsy) those that bode poorly for religion.[4]

Ronald Nash has been perhaps the most zealous Christian advocate of Austrian economic theory. His essay "The Subjective Theory of Economic Value" is an attempt to apply a Christian defense to the value subjectivism at the heart of Austrian economics. However, Nash attempts a description of the relationship between the Christian "world view" and the philosophical constructs of the "Austrian revolution" in economic philosophy that ultimately leaves several questions unanswered:

> [Christians] are undoubtedly correct when they judge that the Bible obliges them to change the personal value scales of themselves and others to bring them more in line with the ultimate values associated with the Christian world view. But as important as this second task may be, it is an activity that falls under a different task than positive economics. Economic exchanges in the real world will mirror only the actual subjective value that individuals have imputed to the goods being exchanged.[5]

First, does Nash's statement imply a critical and inevitable disjunction between the Christian consumer's personal values and her "ultimate values?" His statement could be interpreted as distancing the individual Christian's religiously inspired "world view" from her judgments as a subjective, economic decision maker. Second, is Nash's characterization as a "second task" the Christian's responsibility "to change the personal value scales of themselves and others" also an implication that the Christian's religious identity factors less into her immediate consumption choices than does her "personal order of values"? Finally, would an affirmative answer to the previous question mean that the "first task" of the Christian is to transact in such ways as to further her material well-being and in ways that conform more closely with positive than with normative economics?[6]

Affirmative answers to the above questions would suggest Nash's adherence to the Hayekian model of social morality. For Hayek, the presumed subordination of religious to more utilitarian motives in the immediate context of the market transaction is a principal stimulus to social change. The persistent alteration of traditional values to states more consistent with economic reality is the social dynamic that paves the way for human progress. Similarly, Nash observes the means by which individual values affect economic decision making, stating, "As human beings seek ways to get the most from their limited resources, they are forced to rank their available alternatives. This ranking will reflect the individual's personal order of values."[7] However, "this scale of values is not always something of which the individual is conscious. But whether or not a person happens to be aware of his scale of values, he will always aim at whatever goal or end he regards as most urgent or important at the moment."[8] Nash's suggestion that individuals often transact according to latent sets of values in the immediate context and with limited reflection on their religious or other morally formative traditions is the strongest evidence of his support for Hayek's model of social morality.

An additional insight into Nash's understanding of the moral basis of modern capitalism is found in his assertion, "What transpires in the market will be as moral or immoral as the human beings who are active in the market."[9] Consistent with many Christian libertarians and neoconservatives, Nash minimizes the possibility that the market itself may contribute to the process of value transformation in free societies. He states, "Because the market itself is amoral and does not supply the moral standards to evaluate what transpires within the system, it is a mistake to confuse *economic merit* (the value something has in the market) with *moral merit*."[10] His comment portrays the market not as a value-shaping institution but rather as a value-neutral system of arbitration that draws its moral content from the personal value scales of market participants, which are shaped, secondarily, by the value systems of their respective moral traditions. This view of market neutrality is popular among neoconservatives as evidenced by Father Sirico's characterization of the market as "essentially morally neutral."[11] Casting the market as a neutral arbiter of exchange enables economically conservative Christians to shield it from criticism while laying blame for perceived moral degradation in capitalist societies on other cultural phenomena.

One might counter those who believe in the value neutrality of the market with the observation of three particular values that seem to arise directly from the institution of the market: utility maximization, immediate gratification, and pervasive commodification. Each of these values would appear to be wholly dependent upon the market for their existence. More-over, it is likely not coincidental that scholars have observed the growing dominance of these values in capitalist culture at a time when the reach of the market is expanding dramatically. Christian ethicist Jean Bethke Elsh-tain, for example, has observed what she calls "a pervasive late modern habit of thought that now takes shape as something akin to an all-embracing ide-ology" in the nexus "consumerist-commodifiable." In this realm, "nothing is holy, sacred, or off-limits in a world in which everything is for sale."[12] Elshtain claims that this emerging ideology has created an environment where respectable people from all walks of life clamor for "a free market in nearly everything, even babies."[13]

Demand for a "free market in everything" undoubtedly contributes to the rising influence of immediate gratification, utility maximization, and pervasive commodification in the personal order of values of American consumers. Phillip Yancey has written of the extension of desire for im-mediate gratification to virtually every area of American life: sex, politics, and even religion. He hints at the potential for intergenerational conflict re-sulting from the rise of this social norm, as "short-sited societies spend all their capital at once, leaving nothing for the future."[14] While one could ar-gue that the immediate gratification of particular desires are demanded even of government institutions in totalitarian societies, those positions will in-evitably exist in some normative relationship to the same services supplied by the free market. Globalization has entrenched the market as the standard by which the provisioning of all services is measured, and it is this standard (as much as any other factor) that led to the global demise of Communism. Thus, consumers have no expectation that a full meal will be supplied to a family of four in three minutes by a fast-food restaurant other than that the market has proven its ability to meet that expectation in the past.

Utility maximization also is largely dependent for its existence as a so-cial value upon a means of exchange between the individuals in society. The science of economics holds that economic actors maximize the util-ity derived from a particular bundle of goods and services only over and against alternative bundles; therefore, some medium of exchange must ex-ist to enable consumers to make such determinations. Again, Elshtain sug-gests that this notion of utility maximization has become a dominant value in modern society. She states, "We are called to be utility maximizers" and, "at the same time, to forget or deny or to distort the Christian tradition in order to make that tradition comport with the preference-aggregations ap-proach or, simply to ignore the existence of any tension whatsoever."[15] The pervasive reach of the market and its increasing prominence as a means of interaction between individuals has been critical to the value displacement that Elshtain describes.

Swedish economist Staffan Linder emphasizes the economic characteristics of "time" in reinforcing utility maximization as a social value and contributing to the intensification of consumption relative to other human activities. Because progress has not brought about the increase in leisure time that was once so roundly anticipated, we seek to maximize leisure through the acquisition of consumption goods. Linder notes, "Just as working time becomes more productive when combined with more capital, so consumption time can give a higher yield when combined with more consumer goods."[16] Linder's *The Harried Leisure Class*, written in 1970, contributes eight rather prescient observations of the consequences of rapid economic growth and rising consumption. One of these is that there "will be a declining competitive position for time devoted to the cultivation of mind and spirit." Another of Linder's predictions is that "there will be a curious combination of an increasing attachment to goods in general and, owing to a low degree of utilization and a rapid turnover, an increasing indifference to each of them in particular."[17] Linder's conclusions reinforce Hayek's observation of the gradual displacement of sacred and aesthetic ideals by commercial values, and it implies a value revolution in Western society driven by economic growth in which utility maximization, when applied to leisure, displaces other values that have traditionally engendered the "cultivation of mind and spirit."

Even if one denies the influence of the three "market-determined" values identified above or insists that the source of these values lies outside the market, Hayek's theory of unintended consequences still comes into play. If at the point of the singular transaction it is conceded that all values are supplied exogenously, the cumulative social and moral effects of market transactions still may conflict with the *aggregate* intended results of individual market participants. Christian social theorist Phillip Wogaman observes this phenomenon in the context of human freedom, stating, "While market allocation may appear to place greater premium upon individual decision-making and may appear to maximize freedom of choice in one's economic life, this freedom can be illusory if the result of individual decisions is to create social conditions that undermine one's intentions."[18] Wogaman's observation is consistent with Hayek's conclusion cited in chapter 4 that the "changes to which such people must submit are part of the cost of progress" in which "not only the mass of men but, strictly speaking, every human being is led by the growth of civilization into a path that is not of his own choosing."[19] It is no great leap to suggest that if the growth of civilization

itself can lead to a deterioration of individual freedom even as recognized
by that champion of freedom Friedrich Hayek, then so too can it lead to
degradation of the moral basis of society. And it is important to note that
in Hayek's view, this "cost of progress" results directly from those processes
that advance civilization and not from the deterioration of an independent
moral-cultural sector. Thus, even if it could be proven that the market does
not supply its own values, recognition that market dynamics generate unintended consequences leads to the conclusion that social morality will be reshaped because the market's moral outcomes will not conform to a strict aggregation of its moral inputs.

Michael Novak suggests that any "net" reshaping of social morality by
the forces of the market will be to the "good." In *Free Persons and the Common Good*, he offers a description of the synergistic relationship between the
market and social virtues in a "civilized society":

> A market order is the work of civilization. It depends upon favorable so-
> cial traditions. Those who merely seize what they want, or force their
> own goods upon the unwilling, do not engage in market-exchange; they
> conduct themselves like barbarians. Those who lie, cheat, deal with oth-
> ers rudely, care nothing about their purchasers' satisfaction, preserve their
> products badly, offer their services incompetently, and so on, tear at the
> social tissue that makes a market order civilized. Therefore, a market or-
> der is not simply neutral regarding virtue or vice. It positively reinforces
> certain social virtues, for its dependence upon them is very high.[20]

There are critical dependencies, however, in Novak's idealistic assumptions of "market-exchange" that enable the reinforcement of social
virtues. Producer reputation, for example, seen as an essential component
to any "virtuous" market by the classical economist Adam Smith as well as
by the American Protestant theologian and student of economics Francis
Wayland, would also seem necessary to ensure virtue in Novak's understanding of the market order. Novak recognizes that, at least in certain situations, unscrupulous producers have the ability to "force" their products
and services on consumers, but responsibility for correction of this flaw rests
with "favorable social traditions." He thus minimizes the role of *market structure* as a determinant of virtue vis-à-vis the conditioning of social institutions. Maintenance of producer reputation, however, that is sufficient to in-
ject scruples and quality standards as determinants of success is dependent
upon the existence of a "personal" market where participants understand
that there are consequences to unethical and opportunistic behavior. Technological and financial obfuscation enabled by the complexity of society,

along with the sheer mass of the global economy, have an inherent tendency to mask personal conduct. Nevertheless, Novak implies that the mere existence of markets is evidence of their virtuosity, for the market's "dependence upon [social virtues] is very high."

Novak does recognize the potential for immoral behavior among the individuals and institutions of the market order. For all his praise of corporate structures in his book *Toward a Theology of the Corporation*, Novak acknowledges that businesses sometimes fail to uphold the moral principles that he believes are essential to democratic capitalism:

> Corporations err morally, then, in many ways. They may through their advertising appeal to hedonism and escape, in ways that undercut the restraint and self-discipline required by a responsible democracy and that discourage the deferral of present satisfaction on which savings and investment for the future depend. They may incorporate methods of governance that injure dignity, cooperation, inventiveness, and personal development. They may seek their own immediate interests at the expense of the common good. They may become improperly involved in the exercise of political power. They may injure the conscience of their managers or workers. They are capable of the sins of individuals and grave institutional sins as well.[21]

Taken in bulk, however, Novak's comments are decidedly in favor of the moral requirements and, ultimately, moral sustainability of capitalism and its corporate entities. He writes that a business career "is not only a morally serious vocation but a morally noble one."[22] In addition, the business life is creative because "business is a source of endless personal challenge, testing intellectual and moral mettle in the crucible of practicality."[23] Simple success in the business world "imposes remarkable moral responsibilities."[24] Again, Novak's statements are simply too unconditional, acknowledging neither the wide disparities in morality and nobility among modern capitalism's myriad industries nor the evolving nature of capitalism itself. Indeed, there are many pockets within the capitalist system in which nobility, creativity, and personal challenge are present and which contribute to the character of the employees, customers, and other stakeholders who participate in those markets, but there are also many areas of American commercial culture in which such qualities are noticeably absent. The existence of sweatshops, abortion clinics, the pornography industry, and other commercial institutions that exist within the legal bounds of liberal society cast into doubt Novak's rather general claim of moral nobility for producers and service providers. Recently, the moral dignity of large corporations in general has been called into question by numerous ethical scandals involving corporate executives.[25]

For Novak, this question concerning the morality of the business enterprise is not simply an assessment of the ethics of commercial society; it has far deeper implications. He posits that one of the "injuries" done by those who "do not allow that business is a moral institution" is that "since a healthy capitalist economy is a necessary condition for the success of democracy, they diminish the prospects of the free society."[26] One would hardly think of the Enron whistleblowers, who now must certainly question whether their company was, at least at the executive level, a moral institution, as diminishing the prospects of the free society. Novak's comment provides additional evidence of the extreme to which many Christian defenders of capitalism go in "protecting" the system.

Novak's "idealism" regarding the business enterprise and market exchange ironically reflects the realism that capitalism and its ubiquitous markets can be generalized as virtuous only in a theoretical sense. The reality that markets differ widely in their concentrations of economic power among producers and consumers, and that they also differ in terms of the organizational, financial, and technological sophistication of participating firms; the historical and cultural context in which they exist; and other factors suggests that they will also vary in their capacities to promote social virtues. Moreover, if increases in size and complexity have the ability to obfuscate unethical behavior and mask the reputations of market participants, and given the rise in cultural complexity observed by Roger Shinn and Wolf Häfele,[27] then one might suggest a general decline in the ability of markets to promote social virtues altogether.

At one point in his most famous book, *The Spirit of Democratic Capitalism*, Novak describes the dramatic impact of the democratic capitalist system on religion, stating, "Such an order [democratic capitalism] calls forth not only a new theology but a new type of religion. The institutional force of religion is dramatically altered under it: strengthened in some respects, weakened in others."[28] Elsewhere in the same book, Novak recognizes a different form of interdependence, or perhaps simply dependence, between religious and other moral institutions and those of commerce. Novak writes, "Commercial virtues are not, then, sufficient to their own defense. A commercial system needs taming and correction by a moral-cultural system independent of commerce."[29] But *no moral-cultural system can be independent of commerce* for the reasons articulated by Hayek and implied by Novak himself in the first quotation. Economic transacting by subjective actors in the marketplace does not take place in a vacuum. Its consequences bleed into other institutions and, according to Hayek, ultimately serve as the well-spring of institutional values of religious and moral traditions.

Christian libertarians and neoconservatives often attempt to place distance between the value systems of what they perceive as distinct economic and moral-cultural sectors of society despite Hayek's insistence on the interrelatedness of values in modern culture. Father Sirico, in a lecture given at an Acton Institute conference held in West Cornwall, Connecticut, in November 2001, explained that economic value is different from moral value, principally in that economic value is subjective.[30] Sirico acknowledged that economic decisions "have moral dimensions"; however, true morality, just as freedom, must be oriented outside itself—beyond its immediate context.[31] Sirico recognizes that the social and historical context of markets can contribute to "abuses." He notes, "Each nation and culture will develop a slightly different market culture, a different way of conducting business, of treating others at market, of agreeing to contracts, of treating workers, and so forth."[32] Sirico's admission of cultural influences on particular instantiations of markets leads him to state, "In this sense, we stand opposed to those who define capitalism as the economic and cultural essence that exists in the Western world today. When abuses occur it is a sign that the culture of the market is poorly formed and not in synchronicity with human nature and moral values."[33] But does the market itself impose norms and values that lead to a loss of synchronicity with human nature and moral principles? The rising brand consciousness and desire for immediate gratification observed in American children indicate that the market itself may promote its own ethos at least to impressionable market participants. From what other cultural reservoirs are such values derived if not from the market? Father Sirico also states that we should seek economic growth not for its own sake but rather for "genuine human development, a component of which is economic growth. Genuine human development implies growth that is aimed at human betterment and the furthering of the common good."[34] But does this accurately describe either the modern capitalist economy or the corporation that is one of its principal institutions?

Gloria Zuniga, an economist and senior fellow at the Acton Institute, addresses the most common and "troublesome" charge against the value subjectivism at the heart of Austrian economics: "that it is either consistent with, or an endorsement of, moral relativism."[35] Zuniga dismisses this criticism with the observation that it "conflates economic value with moral value, two wholly distinct species of value."[36] But economic valuations impinge greatly upon "moral value" in markets for abortion, human organs, and genetic customization. The "moral dimensions" of transacting in these markets are undoubtedly capable of altering consumers' basic values by applying price tags to human life. And it would seem that those who insist on placing distance between moral and economic value part company with Hayek on this issue. As demonstrated in chapter 4, all moral values in the Hayekian social model, irrespective of whether they originate in religious or commercial society, ultimately converge at the point where they are deemed to contribute to the dominant social instinct of group persistence. In this way, Hayek notes that it is "an erroneous belief that there are purely economic ends separate from the other ends of life."[37] This was the very reason that Hayek preferred the term "spontaneous order" to "market order": the "system" of free societies is too complex and its boundaries too porous to categorize values or activities as "purely economic."

Christian neoconservative Richard John Neuhaus also attempts (in concert with Novak and Zuniga) to divorce the economic structure of modern society from its moral-cultural establishments in the specific context of consumerism:

> Consumerism is, quite precisely, the consuming of life by the things consumed. It is living in a manner that is measured by having rather than being. As Pope John Paul II makes clear, consumerism is hardly the sin of the rich. The poor, driven by discontent and envy, may be consumed by what they do not have as the rich are consumed by what they do have. The question is not, certainly not most importantly, a question about economics. It is first and foremost a cultural and moral problem requiring a cultural and moral remedy.[38]

Again, the separation of moral-cultural institutions from economic life has the effect of distancing capitalism and the market that is its principal instrument from any perceived moral degradation of society. Cultural and moral establishments, including churches, which ultimately must supply the remedy that Neuhaus seeks, are bathed in capitalist culture. Where do the more competitive values of the modern megachurch come from if not from the market system within which the church's membership interacts on a daily basis? To assign, as Neuhaus and Novak largely have done, the responsibility for morally reforming society to the moral-cultural sphere while restricting the reach of those reforms to exclude the market system is a self-defeating proposition. All social institutions must be scrutinized as to their moral impacts if we are truly to address the problem.

Although Neuhaus references Pope John Paul II to make his point, John Paul might differ from Neuhaus concerning the degree of distance that he places between the moral and economic decisions of individuals. As

Elshtain explains, "John Paul suggests that the richer we get in the consumerist way, the poorer we become in a richly human way. That is why he insists that every decision to buy, spend, or invest is a moral and cultural choice, not just an 'individualist' preference."[39] Elshtain's description of John Paul's views on consumerism implies an understanding of the economic principle of "opportunity cost." The reason for the moral dimension of every human choice involving the exchange of resources is that every human action has an opportunity cost associated with it—the cost of some product, service, or activity foregone. Every action projects some moral value, no matter how subtle, for the reason that it involves *not* having done something else. The decision to purchase a new automobile (as well as the decision to spend ten thousand dollars versus forty thousand dollars) is at once a decision not to tithe that same money to one's church or use it to patronize a strip club. The fact that alternatives in economic decision making will always be present and that they will often not be moral equivalents necessitates, as Elshtain implies of John Paul's attitude toward consumerism, that every consumption decision is necessarily a moral statement.[40]

Zuniga uses the example of a decision to purchase a red versus a yellow hat as illustrating that "not all economic actions are morally relevant." She uses this consumer choice as demonstrating the absence of moral relevance to many consumer decisions.[41] However, assuming no difference in cost between the same style hat in different colors, the lack of moral relevance stems from the fact that no economic resources are exchanged because of this preference. If the red hat costs twenty dollars and the same hat in yellow costs forty dollars, then a moral component is added to the transaction because of the opportunity cost involved in the differential; it becomes a decision to spend an additional twenty dollars for a hat in a certain color and not to use that twenty dollars for another purpose. The range of "other purposes" for the additional money spent (the opportunity cost) will necessarily involve differing moral values: it could be used for another purchase, given to the poor, or whatever.

As noted, the common disjunction between moral and economic values in the "systems" of Christian adherents of Austrian economics is a departure from Hayek's model of social morality. Hayek conceived of no moral value that lay beyond the influence of culture or the institutions of capitalism; thus all social values can and likely will be impacted by economic decision making. Yet libertarians and neoconservatives commonly use Austrian economic theory to give greater moral weight to economic science. For example, Sirico states, "Modern Austrian economists like Wilhelm Röpke, Ludwig von Mises, Henry Hazlitt, F. A. Hayek and Israel Kirzner certainly evince a concern about moral matters, even if on particular points they would part ways with the Church's teaching."[42] First, this broad casting of the net around the Austrian economists groups together rather divergent views on the morality of economic behavior. Certainly Röpke's *A Humane Economy* differs in its moral perspective and tone from Mises' *Liberalism in the Classical Tradition*. In contrast to Mises' austere and often Darwinian statements on social morality, Röpke stated, "My picture of man is fashioned by the spiritual heritage of classical and Christian tradition. I see in man the likeness of God; I am profoundly convinced that it is an appalling sin to reduce man to means . . . and that each man's soul is something unique, irreplaceable, priceless, in comparison with which all other things are as naught."[43] Second, what has been shown of the work of Hayek and Mises does not reflect so much "concern" over moral matters; rather, these theorists have presented well-reasoned explanations for the moral transformations that take place in both free and totalitarian societies. The principal "concern" is over institutional impediments such as government that often deter the advance of progress. In Mises' view, for example, "Everything that serves to preserve the social order is moral; everything that is detrimental to it is immoral."[44] Similarly for Hayek, those rules, values, and behaviors that have proven their contributions to group persistence ultimately will be determined as moral, while those that have not will be rejected. Sirico's statement suggests an unwarranted elevation of the moral component of Austrian theory that could lead to an equally unwarranted confidence by some Christians in the moral sustainability of capitalism based on their understanding (or misunderstanding) of the Austrian model.

Yet, many Christians promote Austrian economic theory as largely consistent with the Christian view of capitalism. Professor Gabriel Zanotti attempts to explain a common "misunderstanding" that has philosophically separated these traditions in his essay "Misesian Praxeology and Christian Philosophy":

> Very few Thomistic thinkers have realized that Austrian economic theory and methodology are capable of establishing a fruitful dialogue with Christian philosophy. Very few Christian thinkers, especially those of the philosophical tradition of Aquinas, have seen the value of such a dialogue. Why? The simple reason is that they reject the neo-Kantian metaphysical agnosticism of Mises and Hayek. However, neither metaphysical agnosticism nor a neo-Kantian theory of knowledge are necessary presuppositions of Mises' theory of human action or Austrian economic methodology.[45]

It is suggested here, however, that group persistence, as the central pillar of Hayek's thought and humankind's dominant instinct in the Hayekian social model, both emanates from and strongly favors an agnostic worldview. This is the irony in Hayek's moral system noted by Graham Walker where he states, "Hayek's ethical position is marked by a striking juxtaposition of agnosticism and reverence [for traditional morals]."[46] Hayek jettisons any notion of teleology in his explication of the processes of cultural evolution in which "groups which happen to have adopted rules conducive to a more effective order of actions will tend to prevail over other groups with a less effective order."[47] He can accept no corollary to his system that an institution or social group may survive in the long run if it willingly (or even unconsciously) puts its own survival at risk for principle. Thus, Hayek's system contains an essential presupposition of group persistence that entails the rejection of other presuppositions, including metaphysical or religious beliefs, which might interfere with institutional survival.

In this vein, literary critic Harold Bloom has perhaps stumbled upon the reason why American society, of all industrial societies, so closely follows the Hayekian moral model, as was demonstrated in chapter 4. He states flatly, "No nation ever has rejected death with an intensity comparable to ours."[48] It would seem consistent that to the extent that the rejection of death exists as a cultural value, and to the extent that the nation follows a strictly subjective path to the good, then it would closely follow Hayek's understanding of moral transformation since individual decisions will favor longevity and the persistence of social groups, subordinating all others. This value thus becomes the principal dynamic and defining characteristic of social change for such a society.

Christians must be careful of too closely aligning their moral systems with the theories of Hayek, not for the fact that he was wrong, but for the likelihood that he was right about the evolutionary nature of morality in a highly subjectivist system of capitalism. If, as Nash implies, Christian values only come into play "secondarily" in such a system, then behavior will indeed conform to dominant instincts, and personal orders of values will favor group persistence. Raw market ethics, absent Christian or other traditional supports, concerns only performance, not intention, and will tend toward the destruction of those groups that do not adhere to its principles. If the Christian faith is in any way opposed to certain values that favor its institutional survival, then it is vulnerable to alteration or even extinction under the Austrian model. For example, if a particular genetic or other biological technology becomes available and is capable of extending the average lifespan one hundred years, but only through the use of techniques that violate one or more defining tenets of the Christian faith, then Hayek's model suggests that the values of individual Christians and ultimately those of its varied traditions must conform, or Christianity will not survive. No persistent religious tradition can collectively defy the dictates of group persistence. Individuals may indeed "martyr themselves" through the rejection of technologies that contradict doctrines of their faith traditions; however, the values of these individuals must be recessive within the group as a whole to ensure the survival of their tradition.

It is in this way that Hayek's agnosticism matters. The unpredictability of social "survival characteristics" insists that for groups to have the potential to endure the evolutionary gauntlet, they must only loosely hold to values that may conflict with their future survival choices. In this context, one can perceive the significance of Hayek's comment from his essay "Religion and the Guardians of Tradition": "Perhaps what many people mean in speaking of God is just a personification of that tradition of morals or values that keeps their community alive. The source of order that religion ascribes to a human-like divinity . . . *we now learn* to see to be not outside the physical world but one of its characteristics."[49] The strength of evolutionary rationalism in Hayek's thought suggests the significance of the phrase "we now learn" not so much as a statement of personal metaphysical belief (or unbelief) but as a systematic result of the process of evolutionary rationalism in the context of free markets. In other words, it is the logical conclusion of a free capitalist order that rejects death with intensity and in which "liberty" is the supreme individual value and "persistence" the highest collective value. Such a society will conform to Hayek's understanding of social value transformation.[50]

That Hayek's understated metaphysical references should factor into his social model and observations of free societies is not surprising. Alfred North Whitehead observed that "every philosophy is tinged with the colouring of some secret imaginative background which never emerges explicitly into its trains of reasoning."[51] However, it is the systematic nature of Hayek's thought that is most relevant. Hayek was, of all economic thinkers, perhaps most consistent in his approach to social phenomena. Yet he minimized all references to his "theories" in favor of his "observations," and he insisted that he did not design anything but merely abstracted principles from observations of the interactions of individuals and institutions in the context of free and totalitarian societies.

Interestingly, in his essay "Of Markets and Morality," Father Sirico observes that the "modern, liberal mindset begins by rejecting revelation, but in the course of its intellectual trajectory it must undermine not merely Biblical truth-claims but any claim to know truth. It does so to allow the individual to impose himself and his opinions on the world, creating God and others in his own image rather than shaping his views according to reality."[52] Sirico further observes, "Theistic agnosticism in this way easily proceeds to moral agnosticism, and eventually, when it has run its course, one emerges as an epistemological agnostic—unable to assert knowledge of anything with certainty. . . . It is an attack on the prerequisite for all intellectual and moral progress—and it is done in the very name of progress."[53] Is Sirico's description of the creeping agnosticism and moral relativism of the "modern, liberal mindset" not strikingly consistent with Hayek's understanding of the theological and moral basis of progress and our ultimate realization that there are no truly absolute values whatsoever? The principal difference appears to be Sirico's unfounded leap from epistemological agnosticism to the individual's loss of choice. In Hayek's understanding, the individual does not lose her capacity to choose, but rather her perspective from which choices are made is altered by the changing dictates of evolutionary rationalism.

Sirico again places distance between the "modern, liberal mindset" and the market, which is absolved of blame for perceived moral decline. Sirico adopts a position consistent with the market's moral neutrality:

> The market and the technological advances that result from it, lack a *telos*—a proper end or purpose toward which this development is oriented. That end or purpose depends upon the human person who initiates economic actions, and who himself has absorbed from somewhere a sense of moral purpose. The market and technology lack the logic to tell us who we are and what we ought to do.[54]

Thus, the market and technology cannot be faulted for any perceived moral degradation in society for the reason that they do not direct us toward any particular end.

The problem is that this view minimizes what the market itself supplies. The market and technology do have a definite ethos and an incontrovertible logic that most typically guides the decision making of human beings. It is centered on the rational calculation that leads to utility maximization, and its telos is *homo economicus*. This view of the human person as reflected in rational choice, public choice, and other theories of human behavior has been dominant within the economics profession for several decades. Such models are morally thin, to be sure; however, adherents boast of their accuracy.

The Modern Dominance of Economic Rationalism

That literally thousands of social scientists base their life's work on intensely rational models of human behavior is perhaps the greatest evidence that the market and its associated technologies do compose a particular telos for the human person and provide a logic for the achievement of that telos. Some scholars are convinced that a simplified view of the individual as a thoroughly rational economic decision maker is in fact most accurate. The "Chicago" and "Virginia" schools of economics, for example, are two of the most prominent schools of economic philosophy, advocating empirical systems of human behavior through what are called the "rational choice" and "public choice" models.[55] Promotion of these theories and the great devotion of many scholars to their explanations for human action has led Christian economist Robert Nelson to conduct an exploration of the "Chicago Project" in an attempt to determine whether "Chicago economics [is] a secular religion in much the same manner as Marxism."[56]

Nelson begins his analysis by examining the core principles of Chicago economics, the primary one being an "article of faith, really—that all the world is driven by self-interested economic rationality. People do things because, on balance, these actions offer them greater positive benefits than the costs incurred."[57] Nothing particularly surprising here, since some variation of this tenet is common to classical, neoclassical, utilitarian, monetarist, and other philosophical schools of economics. However, what differentiates the Chicago project is the extension of the dominant motivation of rational self-interest to virtually every aspect of life. Nelson notes how the Chicago project has produced theories to explain behavior in myriad facets of life, including an "economics of the law, crime, family life, sex, health and education, and so on. In each of these fields, the Chicago project today aims to show how an underlying economic rationality is at work." While it may seem that "tenets of Christian religion, love, morality, and other noneconomic value systems are driving the course of events," the Chicago school holds that "such noneconomic values merely serve to obscure the deeper workings of the forces of self-interested economic rationality."[58]

Nelson uses Nobel laureate and University of Chicago economist Gary Becker's application of public choice theory to the family as a case in point. Becker's project has attempted to distill the underlying rationality of familial relations in order to model family dynamics (or, perhaps more accurately, "mechanics"). Nelson quotes Becker from his Nobel

Prize acceptance speech that what traditionally has been thought to result from family love is in fact motivated by "the incentives to invest in creating closer relations."[59] In *A Treatise on the Family*, Becker states that altruism is more common in the family than in capitalist markets for the reason that "altruism is less 'efficient' in the marketplace and more 'efficient' in families."[60] Even more controversial is Becker's application of calculus to derive demand functions for children in the family and his attempt to determine "marriage-market equilibrium" based on male and female incomes.[61] Becker's larger contention is that virtually all human behaviors—even those most intimate, emotional, and altruistic—can be mathematically modeled because an underlying rationalism stimulated by self-interest guides human actions.

Nelson believes that the universality of such models forms unique "worldviews" that approach the qualities and characteristics of religion. He concludes that the practice of economics, especially as performed on highly definite models of human behavior such as that of public choice theory, "has been associated with various secular religions that are, in essence, competitors to Christianity."[62] According to Nelson, "to be a fully active member of the economics profession may be to join a competitor religion to Christianity, a competitor priesthood."[63] He arrives at the conclusion that Christianity and economic philosophy are competing worldviews—with economics containing multiple worldviews because of its myriad "schools."[64]

Dominance of the economics profession by these intensely rationalistic schools such as Chicago leads some Christian conservatives to Austrian economics for the reason that Hayek and others are willing to concede a "place at the table" for religion as a meaningful economic phenomenon. Some of the Christian scholars addressed here are negative toward the Chicago school for its minimization of the importance of cultural (including religious) influences on human behavior. Michael Novak suggests that the Austrian school has rescued economics from its twentieth-century drift toward mathematical irrelevance:

> During our own century, a school of economics much disdained by the leaders and the general run of professionals in the field (who were more and more attracted to the scientific model, and particularly to the strengths and beauties of mathematics) has restored economics as a field worthy of investigation by moral philosophy. The school is known as the Austrian School, the school of "classical liberals" or, in F. A. Hayek's

preferred description, "Whigs." Let me state the accomplishment of these Whigs starkly: As a result of the inquiries of the Austrian School, it has become clear that economics is at least as much a branch of moral philosophy and the liberal arts as it is a science.[65]

Novak's testament for the "Austrian reformation" in economics is substantiated by an observation by economist Jesus Zaratiegui of rising criticism of the positivistic excesses of neoclassical economics. Zaratiegui notes that many believe the "neoclassical quest for exactness has gone from simplification to the loss of contextual references."[66] Indeed it has. Yet the question must be asked whether the contextual framework of Austrian economics provides a substantive moral foundation that enables a more positive outlook for the sustainability of Christian morality vis-à-vis the Chicago school. Nelson's characterization of Chicago economics and its treatment of religion sheds some light on this question:

> From the perspective of the Chicago School, religion can have a practical function as a particularly effective way of reducing transaction costs in society. Honesty, which religion may tend to promote, is economically efficient for a society because it can greatly simplify the contracting process and in other ways reduce transaction costs. To be sure, there is a free-rider problem in that it may be in each person's interest to live among honest people but to be dishonest (at appropriate times) themselves. However, for the Chicago project that is just another complication to be factored into the theoretical calculations of the economic analysis of "truthfulness."[67]

There is obvious consistency between the utilitarian role that Nelson perceives as assigned to religion by the Chicago school and the quite similar view of religious tradition found in the thought of Hayek that was discussed in chapter 4. In the Chicago model, religion supplies honesty and other values to the market that have tangible economic benefit and serve economic purposes, similar to Hayek's belief that "persistent" religious institutions have arrived at certain values that contribute to the orderly progression of civilization.[68] Where the two schools seem to diverge is that the Chicagoans are more willing to identify those specific religious values that contribute to market efficiency and suggest their *definite* contributions to the good, whereas the Austrians perceive a more indistinct and evolutionary character to religious values that are perceived to benefit material efficiency. Members of the Austrian school leave open the possibility that values, which in the past have contributed to the economic success of various groups, may cease making contributions in the future and be disavowed. Therefore, the role assigned to religious tradition in morally reinforcing modern capitalist society is not widely divergent between the Austrian and Chicago schools of economics. Moreover, both systems are largely dependent upon highly rational understandings of the human person, just as was the constructivist pragmatism of John Dewey. It is simply the *source* of rationality of these three models of social behavior that differ. For Dewey, it was the scientific rationalism built upon human experimentation that resulted from discovery and innovation. For Hayek and Mises, an ultimately indiscernible evolutionary rationalism ensures order in human conduct and enables the sustainability of progress. For members of the Chicago school, a presumed universality of economic rationalism is the dominant motivation to human action. It enables the predictability of individual and social behavior and, thereby, the orderly advancement of civilization.

For both the Austrian and Chicago schools, the market supplies the logic that guides human decision making in most areas of life. It was recognized in chapter 4 that even John Dewey arrived at a subjectivist understanding of human progress built around the "unconscious" forces of "new knowledge" that act upon the individual, with the market being a disseminating source of that knowledge.[69] Given the convergence of these prominent social models around a common rationality supplied by the market, how can Christian conservatives such as Father Sirico deny that the market provides an ethic and logic for human action?

CULTURAL ELITES AND MORAL DETERIORATION

Christian advocates of Austrian economic theory do recognize the disintegration of the family, increases in sexual promiscuity, growth in markets for pornography and illegal drugs, and other symptoms of what is widely perceived as moral deterioration even in the most advanced capitalist societies like the United States. Indeed, all of the economically conservative American Christians discussed here are quite vocal in their observations and criticisms of the "moral slide" of the present generation. Given their sanguine views of the moral sustainability of capitalism, and given its now pervasive reach and the remarkable material progress that has taken place in the past century, how can one explain such deviations from the "model?" If capitalism, as George Gilder suggests, "is simply the essential mode of human life that corresponds to religious truth,"[70] then one would anticipate religious and moral benefits to result from the triumph of the global market system.

The elimination of the market from the list of possible contributory factors to moral decline forces Christian libertarians and neoconservatives to explore other cultural phenomena as detrimental influences. The so-called elite class of liberal society commonly is identified as a morally denigrating force that attempts to steer mainstream culture toward its own permissive values and behaviors. Michael Novak, for example, perceives within the American advertising industry the elitism that contributes to moral deterioration. He states, "It has been wrong—devastatingly wrong—for advertisers *in the name of business* to promote assaults on traditional virtues. These are the muscles, ligaments, sinews of the free society. Cut them and you have paralyzed liberty."[71]

Advertisers undoubtedly have played a part in the perceived vulgarization of American culture over the past several decades. The barrage of newspaper, magazine, television, radio, and now Internet advertising that bombards Americans on a daily basis is increasingly sensationalistic and lascivious. Moreover, slogans and jingles preach self-indulgence to an already intensely self-interested culture. Marketeers and advertisers have a significant incentive to generate demand for their products wherever possible and by whatever means necessary. However, in a market economy, the principal stimulus to production is consumer demand, or at least perceived demand. Thus, the nature of advertising, as any business function, is conditioned by suppliers' perceptions of their customers' demand, and market logic suggests that consumer taste is the dominant factor contributing to the type of advertising that ultimately is produced.

Many neoconservatives single out advertising as an aberrant and especially pernicious source of moral decay in American culture. Yet casting blame on advertisers and other elites for American moral failings reveals some of the same economic naïveté of which they commonly accuse their religious leadership.[72] The idea that advertisers conspire to change social values in order to manipulate American culture to their own designs contradicts conservatives' usual belief in the *responsiveness* of the free market system and their general understanding that subjective choice drives the market economy. People who have worked closely with the marketers and advertisers of the business world recognize them more as sycophants than elitists. They expend massive resources in researching the values and preferences of consumers in order to design their marketing campaigns accordingly. There is no question that advertisers are expert in their ability to tantalize and sensationalize for the purposes of stimulating consumers, but the idea that they "assault" the values and virtues that consumers hold dear in order to sell their products is illogical and uneconomic, not to mention an insult to the American consumer who winds up being a stooge of corporate culture in this scenario.

By assigning such influence to advertisers, Novak has concurrently bestowed upon them the onerous responsibility of defending traditional values, something he expressly does not do with corporations as a whole. Corporations are, for the most part, assigned the singular task of maximizing profits. In the larger context, Novak sees the virtues of capitalism emanating from a remarkably simple source—the drive to profitability. Novak quotes economist Milton Friedman on the subject that, in a free economy, "there is one and only one social responsibility of business—to use its resources and engage in activities designed to increase profits so long as it stays within the rules of the game."[73] But it is unclear how businesses as a whole can bear less responsibility for moral deterioration in society than the advertisers who perform a particular function within those businesses.

Academics and the elite stars of the entertainment industry also draw Novak's ire. He states, "The moral rot evident among Hollywood, television, and rock star elites, and the moral confusion evident in the professoriat seem steadily to be corroding the morals of ordinary people."[74] This consortium of elites has been named by Novak the "adversary culture" to emphasize its value and behavioral conflicts with mainstream American society. According to Novak, the adversary culture "now governs the mainstream in the universities, the magazines, movies, and television. Coincident with its rise is the gradual collapse of the prestige of scientific and technical elites, and even the idea of progress."[75]

Yet the means by which Novak attempts to demonstrate the divide between middle-class and adversary cultures exposes a critical flaw in his own logic. He states, "The hardest part of the moral task we now face is the immense power of the adversary culture. To oppose that power is to risk excommunication from the mainstream."[76] How can one risk excommunication from the mainstream by opposing the adversary elite unless mainstream society is aligned with or sympathetic to that elite? And that is the very point here. While Novak perhaps is referring to the influence of the elite class on mainstream culture, that influence is dependent upon some common value or values between the two groups. The idea that in a free society the cultural mainstream would empower through its votes or pocketbooks an "adversary elite" to which it has no allegiance, for which it has no sympathy, and with which it shares no common value or values is absurd.[77]

Austrian economic theorist Wilhelm Röpke recognized the commensurate culpability of mainstream society in the moral deterioration that accompanies the rise of mass culture:

> If [members of mainstream society] avidly lap up mass slogans, if they surrender to "social religions" as a surrogate for vanishing faith and traditional values, if they take to mass entertainment and mass spectacles almost as to narcotic drugs, they do it not merely to fill the emptiness of their souls. One of the principal reasons why they plunge into the mass is that they are made deeply unhappy by the social enmassment which prizes people out of the fabric of true community. Thrown into society as isolated human beings, literally *indivdua* and human atoms, people hunger for "integration," and they allay this hunger by means of the intoxicating thrills and crowds of mass society. They can no longer live without the radio, press, films, group outings, mass sports, and all the concomitant noise, without the sense of "being in the swim," without the "smell of the herd."[78]

D. Stephen Long agrees that the targeting of elites as responsible for the moral decline of society is an oversimplification. He states, the "notion that some class intentionally opposed to free markets dominates communications networks reveals a weakness in Novak's argument. His three systems [political, economic, and moral-cultural] allow the capitalist market to be free from blame for the consumer culture that it produces and which produces it."[79] Long's statement reflects recognition of the complex interplay of markets, institutions, and individuals that has led to the culture of consumerism. Social elites are no less bound to that cultural phenomenon than is mainstream society.

AN ALTERNATIVE EXPLANATION FOR MORAL DECLINE

One might differ with Long's argument slightly and concede to Novak and other Christian conservatives the possibility of an elite class imposing its values in particular situations where concentrations of market power limit the range of values expressed. Conservatives make stronger arguments for the exorbitant cultural influence of the entertainment and media industries when they base that influence on the market clout resulting from mergers and acquisitions that have contributed to the emergence of giant media conglomerates. One might explain the possibility for such value imposition by placing a "moral twist" on a widely known principle of economics called Say's law, which in its most simple form is generally identified by the phrase "supply creates its own demand." In *A Treatise on Political Economy* (1803), the French political economist Jean-Baptiste Say observed, "All products are consumed sooner or later; indeed they are produced solely for the purpose of consumption, and, whenever the consumption of a product is delayed after it has reached the point of absolute maturity, it is value inert and neutralized for the time."[80] Although Say intended his principle as a contribution to the (at that time) emerging concept of market equilibrium, it nevertheless may be seen to have moral implications. Say recognized that in "each country the wants of the consumer determine the quality of the product."[81] Yet he also observed that the overall economic system has a tendency toward consumption as the result and as an expression of national wealth; thus, "opulent, civilized, and industrious nations, are greater consumers than poor ones, because they are infinitely greater producers."[82] If, however, production is concentrated among few producers in a particular industry of an "opulent" nation, and the mere fact of that nation's wealth promotes a general consumption of commodities supplied to the market *in general*, then one might conjecture that concentrations among producers can have the effect of inducing demand for the commodities they supply. In cases where those commodities are "value shaping," one might also surmise that consumers will adopt values associated with certain products and services in general uniformity with the rise in demand for those commodities. Thus, the mere existence of certain products and services in the marketplace has the possibility of inducing acceptance of values associated with them due to the propensity of an opulent nation to consume.

Of course, even accepting the veracity of Say's law, the ability of a producer to shape the values of consumers is directly proportional to the producer's power in supplying products to the market and keeping them available long enough to influence demand. The extent to which producer values that do not readily conform to consumer values are adopted would appear to be conditioned by their *persistence* in the marketplace. Persistence of particular goods and services, in turn, depends on concentrations of market power that would limit entry of competitors whose products embody values more consistent with those of consumers. Thus, a megamerger in the media industry that results in a single corporation controlling a substantial share of the network news market, for example, would have far greater potential to influence public values than would a news organization that has little market power, no matter how "elitist."

The problem that this logic presents for economically conservative Christians, however, is that their general opposition to government interference in the private sector often causes them to resist public attempts to break up or re-strict powerful firms. Christian libertarian policy analyst Doug Bandow, a sen-ior fellow at the Cato Institute, suggested at an Acton Institute conference in November and December 2001 that government attempts to break up the Mi-crosoft Corporation were ill advised and that the cure of government inter-vention would likely result in greater economic harm than the negative con-sequences resulting from Microsoft's monopoly.[83] Bandow pointed out the legal costs associated with such a challenge and suggested that government was at a disadvantage with respect to legal resources; therefore, it could well lose the case anyway.[84] The pervasiveness of such defeatism virtually ensures the ability of large firms like Microsoft to impose their products and the values as-sociated with those products on consumers. It matters not whether a company like Microsoft is elitist (whatever that term may imply), only that its market power allows its products to persist and influence consumers' *future values* re-gardless of whether they conform to consumers' *present values*.

Other scholars have offered different explanations for the perceived moral decline associated with the structure of markets. One critic who has emphasized the morally deleterious effects of increasingly private con-sumption choices in contributing to the culture of consumerism is conser-vative jurist turned social theorist Robert Bork. In countering Gilder's ar-gument that moral slide results principally from the "centralized control" of television and other broadcast technology, Bork retorts that decentralization spawned by the Internet and other technologies will not have the positive effect on social morality of which Gilder is hopeful. Bork states, "The more private viewing becomes, the more likely that salacious and perverted tastes will be indulged. That is suggested by the explosion of pornographic film titles and profits when videocassettes enabled customers to avoid going to 'adult' theaters. Another boom should occur when those customers don't even have to ask for the cassettes in a store."[85] Bork suggests that it is more the *private nature of consumption* rather than the *centralized manner of production* that has contributed to modern moral decline. He also recognizes the fal-lacy that by merely rejecting products and services that go against traditional values, society can avoid the adverse social and moral consequences engen-dered by these markets. He states the notion that "'if it offends you, don't buy it'—is both lulling and destructive. Whether you buy it or not, you will be greatly affected by those who do. The aesthetic and moral environment in which you and your family live will be coarsened and brutalized."[86]

In his comment, Bork has stumbled upon the realization that makes a seemingly benign belief in the essential moral neutrality of the market a dangerous conception. The idea that the market is an impartial arbiter of values in society suggests that those commodities that enter the market but which contravene the religious and moral principles of large numbers of consumers will be rejected and, ultimately, that producers of such commodities will wither away. However, the moral aspects of Say's law and the resultant coarsening of society observed by Bork, along with Robert Wuthnow's recognition of the rising American belief in the market as a morally positive institution,[87] all suggest that consumers increasingly accept the moral legitimacy of the products and services that enter the marketplace.

Despite his acknowledgment of the effects of private consumption on morality, Bork falls back into the "conservative trap" of blaming elites for society's moral demise:

> Modern liberalism is most particularly a disease of our cultural elites, the people who control the institutions that manufacture or disseminate ideas, attitudes, and symbols—universities, some churches, Hollywood, the national press (print and electronic), much of the congressional Democratic Party, and some of the congressional Republicans as well, large sections of the judiciary, foundation staffs, and almost all the "public interest" organizations that exercise a profound if largely unseen effect on public policy.[88]

The "diseases" of the system as characterized by Bork are not dependent upon a conspiratorial elite for their existence. They are endemic to a system whose definition of progress is subsumed under the assumptions of material insatiability and the exclusivity of subjective valuations of the good. While there unquestionably is a common approach by advertisers, the media, Hollywood, and even political parties to exaggerate or sensationalize their claims in order to attract greater followings, market logic again dictates that these so-called elites must appeal to at least latent values of their respective constituencies in order to survive. The amazing responsiveness of the market system, accented in an era of mass communications, insists that the elites of culture are best understood not as manipulators who are hellbent on transforming the values of the masses, but rather that they seek to radicalize and exploit existing values (perhaps more latent and more base) held by their consumer and constituent groups for material gain. In other words, it is not so much their status as "elites" but as powerful market players that results in their ability to impose values on society. Significantly, this view of consumer culture is also more consistent with Hayek's belief that value changes within institutions are accomplished more efficiently through the transacting of individual members in the wider economy than through the control and guidance of the leaders of those institutions.

In the end, for Novak as well as for Bork, it is the moral-cultural sector that is at fault for society's observed moral deterioration. Novak states, "Our moral-cultural institutions do their job less well than our economic institutions do theirs. The twain are not yet matched. We need a spirituality appropriate for democratic capitalism as it is, and we do not have it."[89] Novak describes the moral-cultural institutions of his tripartite system, including those of religion, as outdated and in need of overhaul. One might also observe Novak's comment as a classic restatement of the cultural lag problem—that the moral-cultural sector lags behind the surging technical-economic sector and must be brought up to speed. Given Novak's rejection of collectivist and interventionist responses to the problem, then, it would seem that the only means to enable society's moral-cultural institutions to "catch up" with its economic and technical advances would be either to accelerate the process of religious and moral adaptation to material advance or to slow the pace of economic development.

Father Sirico identifies "moral evil" as occurring "when the human person has disregarded God."[90] But one must ask which force is most capable of engendering disregard for God in contemporary culture: the influence of the market, the moral suasion of elites, or the coercive force of the state? Was the rise of the culture of death the result of decisions of cultural elites to intentionally direct society into a moral abyss? Is it more realistic to view *Roe v. Wade* as the intention of an elitist Supreme Court to legally enforce a disregard for human life on the whole of society, or was it more likely a response to social changes that have occurred with the rise of modernity? A student of mine was once amazed when I portrayed the free-love generation of the 1970s as more receptive to the legalization of abortion than that of today. He simply could not believe that *Roe* resulted from a cultural revolution that demanded greater freedom in sexual reproduction. It had to be an imposition from on high because of what the alternative would say about the moral state of American society in that period. In many ways, *Roe* was a market phenomenon—a response to consumers of medical services to remove restrictions that limit our "progress." Reflecting on value changes that have reduced the individual to an almost exclusive role as rational actor on the economic stage would suggest that the market as much as any institution has distracted us from higher moral purposes and established an environment that engenders a disregard for God.

President George W. Bush reinforced this loss of dimensionality of the human person in his encouragement of Americans to "consume" as a response to the crisis generated by the terrorist attacks of September 11, 2001.[91] The president's implication that society has progressed to a state where the average American's most important contribution in the event of national crisis is to increase consumption in order to help stabilize the economy acknowledges a new realism—that the traditional fears of American society (communism, nuclear holocaust, disease, social unrest) have shifted to the less tangible and less directly combated fears of quite subtle changes in economic conditions. American culture has evolved in the very way that Hayek theorized to a state where fear of nuclear annihilation has been eclipsed by the fear of fractional dips in gross domestic product. Robert J. Ross and Kent C. Trachte cast the new agents of "terror" in a mold familiar to students of the liberal tradition—a "New Leviathan" not in the form of the state but in a "newly invigorated system of global capitalism":

> The characteristic "terror" of the Old Leviathan was the police power of the state. The characteristic terror of the New Leviathan is unemployment, wage cuts, the fear that a family or a community's aspiration for environmental or economic improvement may cause the agents of the New Leviathan to take their investments to some other place where working people are more vulnerable to the demand of their employers.[92]

Perhaps the most frightening aspect of the New Leviathan that is the global economic system is that it works just as Hayek described. The dwindling importance of collectives in modern capitalism results in an economic order in which there are few guides to production, unfettered consumption is the singular driving force behind "progress," and the "good" is expressed almost entirely at the level of the individual. Except as they are able to achieve market dominance, cultural elites have little capability to force consumers to watch R-rated films, purchase designer fashions, or overindulge at happy hour. The effort involved in "forcing" consumers to partake of products and services that go against their basic values in the highly responsive market environment is a decisive argument against those who assign such motivations to elites. Any serious discussion of moral decline in capitalist society must include at least the possibility that elements of the market system itself may have morally deteriorative effects.

CONCLUDING REMARKS

The pessimistic outlook for the future of Christian morality conveyed in this chapter reflects in part what former Czechoslovakian leader and poet Vaclav Havel describes as the "general unwillingness of consumption-oriented people to sacrifice some material certainties for the sake of their own spiritual and moral integrity."[93] Americans are indeed a consumption-oriented people who, as Harold Bloom describes, reject death with incomparable intensity. But Hayek scholar John Gray has made an observation of socialism that has coequal relevance to capitalism in that it implies not so much the *unwillingness* as the *infeasibility* of a consumption-oriented people to sacrifice for spiritual and moral integrity. Gray posits the "epistemological impossibility" of socialism that, "in the absence of the signals transmitted via the price mechanism," citizens of socialist states are unable to direct their activities to the common good.[94] Chapter 4 demonstrated that human transcendence and human life itself generate no signals that are interpretable by the pricing mechanism; these values are excluded from the "market" determination of the good, which in subjectivist capitalism has become a near-exclusive determinant. Thus, Gray's critique of socialism implies the infeasibility of accounting for human transcendence and other deeply held religious values and beliefs in the context of the modern market economy.

Such a concession might well support the common contention of economically conservative Christians that the moral and economic spheres of society are distinct and to some degree separable, but for one unavoidable fact: *the inability of the market to absorb and represent all values in capitalist society does not deter either the rate or the reach of its advance.*[95] In fact, as Hayek observed, progress itself thrives on material insatiability and moral malleability. Ezra Mishan confirms this maxim with his recognition that a "consuming public that looks as if it might eventually become satisfied with what it has, or a consuming public whose demand is restrained by traditional notions of good taste and propriety, or by firm ideas of what is right and wrong, will not serve. This required insatiability even in an age of reckless abundance can be ensured only by undermining traditional restraints, by subverting cultural norms, and by encouraging promiscuity."[96]

Despite the observations of Hayek, Mishan, and others, the Christian scholars discussed here are generally unconvinced by arguments of the market system's encroachments on morality. They perceive moral decline in advanced capitalist societies as resulting principally from the domination of elites that has divided our modern civilization into mainstream and adversary cultures. Moral deterioration occurs as the elite class, utilizing its disproportionate influence, displaces with its permissive values the more traditional mores of mainstream society. The question they have not answered is from whence this influence originates in a highly subjectivist order in which the responsiveness of the market to consumer demand is considered the most significant contribution to the greatest economic achievements of history—the defeat of communism and the rise of the global economic order. This market responsiveness that has been so critical to the ideological defeat of collectivism ironically stops short of supplying adequate and accurate feedback on consumer values at the very point where those values begin to deteriorate.

Perhaps the arrival of these Christian social thinkers at seemingly inconsistent positions results from their unwillingness to believe that our conception of progress and even elements of the market itself may contribute to moral decline. Their recognition that even more insidious and morally corrosive elements are imbedded in collectivist systems undoubtedly inspires such denial. And this is a major part of the problem: the capitalist-socialist debate has been cast in such dichotomous terms that it has instilled resignation to capitalism's flaws and limited discussions over the relevance of religious principles to economic life. This, in turn, has contributed to the incessant drive toward simplification in economics for the purpose of developing models that enable prediction, which ultimately ends in an anthropological interpretation of humankind that is dangerous to our religious self-understanding. *Homo economicus*, derived either from the rational utility maximizer of neoclassical theory or as the endpoint of Hayek's evolutionary rationalism, stands unchallenged as the most accurate representation of the human person.

No rational theory of human behavior derived from social science can offer a solution, for it is the modern dominance of rationalism that is the problem. Theology would seem to offer the greatest hope, but it must be a theology that exhibits both a holistic and realistic understanding of the human person. While one might agree with Michael Novak that the "theology of economics is at present the least sophisticated branch of theological inquiry,"[97] this assessment seems to discount, as most others have done, Christian economic thought such as that of Reinhold Niebuhr, G. K. Chesterton, and Pope John Paul II. Succeeding chapters will demonstrate that the unique theological economics of these three men offers hope for a redemptive economy capable of sustaining traditional morality and the Christian conception of the human person.

NOTES

1. Hayek's claim that civilization advances through the replacement of old by new "principles" to the disregard of those "indignant moralists" of religious traditions is pertinent here. See Friedrich Hayek, *Law, Legislation and Liberty*, vol. 3, *The Political Order of a Free People*, 2nd ed. (Chicago: University of Chicago Press, 1981), 165–66. See also

"Religion and the Guardians of Tradition," in *The Collected Works of F. A. Hayek*, vol. 1, *The Fatal Conceit: The Errors of Socialism*, ed. W. W. Bartley III (Chicago: University of Chicago Press, 1988), 139–40.

2. The word "inadvertently" is inserted here to reflect the fact that MacIntyre himself does not advocate the liberal solution. His more "republican" answer to the problems plaguing modern society includes a segmentation of mass polities into more manageable, virtuous, and value-consistent communities. He states, "What matters at this stage is the construction of local forms of community within which civility and the intellectual and moral life can be sustained through the new dark ages which are already upon us." Alasdair MacIntyre, *After Virtue: A Study in Moral Theory*, 2nd ed. (Notre Dame, IN: University of Notre Dame Press, 1984), 107, 263.

3. Quoted in an interview with Rodney Clapp, "Where Capitalism and Christianity Meet," *Christianity Today* 27 (February 4, 1983): 27.

4. One recalls Novak's statement, "Hayek's work, both in its genius and in its errors, has been sorely neglected by Catholic social thinkers." See Novak, *Free Persons and the Common Good* (Lanham, MD: Madison Books, 1989), 86. Yet the lack of specificity as to "where Hayek erred" contributes to speculation on the disjunction between Hayekian and Christian views of morality contained in this chapter.

5. Ronald H. Nash, "The Subjective Theory of Economic Value," in *Biblical Principles of Economics: The Foundations*, ed. Richard C. Chewning (Colorado Springs, CO: NavPress, 1989), 84.

6. Positive economics most commonly is defined as the science of economics that records and correlates observed economic phenomena and verifiable cause-effect relationships in the "real world" as Nash describes. By contrast, normative economics takes into account the values held by market participants and allows estimation over "what should be" the consequences of economic behavior.

7. Nash, "The Subjective Theory of Economic Value," 90.

8. Nash, "The Subjective Theory of Economic Value," 90. One notes consistency between Nash's statement and that of Ludwig von Mises that regardless of cultural influences, individuals transact in such ways as to attain the most "favorable physiological conditions possible." In his famous work *Human Action*, Mises observed that while the individual "is capable of dying for a cause," institutions are far less capable of engendering sacrifice. Mises stated, "as soon as a religious community enters the field of political action and tries to deal with problems of social organization, it is bound to take into account earthly concerns, however this may conflict with its dogmas and articles of faith. No religion in its exoteric activities ever ventured to tell people frankly: The realization of our plans for social organization will make you poor and impair your earthly well-being." See Ludwig Mises, *Epistemological Problems of Economics*, trans. George Reisman (Princeton, NJ: D. Van Nostrand Company, 1960), 38; and *Human Action: A Treatise on Economics*, 3rd rev. ed. (Chicago: Henry Regnery Company, 1949), 183–84.

9. Ronald H. Nash, *Social Justice and the Christian Church* (Milford, MI: Mott Media, 1983), 57.

10. Nash, *Social Justice and the Christian Church*, 57 (emphasis author's).

11. Sirico states, "A clear understanding of what is meant by a market economy is rarely grasped. The market, while possessing practical virtues, remains essentially morally neutral, and thus needs a broader framework in order to operate ethically." Robert A. Sirico, "The Mystery and Morality of Markets—Explained!" *Acton Commentary*; available

from the Acton Institute website at www.acton.org/research/comment/comment.html (accessed October 18, 2001).

12. Jean Bethke Elshtain, *Who Are We? Critical Reflections and Hopeful Possibilities* (Grand Rapids, MI: William B. Eerdmans, 2000), 47. Elshtain references Marilynne Robinson who, "in a lively essay on Darwinism, shows the ways in which Darwinian presuppositions fed one school of economics (as the 'dismal' science), namely, the Malthusian school. A constitutive feature of this approach is the insistence that: 'There is no such thing as intrinsic worth. No value inheres in whatever is destroyed, or destructible.'" See Marilynne Robinson, *The Death of Adam* (New York: Houghton Mifflin, 1998), 33; cited in Elshtain, *Who Are We?* 47.

13. Elshtain, *Who Are We?* 47–48.

14. Phillip Yancey, "Why Not Now?" *Christianity Today* 40 (February 5, 1996): 112.

15. Elshtain, *Who Are We?* 59.

16. Staffan Burenstam Linder, *The Harried Leisure Class* (New York: Columbia University Press, 1970), 4, 134.

17. Linder, *The Harried Leisure Class*, 143–44.

18. J. Phillip Wogaman, "Theological Perspectives on Economics," in *Morality of the Market: Religious and Economic Perspectives*, ed. Walter Block, Geoffrey Brennan, and Kenneth Elzinga (Vancouver, BC: Fraser Institute, 1985), 48.

19. See Friedrich A. Hayek, *The Constitution of Liberty* (London: Routledge and Kegan Paul, 1960), 52; quoted in David T. Koyzis, "Progress as an Object of Faith in the Thought of Friedrich A. von Hayek," *Christian Scholars Review* 12 (1983): 146, 147.

20. Novak says that it is "an analytic mistake to view markets solely for their effect on the individual; their role is social." See Michael Novak, *Free Persons and the Common Good* (Lanham, MD: Madison Books, 1989), 105, 107.

21. Michael Novak, *Toward a Theology of the Corporation* (Washington, DC: The American Enterprise Institute, 1990), 57. Novak further confesses that, "like all other regimes, democratic society has inherent weaknesses and maintaining high moral ideals in its central institutions is one of them." Novak, *Business as a Calling: Work and the Examined Life* (New York: The Free Press, 1996), 52; and *The Spirit of Democratic Capitalism* (New York: Simon & Schuster, 1982), 121.

22. Novak, *Business as a Calling*, 13.

23. Novak, *Business as a Calling*, 36.

24. Novak, *Business as a Calling*, 135.

25. The Enron/Andersen scandal became public during the writing of this book in which it was disclosed that the Enron Corporation, with the aid of its auditor, Arthur Andersen LLP, had apparently deceived stockholders and financial analysts regarding its financial condition by concealing massive losses within rather dubiously formed partnerships. Many employees of the company lost much of their retirement savings when these practices were disclosed and the value of the company's stock tumbled. See Novak, *Business as a Calling*, 159. See also "Enron and Immorality," *America* 186 (February 11, 2002): 3.

26. Novak, *Business as a Calling*, 159.

27. Shinn's exploration of Wolf Häfele's theory of "hypotheticality," the idea that the number and magnitude of potential consequences to human action is growing exponentially, thereby leading to increasing uncertainty, was discussed in chapter 4. See Wolf Häfele, "Hypotheticality and the New Challenges: The Pathfinder Role of Nuclear

Energy," *Anticipation* (World Council of Churches) 20 (May 1975), reprinted from *Minerva*, July 1974; cited in Roger Lincoln Shinn, *Forced Options: Social Decisions for the 21st Century* (San Francisco: Harper & Row, 1982), 9.

28. Novak, *The Spirit of Democratic Capitalism*, 69. Novak states, "A capitalist economy brings with it—has as its precondition—a new morality. A capitalist economy is not merely a functional relation to production. It has its own spirit and social logic, conveys new ideals, offers a new set of commandments and prohibitions." See Novak, *Freedom with Justice: Catholic Social Thought and Liberal Institutions* (San Francisco: Harper & Row, 1984), 14.

29. Novak, *The Spirit of Democratic Capitalism* (New York: Simon & Schuster, 1982), 121. Novak is somewhat inconsistent on this point. In other writings he suggests critical interdependence between the elements of his tripartite system. At one point he says that it is the "moral-cultural system [that] is the chief dynamic force behind the rise both of a democratic political system and a liberal economic system." See Novak, *The Spirit of Democratic Capitalism*, 185.

30. Recorded in notes taken from a presentation by Robert Sirico at the Acton Institute's "Toward a Free and Virtuous Society Conference," West Cornwall, Connecticut, November 29, 2001.

31. Sirico presentation at "Toward a Free and Virtuous Society Conference."

32. Sirico, "Free Markets and the Profit of Solidarity"; available from the Acton Institute website at www.acton.org/programs/speeches/freemarkets.html (accessed February 28, 2001).

33. Sirico, "Free Markets and the Profit of Solidarity," 3.

34. Sirico, "Free Markets and the Profit of Solidarity," 3.

35. Gloria L. Zuniga, "Truth in Economic Subjectivism," *Journal of Markets and Morality* 1 (October 1998); available from the Acton Institute Website at www.acton.org/publicat/m_and_m/1998_Oct/zuniga.html (accessed October 15, 2001).

36. Zuniga, "Truth in Economic Subjectivism."

37. Hayek, *The Road to Serfdom* (London: George Routledge & Sons, 1944), 44.

38. Richard John Neuhaus, *Doing Well and Doing Good: The Challenge to the Christian Capitalist* (New York: Doubleday, 1992), 52–53; quoted in Patricia Donohue-White, "Controversy: Does the Free Market Undermine Culture? A Response to D. Eric Schansberg," *Journal of Markets and Morality* 2 (Spring 1999); accessed at Acton website at www.acton.org/publicat/m_and_m/1999_spr/schanberg2.html.

39. Elshtain, *Who Are We?* 45.

40. This conception of opportunity cost is also the reason why Zuniga's illustration using a choice between hats of different colors that presumably cost the same amount does not reflect the moral dimensions of economic decisions. It is true that if there is no cost difference between alternatives, then there often will be no moral dimension to that decision. However, if a red hat costs even one dollar more than a yellow hat, then the decision to purchase the red hat has a moral component for the reason that it is a decision not to use that dollar for some other purpose that likely will not be its moral equivalent.

41. Zuniga, "Truth in Economic Subjectivism."

42. Robert A. Sirico, "Mater et Magistra (1961)," in *A Century of Catholic Social Thought*, ed. George Weigel and Robert Royal (Washington, DC: Ethics and Public Policy Center, 1991). Sirico cites a "representative selection of their works" to substantiate

his claim of the moral concern of the Austrian economists. He lists Wilhelm Röpke, *A Humane Economy* (Chicago: Regnery, 1960); Ludwig von Mises, *Liberalism in the Classical Tradition*, 3rd ed. (San Francisco: Cobden Press, 1985); Henry Hazlitt, *The Foundations of Morality* (Lanham, MD: University Press of America, 1988); and F. A. Hayek, *The Fatal Conceit: The Errors of Socialism* (Chicago: University of Chicago Press, 1988).

43. By contrast with the thought of both Mises and Hayek, Röpke's philosophy exhibited a true appreciation of the importance of theism to social order and a fear of what would fill the void once belief in God has been eradicated by progress and the "enmassment" of culture. See Röpke, *A Humane Economy*, 5, 9.

44. Ludwig von Mises, *Liberalism in the Classical Tradition*, trans. Ralph Raico (Irvington-on-Hudson, NY: Foundation for Economic Education, 1985), 34; quoted in Michael Novak, *Free Persons and the Common Good*, 162.

45. Gabriel J. Zanotti, "Misesian Praxeology and Christian Philosophy," *Journal of Markets and Morality* 1 (March 1998); available from the Acton Institute website at www.acton.org/publicat/m_and_m/1998_Mar/zanotti.html (accessed March 11, 2002).

46. Graham Walker, *The Ethics of F. A. Hayek* (Lanham, MD: University Press of America, 1986), 24.

47. A footnote from this quotation by Hayek in *Rules and Order* explains that the idea of groups "prevailing" does not imply direct competition or clashes between groups in which victors exhibit obvious traits that contribute to their persistence; rather, members of prevailing groups often will not know "to which peculiarity they owe their success." See Hayek, *Law, Legislation and Liberty*, vol. 1, *Rules and Order* (Chicago: University of Chicago Press, 1973), 99n7.

48. Harold Bloom, *The American Religion: The Emergence of the Post-Christian Nation* (New York: Simon & Schuster, 1992), 257.

49. Friedrich A. Hayek, "Religion and the Guardians of Tradition," in *The Fatal Conceit*, 139–40 (emphasis added).

50. As noted in chapter 3, Robert Bellah and the other authors of *Habits of the Heart* observed, "Freedom is perhaps the most resonant, deeply held American value." See Robert Bellah et al., *Habits of the Heart: Individualism and Commitment in American Life* (New York: Harper & Row, 1985), 23.

51. Alfred North Whitehead, *Science and the Modern World* (New York: Macmillan, 1929), 11; quoted in Roger L. Shinn, "From Theology to Social Decisions—and Return," in *Morality of the Market: Religious and Economic Perspectives*, ed. Walter Block, Geoffrey Brennan, and Kenneth Elzinga, 175–95 (Vancouver, BC: Fraser Institute, 1985), 176.

52. Robert A. Sirico, "Of Markets and Morality," *Religion & Liberty* 7 (July–August 1997); available from the Acton Institute website at www.acton.org/publicat/randl/97jul_aug/sirico.html (accessed March 11, 2002).

53. Sirico, "Of Markets and Morality."

54. Sirico, "Of Markets and Morality."

55. Public choice theory, which essentially is the application of rational choice models in the context of the public sector, originated in the work of Nobel Prize–winning economist James Buchanan and his colleague Gordon Tullock at Virginia Polytechnic Institute and State University in the 1960s. For a summary of public choice theory, see Tibor R. Machan, "Public Choice Theory: Not the Whole Story"; available from the

Liberty Haven website at www.libertyhaven.com/theoreticalandphilosophicalissues/publicchoice/publictheory.html.

56. Robert H. Nelson, "Economic Religion versus Christian Values," *Journal of Markets and Morality* 1 (October 1998); available from Acton Institute website at www.acton.org/publicat/m_and_m/1998_Oct/nelson.html (accessed February 20, 2002).

57. Nelson, "Economic Religion versus Christian Values."

58. Nelson notes, "Economics formerly observed what might be called 'stopping points'—demarcations of subject areas where economic rationality was not considered to operate. The Chicago project, in essence, seeks to abolish all stopping points. For those who believe that there are things in life that are sacred and beyond the workings of self-interested rationality, the Chicago project sees such attitudes as part of a superficial ideological 'cover' for the underlying true workings of economic forces." See Nelson, "Economic Religion versus Christian Values."

59. Nelson, "Economic Religion versus Christian Values."

60. Gary Becker, *A Treatise on the Family* (Cambridge, MA: Harvard University Press, 1981), 194. For a summary of Becker's ideas on altruism in families, see the section of his book entitled "Altruism in the Family and Selfishness in the Marketplace," in *A Treatise on the Family*, 194–98.

61. Becker, *A Treatise on the Family*, 93–112, 38–65.

62. Nelson states, "Economics offers a worldview of its own, or multiple worldviews, according to the specific economic school. Economics is thus part of an overall value system, really a theology of a secular sort." See Nelson, "Economic Religion versus Christian Values."

63. See Nelson, "Economic Religion versus Christian Values."

64. Nelson also suggests that more active engagement by religious scholars in the economics profession might lead to the development of many more schools of economic thought to include "a Catholic economics, a Lutheran economics, a Calvinist economics, an Islamic economics, a Buddhist economics, and so forth." See Nelson, "Economic Religion versus Christian Values."

65. Michael Novak, "Economics as Humanism," *First Things* 76 (October 1997): 18.

66. Jesus M. Zaratiegui, "The Imperialism of Economics over Ethics," *Journal of Markets and Morality* 2 (Fall 1999); available from the Acton Institute website at www.acton.org/publicat/m_and_m/1999_fall/zaratiegui.html (accessed January 22, 2002).

67. Nelson, "Economic Religion versus Christian Values." Transaction costs in economics typically are defined as those costs associated with the transferal of property rights via an exchange transaction. "Free riders" are third-party beneficiaries to exchange who incur no direct costs themselves. Public television viewers who do not contribute to public television stations are commonly used as examples of free riders. For an interesting treatment of the free rider problem in the context of religion, see Joe L. Wallis, "Church Ministry and the Free Rider Problem: Religious Liberty and Disestablishment," *The American Journal of Economics and Sociology* 50 (April 1991): 183–96.

68. Hayek observed, "The belief in spirits that punished transgressors led [behavioral] restraints to be preserved." See Hayek, "Religion and the Guardians of Tradition," 136.

69. Dewey, *A Common Faith* (New Haven, CT: Yale University Press, 1934), 62.

70. Quoted in an interview article with Rodney Clapp, "Where Capitalism and Christianity Meet," *Christianity Today* 27 (February 4, 1983): 27. In the same article, Clapp states that Gilder "shifts the blame [for moral deterioration] to secular humanism

and the failure of moral guardians such as the church. He will not allow that some flaw within the economic system itself might lead to an unjust distribution of wealth or the dissolution of society's moral discipline." See Clapp, "Where Capitalism and Christianity Meet," 24.

71. Novak, *Business as a Calling*, 159 (emphasis author's). Aside from the seeming inadvisability of placing responsibility for the protection of traditional values on advertisers, Novak's statement also lacks economic logic. Advertisers earn their keep in the American economic system by being in tune with consumer values and not by constructing elaborate plots to reinvent them. The market responsiveness of which Novak and other conservatives are so admiring in other contexts is the strongest argument against their contention that advertising actively works to subvert the values of the American people.

72. Novak notes that virtually every papal reference to liberalism (in its classical usage) prior to John Paul II was pejorative. A critical flaw of the papal tradition is that it is "clearer in what it condemns than in what it commends." See Novak, *Freedom with Justice: Catholic Social Thought and Liberal Institutions* (San Francisco: Harper & Row, 1984), 29, 33–35.

73. Milton Friedman, *Capitalism and Freedom*; quoted in Novak, *Business as a Calling*, 140–41.

74. Michael Novak, *The Catholic Ethic and the Spirit of Capitalism* (New York: The Free Press, 1993), 205.

75. Novak, *The Catholic Ethic and the Spirit of Capitalism*, 212.

76. Novak, *The Catholic Ethic and the Spirit of Capitalism*, 212.

77. Father Sirico describes this general empowerment of mainstream culture by the market in an excellent article on the DreamWorks production of the movie *The Prince of Egypt*. Sirico lauds the faithfulness of the production to the biblical story and is hopeful that the movie will "forecast a return to faith in popular culture." Moreover, the success of the production leads him back to a basic principle of the market economy that "generally, the market reflects rather than leads the culture." See Sirico, "The Return of Faith on Film," *Religion & Liberty* 9 (January–February 1999); available from the Acton Institute website at www.acton.org/publicat/randl/99jan_feb/sirico.html.

78. Röpke, *A Humane Economy*, 57.

79. D. Stephen Long, *Divine Economy: Theology and the Market* (New York: Routledge, 2000), 16.

80. Jean-Baptiste Say, *A Treatise on Political Economy, or the Production, Distribution, and Consumption of Wealth*, Reprints of Economic Classics Series (New York: Augustus M. Kelley, 1964), 388.

81. Say, *A Treatise on Political Economy*, 390. It is recognized that Say's law is not being used in exactly the way he intended. Say understood that value inheres in the individual consumer, yet he recognized that the system tended toward a clearing of the "cycle" of goods such that wealth can be expanded. As an economic theorist, Say is a transitional figure between the classical view of value inhering in products themselves and the Austrian understanding that all value is derived from the subjective judgments of consumers.

82. Say, *A Treatise on Political Economy*, 391.

83. Comments taken from Doug Bandow's presentation at the Acton Institute's "Toward a Free and Virtuous Society" conference in West Cornwall, Connecticut, December 1, 2001.

84. Bandow's presentation at the Acton Institute's "Toward a Free and Virtuous Society."

85. Robert H. Bork, "Hard Truths about the Culture War," *First Things* 54 (June–July 1995): 20.

86. Bork, "Hard Truths about the Culture War."

87. Wuthnow's recognition of most Americans' belief in the market as an essentially moral institution was noted in chapter 2. See Robert Wuthnow, *The Restructuring of American Religion: Society and Faith since World War II* (Princeton, NJ: Princeton University Press, 1988), 263.

88. Bork, "Hard Truths about the Culture War," 21.

89. Novak, *The Spirit of Democratic Capitalism*, 140.

90. From a comment by Sirico in *The Theology of Welfare: Protestants, Catholics, & Jews in Conversation about Welfare*, ed. John G. West Jr. and Sonja E. West (Lanham, MD: University Press of America, 2000), 68.

91. In fairness, President Bush also called upon Americans to commit to service in their communities. Yet, a frequent comment made not only by the president but also by other politicians and dignitaries was that Americans should go about their lives as usual, enjoying travel, entertainment, shopping, and other activities as consumers. For more on the president's comments, see "Soothing Words: In Speech, Bush Seeks to Reassure Nation, Urges Security Volunteers," *ABC News* (November 8, 2001); available at http://more.abcnews.go.com/sections/politics/dailynews/bushspeech011108.html.

92. Robert J. Ross and Kent C. Trachte, *Global Capitalism: The New Leviathan* (Albany: State University of New York Press, 1990), 2–3; quoted in D. Stephen Long, "A Global Market—A Catholic Church: The New Political (Ir)realism," *Theology Today* 52 (October 1995): 360.

93. Quoted in Francis Fukuyama, *The End of History and the Last Man* (New York: The Free Press, 1992), 169.

94. John Gray, *Hayek on Liberty* (Oxford: Basil Blackwell Publishers, 1984), 40.

95. Röpke stated, "The curse of commercialization is that it results in the standards of the market spreading into regions which should remain beyond supply and demand. This vitiates the true purposes, dignity, and savor of life and thereby makes it unbearably ugly, undignified, and dull." See Röpke, *A Humane Economy*, 128–29.

96. Ezra J. Mishan, "Religion, Culture, and Technology," in *Morality of the Market: Religious and Economic Perspectives*, ed. Walter Block, Geoffrey Brennan, and Kenneth Elzinga, 279–312 (Vancouver, BC: Fraser Institute, 1985), 304.

97. Novak, *Toward a Theology of the Corporation*, 27. Novak has also stated, "Looking ahead to the twenty-first century, we can expect to see the disciplines of economics and theology (and philosophy) come closer together in the study of many common materials—especially those of human choice." See Novak, *The Catholic Ethic and the Spirit of Capitalism*, 92.

II

ENVISIONING A MORALLY
REDEMPTIVE ECONOMY

6

REINHOLD NIEBUHR'S
ECONOMIC REALISM

American Christians have struggled mightily to say something distinctively Christian about economic life. Chapter 2 chronicled the history
of this struggle from the "Christian republicanism" of the American founding to the "clerical laissez-faire" period of the American frontier to the era
of the Social Gospel and Christian socialism at the turn of the twentieth
century. More recently, Christian libertarians and neoconservatives found
what they believe to be common principles between their faith and the theories of Austrian liberalism. Each of these unique syntheses has attempted
to cast a Christian light on secular ideas of social organization in the hope
that a resolution of tensions between religious and economic life will yield
the fullest possible actualization both of the Christian community and the
individual in the context of a moral and prosperous society.

Protagonists of past attempts at "theological economics" have had the
best of intentions. For, if the Christian religion is indeed the truest expression of the nature of the person and of her relationship to the Creator and
to her fellow human beings, then an economic system that draws upon that
wisdom logically would enable the greatest possible fulfillment of the individual and contribute social structures that are morally (and perhaps even
materially) more sustainable than systems founded on less accurate religious
and philosophical worldviews. However, chapter 2 demonstrated significant
problems in past attempts to integrate Christian theology with economic
philosophy that ultimately undermined these visions. Despite dreams of
moral and economically productive societies, efforts to wed Christian doctrine with economic principles inevitably have devolved into Christian
sanctification or vilification of the social order and have often resulted in a
decline of the church's prophetic voice on social issues.

This chapter will demonstrate that the economic realism of Reinhold Niebuhr offers something distinctively different from past attempts at synthesis for its very *lack* of a unified theory of religious and economic life. Niebuhr's insistence that "there is no 'Christian' political or economic system,"[1] as reinforced by the central premise of his realism that "ideal" social structures are not possible in history, enables a starting point that departs radically from other efforts at "Christian economics." Niebuhr's understanding of the Christian person as both spirit and creature whose fulfillment is realized in community and whose transcendent freedom "accounts for both the creative and destructive possibilities in human history,"[2] offers a foundation capable of avoiding the collectivist utopianism of Christian socialists and the subjectivist utopianism of Christian libertarians:

> To know both the law of love as the final standard and the law of self-love as a persistent force is to enable the Christian to have a foundation for a pragmatic ethic in which power and self-interest are used, beguiled, harnessed and deflected for the ultimate end of establishing the highest and most inclusive community of justice and order.[3]

Niebuhr's development as a social theorist was, by his own description, "torturous" in its necessary adjustment from his "original Protestant heritage of individualism and perfectionism through a world depression and two world wars to the . . . realities of a highly technical and collective culture."[4] He vacillated throughout his life in assessing the justice and moral sustainability of various social orders, yet the depth of his convictions insisted that his philosophical wavering was never whimsical. He altered his views only after exhaustive examinations of the virtues and vices of each system that focused on their respective contributions to a Christian conception of the good. If nothing else, the breadth of his social analysis must be commended. Niebuhr's considerable intellect, his remarkable ability to abstract and synthesize, his unique conception of history, and his undeniable determination to resolve the unresolvable attest to the profundity of his social thought.

All attempts to "bring forth Niebuhr" and to use him for the construction of any social model face the unavoidable charge that he was no more than an artful and eloquent critic of society. Niebuhr's pessimistic philosophy and the dialectical nature of his criticism suggest to some that nothing can be drawn from his work other than the utter hopelessness of humankind in history as ameliorated only by the faith in an ultimate redemption that transcends that history. This chapter will demonstrate that

Niebuhr was no brooding cynic. Cynicism was never a part of Niebuhr's realism, for he exhibited remarkable energy in the pursuit of uniquely Christian answers to society's most intractable problems. Ironically, Niebuhr's realization of the hopelessness of humankind's situation in nature and history—the very pessimism by which his critics attempt to render his work unusable—will be presented as an invaluable tool for the construction of social structures that are uniquely capable of sustaining Christian morality.

Attempts to co-opt the thought of Reinhold Niebuhr inevitably elicit another question that has stymied past efforts to build upon his work: which Niebuhr? Does one use the youthful and liberal idealist who became disillusioned with the ethics of industrial capitalism through his confrontations with Henry Ford's corporate empire? Or should one invoke Niebuhr the Christian socialist, leader of the Fellowship of Socialist Christians and expert in the use of Marxist theory to reveal the injustices of liberal culture? Perhaps Niebuhr the elder statesman of Christian realism, resigned to capitalism's material and moral superiority to socialism but disillusioned by its near exclusive reliance on self-interest to direct society to the "good," is a more proven resource. His biographer Richard Wightman Fox has suggested the futility of attempts to bring Niebuhr into contemporary discourse and speculate on what he would say about the myriad cultural issues that confront us. Fox states that Niebuhr's "social and political views cannot be ripped out of their context and pressed into service today. It is futile to wonder what he would have said today about Central American revolutions, about 'free enterprise,' about the women's movement. He would have evolved so much, so unpredictably, over the last quarter-century."[5]

But one might take issue with Fox and suggest that if the core of Niebuhr's social philosophy can be shown to be consistent despite changes in his life experience and his political allegiances, then those "timeless" principles may well be useful today in the development of social philosophy. Niebuhr's intellectual development spanned a remarkable period of history that witnessed the Industrial Revolution, both world wars, the Great Depression, and the Cold War. That same period saw the rise of the Social Gospel and the Gospel of Wealth, Christian socialism, the Marxist ideology of liberation theology, and the beginnings of Christian libertarian movements. Despite his drift between liberal and collectivist ideals, Niebuhr's social thought demonstrates remarkable consistency for someone so politically malleable at the surface. He offered insightful critiques of socialism from the capitalist perspective and capitalism from the socialist perspective, and he never shied away from criticism of both capitalism and socialism from the Christian perspective. Yet

he relied upon consistent principles for those criticisms that reveal a frequently overlooked uniformity to his social philosophy.[6]

REINHOLD NIEBUHR'S ECONOMIC DEVELOPMENT

It is difficult to pinpoint the exact stage of Reinhold Niebuhr's intellectual
development at which he became a serious economic thinker. Even as a boy
of twelve or thirteen, he was highly industrious, working before and after
school at Denger's Grocery Store in his boyhood town of Lincoln, Illinois.[7]
Reinhold's intellectual gifts were already evident by the time his father,
Gustav, died in 1913 and financial responsibilities within the Niebuhr family shifted. Initially, that shift was onto the shoulders of his older brother
Walter who had achieved some success as a newspaper reporter and editor.[8]
Reinhold's responsibilities, too, were elevated by his father's passing, but
those duties were directed toward preserving his father's ministry at the small
St. John's Church in Lincoln and later to his studies at Yale Divinity School.

The pulpit offered Niebuhr an opportunity to reflect on more than the
Christian theology and history that he had learned at Yale. He ran headlong
into hard economic realities that provided Niebuhr an opportunity to employ an uncommon social discernment. He recognized the flaws in secular
solutions to the "social problem" that resulted from an idealistic view of human nature and a simplistic reliance on human reason or some "natural harmony" to rectify injustices. Fox suggests that for young Pastor Niebuhr, the
paradox between the ideal and the real in economic life was most evident
in the seemingly unending struggle for power between capital and labor:

> The raging battle between capital and labor was caused, [Niebuhr] as-
> serted, by human selfishness. . . . But socialism was no better than cap-
> italism since it merely put the selfishness of the "underclass" in place of
> that of the "upper classes." As long as most people were selfish there
> could be no solution. Capitalists would have to "voluntarily release some
> of their fat profits, . . . to lose themselves for their employees." On both
> sides love was the answer. The twenty-one-year-old Lincoln pastor be-
> lieved love and self-sacrifice to be both the essence of the individual's
> faith and the basis of a social program—liberal sentiments that he would
> later deride as "utopian."[9]

Niebuhr believed that economic battles between social classes were
due principally to human selfishness, and collective efforts to resolve these
conflicts and their resultant injustices commonly created other injustices.

Where Fox perhaps exaggerates Niebuhr's position is in his statement that "on both sides love was the answer"; for, although Niebuhr preached the law of love vigorously from the pulpit, it is debatable whether he ever truly believed that a society built on Christian love was a realizable goal in human history. Niebuhr inherited much of the liberal optimism of the Social Gospel, yet he recognized the flawed feudal, mercantile, capitalist, and socialist economic orders that history had produced. Each resulted in varying degrees of social justice, yet all had fallen short of the Christian ideal of love, as Henry Clark observes:

> From the very beginning, Niebuhr was not exactly typical of the Social Gospel preachers, and as time passed and his tendency to be both empirical and pragmatic asserted itself, he was increasingly inclined to define both ends and means in a significantly different way. Like [Walter] Rauschenbusch, Niebuhr realized that class consciousness was an essential ingredient in a realistic social analysis, and he knew that countervailing power would be required to secure results which preaching the love of Jesus to the bosses would never achieve.[10]

While Niebuhr understood that all social systems fall short of the Christian ideal, he was equally convinced that some fall shorter than others. It was in light of this conviction that the variability in his social philosophy ultimately would be exposed. However, even during the most Marxist stage of Niebuhr's economic development, he was never utopian about the justice that could be achieved through the socialization of property. Likewise, during his liberal periods, Niebuhr was equally if not more skeptical about the proposition that the unfettered operation of the free market could bring about justice. At various times in his life, he was more or less sanguine that particular economic systems could engender something approaching a Christian "harmony of life with life," and he came to characterize love as an unattainable ethos for any political or economic order; yet, as an ideal, it was indispensable to prevent the drift toward some naturalistic or totalitarian system.[11]

Whatever idealism may have existed in Niebuhr's early social philosophy undoubtedly was tempered during his thirteen-year pastorate at the Bethel Evangelical Church in Detroit, Michigan. Niebuhr arrived at Bethel immediately following his graduation from Yale in 1915. Ironically, Niebuhr's ambitions for the church and his determination to expand it beyond its near exclusive German-American ethnic makeup led to a more willing embrace of American capitalism.[12] Fox observes the paradox in Niebuhr's criticism of commercial society from the pulpit and his willingness to employ commercial methods in his practical duties as minister, noting that while Niebuhr denounced "the spirit of commercialism [that] has invaded the church and vulgarized it," he also made efficient use of the advertising medium to promote Bethel's services and his own sermons to the wider Detroit community.[13]

The global backdrop to Reinhold Niebuhr's economic education in Detroit was the First World War. Like those of many of his contemporaries, Niebuhr's political and economic ideas were hardened in the collective disillusionment spawned by global conflict. The reality that national egotism could produce brutality on such a horrific scale directly challenged his youthful, liberal idealism. His biographer Ronald Stone believes that Niebuhr came to view the Great War like most conflicts, as a battle for economic rather than political or military supremacy: "The primary causes of [World War I] were regarded as economic. Possible economic gains for the nation were not worthy of the sacrifice of individuals."[14]

Niebuhr never gave up the idea that, in general, political discourse exhibits a more exalted character vis-à-vis the more raw and instinctual expressions of the economic realm. His statement that "political society is a more self-conscious and a more conscious society than economic society"[15] suggested that the idealism so prevalent in political philosophy tended to obscure the more base realities of economic life. People of privilege would forever attempt to use political institutions to secure their material advantages while the underclass would just as consistently seek redress of perceived injustices through those same political structures. This realization meant for Niebuhr that the economic realm forever would have greater difficulty than the political in maintaining the idealism that is critical in assessing the virtues and limitations of myriad "realisms" that emerge in history. This belief that some ideal must be retained as an instrument for the assessment of the real is a crucial aspect of Christian realism that is frequently misunderstood. Only through perpetual comparison with religious or even lesser ideals can "real" political and economic systems be assessed.

Lack of understanding of this relationship between the ideal and real in Niebuhr's philosophy has led to distortions of his social thought. Niebuhr consistently utilized this dialectical method of social analysis, but both admirers and critics have often mistaken elements of his writing as foundational; thus they tend to overstate his position as a liberal, socialist, conservative, or whatever label they attempt to apply. A sampling of economic ideas from various periods of Niebuhr's life reveals profound questions about the justice that can be attained through the market in his supposedly "liberal" periods, just as it reveals sharp criticisms of what might be accomplished through the socialization of property during his socialist phase. In *Reflections on the End of an Era* (1934), Niebuhr's self-described "most Marxist work," he criticizes both the "mechanistic collectivism" of communism *and* the "mechanistic individualism" of liberal society.[16] He observed that both fall short of the "organic collectivism" that is attainable in social organization, the most tangible approximation of which he observed in the class relations of Great Britain.[17]

For Niebuhr, the mechanical relations of American society in the 1920s, as dictated by its intense individualism, were particularly repugnant. The hard realities that Niebuhr experienced as a minister in Detroit caused him to ratchet down his social optimism. Stone casts Henry Ford as the protagonist of that change. Stone observes that Ford "became a symbol to Niebuhr of America's technical genius and social ineptitude."[18] Ford represented the worst of the capitalist class, the very reason for the rise of socialism, and a classic example of the boundlessness of economic interest. He also symbolized the ability of the establishment to mask the often ugly economic relations of early industrial capitalism. Charles C. Brown, in his book *Niebuhr and His Age*, captures the tension between the two men that would forever shape Niebuhr's worldview:

> It was the heyday of Henry Ford, who became a folk hero as his Model T rolled off the assembly lines in Detroit and put the nation on wheels. Less visible to the public were the hardships of Ford workers and their families. After visiting the coke oven in the Rouge plant, five miles southwest of Bethel Church, Niebuhr wrote in his diary: "The heat was terrific. The men seemed weary. . . . Their sweat and their dull pain are part of the price paid for the fine cars we all run." In pieces for *Christian Century* readers in 1926 and 1927, he presented facts contradicting Ford's self-promoted image as a benevolent industrialist: his supposedly generous five dollars a day obscured assembly-line speedups that exhausted older men, retooling layoffs without pay, the absence of any pensions, the discharging of sick employees and then rehiring them at beginning wages, and the burdening of local charities with Ford workers unable to make ends meet.[19]

Niebuhr believed that the credit given Ford for benevolence toward his employees was wildly exaggerated. His own research revealed the less flattering truth—while Ford did raise wages, in other ways he created misery for his workers.[20] Thus, from the perch of his pastorate in Detroit, Niebuhr was able to observe two phenomena that drastically influenced his economic thought: "the shortcomings of Henry Ford's widely acclaimed 'benevolent paternalism' and the weaknesses of the Church as a social change agent."[21]

The Period of Economic Radicalism

Realization of the powerlessness of idealism against the intractability and ruthlessness of economic power prompted a radical shift in Niebuhr's economic philosophy. It is also likely that his move to New York City's Union Theological Seminary in 1928 freed Niebuhr somewhat from his intense devotion to local causes and enabled him to reflect in the abstract on some of the hard economic realities he had witnessed in Detroit. Niebuhr published an article immediately preceding the start of the Great Depression that, for the first time, offered a rather systematic account of capitalism's flaws. In "Why We Need a New Economic Order," Niebuhr exhibited an uncanny grasp of economic theory for a theologian untrained in the social sciences. Paul Merkley derives from that essay some of the influences that contributed to Niebuhr's largely self-taught economic education:

> Niebuhr had obviously read and understood the history of capitalism's origins. We have already noted his acquaintance with the works of Max Weber. . . . There is as well a large debt obvious to R. H. Tawney's *Religion and the Rise of Capitalism*.[22] One could hardly hope for a clearer description of the fundamental flaw of the American economy which would lead in a very few months to the great depression: "As industry continues to perfect its machines it arrives at a production capacity which the wants of the community cannot absorb except the buying power of the workers is greatly increased. . . . With his present buying power the worker cannot absorb the products of his own toil. . . . When competitive industry deals with this problem it easily aggravates it, for it meets the problem of restricted markets by lowering wages and cutting wages, thus further restricting the buying power of the public."[23]

Niebuhr's engagement with the structural flaws that had precipitated worldwide economic depression led him directly into his radical period of social philosophy and activism in the 1930s. The breadth of his reading and scholarly interests introduced him to the theories of British economist John Maynard Keynes, who had identified the "demand problem" in the specific case of Germany during the reparation period between the world wars. Niebuhr grasped the underlying causes of global economic problems, some of which were unrecognized by professional economists. However, his dire reflections on capitalism in the aftermath of the Great Depression caused him to exaggerate certain of its flaws. For example, although he rightly characterized "inadequate aggregate demand" as the principal cause of the Depression, he went further by drawing the Marxian conclusion that this condition was endemic to the capitalist system, stating, "Mass production requires mass consumption; and capitalism is unable to provide mass consumption."[24]

Niebuhr's conclusion that an asynchronous condition existed between capitalism's ability to produce goods and its capacity to generate (and distribute) the wealth necessary to consume them must be viewed in its historical context. First, this was an accurate assessment of the immediate problems of the 1930s and easily lent itself to generalization. Second, the fact that many European economists were arriving at much the same conclusion would tend to reinforce the convictions of a theologian who dabbled (though quite adroitly) in economic theory. Finally, industrial capitalism was still a relatively new cultural phenomenon in the 1930s and simply had never demonstrated the ability to achieve a distribution of wealth that would enable consumption to match the increasing levels of output that were being generated in nations with vast resources like the United States. Whatever the reasons, by the early 1930s, Niebuhr, like other social thinkers, tended to view this flaw in capitalism as endemic and turned for a potential solution to the Marxism that had begun to make significant inroads in European culture.

That Niebuhr warmed to the economic theories of Karl Marx early in the 1930s is unquestioned; however, the extent to which he courted Marxist ideas is the subject of much debate. Merkley, for example, places considerable emphasis on Niebuhr's Marxist leanings, stating that after the dissolution of one of Niebuhr's favorite sounding boards, the journal *World Tomorrow*, "the Christian Marxist message was carried over to a new paper founded by Reinhold Niebuhr in 1936, called *Radical Religion*."[25] Indeed, Niebuhr's journal (which actually printed its first edition in Autumn 1935) exhibited a decidedly Marxist taint. Its first issue included articles like "Is Religion Counter-Revolutionary?" by Niebuhr himself, Paul Tillich's "Marx and the Prophetic Tradition," and "A Labor Party" by Francis Henson. Niebuhr saw Marxism as an insightful platform from which to launch his criticisms of capitalist culture, and he adopted a Marxist paradigm and used decidedly Marxist language in his critiques.

During his qualified embrace of Marxist philosophy in the 1930s, Niebuhr always recognized the flaws in its assessment of human nature and its exaggeration of property as the near exclusive source of injustice in society. Niebuhr's attraction to Marxist social theory never approached the utopianism of other so-called Christian Marxists such as Harry F. Ward. In fact, Merkley suggests that Niebuhr was not so much smitten by Marxism for its social "truths" or utopian aspirations as he was drawn to it by the "religious" level of commitment that it inspired in its adherents.[26] Niebuhr's pessimism simply favored what he considered to be Marxism's more somber view of humankind's historic struggle.

Niebuhr's attraction to Marxist philosophy stemmed from his search for a platform from which to critique the causes both of World War I and the Depression. His belief in the underlying *economic* causes of wars, as Stone observed, and his recognition of the intractability of human selfishness pushed his thought toward the socialization of property, not as a panacea, but as an inevitable outcome for industrial societies. In his article "Socialism and Christianity," written in 1931, Niebuhr was even more condemnatory toward what he saw as the prime offending institution of industrial capitalism:

> The chief root of economic and social inequality in the present social order is the unqualified right of private property, sanctified by law and custom and made irrelevant by the facts of contemporary civilization. The absolute right of private property has been made irrelevant because a factory in which a thousand men work is not in fact private property. It represents a social process which affects the weal and woe of many people; and society is therefore bound to interfere in more and more ambitious terms with the "freedom" of the owner in the interest of the many whose welfare depends upon the manner in which this social process is managed.[27]

The complexity in Niebuhr's conception of property is significant. It necessitated that he reject any "absolute" right to private property as commonly advocated by the conservatives, yet it was also the reason why Niebuhr never became convinced that the socialization of property could overcome the injustices that he had observed as a pastor in Detroit. The sinful self stands in opposition to all efforts to achieve justice; collective ownership of property can neither tame the transcendent will nor eradicate the sin resulting from it. Still, Niebuhr's optimism about the prospects for political and economic remedies to social problems undoubtedly peaked during his Christian socialist period in the 1930s. At that time, he was at the center of reform efforts by Christians who were convinced that socialism was inherently more compatible with the spirit of the gospels than was capitalism. One such group was the Fellowship of Socialist Christians (FSC), a successor organization to the Fellowship for a Christian Social Order that had formed around a nucleus of gifted Christian social thinkers, including YMCA "social evangelist" Sherwood Eddy.[28] Added to the ranks of the FSC in 1930 and 1931 were Niebuhr and fellow socialist Christians John Bennett, Roswell Barnes, Francis Henson, and Frank Wilson.[29] As Fox observes of Niebuhr's affiliation with the FSC, "Niebuhr *was* the FSC: head organizer, editorial director, guiding spirit, perennial leader by silent acclamation."[30]

Niebuhr's emerging realism, however, precluded a wholehearted embrace of socialist philosophy. The pragmatism of his social thought required that he adjust to changing political and economic realities. The death of Niebuhr's socialist convictions may have been presaged in a letter from his brother Richard in September 1936, in which Richard informed his brother of the reasons why he was resigning his membership in the Socialist Party. In the letter, Richard stated,

> I am a bourgeois, I make my life by capitalism, I live like a bourgeois, I think like one and I am in [the] wrong. That doesn't make the proletarian right by a long shot. And my business is not to try to change sides but to admit that I am wrong, to live in daily repentance, and to know that something is happening all the time whether or not I "do anything about it."[31]

Although Reinhold Niebuhr would continue his membership in the Socialist Party until 1940, by the late 1930s, he had already begun an ideological transition from Christian socialism to the progressivist liberalism of Franklin Delano Roosevelt's New Deal.

The Moderating Influence of the New Deal

From its inception, Reinhold Niebuhr had been a critic of virtually everything that Franklin Roosevelt's administration had proposed for economic relief. As late as 1938, Niebuhr wrote that Roosevelt's "program reveals how impossible it is to heal the ills of modern capitalism within the presuppositions of capitalism itself."[32] Yet, despite his protests of Roosevelt's progressive policies in *Radical Religion* and elsewhere, the tide began to change around 1940. Niebuhr began to discern the possibility of a "third way" to materially and morally sustainable growth through the progressivist agenda of an administration that he once labeled "brazenly dishonest."[33] Brown notes that by the early 1940s, Niebuhr "saw the New Deal, especially its labor laws and welfare measures, had significantly reformed American capitalism, and thereafter he became a persuasive apologist for Roosevelt's mixed economy as more just and realistic than Marxism or laissez-faire."[34]

Despite his earlier criticisms, the New Deal ultimately appealed to Niebuhr for obvious reasons. It required American Christians and other citizens to engage the "creative center" of life with the myriad resources available to navigate the problems of a complex industrial society. In a sense, the New Deal was a formal rejection of the utopianism both of socialists and conservatives. Roosevelt's plan necessitated intervention to correct the injustices resulting either from market outcomes or from previous government attempts to arbitrate conflicts over rights and resources. It was more realistic than either socialism or laissez-faire capitalism because it reflected that neither central planning nor the market was a total solution; checks and balances were necessary to correct injustices that emerged from a too-pure reliance on either method of social organization.

The influence of Roosevelt's policies on Niebuhr's social thought is evidenced by the fact that he had clearly broken all political ties with socialism by 1944. Moreover, 1944 was the year in which Niebuhr wrote his most "economic" treatise, *The Children of Light and the Children of Darkness.* The book's thesis became a defining principle of Christian realism with its assertion that both liberals and Marxists fall into the same category as "children of light." Liberals demonstrate a naive optimism "in the possibility of achieving an easy resolution of the tension and conflict between self-interest and the general interest," while Marxists believe that "after the triumph of the lower classes of society, a new society would emerge in which exactly that kind of harmony between all social forces would be established."[35] Niebuhr expertly interlaced theological and economic principles to make his case. He exposed the common philosophical flaws of Marxism and capitalism, noting that both expose "the error of a too great reliance upon the human capacity for transcendence over self-interest."[36] More egregious and potentially destructive was "their common effort to understand man without considering the final dimension of his spirit; his transcendent freedom over both the natural and historical process in which he is involved."[37]

In *The Children of Light,* Niebuhr attempted to ground a theory of property—the commercial institution that he believed even as an "ex-socialist" to be at the center of most economic conflicts—in the Christian doctrine of the "Fall of Man":

> The Christian, as the Stoic, theory presupposes an ideal possibility of a perfect accord between life and life which would make a sharp distinction between "mine" and "thine" unnecessary. The sinful selfishness of

men, however, had destroyed this ideal possibility and made exclusive possession the only safeguard against the tendency of men to take advantage of one another. Such a theory has the advantage of viewing the "right" of property with circumspection and of justifying it only relatively and not absolutely.[38]

Niebuhr's complex theory of property and his recognition of its social character led him to conclude that as opposed to past economic conflicts, modern struggles are not competitions over self-preservation but rather "conflicts of rival lusts and ambitions."[39] This observation spoils utopian aspirations on both sides, for Marxism "expects men to be as tame and social on the other side of the revolution as Adam Smith and Jeremy Bentham thought them to be tame and prudential on this side of the revolution."[40] Niebuhr insisted that there can be no final resolution of the social problem, for a "conservative class which makes 'free enterprise' the final good of the community, and a radical class which mistakes some proximate solution of the economic problem for the ultimate solution of every issue of life, are equally perilous to the peace of the community and to the preservation of democracy."[41] This pessimism led Niebuhr to posit the necessity of a political and economic "third way" for the Christian that avoids utopian aspirations and denies the possibility of natural harmonies in the social order forged either by the market or by systems of central planning.

In a 1949 essay written as a defense of an economic position paper produced by the World Council of Churches in Amsterdam, Niebuhr reinforced his view of the common and foundational flaws of both capitalism and socialism. He noted the false promises of both systems, where "one made the promise that justice would be an inevitable by-product of freedom and the other that freedom would be an inevitable by-product of the socialization of property."[42] More novel, however, was Niebuhr's contention that a "cult of freedom" was forming in American culture that sought to transform liberty from a political to a "religious" value. Niebuhr stated that the "very secular idea" that "when each man seeks his own he serves the commonweal" is the conception "which lies at the foundation of America's uncritical devotion to freedom and its uncritical belief that justice flows automatically from freedom."[43] The Austrian philosophers were among those who constituted the "cult" and who proselytized by spreading fear of the "slippery slope" toward collectivism that resulted from socially constructivist policies. Niebuhr stated, "The creative middle ground is always rejected on the ground that any venture in the direction of planning will start us on the slippery slope toward communism." He referred to a pamphlet by The Foundation for Economic Education in which Austrian economist Henry Hazlitt declared that to reject laissez-faire is to reject the free market.[44]

Niebuhr's essay, "The Cult of Freedom," also laid out principles to support his contention that the potential for injustice is greater in socialist than in capitalist society. Niebuhr attributed this difference to those "vast concentrations of power, which under capitalism are mainly economic and under communism are both political and economic."[45] Tolerable economic inequalities are more desirable than government attempts to force equality, for "Christianity has long known, as Marxism does not, that there must be functional inequalities in society and that inequalities of reward may also be necessary to incite men to full performance of their function."[46] These conclusions contributed to Niebuhr's rebirth as a political and economic "realist" in the late 1940s.

The Maturing of Niebuhr's Realistic Liberalism

Development of Niebuhr's realism in the direction of more liberal ideals continued throughout the 1940s and 1950s and was no doubt reinforced by the intensity of the Cold War. Niebuhr contended that the global standoff between Russia and the West was "a conflict between justice and injustice, or at least between freedom and totalitarianism."[47] He was especially critical of Russia's manipulation of Germany during this period, noting, "As divided Germany sinks into economic misery, Russia hopes to conquer her ideologically by attributing this misery to capitalistic exploitation."[48] The former Marxist critic of liberalism witnessed firsthand the iron rule of a Communist nation in a world recovering from global conflict, which reinforced his understanding of the need for a third way in economic life.

Niebuhr consistently articulates this third-way ideal from the early 1950s, although he does appear to grow increasingly fond of the American model of social organization in his later writings. He rejects absolute economic freedom because of its limitations with regard to social justice, yet he also recognizes that socialization or even excessive regulation of the economy tends to destroy individual initiative. In a passage from "Theology and Political Thought in the Western World," he expresses what some scholars have described as his "mature" view of the relationship between Christianity and the social order:

> We have now come to the fairly general conclusion that there is no "Christian" economic or political system. But there is a Christian atti-

tude toward all systems and schemes of justice. It consists on the one hand of a critical attitude toward the claims of all systems and schemes, expressed in the question whether they will contribute to justice in a concrete situation; and on the other hand a responsible attitude, which will not pretend to be God nor refuse to make a decision between political answers to a problem because each answer is discovered to contain a moral ambiguity in God's sight. We are men, not God; we are responsible for making choices between greater and lesser evils, even when our Christian faith, illuminating the human scene, makes it quite apparent that there is no pure good in history; and probably no pure evil, either. The fate of civilizations may depend on these choices.[49]

By 1955, Niebuhr's realism had evolved to incorporate, perhaps reluctantly, one of the central tenets of liberal philosophy. "A wise self-interest," he stated, "which can find the point of concurrence between a particular and general interest should represent the *summum bonum* of the community rather than sacrificial love."[50] While his pragmatism had exposed the utopian dreams of socialists and capitalists alike, Niebuhr understood that one system was more offensive to justice than the other. Christian realism recognized the contribution of self-interested action to the achievement of the good in a way that Christian socialism did not. In a mood of reflection in 1959 on his youthful "error" in judgment, Niebuhr wrote that he and other Christian socialists of an earlier era "became involved in a politics which made an absolute distinction between the innocent poor and the guilty rich. We were thus led astray by a genuine religious and ethical impulse into utopian politics."[51]

The "third way" necessitated by Niebuhr's realization of the inherent flaws of all social systems caused him to place increasing reliance on the "balance of power" as a principle for the achievement of harmony between the competing interests in society. Niebuhr's friendship with the economist John Kenneth Galbraith resulted at least in part from their common faith in the potency of "countervailing power" to contribute some approximation of justice.[52] Niebuhr stated in 1957 that the "organized power of labor has come more to increase the health of both our economic and political life than any other factor. . . . It is a New Deal achievement that the two giants (big business and big labor) are fairly evenly balanced. That solves the overall problem of justice."[53] This uncharacteristically optimistic statement revealed what he believed was the potential of a careful balancing of the prideful and power-seeking interests in society in solving the intractable problem of social justice.

In his 1965 book, *Man's Nature and His Communities*, Niebuhr offers a commentary on his youthful socialist idealism and an introspective review of his life's work. The book contains few original economic ideas; however, it does refute those who contend that Niebuhr had become fully convinced of the virtues of liberalism in his later years. Niebuhr's concession to liberalism is found in his acknowledgment that self-interest is the principal guiding force of human history. Yet his pronouncement was decidedly melancholy; the dialectical nature of his thought would never allow him to ignore the social "discipline" necessary to temper the power of self-seeking. Niebuhr had confessed the error of his socialist ways but retained his fundamental assessment of human nature and the institutions that form to contain it.

A CHRISTIAN REALIST'S THEORY OF VALUE

When seen in relation to the rational models of human behavior discussed in chapter 5, defensible arguments can be made that the value theories of both Austrian liberalism and Christian realism are "organic" in the sense that they recognize cultural, historical, and other influences on human conduct that defy mathematical replication and prediction. For Hayek, this organicism that defies rationality is born of sheer complexity—social dynamics that are beyond the explanatory powers of individual or collective reason. One recalls Hayek's comment that the "facts which result from certain values being held are not those to which the values which guide the actions of several individuals are attached, but a pattern comprising the actions of many individuals, a pattern of which the acting individuals may not even be aware . . . and which was certainly not the aim of their actions."[54] Yet, while Hayek insists that complexity often renders social dynamics and their consequences indiscernible, he is equally insistent that the goal of group persistence is the dominant motivation to human behavior. This *ultimate value* in Hayek's system has the possibility of leaving in its wake elements of moral traditions (even whole traditions themselves), transcendent conceptions of the human person, and other values that would, if accurate, seem to threaten Christianity and other faiths.

Reinhold Niebuhr's value theory stems from another source that transcends cultural and historical boundaries and embraces a differing view of the person and the need for a teleological foundation to life. Niebuhr stated, "Only if things are related to each other organically in a total meaningful existence can it be claimed that they have value."[55] While nature and culture establish the limits to Hayek's naturalism, according to Niebuhr, "the individual man has a uniqueness which nature does not know. This uniqueness must be appreciated poetically and imaginatively rather than scientifically."[56] It is at various "levels of freedom" that human beings express their values. While the biological individual is subject to analytical investigation, the nonbiological self is not: "Every effort to make [the self] an object among other objects reduces its stature. The transcendent and responsible self is not known and cannot be known."[57]

Niebuhr, just as some adherents of Austrian economics, detested increasingly popular theories of human behavior such as those that would later form the basis for rational choice and public choice models. He observed the same flaw in the works of early classical economists who "obscured the effect of ethnic loyalties and cultural restraints and geographic restrictions upon human activity and gave us an oversimplified and false picture of 'economic man.'"[58] Niebuhr insisted that despite elaborate claims on behalf of science and its ability to clarify the infinitely complex subject of human culture, a rigorous application of science "means a denial of everything which is characteristically human."[59]

Niebuhr's recognition of the cultural and historical ignorance of purely empirical models of classical economics brings him to Hayek's level of understanding of the complexity of the human person and the nature of value. Yet Niebuhr goes further. He understands that the "self-transcendent" nature of the human person extends beyond Hayek's projection of the subjective economic actor who remains largely bound to the dictates of group persistence and the dominant societal value of economic growth. Self-transcendence enables the human being to stand outside culture and history and to make decisions that defy not only reason but individual instinct and social mores as well. This transcendent perspective affects the individual's values by sheltering her moral sense from the pressures of mere survival. Both personal values and the individual's ability to value are influenced by the "I-Thou" relationship— the "turning of the self from itself as the center of its life to God and the neighbor"—that defies scientific explanation.[60]

Reinhold Niebuhr was indebted to his brother Richard for many insights into the nature of value that ultimately coalesced within his own understanding of Christian realism. Richard's essay "The Center of Value," which appeared in his book *Radical Monotheism and Western Culture*, offered perhaps the most complete examination of value from the perspective of a Christian realist ever presented. The starting point for Richard's exploration of this aspect of human existence was what he termed the "center of value." All value systems, irrespective of their relational or relativistic claims, possess such a center, for "good," which is the ultimate objective, can only be comprehended in the context of "good for what or whom." Thus, the center that is the "what or whom" must exist for valuations to have meaning, even in systems that profess a detached objectivity:

> Though relational value theory is not psychologically relativistic it is evidently dogmatically relativistic since it is necessary to take one's standpoint with or in some being accepted as the *center of value* if one is to construct anything like a consistent system of value judgments and determinations of what is right.[61]

Therefore, systems of political economy identify (often implicitly) their centers of value as a basis for their necessarily relational systems that appropriate society's resources and approximate some conception of social justice. In Communism, the proletarian class serves as that center of value, while in Austrian liberalism, all value is perceived to emanate from the subjective economic actor in market exchange.

The Christian realist is aware of the necessity for standards of value in economic systems, yet she is also aware that such standards are relative and, to some extent, arbitrarily chosen. Each culturally conceived and historically conditioned center of value has contributed to greater or lesser achievements toward the "end" of social orders that is "justice." Each is flawed because it falls short of the *ultimate* center of value that is the Creator. Richard noted that at times in history, singular values such as "knowledge" have been identified as the center of value; however, "more frequently the relational value theories . . . are caught up in a polytheism which posits two or more centers of values."[62] By contrast, the value theory of monotheism establishes first a central value theory centered in God but then proceeds to acknowledge the need for countless relative and temporal value systems that make greater or lesser contributions to worldly justice. A monotheistically centered system of value demonstrates not only compatibility with "objective relativism in value analysis" but actually requires it because ultimate morals and principles are found in God alone. The extension of this truth to the realm of social order insists that "the absolutizing of anything finite is ruinous to the finite itself."[63]

Richard Niebuhr offered an eloquent defense against the common charge that the value system of monotheism is uncritically dogmatic, turning the table on critics by pointing instead to the dogmatism of relative systems of politics and economics:

> Uncritical dogmatism is the practice of those explicit or disguised relational systems of thought about the good which arbitrarily choose some limited starting point [man, society, or life] for their inquiries and either

end with the confession that value is an irrational concept which must nevertheless be rationally employed because nature requires this, or otherwise rule out of consideration great realms of value relations as irrelevant. Critical thought based on theocentric faith has no quarrel with the method of objective relativism in value theory and ethics. It objects only but strongly to the religious foundations of these relativisms.[64]

Thus, it is the concurrent absolutizing and minimizing of finite centers of value in necessarily relative systems of social organization that the Christian realist finds objectionable.

The tendency of scientifically constructed social systems to reduce the individual in order to fit her into some rational scheme is observed in both subjectivist and collectivist theories. Classical liberalism, which serves as the philosophical foundation of modern capitalist society, collapses the person into a role as a near slave to self-interest, while collective systems minimize the self-regarding impulse and exaggerate the altruistic nature of the individual in order to make a propertyless society feasible. Richard and Reinhold both agreed that these flaws in both capitalist and collectivist systems are evidence that the theories of value that emerge from science or philosophy are necessarily incomplete and, worse, inaccurate. Reason has its limitations; therefore, the arts and sciences, along with the institutions to which they give rise and that rely exclusively on human reason for their insights into "man and his history," necessarily must be limited as well.

Although Reinhold Niebuhr identified social groups as critical in the dissemination of values that is the principal function of any system of political economy, he also understood their inherent limitations as cultivators of "individual" values. Niebuhr's social thought was formed in a time when, as Fox notes, society greatly differentiated between the "public sphere of work and politics" and the "value-creating" private sphere (principally the family and the church).[65] Thus, Niebuhr's acknowledgment of the limitations of the value-creating potential of social groups is a defining element of his economic realism and the reason why institutions of the "public realm"—the market, corporation, government, trade union, and the like—are inappropriate for the inculcation of ultimate values. In his essay "Niebuhr's World and Ours," Fox describes this aspect of Niebuhr's value theory:

> [The public realm] was not a place to cultivate ultimate human values but the place to effect production, maintain order, and distribute or redistribute opportunity. There were certainly "values" appropriate to the social and political arena but they were second-order values of tolerance,

dispassionate intelligence, and the exercise of judgment in the pursuit of freedom and equality. As Niebuhr has always put it, justice, not love, was the goal of the Christian in society.[66]

Consistent with Hayek, Niebuhr recognized the general inability of social groups to make sacrifices that jeopardize their existence, which limits the range of values that groups are able to cultivate in their respective members. Moreover, Niebuhr's belief that sin is the denial of human finitude insisted that institutions are more susceptible to sinful conduct, for as Niebuhr and Hayek both observed, human collectives are principally about survival. Thus, to the extent that collectives or other institutions, including the market and its associated technologies, advance the possibility of escaping one's finite existence, they may be seen as having a corrupting influence on individual values.

The additional complexity inherent in the interplay of personal and social values and Niebuhr's consistent demarcation between the first-order values of the transcendent realm and those second-order values of society suggests that a simple aggregation of individual preferences as expressed in the market will not suffice as the primary expression of value for Christians. Primary values must always seek the "good" from the transcendent perspective, and good is always found in the "harmony of the whole on various levels."[67] Harmony, in turn, must be established among the competing interests in society—among both individuals and the groups to which they belong.

In *The Democratic Experience*, coauthored with Paul Sigmund in 1969, Niebuhr expressed an appreciation for enlightened self-interest as a creative force in history, stating, "History is fashioned by a clash and competition of powers which are armed with ideas related to interests but frequently and fortunately also creative for the community as a whole."[68] To the extent that the market arbitrates clashes between powers and minimizes the need for coercive force, it serves a vital function in facilitating the arbitration of social values and a collective expression of the good. Yet even after Niebuhr's transformation from Christian socialist to realistic liberal, he continued to recognize "that many cherished values of civilization are not protected by the operations of a 'free market' . . . and that there are conflicts in society which are not composed within the limits of a self-regulating competition."[69] The market can serve society as a less onerous arbitrator of scarce resources and social values vis-à-vis government institutions, but there are limits.

In one of his early forays into the nature of value, Niebuhr devoted an entire chapter of his book *Beyond Tragedy* to an exploration of his partial point of agreement with German philosopher Friedrich Nietzsche that

Christianity "transvalues" history. In other words, Christianity's hierarchy of values as best articulated in the gospels exists largely in inverse relationship to those values that have been validated by historical outcomes. Niebuhr referenced the beatitudes, the letters of St. Paul, and other biblical sources to prove his point, yet Niebuhr disagrees sharply with Nietzsche in that he perceives a healthy purification in the periodic upwelling of religious values that Nietzsche sees as harmful to society:

> If history should itself turn over its own values and periodically cast the mighty from their seats and exalt them of low degree, this would happen only because history is forced partly to validate, though it usually defies, the standards of the Kingdom of God. History is nature; and in nature the strong devour the weak and the shrewd take advantage of the simple. But human history is more than nature. It is a realm of freedom where the inequalities of nature are accentuated by human imagination until they become intolerable and destroy themselves.[70]

The transvaluation of history by Christianity serves periodically to restore God as the center of value, and it establishes a more reliable basis for human valuations than the relational and naturalistic systems of political economy. Ronald Stone generalizes this critical difference between Christian realism and "classical culture" (and, it will be added here, the classical liberal tradition), stating that Reinhold Niebuhr's "insistence upon a linear interpretation of history, stressing the uniqueness of events and finding tentative meanings within the process of reserving the final meaning of history for the judgment of God, provided the church with intellectual resources that classical culture lacked."[71] Christianity's recognition of the individual's capability to assess "historical meanings" from a self-transcendent perspective enables a more comprehensive conception of value and a greater possibility for a morally redeeming economic system than economic philosophies based purely on scientific conceptions of the human person.

THE BALANCE OF POWER AND ITS CONTRIBUTION TO JUSTICE

No single regulative principle consistently played upon Reinhold Niebuhr's economic mind so much as did the notion that social harmony is best achieved and human personality best preserved through maintenance of a balance of power among the various interests of society. Franklin Roosevelt's

New Deal revealed for Niebuhr the relative truth that an equitable distribution of power in society is necessary for any approximation of justice. Moreover, it convinced him of the feasibility of the mixed economy. He stated that the New Deal provided more than minimal social securities through the intervention of the state; what was more important was that it enabled organized labor "to set power against power. For justice in a sinful world demands an equilibrium of power."[72]

In truth, Niebuhr believed that he was contributing to the achievement of an equitable distribution of power in American society when he joined the Socialist Party in the 1920s. His understanding of the complex relationship between politics and economics entered into his reasoning. As a socialist, Niebuhr believed that "the creeds and institutions of democracy have never become fully divorced from the special interests of the commercial classes" that were intent on destroying the political power that could restrain them.[73]

In 1941, as Niebuhr was in transition from his Christian socialism to what ultimately would be described as Christian realism, he authored his greatest theological work, *The Nature and Destiny of Man*. It was in this book that Niebuhr solidified his theoretical understanding of power relations in human communities and offered theological principles upon which his later political and economic thought would be founded. His first and most foundational theorem was that "power is the product of spirit. It never exists without an alloy of physical force but it is always more than physical compulsion."[74] Recognition of the spiritual aspect of power is a clear break with his emphasis on its economic and more physical nature articulated in *Moral Man and Immoral Society*, and it leads directly to Niebuhr's understanding of the basis of community:

> The power which determines the quality of the order and harmony is not merely the coercive and organizing power of government. That is only one of two aspects of social power. The other is the balance of vitalities and forces in any given social situation. . . . No social or moral advance can redeem society from its dependence upon these two principles.[75]

Dynamic forces are at work that defy rational attempts to regulate their consequences. Equilibrium attained by the interaction of these forces largely determines the degree of justice that can be realized within a particular society. Justice often is deified by idealists or derided as unattainable by the most extreme realists, yet it must exist in some form for society to maintain cohesion. The quality of justice is determined by the proportionality of competing power interests, because "all historic forms of justice and injustice are determined to a much larger degree than pure rationalists or idealists realize by the given equilibrium or disproportion within each type of power and by the balance of various types of power in a given community." Thus, "it may be taken as axiomatic that great disproportions of power lead to injustice, . . . while the diffusion of political power has made for justice."[76]

Among the idealists were both libertarians who insisted that an equitable distribution of power would form naturally where government is removed from all but the most basic social responsibilities, and collectivists who asserted that human reason is capable of planning justice from the vantage of a central authority. Niebuhr's insight that libertarians exaggerate the ability of natural harmonies in the economic system to minimize disproportions of power in society while the socialist solution to the "power problem" actually exacerbates it is consistently articulated in his economic writings after 1940. He recognized the "power impulse" in all human institutions, rising from that which is observed in the "external relations" of families to its peak in the near purely egoistic nation-state. He observed, "The power impulse of the nation is, in fact, so strong, and its sense of a higher loyalty so weak, that only an irrelevant idealism would speculate about the possibility of the nation subordinating its national interest to that of an overarching culture."[77] Progressively higher-level institutions have greater difficulty in subordinating their values, ideals, and ambitions for the sake of a perceived greater good. This fact plus the growth of mass society led Niebuhr to conclude that a realistically crafted balance of power is necessary to prevent the domination of self-regarding groups.

Democratic capitalist principles and institutions were increasingly important but necessarily insufficient instruments for the realization of justice in society. Niebuhr did come to view democratic government in its uniquely American form as especially effective in the diffusion of social power. He recognized the policies of the Roosevelt administration, in particular, as the truest realization of the Founders' vision, which had discerned this need for balance among political and economic powers. For all his contempt for the natural harmony theories of the liberals, he began as early as 1944 to see that certain forces were at work in the market system that tended to equilibrate interests. In *The Children of Light and the Children of Darkness*, he stated, "We must be careful to preserve self-regulating forces that exist in the economic process. If we do not, the task of control becomes stupendous and the organs of control achieve proportions which endanger our liberty."[78] Niebuhr acquired a preference for "natural" balances of economic power over what he had come to recognize as the inherently coercive and often damaging force of governmental authority.

Niebuhr's views in the mid-twentieth century were evolving toward the creative center in the economic debate, and he began to perceive the American system of democratic capitalism as moving in the same direction. By the 1950s, Niebuhr believed that American society was well on its way to attaining a finely crafted balance that would secure a stable harmony based on an underlying sense of justice. The successes of the New Deal (especially in the empowerment of labor) and the rising influence of intellectuals of the same bent as his good friend John Kenneth Galbraith were serving to negate the traditional dominance of big business in American society:

> The new industrial unions were so successful in setting collective power against collective power, and the companies proved themselves, in the end, so flexible in coming to terms with the unions, that long term contracts with escalator clauses, allowing for increased wages according to the price index, and an annual bonus for higher productivity are now established procedure.[79]

Democratic institutions established the foundation for American achievements. In *A Nation So Conceived*, Niebuhr and coauthor Alan Heimert observed that in the early twentieth century, the United States and other democratic nations attained greater equality through universal suffrage and other principles but were now in need of "an equilibrium of power in the economic realm itself."[80] While Niebuhr and Heimert lauded the steps undertaken to achieve a stable equilibrium in American society, they were also mindful that such balances are easily destroyed, especially by technological change. They recognized particularly the "problem" that automation posed for industry and wrote of the demise of collective bargaining in an "era of rapid automation," which imperiled the community by institutionalizing the disproportion of power between management and labor.[81] Even during the most promarket stages of his economic development, Niebuhr believed that the collective voice of labor was critical to political as well as economic stability.

Christianity, in particular, is instructive to the development and maintenance of a balance of power among social groups that is critical to the achievement of justice. Prophetic Christianity, unlike modern liberalism, "knows that the force of egoism cannot be broken by moral suasion and that on certain levels qualified harmonies must be achieved by building conflicting egoisms into a balance of power."[82] Moreover, religion in gen-

eral "faces many perils to the right and to the left in becoming an instrument and inspiration of social justice. Every genuine passion for social justice will always contain a religious element within it."[83] Niebuhr's recognition of this religious element of social justice led him to emphasize the
impacts of social, political, and economic institutions on the complex relationship between human and divine personality. Maintenance of a balance
of power in society serves to establish social equilibrium, but it was just as
important for Niebuhr that such a balance would stave off encroachments
upon the individual by necessarily flawed and self-seeking collectives, which
at their core advanced forms of naturalism and threatened the Christian
conception of personality.

THE MORAL AND SOCIAL
CONSEQUENCES OF "TECHNICS"

The inclusion of this category as among the more "consistent" elements in
Reinhold Niebuhr's economic thought is likely to raise a few eyebrows.
Niebuhr's writings throughout much of his lifetime exhibited a near obsession not with technology itself but with its social and moral outcomes, yet
some of Niebuhr's contemporaries as well as several Niebuhr scholars are
convinced that he was inconsistent in his appraisal of the cultural effects of
technological change. For example, the perception of Niebuhr's increasing
acceptance of the potential for technology to contribute to justice in developing nations caused the Protestant missionary M. M. Thomas to question Niebuhr's "conversion" in light of his past experiences:

> When [Niebuhr] emphasized "technical efficiency," did he forget that
> increased technical efficiency in Detroit brought increased oppression
> and that it might do the same in the Third World if it was not coupled
> with social transformation for justice? Or by this time [1952] did he ac-
> cept the ideology of the American free enterprise system that techno-
> logical modernization under America's leadership was for the ultimate
> good of all?[84]

The answers to Thomas's questions can be arrived at only with some
difficulty. While it is true that Niebuhr appears to have become more sanguine over time regarding the technical society's potential to achieve justice,
he consistently voiced fears over the moral and spiritual effects of rapid
technological change. In 1927, Niebuhr offered a rather dire assessment of

technology's cultural effects in his book *Does Civilization Need Religion?* stating, "Western civilization is enslaved to its machines and the things which the machines produce. Spiritual forces are emancipated from the forces of nature only to become the victims of a mechanized civilization."[85] More than thirty years later in an essay on Russian and American imperialistic zeal in the Cold War, Niebuhr stated that American hegemony "offers some real hazards since we are probably too technocratic and too interested in high living standards that will seem vulgar to the poor nations ambitious to escape the deprivations of agrarian poverty."[86] Niebuhr's anxiety over the U.S. obsession with technical hegemony was not simply a concern about national image. He was troubled more about technology's impact on the spiritual and moral health of the nation.

Early on, Niebuhr tended to view technology as altering the distribution of power in society, which necessarily invites political responses. The necessity for state intervention to ensure justice in societies that are both democratic and technical results from the fact that "human freedom expresses itself destructively as well as creatively, and that an increase in human freedom and power through the introduction of technics makes the achievement of justice more, rather than less, difficult than in non-technical civilizations."[87] Niebuhr's dogmatism in portraying the greater difficulty of achieving justice in technical society waned as his social thought matured; however, he continued to maintain that the advance of technology complicates the realization of social justice.

Closer examination of Niebuhr's economic writings reveals that he was more inclined toward placing blame for injustices on human failings and inadequacies in the political and economic order rather than on technical advance itself. Technology only amplifies the ability of human beings to exploit one another. In *The Nature and Destiny of Man*, he observed that greed, "as a form of the will-to-power has been a particularly flagrant sin in the modern era because modern technology has tempted contemporary man to overestimate the possibility and the value of eliminating his insecurity in nature. . . . This [bourgeois] culture is constantly tempted to regard physical comfort and security as life's final good and to hope for its attainment to a degree which is beyond human possibilities."[88] Thus, for Niebuhr, technology only magnifies humankind's predisposition toward self-seeking and self-reliance at the expense of dependency on the Creator.

Just as technology has the power to amplify sins of the individual resulting from the prideful ambitions of the human will, so too can it damage communities and heighten the injustices that flow naturally from inherently flawed social structures. Niebuhr expressed this belief in his 1948 essay

"God's Design and the Present Disorder of Civilization," in which he stated that the rise of modern industry was contributing to the "destruction of community" in the United States, an effect that was spreading to the rest of the world. Niebuhr again asserted his understanding of the true source of the cultural tension that accompanies technological change, stating, "To attribute the social confusion of our era to the introduction of technics is . . . to give only the negative cause of our discontent. The more positive cause has been the failure of men and nations either to desire or to achieve a tolerable justice within the new conditions created by expanding technical power."[89] Technology can only amplify the justice or injustice already present in a given social order; it is not itself the source of injustice or disorder.

One aspect of technics that is commonly overlooked is its tendency to attenuate the social and psychological effects of human mortality, which erodes the uniqueness of the human person by denying an essential fact of her existence. "A culture which is so strongly influenced by both scientific concepts and technocratic illusions," he stated, "is constantly tempted to annul or to obscure the unique individual."[90] Hence Niebuhr came to the realization that personality and its transcendent nature are put at risk by technological change.

At the core of Niebuhr's pessimism regarding the cultural effects of technical advance was his recognition that technics is forever forging new dependencies between individuals and groups in society. Technological forces increasingly shape social relationships and displace the character of their traditionally organic associations with its own rationalism. He stated, "Every age, and more particularly the age of technics, has confronted men with the problem of relating their lives to a larger number of their fellowmen. The task of creating community and avoiding anarchy is constantly pitched on broader and broader levels."[91] Among the social hazards of technics was a phenomenon in industrial societies similar to that for which Joseph Schumpeter coined the term "creative destruction."[92] In 1945, Niebuhr stated,

> Technics in production have shattered old forms of justice and made the achievement of new ones difficult. The modern machine becomes larger and larger as it becomes more and more efficient. It long since has divorced the skill of the worker from his tool. It has to a certain degree divorced the worker from his skill, which is now increasingly in the machine. It has thus made the worker powerless, except insofar as common organized action has given him a degree of social and political power.[93]

Niebuhr's thought became more ambiguous respecting technological change during World War II. As early as 1942, he discerned the myriad and often conflicting influences of technics and its ability to alter society's fine balances even as it has the potential to forge a "world community through economic interdependence." But he feared that this new international community could devolve into "a state of international anarchy" without the political instruments necessary to control it. He perceived two principal sources of the indeterminate effects of technological advance. First, technics increases the interdependence of humankind, a force that he understood to be in conflict with the coterminous rise of individualism in industrial society. He noted that a "particularly pathetic aspect of this ideal of individual self-sufficiency is given by the fact that early bourgeois culture was the childhood of a technical civilization in which men would become intimately related to, and dependent upon, vaster and vaster historical forces."[94] Second, technology works in favor of the centralization of economic power, a phenomenon that he witnessed firsthand through the development of techniques of mass production in the automobile industry in Detroit.

Technology always brings with it the danger of idolatry, and its power has the potential to accentuate factionalism. He insisted that modern civilization "may perish because it falsely worshipped technical advance as a final good. One portion of a technical society may harness techniques to the purpose of destruction and vent its fury upon another portion of the civilization, which has grown soft by regarding the comforts yielded in such great abundance by a technical age, as the final good."[95] This idolatrous allure of technology is observed in the American preoccupation with "cheap technocratic approaches to the tragic historical drama in which we are all involved."[96] The vulgarization of human culture inspired by technics only compounds the general complexity that technology adds to the resolution of already difficult cultural problems.

Technology, like the once seemingly limitless expanse of the American frontier, has a way of postponing, even obfuscating, ultimate issues. Niebuhr noted that when "the frontier ceased to provide for the expansion of opportunities, our superior technology created ever new frontiers for the ambitious and adventurous." But he went on to assert that the economic advances enabled by technics could not serve as a palliative for our moral and social problems. "This expansion cannot go on forever," he wrote, "and ultimately we must face some vexatious issues of social justice."[97] Those "vexatious issues" arise from the fact that society experiences "the law of diminishing returns in the relation of technics and efficiency to the cultural life."[98] The complex nature of the human person as a rational, social, and spiritual being insists that there are limits to the satisfactions that technical solutions can provide.

Yet there is evidence to substantiate M. M. Thomas's claim that Niebuhr became more ebullient about the prospects of modern technical society with respect to justice. Where Niebuhr's ideas on technology were transformed was in his growing appreciation of its ability to raise living standards and, in some cases, to empower less privileged members of society. Niebuhr came to understand the influence of technics as many sided rather than his earlier and simpler estimation of its tendency to centralize power and accentuate human interdependence. By the 1960s, Niebuhr believed that the increased productivity spawned by technological innovation had negated and perhaps even overcome technics' more negative cultural effects. For example, Niebuhr recognized the lack of technical skill as one factor contributing to poverty among blacks in America, with the obvious implication that technical training could help prevent economic damage to the black community caused by technical advance, as that observed in the deskilling of Southern blacks through the mechanization of cotton farming.[99]

In *Man's Nature and His Communities*, Niebuhr continued to associate technics with the cause of human rights, and he suggested that technology helped to demonstrate that rights for blacks and other minorities are in the interest of the nation. In lobbying for federal training programs, he stated, "an increasing technical culture needs trained manpower. . . . Hence the retraining program of the federal government and also its anti-poverty program are clearly inspired, at least in part, by the nation's concern for its economic advantages."[100] Yet, in the same period, Niebuhr targeted one of America's proudest technological achievements as an illustration of a national moral lapse. Regarding the first moon landing, Niebuhr stated, "I have a proper pride in the technical achievement"; however, he went on to say that its priority over more pressing problems "represents a defective sense of human values" since the nation's "inner cities are decaying" and the space program deflects resources from those more serious problems.[101] This event reinforced Niebuhr's conclusion that technics can be morally misdirected and that it has a way of opening up pockets in society for exploitation.

Niebuhr's "mixed view" of the totality of social and moral effects of technological change resulted from his impression of relative changes in the cultural forces that accompany the introduction of various technologies. Yet Niebuhr's understanding of the general, and often conflicting, effects of technics on society may be discerned with relative clarity, that technology:

- tends to centralize economic power among those who control it;
- empowers certain groups that have traditionally been disenfranchised;

- increases human interdependence and makes possible a world community;
- acts to "deskill" workers as automation encroaches upon the workplace;
- raises standards of living through enhanced production;
- captivates consumers with its technical gadgetry and flood of new goods;
- complicates the attainment of justice by continually recasting individual and group relationships; and
- tempts human beings into complacency and a belief in their own self-sufficiency.

These general consequences of technological change are consistently articulated despite shifts in Niebuhr's political and economic philosophy. What does change, however, is the relative strength of these forces as conditioned by the social and historical contexts of societies impacted by technology. At certain stages in development, a particular culture's ability to raise living standards and empower labor via technology will override the tendency of technics to centralize economic power and deskill specific labor classes. Thus, for Niebuhr, the social and moral impacts of technology on human culture were uncertain but most decidedly not neutral.

THE NEED FOR CONTINUAL REASSESSMENT OF PROPERTY AND OWNERSHIP

Economically conservative readers likely cringed when encountering the section heading above. Capitalism's global triumph presumably involved a once-for-all settlement of the property question. Yet Christian realism's reliance on a monotheistic value theory that acknowledges only God as absolute and infinite relegates all systems of political economy to the temporal and finite. Values and principles within those necessarily relative systems of thought, including specific conceptions of property and ownership, are themselves relative and thus subject to revision. Consistent with this idea, Reinhold Niebuhr articulated the need for continual reassessment of the institution of property and the conception of ownership even after dropping his affiliations with the Socialist Party in 1940. Social and technological change opens up pockets of injustice within society that require redress.[102] While Niebuhr came to recognize the Marxist ideal of the propertyless society as a serious mistake stemming from Marx's emphasis on property as the singular source of social injustice, he continued to believe that property is a far more complex phenomenon than most capitalists acknowledge.[103]

Compounding the problems of property's dynamic nature and the static conception of ownership was the inadequacy of legal and other instruments to represent the true complexity of these concepts. Legal expressions of property are limited by reason, language, and utilitarian necessity because too-expansive definitions of property are presumed to confound market logic. However, they become inaccurate or antiquated as interdependency grows in society and as technology obscures or distorts underlying claims to possession. Niebuhr stated, "The bourgeois mind, . . . , has been the victim of illusions caused by the contrast between the private character of its 'tokens' of property and the social character of the real wealth which these tokens and counters signify."[104] Simplification of the true nature of ownership is a critical flaw that has contributed to a loss of social organicism and to a concurrent rise of injustices brought about by an excessively legalistic and hence insufficiently social view of "property."

The rise of the managerial class further complicated the character of ownership in both socialist and capitalist societies. By the 1960s, Niebuhr had changed course from his early emphasis on property as a principal source of injustice to the view that managerial power was the principal threat. In *The Democratic Experience*, he stated, "The managerial economic system that developed in both Communist and capitalist cultures revealed that the power of the manager over the economic process is greater than the power of ownership, whether it be by a private concern or the government."[105] Thus, Niebuhr viewed the rise of the managerial class as a reason for growing concentrations of power in both democratic and collectivist societies. Managers separate owners from that which is owned, with the result that they empower themselves and advance their own interests. In capitalism, this results in the problems of absentee ownership, while in socialist societies, a "pathetic consequence" of the growth in managerial power is "that the workers of a socialized concern, who are in theory the common owners of the property" are "prevented from holding any significant power."[106]

Niebuhr's assessment of the complex ownership and managerial structure of the American factory in the first half of the twentieth century and the failure of institutions to adapt to new realities has relevance to contemporary corporate forms and to certain problems that have emerged recently in the governance of large corporations. To begin, there is considerable evidence that the composition of ownership in American corporations has changed dramatically in recent years. The rise of employee stock ownership plans (ESOPs), 401(k) plans, and various programs offering stock options to employees suggests that employees own their companies to a greater extent today than ever before. Corey Rosen, cofounder of the National Center for Employee Ownership, notes that during the last twenty years, around fifteen million American workers have acquired stock in their companies through employee ownership plans, around two-thirds of which are publicly traded. Employees control over 5 percent of the stock in about 1,000 of the roughly 7,000 publicly traded companies, with a median ownership of about 10 percent to 15 percent. In addition, employees own stock in approximately 12,000 privately held firms, with a median ownership of around 30 percent in 8,500 privately held firms through ESOPs, "and employees own or will own a majority of the stock in about 3,000 of these companies."[107]

One might assume that the rise in employee ownership of corporations would mean a greater diversity in governance structures and a more broad-based representation of values from among the diverse ownership community. However, despite these dramatic changes, Rosen observes, "this extensive employee ownership does not usually translate into employee involvement in corporate-level decisions. Only a handful of public companies with broad employee ownership have employee representation on their boards, and only about 5% to 10% of the privately held companies have such representation."[108] The statistical evidence suggests that governance structures of many large corporations exist largely as remnants from earlier corporate forms that no longer represent the range of interests that make up the modern firm's ownership community. Niebuhr offered an explanation for this phenomenon where he observed the acquiescence of Americans to an oligarchic corporate ethic:

> The situation, in which a majority of the American people acquiesced through the end of the [nineteenth] century, is not adequately characterized as simply a decision to let business alone. What defined the age was rather a fairly consistent commitment to encouraging the wealth-producing enterprise of the nation—and doing so, not according to a studied plan, but on the assumption that those individuals and corporations who controlled industrial capital best understood the nation's needs.[109]

Perhaps there was a time in the industrial history of the United States when only a handful of Americans had the know-how to run large corporations and possessed a sufficiently universal perspective to assess the "nation's needs"; yet that deficiency of managerial talent has abated, and today a large percentage of employees at all levels of corporations are highly educated and have wide-ranging expertise. Despite the changes in composition in corporate ownership noted by Rosen and the perceived broadening of executive talent in the United States, the archaic structure of corporate governance still predominates and has led to significant abuses of power. Although the book is somewhat dated, economist John Munkirs' *The Transformation of American Capitalism* explores the extent to which the boards of directors of American corporations are both "intralocked"—where linkages exist between directors of corporations within a single industry—and "interlocked," denoting linkages among directors across industries.[110] What results from this structure is that boards of directors become "functional planning instruments" that coordinate production processes not only for entire industries but, in effect, for the national economy. Munkirs points out both the good and bad effects of the natural formation of this system that he describes as "centralized private sector planning," and he recognizes that it is stimulated by the rise of financial and technological interdependence in the increasing complexity of the modern economy.[111]

If Munkirs' observations are accurate, then the idea that American corporations reflect a broad diversity of interests (and thus values) is exaggerated due to the concentrations of power in corporate culture. The Enron/Andersen scandal appears to have resulted from the ethical failures of a few executives, the collusion of one or two partners from an outside consulting firm, and the negligence of the Enron Corporation's board of directors.[112] It serves as evidence of Munkirs' thesis and demonstrates the extent to which concentrations of power exist within American corporations despite more widespread distribution of ownership. At Enron, the concentration of managerial power and lack of oversight by the board created a situation where the unethical conduct of a few individuals led to the collapse of a company of tens of thousands of employees. The company misrepresented its financial position, spinning off huge losses into secretive partnerships, engaging in deceitful accounting practices, and misleading investors and employees into believing in the health of the company.

A Christian realist perspective on the Enron/Andersen scandal would point to its inevitability. Concentrations of power in large institutions combined with an environment of immense complexity and given the ever-present condition of human sin will inevitably lead to abuses. Moreover, the drive for profits that has consumed the American economy over the past two decades at the expense of holistic conceptions of economic growth conditions the business environment in favor of such abuses. Scandals such as Enron signify the failure of the modern corporation to adjust its management structure to accommodate the contemporary composition of corporate ownership. Evidence indicates that management has remained centralized even as ownership has been disseminated among employees as well as institutional and individual investors. This divergence between management and ownership suggests the potential for corporate action in the form of financial dealings, service offerings, and other operations that do not reflect the collective values of the diverse interests that own the corporation.

The magnitude of corporate scandals in American business indicates that there must be more reflection on the composition of corporate boards to ensure that they accurately reflect the values and interests of the ownership community. While some have suggested that the cronyism of American corporate culture is fading, there is still evidence that much power is concentrated in the upper echelons of the business hierarchy. It is in the best interests of "democratic capitalism" to ensure that owners are represented in the guidance of firms to the extent that they own them. But Michael Novak has argued persuasively that corporations cannot be run like democratic governments.[113] Indeed, the realist recognizes the infeasibility of including all interests in the day-to-day decision making of the corporation. However, some conservatives take this argument so far as to shield from scrutiny concentrations of power control within corporations under the notion that they are necessary for its efficient operation. This protectionism only postpones growing problems caused by the division of ownership and control.

The necessary reassessment of property and ownership must be a continual process stimulated by social and technical changes that inevitably make old views obsolete. There can be no once-for-all settlement of these questions for the reason that property and ownership, like all human institutions, are finite, imperfect, and contingent constructs that vary with unique cultural and historical circumstances. The very rule by which conservatives (neo- and otherwise) discredit central planning—the fact that human reason is limited and that human beings cannot foresee the future—is also the reason why the property question cannot be settled "absolutely." The impossibility of envisioning the ways in which social and technical changes will impact our understanding of property insists that such definitions must remain somewhat fluid. Increasing conflicts over intellectual property rights and the current controversy over the patenting of human genetic "property" that were unforeseen only a few years ago suggest that "creative destruction" in the realm of property rights is a very real phenomenon and will remain a fixture in the modern economy for the foreseeable future.[114]

The individualistic conception of property and ownership that exists in modern capitalist society has begun to threaten more than the proliferation of injustices. It could well endanger civilization itself if that attitude continues to ignore the growing interdependencies spawned by technology that Niebuhr recognized. A case in point was highlighted in the Public Broadcasting System's production of the documentary "Organ Farm" that appeared in its *Frontline* series. The documentary dealt with the emerging technology of xenotransplantation—the transfer of genetically modified cells and organs between species—that was discussed briefly in both the introduction and chapter 4. The documentary recorded that five individuals participated in the initial trial and that each was required to sign a quite "extraordinary" consent form in which they agreed to have only "safe sex" for the remainder of their lives, to submit lists of their sexual partners to the Food and Drug Administration, and "to agree to follow-up for life and to [allow] access to their tissues after death . . . to determine if their death had anything at all to do with the xenotransplant."[115] Moreover, they received emphatic disclaimers from members of the research staff about the hazards of the genetic experiments. Neurologist Galen Henderson reflected on a conversation with one of the patients in the trial:

> It's quite scary. You know, [ten] years from now, could something bad happen as a result of her transplantation? Yes. Will there be any treatment for her? I told her that it's possible, but probably not. We don't know. We just don't know. And we want her to understand and the rest of the family to understand that we don't know.[116]

But the unknowns of xenotransplantation extend beyond the immediate patients involved in the trial. The documentary recorded that prominent scientists have voiced serious concerns over the public health risks associated with xenotransplantation based on fears that infectious agents might develop that are resistant to known treatments and spread to the general population. The PBS Internet website references a paper published in the journal *Nature Medicine* by a group of concerned scientists who have called for a moratorium on such experiments, citing inadequate methods of obtaining "public consent" for experimentation.[117] These scientists, in effect, have observed that the intensity of the individualist ethic in modern capitalist society has left open certain gaps in which collective interests are undefended. In the case of the xenotransplantation trials, a contract (patient consent) is enacted between one party (the patient) who desperately seeks treatment for a life-threatening disease and another party (the research team) that has a significant incentive to realize the fruition of years of research work; yet this contract takes place without representation from the public and despite the fact that it can have negative consequences for public health. The consent agreement is a reflection of the degree to which the externalities to private contracts (just as Niebuhr's observation of the social nature of property) are disregarded in American society.[118] It also suggests that legal and other instruments that represent the interests of various parties can become obsolete given the pace of technological change, just as Niebuhr observed.

Both the Enron scandal and the xenotransplantation trial illustrate a growing problem in American society due to the explosion of social and technological complexity that is perhaps best phrased as a question: Given the rising interdependencies and concurrent depersonalization of contemporary culture, how does society ensure that affected parties to myriad and increasingly complex transactions are involved in decision making or, at the very least, are informed of the decisions made? In the case of Enron, a select few individuals made far-reaching decisions that greatly damaged not only the corporation but the entire American economy without the consent of affected parties who had much at stake in these decisions. More egregious, not only were these disenfranchised groups not party to the decision-making process, they were not even informed of most decisions that would have enabled them to make value judgments and to act on those judgments (i.e., to change employment or sell company stock).[119] Similarly, the PBS documentary demonstrated that consent agreements to genetic experiments expose the public to risk without adequately enabling the public to be included in decision making or adequately informing the public of the risks involved.

Applying the Christian realist's understanding of the relational and finite nature of all human institutions points out the danger of the sacralization of property and the undue reverence for "private" transacting that exist in modern capitalism. That danger is consistent with the elevation of any value to a status inappropriate for any flawed, relational system of exchange. Thus, the first step suggested by Christian realism is an attitudinal one—to "pull to earth" the values, principles, and processes of necessarily flawed human systems and place them under a process of continual review. At the institutional level, attempts to reform modern capitalism get sticky; the Christian realist acknowledges that those who support public intervention in private business inevitably go too far in their confidence in human reason, just as conservatives err in placing too much faith in the natural harmonies of the market order.

A unique institution that conforms to several of Christian realism's philosophical principles and that has been implemented successfully in several European nations is the "consensus conference" format for deliberating socially and morally controversial issues. The idea behind the consensus conference is to enable a great diversity of affected parties to express their views on the implementation of particular technologies, the enactment of social policies, or other controversial issues. Most consensus conferences are made up of a steering committee, a panel of ten to sixteen citizens, a group of experts who provide testimony before the panel, and a facilitator who handles conference preparation and administration and frequently aids in the preparation of a final report.[120] Denmark has been one of the most successful and innovative countries in implementing this forum. According to Richard Sclove, between 1987 and 1996, "the [Danish] Board of Technology [organized] 12 consensus conferences on topics ranging from genetic engineering to educational technology, food irradiation, air pollution, human infertility, sustainable agriculture, and the future of private automobiles."[121] The Danish board has been highly innovative in its approach to the consensus conference, and it was the Danes who advanced the concept of using "lay citizens" rather than "experts" as participants.[122]

Great Britain, Norway, France, New Zealand, and several other countries also have adopted the consensus conference model for the public deliberation of sensitive issues such as radioactive waste management, air pollution, and gene therapy.[123] While certain industries (principally health care) and public institutions within the United States have implemented this conference format for the deliberation of issues, the tendency has been more to involve "experts" rather than the general population and to hold specialized conferences on highly technical subject matter. Other countries employing this idea have been more inclusive both in the topics and structure of the conferences conducted.

Significantly, the consensus conference initiative conforms to virtually all of the economic principles derived for Christian realism in this chapter. First, it draws value judgments on technological and other issues from a wider base than can be expressed through the market, private contracting, board meetings, or other forums. Second, it applies a critical eye to the potential social and moral consequences of technological change that the market generally does not provide. Third, it brings individual citizens out of their most common roles as consumers and gives them a position of communal responsibility where their social and moral consciences have at least the opportunity to supercede their material interests. Fourth, it serves to facilitate the continual reassessment of the notions of property and ownership that Niebuhr desired. Finally, it works to achieve a balance between various interests in the community and the nation in the pursuit of economic progress.

CONCLUDING REMARKS

The breadth of Niebuhr's social knowledge and his insight into human nature and the institutional complexities that underlie the sources of political and economic conflicts is remarkable for someone who, though he always demurred the title, is remembered to history as a "theologian." Unlike the Harvard-educated Jesuit Bernard Dempsey and others in the history of theological economics, Niebuhr was untrained in economics and in the social sciences generally.[124] He was quite simply "the natural" when it came to social philosophy. The amazing range of his interests and his uncommon energy and intellect combined to inspire unique ideas about the underlying causes of social conflicts, many of which he identified as economic. Moreover, the intensity of the connection between politics and economics in Niebuhr's social thought insists that to the extent that he is credited as a political philosopher, so too must he be acknowledged as an economic theorist. Niebuhr understood that the structure of political institutions resulted principally from the attempts of the various interests in society to secure or advance their positions over and against the efforts of other groups. For Niebuhr, it was the interplay of these largely economic forces that resulted in the political structures of nations.

Niebuhr himself undoubtedly would concede that history played a large part in whatever modest success he would attribute to himself as a social theorist. That he lived during periods when humankind made quantum leaps in its standard of living yet concomitantly utilized its technical achievements to perpetrate unprecedented brutality provided Niebuhr's uncommon intellect with a historical context in which it could flourish. He witnessed both world wars in relative youth and was able to reflect on those experiences from the vantage of a seasoned Cold War veteran many years later. He observed firsthand the transformation of human culture brought about by the Industrial Revolution, just as he witnessed social disintegration in the depths of the Great Depression. He recognized the allure of political and economic utopianism by having stood at its threshold as a Christian socialist; and, while his realism never permitted him the luxury of belief in the Kingdom of God on Earth as espoused by his Social Gospel predecessors, he also never lost the ideal of the "impossible possibility." Niebuhr, by the very chronology of his life, enjoyed unique historical "advantages" from which to plumb the depths of human despair and from which to analyze humankind's greatest accomplishments.

That enormous range of experience insisted that the central purpose of any Christian-inspired economic system must be the preservation of the individual personality and traditional morality so as to enable a society that is morally as well as materially sustainable. A morally redemptive economy requires the Christian to find a third way that sacrifices her values neither to the pure self-interest of laissez-faire or to the authoritarian ideals of collectivism. Such systems have inevitably required concessions to simple, naturalistic schemes that advance reductionist views of the person and sacrifice religious values for material success. The third way is admittedly more difficult, but the enormity of the task must never preclude its undertaking, least of all by Christians, who are called to embrace the creative center using the enormous resources of their religious heritage.

NOTES

1. Niebuhr follows this statement with a caveat, noting, "But there is a Christian attitude toward all systems and schemes of justice." See Reinhold Niebuhr (hereafter RN), "Theology and Political Thought in the Western World," in *Faith and Politics: A Commentary on Religious, Social and Political Thought in a Technological Age*, ed. Ronald H. Stone (New York: George Braziller, 1968), 56.

2. RN, *The Children of Light and the Children of Darkness: A Vindication of Democracy and a Critique of Its Traditional Defense* (New York: Charles Scribner's Sons, 1944), 59.

3. RN, "Christian Faith and Social Action," in *Christian Faith and Social Action*, ed. John A. Hutchison (New York: Charles Scribner's Sons, 1953), 241.

4. RN, *Man's Nature and His Communities: Essays on the Dynamics and Enigmas of Man's Personal and Social Existence* (New York: Charles Scribner's Sons, 1965), 16.

5. Richard Wightman Fox, *Reinhold Niebuhr: A Biography* (New York: Pantheon Books, 1985), 295. See also Charles McDaniel, "Friedrich Hayek and Reinhold Niebuhr on the Moral Persistence of Liberal Society," *Journal of Interdisciplinary Studies* 16, nos. 1–2 (2004): 145–46.

6. McDaniel, "Friedrich Hayek and Reinhold Niebuhr," 146.

7. Fox, *Reinhold Niebuhr: A Biography*, 10.

8. Walter helped his younger brother financially during Reinhold's studies at Yale Divinity School, where he concentrated principally on theology and history in his preparation for the ministry. See Fox, *Reinhold Niebuhr: A Biography*, 8–10, 37–40.

9. Fox, *Reinhold Niebuhr: A Biography*, 23.

10. Henry B. Clark, *Serenity, Courage, Wisdom: The Enduring Legacy of Reinhold Niebuhr* (Cleveland: The Pilgrim Press, 1994), 45.

11. In *An Interpretation of Christian Ethics*, written as the substance of his presentation at the Rauschenbusch Memorial Lectures at Colgate Rochester Divinity School in 1934, Niebuhr stated that the "law of love is involved in all approximations of justice, not only as the source of the norms of justice, but as an ultimate perspective by which their limitations are discovered." However, it does not serve as a realistic possibility for any social system. Simply put, the "finite condition" of humanity precluded the "law of love" as a possibility for any social order. See RN, *An Interpretation of Christian Ethics* (New York: Harper & Brothers, 1935; reprint, New York: Meridian Books, 1956), 128, 134, 120.

12. Paul Merkley observes that when Niebuhr arrived at Bethel in 1915, the total church membership was 65 German Americans. By 1928, the church had grown to a much more ethnically diverse congregational size of 656. See Paul Merkley, *Reinhold Niebuhr: A Political Account* (Montreal and London: McGill-Queens University Press, 1975), 8–13.

13. RN, "What Are the Churches Advertising?" *Christian Century* (November 27, 1924): 1532–33; quoted in Fox, *Reinhold Niebuhr: A Biography*, 67.

14. Ronald H. Stone, *Reinhold Niebuhr: Prophet to Politicians* (Nashville: Abingdon Press, 1972), 49.

15. RN, "Editorial: Politics and Economics," *Christianity and Society* 7 (Autumn 1942): 8.

16. RN, *Reflections on the End of an Era* (New York: Charles Scribner's Sons, 1934), 93–94. Niebuhr referred to *Reflections* as his "most Marxist work" in a personal interview with Ronald Stone on March 10, 1967; cited in Stone, *Reinhold Niebuhr: Prophet to Politicians*, 61.

17. RN, *Reflections on the End of an Era*, 51. Merkley notes that in the early 1920s, "Niebuhr, not yet a socialist but already convinced that the continuance of western civilization required an early satisfaction of the just demands of the working-class by the possessing classes, discovered—or thought he discovered—the secret of social reconciliation in the British political arena. That discovery had moved him to predict that the 'Christian political party' that America must have would be like the Labour Party." See Merkley, *Reinhold Niebuhr: A Political Account*, 116.

18. Stone, *Reinhold Niebuhr: Prophet to Politicians*, 27. Fox also detects Niebuhr's disillusionment with American corporate culture and its industrial moguls, stating that to Niebuhr, "Ford was a man of limitless authority whose spirit was as mechanical as his product. His identification of his own and God's purposes was so complete that he was a danger to civilization." See Fox, *Reinhold Niebuhr: A Biography*, 109–10.

19. Brown notes local clergyman Samuel Marquis' attempt to publish a book exposing the fledgling automobile industry's abuses. According to Niebuhr, Ford bought up most of the copies of Marquis' book to prevent its revelations from reaching the public. See Charles C. Brown, *Niebuhr and His Age: Reinhold Niebuhr's Prophetic Role in the Twentieth Century* (Philadelphia: Trinity Press International, 1992), 27.

20. Two articles in which Niebuhr attempts to expose Ford's "deception" of the public are found in the journal *Christian Century*: "How Philanthropic is Henry Ford?" *Christian Century* 43 (December 9, 1926): 1516–17; and "Ford's Five-day Week Shrinks," *Christian Century* 44 (June 9, 1927): 713–14; cited in Brown, *Niebuhr and His Age*, 270n39. In these, Niebuhr describes Ford's lack of a pension program, its frequent and prolonged layoffs during "retooling" periods, and its grinding work schedule that makes old men out of young ones.

21. Clark, *Serenity, Courage, Wisdom*, 45–46. Merkley says that "Ford's claims regarding his own philanthropy were almost complete eye-wash," and Niebuhr took it as a personal challenge to expose this fraudulent image "by means of some cases studies from his own parish, and some plain arithmetic." See Merkley, *Reinhold Niebuhr: A Political Account*, 34, 239n60.

22. R. H. Tawney, *Religion and the Rise of Capitalism*, first published in 1926.

23. RN, "Why We Need a New Economic Order," *World Tomorrow* (October 1928): 395–98; quoted in Merkley, *Reinhold Niebuhr: A Political Account*, 52.

24. RN, *Reflections on the End of an Era*, 24.

25. Merkley, *Reinhold Niebuhr: A Political Account*, 99.

26. See Merkley, *Reinhold Niebuhr: A Political Account*, 88. Internal quotation taken from Niebuhr, "The Religion of Communism," *Atlantic Monthly* (April 1931): 462–70.

27. RN, "Socialism and Christianity," *Christian Century* 48 (August 19, 1931): 1038.

28. Fox, *Reinhold Niebuhr: A Biography*, 75.

29. Fox, *Reinhold Niebuhr: A Biography*, 128–29.

30. Fox, *Reinhold Niebuhr: A Biography*, 167 (emphasis author's).

31. Letter from H. Richard Niebuhr to Reinhold Niebuhr, September 16, 1936; quoted in Fox, *Reinhold Niebuhr: A Biography*, 177. In Clark's interpretation of the letter, he paraphrases Richard's "obvious" conclusion, stating, "'if there is no hope for us in the temporal,' then it makes no sense to keep on preaching a gospel of societal transformation." See Clark, *Serenity, Courage, Wisdom*, 62.

32. RN, "The Domestic Situation," *Radical Religion* 3 (Editorial: Summer 1938); quoted in Merkley, *Reinhold Niebuhr: A Political Account*, 107.

33. RN, "Editorial: The Relief Situation," *Radical Religion* 2 (Summer 1937); and "Editorial: Roosevelt's Merry-Go-Round," *Radical Religion* 3 (Spring 1938); cited in Merkley, *Reinhold Niebuhr: A Political Account*, 107.

34. Brown, *Niebuhr and His Age*, 6–7.

35. Niebuhr described Smith's concept of the "invisible hand" as "the power of a pre-established social harmony, conceived as a harmony of nature, which transmutes conflicts of self-interest into a vast scheme of mutual service." In this belief, Smith "clearly belongs to the children of light." See RN, *The Children of Light and the Children of Darkness*, 2, 25–26, 31.

36. Niebuhr acknowledged that human beings have the capacity to transcend self-interest, for, "If there were not [such a capacity], any form of social harmony among men would be impossible." However, both Marxist and laissez-faire philosophy exaggerate the ability to achieve and sustain it. See RN, *The Children of Light and the Children of Darkness*, 39.

37. RN, *The Children of Light and the Children of Darkness*, 59. See also McDaniel, "Friedrich Hayek and Reinhold Niebuhr," 147.

38. RN, *The Children of Light and the Children of Darkness*, 91. Niebuhr also observed that Roman Catholic thought gradually lost the "ideal possibility of a propertyless state" and this omission contributed to property attaining "an absolute, rather than a relative" status. See RN, *The Children of Light and the Children of Darkness*, 94.

39. RN, *The Children of Light and the Children of Darkness*, 28.

40. RN, *The Children of Light and the Children of Darkness*, 61, 59.

41. RN, *The Children of Light and the Children of Darkness*, 148–49.

42. RN, "The Cult of Freedom in America," *Christianity and Crisis* 9 (February 7, 1949): 4.

43. RN, "The Cult of Freedom in America," 7.

44. RN, "The Cult of Freedom in America," 4, 5. See also McDaniel, "Friedrich Hayek and Reinhold Niebuhr," 148.

45. RN, "The Cult of Freedom in America," 4.

46. RN, "The Cult of Freedom in America," 4, 7.

47. RN, "The Conflict between Nations and Nations and between Nations and God," *Christianity and Crisis* 6 (August 5, 1946) in *Love and Justice: Selections from the*

Shorter Writings of Reinhold Niebuhr, ed. D. B. Robertson (Philadelphia: Westminster Press, 1957), 161; cited in Brown, *Niebuhr and His Age*, 125–26.

48. RN, "The Fight for Germany," *Life* (October 21, 1946): 65–68, 70, 72; cited in Brown, *Niebuhr and His Age*, 127.

49. RN, "Theology and Political Thought in the Western World," in *Faith and Politics: A Commentary on Religious, Social and Political Thought in a Technological Age*, ed. Ronald H. Stone (New York: George Braziller, 1968), 56.

50. RN, *The Self and the Dramas of History* (New York: Charles Scribner's Sons, 1955), 235.

51. RN, "Biblical Faith and Socialism: A Critical Appraisal," in *Religion and Culture: Essays in Honor of Paul Tillich*, ed. Walter Leibrecht (New York: Harper's, 1959), n.p.; cited in Merkley, *Reinhold Niebuhr: A Political Account*, 87.

52. Niebuhr's association with Galbraith was through their common membership in the Americans for Democratic Action, a group formed in 1947 that espoused moderately socialist policies. See Merkley, *Reinhold Niebuhr: A Political Account*, 154–55, 179.

53. RN, "The Teamsters and Labor's Future," *New Leader* (August 26, 1957); quoted in Merkley, *Reinhold Niebuhr: A Political Account*, 177–78. Merkley notes the argument is further developed in "The Meaning of Labor Unity," *New Leader* (March 28, 1955); and RN and Alan Heimert, *A Nation So Conceived: Reflections on the History of America from Its Early Visions to Its Present Power* (New York: Scribner's, 1973), 118–22; cited in Merkley, *Reinhold Niebuhr: A Political Account*, 267n17.

54. Friedrich A. Hayek, *Law, Legislation and Liberty*, vol. 1, *Rules and Order* (Chicago: University of Chicago Press, 1973), 110.

55. RN, "The Truth in Myths," in *Faith and Politics: A Commentary on Religious, Social and Political Thought in a Technological Age*, ed. Ronald H. Stone (New York: George Braziller, 1968), 17.

56. RN, "The Tyranny of Science," *Theology Today* 10 (January 1954): 466.

57. Niebuhr continued by stating that the nonbiological self "is like a peak of a mountain above a cloud. It is almost as 'noumenal' as the mystery of God." See RN, "The Tyranny of Science."

58. RN, "The Tyranny of Science," 470.

59. RN, "The Tyranny of Science," 471.

60. RN, "The Tyranny of Science," 471. According to Niebuhr, "No 'I' can be an 'I' without a 'Thou.' In this way we grow into selfhood." Niebuhr illustrated this point using the example of marriage; for, "if a man says by way of calculation, 'I need to fulfill myself by finding a mate,' he can hardly do so." From a sermon given at Harvard University in 1951, quoted in June Bingham, *Courage to Change: An Introduction to the Life and Thought of Reinhold Niebuhr* (New York: Charles Scribner's Sons, 1972), 39.

61. See H. Richard Niebuhr, "The Center of Value," in *Radical Monotheism and Western Culture* (New York: Harper & Row, 1960), 109 (emphasis author's).

62. H. Richard Niebuhr, "The Center of Value," 111. One might observe this value center "polytheism" in Austrian economics, for, in addition to the subjective individual in market exchange, another center emerges through social dynamics at the institutional level in the determination of those values that contribute to the Hayekian notion of "group persistence."

63. H. Richard Niebuhr, "The Center of Value," 112–13.

64. H. Richard Niebuhr, "The Center of Value," 113.

65. Richard Wightman Fox, "Niebuhr's World and Ours," in *Reinhold Niebuhr Today*, Encounter Series, ed. Richard John Neuhaus (Grand Rapids, MI: William B. Eerdmans, 1989), 5.

66. Fox, "Niebuhr's World and Ours." Fox's statement reinforces Niebuhr's differentiation between what he termed the "prudential ethics" of the social order and "transcendent morality" that exists in the connection between human and divine personality.

67. By contrast, "evil is always the assertion of some self-interest without regard to the whole." See "Niebuhr's World and Ours," 9.

68. RN and Paul E. Sigmund, *The Democratic Experience: Past and Prospects* (New York: Frederick A. Praeger Publishers, 1969), 83–84. Although Niebuhr coauthored the book with Paul Sigmund, the introduction makes clear that Niebuhr wrote the first half of the book from which this quotation is taken.

69. According to Niebuhr, this limitation of the market was often ignored in liberal theory, which "was strangely blind to the factor of power in man's social life" and "was informed by an economic rationalism which tended to equate every form of self-interest with economic interest." RN, "The Christian Faith and the Economic Life of Liberal Society," in *Goals of Economic Life*, ed. A. Dudley Ward, 433–59 (New York: Harper & Brothers, 1953), 435.

70. RN, *Beyond Tragedy: Essays on the Christian Interpretation of History*, Essay Index Reprint Series (New York: Charles Scribner's Sons, 1937; reprint, Freeport, NY: Books for Libraries Press, 1971), 200.

71. Ronald H. Stone, *Reinhold Niebuhr: Prophet to Politicians*, 105.

72. RN, "Walter Rauschenbusch in Historical Perspective," in *Faith and Politics: A Commentary on Religious, Social and Political Thought in a Technological Age*, ed. Ronald H. Stone, 33–45 (New York: George Braziller, 1968), 41.

73. RN, *Moral Man and Immoral Society* (New York: Charles Scribner's Sons, 1932), 14.

74. RN, *The Nature and Destiny of Man*, vol. 2, *Human Destiny*, one-volume ed. (New York: Charles Scribner's Sons, 1949 [orig. pub. 1941]), 20.

75. RN, *Human Destiny*, 257–58.

76. RN, *Human Destiny*, 262.

77. RN, *Man's Nature and His Communities*, 76.

78. RN, *The Children of Light and the Children of Darkness*, 76.

79. RN, "The Meaning of Labor Unity," in *A Reinhold Niebuhr Reader: Selected Essays, Articles, and Book Reviews*, comp. and ed. Charles C. Brown, 89 (Philadelphia: Trinity Press International, 1992; originally published in *The New Leader* 38 [March 28, 1955]).

80. RN and Heimert, *A Nation So Conceived*, 120.

81. RN and Heimert, *A Nation So Conceived*, 121–22.

82. RN, *An Interpretation of Christian Ethics* (New York: Harper & Brothers, 1935; reprint, New York: Meridian Books, 1956), 106–7.

83. RN, *Moral Man and Immoral Society* (New York: Charles Scribner's Sons, 1932), 80.

84. M. M. Thomas, "A Third World View of Christian Realism," *Christianity and Crisis*, February 3, 1986, 10.

85. RN, *Does Civilization Need Religion? A Study in the Social Resources and Limitations of Religion in Modern Life* (New York: The Macmillan Company, 1927), 172.

86. RN, "Coexistence under a Nuclear Stalemate," in *A Reinhold Niebuhr Reader: Selected Essays, Articles, and Book Reviews*, comp. and ed. Charles C. Brown, 103 (Philadelphia:

Trinity Press International, 1992; originally published in *Christianity and Crisis* 19 [September 21, 1959]: 121–22).

87. RN, "God's Design and the Present Disorder of Civilization," in *Faith and Politics: A Commentary on Religious, Social and Political Thought in a Technological Age*, ed. Ronald H. Stone, 103–18 (New York: George Braziller, 1968), 110.

88. RN, *The Nature and Destiny of Man: A Christian Interpretation*, vol. 1, *Human Nature*, one-volume ed. (New York: Charles Scribner's Sons, 1949 [orig. pub. 1941]), 191.

89. RN, "God's Design and the Present Disorder of Civilization," 108. Niebuhr further stated, "Our problem is that technics have established a rudimentary world community but have not integrated it organically, morally or politically." See RN, "The Illusion of World Government," in *Christian Realism and Political Problems* (New York: Charles Scribner's Sons, 1953; reprint, Fairfield, NJ: Augustus M. Kelley Publishers, 1977), 15.

90. RN, *The Irony of American History* (New York: Charles Scribner's Sons, 1952), 8.

91. Moreover, Niebuhr sees community as "an individual as well as social necessity; for the individual can realize himself only in intimate and organic relation with his fellowmen. Love is therefore the primary law of his nature; and brotherhood the fundamental requirement of his social existence." See RN, *Human Destiny*, 244–45.

92. Schumpeter's theory of "creative destruction" was discussed in chapter 1. See also Joseph A. Schumpeter, *Capitalism, Socialism and Democracy*, 3rd ed. (New York: Harper & Brothers, 1950), 83–88.

93. RN, "Will Civilization Survive Technics?" in *A Reinhold Niebuhr Reader: Selected Essays, Articles, and Book Reviews*, comp. and ed. Charles C. Brown, 33–42 (Philadelphia: Trinity Press International, 1992), 35.

94. RN, *The Children of Light and the Children of Darkness*, 52.

95. RN, *Human Destiny*, 304.

96. RN, "Our Country and Our Culture," *Partisan Review* 19 (May–June 1952): 303.

97. RN, *The Irony of American History*, 29.

98. Moreover, "we seek a solution for practically every problem of life in quantitative terms; and we are not fully aware of the limits of this approach." See RN, *The Irony of American History*, 59–60. For a discussion of diminishing returns related to technology, see Orio Giarini and Henri Louberge, *The Diminishing Returns of Technology: An Essay on the Crisis in Economic Growth*, trans. Maurice Chapman (New York: Pergamon Press, 1978).

99. Still, his persistent dialectical analysis required that he balance this notion with the observation that "color prejudice among white workers and in firms accounts as much for the high rate of Negro unemployment as does the defective education of Negro youths." See RN, "The Negro Minority and Its Fate in a Self-Righteous Nation," in *A Reinhold Niebuhr Reader*, 121 [originally published in *Social Action* 35 (October 1968): 53–64].

100. RN, *Man's Nature and His Communities*, 104–5.

101. "Reactions to Man's Landing on the Moon Show Broad Variations in Opinion—Some Would Forge Ahead in Space, Others Would Turn to Earth's Affairs: Reinhold Niebuhr," *New York Times*, July 21, 1969, 7; quoted in Brown, *Niebuhr and His Age*, 241.

102. For example, see RN, "The Sickness of American Culture," *The Nation* 166 (March 6, 1948): 267–70; and "Ideology and the Scientific Method," in *Christian Realism and Political Problems*, 75–94 (New York: Charles Scribner's Sons, 1953; reprint, Fairfield, NJ: Augustus M. Kelley Publishers, 1977).

103. Niebuhr stated, "Property is not as simply the servant of justice as the liberal creed assumes and not as simply the basis of all evil as the Marxist creed avers." See RN, "Christian Faith and Social Action," in *Faith and Politics: A Commentary on Religious, Social and Political Thought in a Technological Age*, ed. Ronald H. Stone (New York: George Braziller, 1968), 124.

104. RN, *The Children of Light and the Children of Darkness*, 102.

105. Niebuhr wrote *The Democratic Experience* with Paul Sigmund; however, the introduction makes clear that Niebuhr authored the first half of the book. See RN and Paul E. Sigmund, *The Democratic Experience: Past and Prospects* (New York: Frederick A. Praeger, 1969), 5.

106. RN, "Why Is Communism So Evil?" in *Christian Realism and Political Problems*, 33–42 (New York: Charles Scribner's Sons, 1953; reprint, Fairfield, NJ: Augustus M. Kelley Publishers, 1977), 36.

107. Data taken from an excerpt from the introduction to Corey Rosen, *Corporate Governance in ESOP Companies* [publication information not given]; available from the National Center for Employee Ownership website at www.nceo.org/pubs/corpgov.html (accessed June 9, 2002).

108. Corey Rosen, *Corporate Governance in ESOP Companies*.

109. RN and Alan Heimert, *A Nation So Conceived*, 76–77.

110. This is an oversimplification of Munkirs' work, which attempts to demonstrate how the system of "centralized private sector planning" (CPSP) has developed in the U.S. economy to compensate for the absence of formal planning processes in capitalism. His thesis is important here because it recognizes that concentrations of control in corporate governance arise "naturally" without ill intent. See John R. Munkirs, *The Transformation of American Capitalism: From Competitive Market Structures to Centralized Private Sector Planning* (Armonk, NY: M. E. Sharpe, 1985), 3–7, 80–89.

111. Munkirs, *The Transformation of American Capitalism*, 178–79.

112. The Enron/Andersen scandal involved the collusion between the energy company Enron and its auditor, Arthur Andersen LLP, with the intention to deceive stockholders and financial analysts regarding its financial condition by concealing massive losses within secretive partnerships. Many employees and investors in the firm suffered huge losses when the company's alleged fraudulent accounting practices were disclosed and the value of the company's stock tumbled. See also "Enron and Immorality," *America* 186 (February 11, 2002): 3.

113. Novak states, "To organize industry democratically would be a grave and costly error, since democratic procedures are not designed for productivity and efficiency." See Michael Novak, *The Spirit of Democratic Capitalism* (New York: Simon & Schuster, 1982), 178.

114. For a "Lockean analysis" of property rights to human organs and tissues, see Margaret S. Swain and Randy W. Marusyk, "An Alternative to Property Rights in Human Tissue," in *Life Choices: A Hastings Center Introduction to Bioethics*, 2nd ed., ed. Joseph H. Howell and William Frederick Sale (Washington, DC: Georgetown University Press, 2000), 484–93. See also House Committee on the Judiciary, Subcommittee on Courts and Intellectual Property, *Gene Patents and Other Genomic Inventions*, 106th Cong., 2nd sess., 2000, committee print.

115. Dan Salomon, M.D., transplant biologist for the Scripps Research Institute; quoted in "Organ Farm" documentary transcript; available from the Public Broadcasting System website at www.pbs.org/wgbh/pages/frontline/shows/organfarm/etc/

script1.html (accessed June 10, 2002). Part 1 aired on March 27, 2001, and part 2 on April 3, 2001.

116. Salomon and other members of the research staff generally echoed Henderson's sentiments on the "unknowns" of xenotransplantation. See Salomon, "Organ Farm."

117. F. H. Bach, J. A. Fishman, et al., "Uncertainty in Xenotransplantation: Individual Benefit versus Collective Risk," *Nature Medicine* 4 (1998): 141–44; cited in Salomon, "Organ Farm."

118. Each of the five participants in the xenotransplantation trial addressed in the PBS documentary was in the advanced stage of a serious (typically neurological) disease that was untreatable with conventional methods. See "The Patients" at www.pbs.org/wgbh/pages/frontline/shows/organfarm/etc/script1.html. Externalities are defined as those external consequences to market transactions not accounted for within the market transactions themselves. Pollution often is used as an example of an externality. In the case of a coal-fired power plant, for instance, the air pollution produced is not considered to be fully accounted for in either the transactions that lead to the production of electricity nor in those transactions that enable its consumption. Thus, the air pollution produced, to the extent it is not accounted for by other means (i.e., environmental "taxes" or fines) is an externality in the production of electricity.

119. One of the most disturbing facts of the Enron case was that company executives continued to profess the financial health of the company and encourage employees and investors to purchase company stock until just a few weeks before revelations of its fraudulent accounting practices. For an interesting perspective on the Enron/Andersen scandal, see Curtis C. Vershoor, "Were Enron's Ethical Missteps a Major Cause of Its Downfall?" *Strategic Finance* 83 (February 2002): 22–24.

120. Robert Hudspith, "Using a Consensus Conference to Learn about Public Participation in Policymaking in Areas of Technical Controversy," *Political Science & Politics* 34 (June 2001): 313–17; available from WilsonSearchPlus (accessed June 10, 2002).

121. Richard Sclove, "Town Meetings on Technology," *Technology Review* 99 (July 1996): 24–31; available from WilsonSearchPlus (accessed June 7, 2002).

122. Ironically, Hudspith notes that the "Danes based their model on consensus development conferences begun by the U.S. National Institutes of Health in 1977 to deal with issues concerning breast cancer screening." Hudspith cites the National Institutes of Health's consensus development conference website at http://odp.od.nih.gov/consensus as his source. See Hudspith, "Using a Consensus Conference to Learn about Public Participation," 313–14. The American system has largely remained confined to expert panels and the healthcare industry, which has limited its reach and effectiveness in the United States while European nations have expanded on this concept.

123. Available from the United Kingdom's Centre for Economic and Environmental Development (CEED) website at www.ukceed.org/conference/consensus_index.htm (accessed June 10, 2002).

124. Dempsey is discussed in chapter 2. For an introduction into the theological economics of Bernard Dempsey, see D. Stephen Long, *Divine Economy: Theology and the Market* (New York: Routledge, 2000), 195–205. See also Bernard Dempsey, *The Functional Economy* (Englewood Cliffs, 1958).

7

G. K. CHESTERTON'S DISTRIBUTISM

Whatever is to be the future of values, it is certain that global capitalism will be formative in the outcome. Whether the expansion of markets to remote corners of the world collapses the barriers of traditional societies and brings civilization into harmony around the values of liberalism, or that same force spawns violent reaction and a retreat to tribalism, fundamentalism, or other "primitive" orders, globalization will act as a principal protagonist. Religious and other traditions will come under increasing pressure brought about by the persistence of economic determinism.

This reality suggests that events of the past may illuminate the possibilities of the future. It has been shown that although the twentieth century began with a value center in the scientific rationalism of John Dewey and the progressives, it concluded with the philosophical dominance of the Austrian economist Friedrich Hayek and his theories of the spontaneous order, the unintended consequences of human action, and the superiority of subjective vis-à-vis collective valuation. No social theorist was as adept in explaining the value transformations that occur in "free societies" as was Hayek. It was a gift that would earn him the Nobel Prize and an intensely loyal following of academics, politicians, industrialists, and, perhaps oddly, many religious leaders. Despite the intensely naturalistic moral philosophy of Hayek, contemporary Christian social thinkers from Catholic priests to Reformed theologians have been caught up in this vindication of the Austrian liberal tradition. The principles of Austrian economics provide an alternative to the socialist idealism that history has exposed as materially deficient and morally flawed. Moreover, Hayek and his colleagues conceded the value of traditions, even religious ones, which progressives had denied and even ridiculed in predicting the eventual extinction of "superstition" by the advance of science.

This sea change in social theory that has been chronicled in the early chapters of this book was critical to the ideological triumph of democratic capitalism. Hayek's classic *The Road to Serfdom* provided a theoretical framework for the deconstruction of socialism and offered a masterful explanation for capitalism's ascendancy. He demolished the pretensions of Marxism and the idea that societies could be rationally and centrally planned:

> The tragedy of collectivist thought is that, while it starts out to make reason supreme, it ends by destroying reason because it misconceives the process on which the growth of reason depends. It may indeed be said that it is the paradox of all collectivist doctrine and its demand for "conscious" control or "conscious" planning that they necessarily lead to the demand that the mind of some individual should rule supreme—while only the individualist approach to social phenomena makes us recognize the superindividual forces which guide the growth of reason. Individualism is thus an attitude of humility before the social process and of tolerance to other opinions and is the exact opposite of that intellectual hubris which is at the root of the demand for comprehensive direction in the social process.[1]

Individualism has indeed triumphed over collectivism. Yet this overwhelming ideological victory that concluded the past century inflicted collateral damage—that being the denigration of collective "moral" guidance to the good that occurred even as the idea of collective "rational" guidance was utterly obliterated. All forms of idealism—Christian and secular, moral and rational, good and bad—have been subordinated to the material and moral outcomes of the market system. In the United States, for example, we no longer consider the economic conditions under which moral traditions will flourish, despite the presence of that ideal in the nation's religious and Enlightenment traditions. The economic system is largely absolved from moral responsibility, while "directive" energy is targeted at the political and legal order. Yet it is in the economic realm today where values primarily are formed and reformed as technological changes and economic advances challenge our understandings of personhood, God and creation, the role of the church, and the need for a public morality.

The prodigious British author G. K. Chesterton was one of the first to warn of the social and moral dangers of modernity and the phenomenon that has come to be known as globalization.[2] Chesterton, along with intellectuals and artists like Hillaire Belloc, Craig Gill, Arthur Penty, and Harold Robbins, crafted an amorphous social philosophy they named "distributism" as a response to growing concentrations of economic power and the perceived drift toward anomie in the Industrial Revolution. Like Hayek, Chesterton recognized the danger of socialist idealism in an era of economic exploitation, but they differed regarding what should be the appropriate response. Chesterton insisted that some vision must substitute for collectivist utopianism; a society sans teleology makes the determination of progress impossible and engenders a deterministic materialism not unlike that of the socialism he abhorred. For Hayek and others in the Austrian tradition, collective imposition of idealism in any form, religious or secular, represented the corruption of reason and the inevitable destruction of liberty.

Because of the penetration of Hayek's ideas into the heart of contemporary Christian social thought, contrasting Chesterton's and Hayek's views on progress opens a unique window into the future of values. Such analysis demonstrates the profound investment of Western Christians in liberalism and its capitalist engine, not simply for the allocation of material goods and the determination of worldly justice, but as the source for what is moral, good, and true. What has emerged over the past quarter century is a natural theology of the market that is accessible to all, consistent in method, and appealing to an innate sense of justice while remaining largely indifferent to social and moral outcomes.

DISTRIBUTISM: AN IDEALIZED ABSURDITY

The distributist movement that began in England in the late nineteenth century has escaped precise definition. One reason for the ambiguity is that distributism was not so much a social philosophy as a negation of much social theory that existed in the turbulent period of the Industrial Revolution. The principal objects of its critique were the dehumanizing concentrations of power in English industrialism and the utopian schemes of socialists who imagined the socialization of property to be a panacea for all ills. Ironically, distributism was equally vulnerable to the charge of promulgating a silver bullet for the social problem in its calls for the redistribution and equalization of property. In Chesterton's view, reapportioning wealth would enable a noble and propertied peasant class to emerge as the ballast of English culture, preserving its rich traditions. His idea that such redistribution might be accomplished without coercion was a particular object of ridicule. He seemed to believe that England's corporate moguls and landed aristocrats would willingly divest if they were offered rather modest incentives and could be persuaded of industrialism's harm to English life.

For the most part, distributists avoided crafting policy statements or laying out specific plans of action. Critics were vicious in attacking even their unstructured economic ideas—to add specificity would only spawn more attacks and deflect attention from one of their central goals: to expose the teleologically defeatist attitudes prevalent in modernity. However, Arthur Penty composed a *Distributist Manifesto* at the twilight of the movement in 1937, well after Chesterton had developed six fundamental principles in his essay "A Misunderstanding about Method." Those principles included the taxation of contracts "so as to discourage the sale of small property to big proprietors and encourage the breakup of big property among small proprietors"; moreover, he advocated the "protection of certain experiments" in the development of small-propertied communities to counter the concentration of wealth resulting from industrialization.[3] Such experiments might require government support via tariff, but that was the extent of coercion that Chesterton entertained.

Distributism was, above all, a remarkable debate about values. It highlighted modernity's principal weakness by pointing out the conspicuous avoidance of discussions regarding the common good. Chesterton detected this flaw in what he perceived as a radical alteration of social discourse that accompanied the Industrial Age:

> Every one of the popular modern phrases and ideals is a dodge in order to shirk the problem of what is good. We are fond of talking about "liberty"; that, as we talk of it, is a dodge to avoid discussing what is good. We are fond of talking about "progress"; that is a dodge to avoid discussing what is good. We are fond of talking about "education"; that is a dodge to avoid discussing what is good. The modern man says, "Let us leave all these arbitrary standards and embrace liberty." This is logically rendered, "Let us not decide what is good, but let it be considered good not to decide it." He says, "Away with your old moral formulae; I am for progress." This, logically stated, means, "Let us not settle what is good; but let us settle whether we are getting more of it."[4]

Chesterton's obvious resentment over the decline of teleological thinking in the age of industry differs markedly from Hayek's later comments on the futility of such deliberations—that discourse on the "good" is inevitably eclipsed by the subjective valuations of individuals engaging in the spontaneous order. Thus, it is ironic that the Austrian economic tradition owes a considerable debt to the distributist movement. Hayek credited Belloc's *The Servile State* as a source of inspiration for *The Road to Serfdom*, and he quoted Belloc in an epigraph to chapter 7: "The control of the production of wealth is the control of human life itself."[5] This statement serves to bind the two philosophies, but it also exaggerates aspects of both; for Hayek was not so indifferent between state and private control as the statement implies, and Chesterton would not have conceded such *absolute* control of human life to the economic order as Belloc apparently did. Still, distributism and Austrian liberalism share several common values: disdain for centralization and specialization, respect for the value of tradition, and a view of scientific (thus artificial) constructions of society as hopeless exercises in rationalistic pretension. Distributists could warm to Hayek's statement that "the rationalist whose reason is not sufficient to teach him those limitations of the powers of conscious reason, and who despises all the institutions and the customs which have not been consciously designed, would thus become the destroyer of the civilization built upon them."[6]

But distributism and Austrian liberalism are different in ways that add greater definition to both and inform the present discussion on the future of values. Chesterton could not stomach simplistic views of "progress" that were based purely on monetary or other measures of material affluence. He could never have agreed with a statement like that by Hayek's mentor, Ludwig Mises, that "no religious or ethical tenet can justify a policy that aims at the substitution of a social system under which output per unit of input is lower for a system in which it is higher."[7] Indeed, Chesterton's writings reflect great concern with the abuses and distractions of wealth, and he often entertained the idea that a society that exhibits declining material standards may actually be "progressing" if viewed holistically. He came to believe that Christianity offers the greatest vantage from which to appraise the essential characteristics of social progress.

A more subtle distinction that divides distributists from the Austrians is their respective views on tradition. While both groups value religious and moral traditions as formative in ways beyond the comprehension of human reason, for Hayek that value ends at the point of the individual decision. Participants are guided by traditional values in choosing among alternative courses of action; however, those influences are ultimately subordinated to the aggregation of subjective choices in the spontaneous order, which reshapes the institutional values that informed the original decisions. Traditions have little importance in assessing the "outcomes" of decision making in free societies. Collective reflection on past norms, values, and practices serves little purpose but to satisfy the psychological need for nostalgia. Hayek never questions the right or, in a strange sense, even the utility of individuals espousing transcendent values that are inaccessible to some. What he says is that none of these beliefs can persist unless they are proven to contribute to the material health and well-being of the institutions that espouse them. For Chesterton, such an evolutionary moral system defied the definition and purpose of tradition, which is to project the wisdom of the ages not only to inform human action but also to establish *absolute* boundaries for individual and collective behavior. He believed that certain truths existed beyond the machinations of culture, as best exemplified by the transcendent beliefs of the Christian faith.

If distributism is absurd for its impracticality, Chesterton thought capitalism absurd for its plethora of contradictions. His famous passage from the essay "On a Sense of Proportion" attempts to point out the self-delusions of the modern capitalist:

> He puts on his curious and creative hat, built on some bold plan entirely made up out of his own curious and creative head. He walks outside his unique and unparalleled house, also built with his own well-won wealth according to his own well-conceived architectural design, and seemingly by its very outline against the sky to express his own passionate personality. He strides down the street, making his own way over hill and dale towards the place of his own chosen and favourite labour, the workshop of his imaginative craft. He lingers on the way, now to pluck a flower, now to compose a poem, for his time is his own; he is an individual and free man and not as these Communists. He can work at his own craft when he will, and labour far into the night to make up for an idle morning.[8]

Chesterton's sardonic sortie into industrial life was intended to demonstrate that capitalism has failed even at its fundamental purpose—to release the individual from the shackles of collectivist obligation. His intent is to show that each point along the capitalist's journey is marked by contradictions (and thus restrictions) on his personality, his creativity, his resiliency—basic freedoms that industrialism has denied and that most men have conceded.

It was to Chesterton's credit that, even in such an early stage of modern capitalism, he recognized what many contemporary libertarians and neoconservatives do not: once economic power has become concentrated to such a degree as to require a mass bureaucracy with its conformity of behavior, it matters little whether the source of concentration is government, a "private" corporation, or even a dominant ideology. Chesterton observed ironically, "Capitalism has done all that Socialism threatened to do." He notes with sarcasm that to a clerk "in a world of private enterprise and practical individualism," it would make no difference "if his job became a part of a Government department tomorrow. He would be equally civilized and equally uncivic if the distant and shadowy person at the head of the department were a Government official."[9] The clerk has exactly "the sort of passive functions and permissive pleasures that he would have in the most monstrous model village." He "moves everywhere in ruts" and "thinks in terms of wages; that is, he has forgotten the real meaning of wealth. His highest ambition is getting this or that subordinate post in a business that is already a bureaucracy."[10] Thus, for Chesterton, socialism and capitalism differ in method and implementation, but they have similarly destructive effects upon the individual.

Chesterton was also prescient in recognizing the misemployment of millions in a mass economy where the demands of economic survival often dashed human passion and the ability to employ one's true talents. He described the "cogitating cogs" of the industrial machine as the "men who remain in subordinate and obscure positions because their private tastes and talents have no relation to the very stupid business in which they are engaged."[11] Modernity has necessitated a mass "sell out" where individuals neglect their true abilities in pursuit of one illusory value—physical security—that has trumped all others to the detriment of humanity's marvelous diversity.

Any number of considerations renders Chesterton's distributism "out of order" in the politically correct parlance of contemporary discourse. His medievalism that included reverence for the nobility of lords and Crusaders is well known, as was his anti-Semitism. In addition to these demerits, the more substantive issues of distributism's lack of "realism," its resistance to systematization, and the fact that the primary object of its attack—the absence of a small-propertied class—has largely been rectified in advanced countries through the wealth-generating capability of modern capitalism, suggest a philosophy devoid of relevance. Yet scholars have been unable to dismiss this "ism" in the manner of socialism or anarchism. Something in the thought of Chesterton and others in the distributist fold continues to attract Christian social theorists, in particular, to their enigmatic propositions.

But neither has distributism's persistence as an odd object of inquiry led to its invigoration as social theory. Despite the fact that Chesterton aggressively wrote against both the material and moral flaws of socialism, his willingness to *conceive* of wealth redistribution by some largely undefined method of national agreement was sufficient to restrict his social thought from the mainstream. His outspokenness on the harm of wealth concentration put him at odds with "Christian-capitalists" who made considerable gains in synthesizing religious and economic values around the natural theology of the market. Moreover, distributism has often been mischaracterized as collectivist or has simply been cast into the lot of "social constructivism" along with the progressivism of John Dewey and the New Deal policies of Franklin Roosevelt.

Michael Novak offers an observation that tempers such distortion by category: "Distributism does not insist upon equality in capital; its point is liberty and independence."[12] Where distributism is uniquely insightful is in its understanding of those forces that restrict liberty and limit independence, and it is this insight where distributism can be important to any discussion on the future of values. Government is an institution that can and indeed has restricted the liberty and autonomy of citizens, but it is far from the only one. Technocracy, urbanization, bureaucracy, monopoly, and bigotry—all these forces conspire to prevent the self-actualization of the individual and thus limit the potential of society.

"Progress and Proportion"

Chesterton's essay of the above title, published in May 1924, was an attempt to explain the disillusionment of intellectuals in the aftermath of the Great War. It was a theme on which Chesterton had written extensively even before the war and would continue to articulate for the balance of his life. He insisted that the term "progress" cannot stand alone unadorned. Those who cast about progress as a panacea meant only that society had become, through advanced techniques and technological development, capable of producing "more" but unable to answer the critical question, "More of what?"

The modern notion of progress was, for Chesterton, relativistic in its essence: "simply a comparative of which we have not settled the superlative." He offered an indictment of its ubiquitous application with the recognition that "we meet every ideal of religion, patriotism, beauty, or brute pleasure with the alternative ideal of progress—that is to say, we meet every proposal of getting something that we know about, with an alternative proposal of getting a great deal more of nobody knows what."[13] Not that progress was an inherently dirty word for Chesterton; to the contrary, "Progress, properly understood, has, indeed, a most dignified and legitimate meaning. But as used in opposition to precise moral ideals, it is ludicrous."[14]

True progress must conform to a particular composition of religious, technological, artistic, commercial, educational, and other values that give it an essential "proportion" in light of some teleological ideal. Traditional societies, even Chesterton's rapidly industrializing England, possess institutional structures capable of throttling material advance to levels where the value adjustments necessitated by development can be achieved with minimal disruption to the established life of citizens. The Anglican Church or a

British labor union could rightfully challenge some new technology, not to inhibit progress but rather to moderate the pace of change to a level at which the social and moral impacts of those changes could be addressed. Chesterton's gripe was that this rarely happened—these institutions faded into the background and trusted in the progress of the progressives that was, ironically, much like that of the capitalists. A society's material development must be realized in concert with at least an implicit teleological view held by its members, thereby assuring the retention of defining social values.

Chesterton insisted that certain developments threatened "progress rightly understood" with "progress for progress's sake." Society's infatuation with its technical prowess resulted in attempts to apply scientific reason even to unscientific questions and was a source of society's disproportionate progress. Some cultural problems might better be corrected by a dose of poetry than by an advance in chemistry. Chesterton's straw men for these criticisms were *illuminati* like the prodigious and respectable (though misguided) H. G. Wells and George Bernard Shaw. They were exemplars of confidence in the power of human reason. Concerning Wells, Chesterton stated that he "is not quite clear enough of the narrower scientific outlook to see that there are some things which actually ought not to be scientific. He is still slightly affected with the great scientific fallacy; I mean the habit of beginning not with the human soul, which is the first thing a man learns about, but with some such thing as protoplasm, which is about the last."[15]

Progress cannot be measured strictly in mortality rates or per capita income because these criteria in no way reflect the condition of the human spirit. In "The Wheel of Fate," Chesterton insisted that advances in material standards must retain an essential connection to human happiness:

> There is no obligation on us to be richer, or busier, or more efficient, or more productive, or more progressive, or in any way worldlier or wealthier, if it does not make us happier. Mankind has as much right to scrap its machinery and live on the land, if it really likes it better, as any man has to sell his bicycle and go for a walk, if he likes that better. It is obvious that the walk will be slower, but he has no duty to be fast. And if it can be shown that machinery has come into the world as a curse, there is no reason whatever for our respecting it because it is a marvelous and practical and productive curse. There is no reason why we should not leave all its powers unused, if we have really come to the conclusion that the powers do us harm.[16]

A society's ability to balance property and control machinery was for Chesterton the principal measure of its "sanity." The insane society, by implication, is technologically deterministic and values bigness, allowing concentrations of power to govern its property structure. His collection of essays entitled *The Outline of Sanity* was the most explicit statement of his economic ideas, emphasizing that cultural sanity requires a method by which members of the society come together to direct themselves toward some purposeful end. Insanity creeps in where a society relinquishes its teleological responsibility for some rational utopian vision (e.g., socialism) or resigns itself to "monopolist momentum" and allows some plutocracy to manage the aspirations of the many (e.g., capitalism).[17]

Specialists and Specialism

The direction of modern progress leads to "a gradual increase everywhere of the specialist over the popular function." Specialists were, to Chesterton, those materialists who applied "reason in the void"—rootless individuals fascinated by logic and driven by a quest for certainty that is unattainable. Their goal is the eradication of mysticism, a principal buttress against the persistent danger of insanity. His appreciation for the values of the "ordinary man" resulted directly from this peril, for the ordinary man "has always left himself free to doubt the gods; but (unlike the agnostic of to-day) free also to believe in them. He has always cared more for truth than for consistency."[18] Chesterton, the master of irony, likely would have observed of contemporary American culture that despite the rise of terrorism, the persistence of incurable disease, and the intractability of crime, we are the most "secure" people of world history. Yet we crave—indeed, it is the entire focus of our lives and source of our values—even greater security. The cost of this monistic existence is the death of poetry and romance, and unless we can right the ship, perhaps the death of religious idealism as well.

Chesterton decried not only increasing specialization but the spread of a toxic individualism that dismantles millennia-old forms of community with alarming speed: "Once men sang together round a table in a chorus," he stated; "now one man sings alone, for the absurd reason that he can sing better. If scientific civilization goes on (which is most improbable) only one man will laugh, because he can laugh better than the rest."[19] What the "modern" individual values is thus the product of her narrowing field of vision on the culture in which she toils. What is lost is original, holistic thinking capable of transforming life. Religion and philosophy are potential answers but also potential dangers. Chesterton conceded that religious and philosophical beliefs are "as dangerous as fire, and nothing can take from them that beauty of danger"; but such beliefs are necessary risks because there is "only one way of really guarding ourselves against the excessive danger of them, and that is to be steeped in philosophy and soaked in religion."[20] Ideas are indeed perilous, yet even more dangerous are the narrow ideas of the specialist than the broad ideas of the theologian or philosopher.[21]

This concern with "specialism" was an area in which Chesterton and Hayek agreed to some extent. Hayek associated specialization with the chimera that was the subject of his life's work: social planning. He described the "illusion of the specialist" that "in a planned society he would secure more attention to the objectives for which he cares most." That flawed logic works in combination with another fallacy: the belief "that our personal order of values is not merely personal but that in a free discussion among rational people we would convince the others that ours is the right one."[22] Chesterton could agree with Hayek on the inanity of a rationally planned society; where they differed was that Chesterton was one of those who believed most men would come to value what he valued if they were liberated from the day-to-day struggle for survival. He believed that people will opt for a conception of the good that balances their spiritual, physical, moral, and emotional needs once basic material concerns have been lifted. This conviction exists as a *first principle* of progress that is dependent upon "the construction of a definite philosophy of life. And that philosophy of life must be right and the other philosophies wrong."[23] For Hayek, there are no first principles beyond survival. The "right" philosophy is not an ideal toward which we strive but an unintended consequence of the fight for institutional preservation in the evolution of human culture.

Concern with the cultural effects of complexity and specialization led Chesterton to contemplate various methods of simplification. Small and simple were for G. K. infinitely more compatible with a Christian ethic than large and complex. Although he avoided economic terminology (or, more often, castigated it with his acerbic wit), one might describe Chesterton's view as a matter of "opportunity cost," that the time spent combating a cumbersome bureaucracy or managing a business concern or tinkering with some overly complex machine was necessarily time not spent attending to the spiritual, moral, and aesthetic needs of human existence. That "more" of certain commodities would contribute to social development could not be known without reflection on the present state of society in the light of some teleological ideal. This visualization must be accomplished within confines of scale that limit the domination of any particular aspect of life by another. Industrialists, just as the wage earners they lorded over, contributed to disproportion for the reason that neither was able to *idealize* their own existence. The former were busy attending to their enrichment, while workers were immersed in a basic struggle for subsistence. The answer, according to Chesterton, was the ability of both classes to understand their plight, to accede their control over the situation, and to come to terms on the redistribution of property necessary to restore the harmony of life with life that existed in preindustrial civilization.

Price and Value

Also contributing to disproportion in progress is modernity's radical elevation of trade, which "is all very well in its way, but trade has been put in the place of Truth."[24] Chesterton noted that trade, "which is in its nature a secondary or dependent thing, has been treated as a primary or independent thing; as an absolute."[25] He conceded that in normal civilizations, "the trader existed and must exist. But in all normal civilizations the trader was the exception; certainly he was never the rule; and most certainly he was never the ruler. The predominance which he has gained . . . is the cause of all disasters of the modern world."[26] Businessmen live lives wildly out of proportion because of their reduction of life's complexities to satisfaction via commodity; thus, the commercial transaction has become a sacred activity.

Elevating the status of the businessman necessarily elevates his values, especially the notion "that things are to be judged by the price and not by the value." Chesterton concluded, "Since Price is a crazy and incalculable thing, while Value is an intrinsic and indestructible thing, they have swept us into a society which is no longer solid but fluid."[27] Such could be interpreted as an indictment of a Hayekian world in which values are formed, reformed, and eradicated in the spontaneous order as facilitated by the market. Yet Chesterton is not so far outside the economic mainstream as one might think in his willingness to question the price-value relationship. One is reminded of economist Frank Knight's observation on the inadequacy of the price mechanism that the "final results diverge notoriously from the ethical standards actually held. No one contends that a bottle of old wine is ethically worth as much as a barrel of flour, or a fantastic evening wrap for some potentate's mistress as much as a substantial dwelling-house, though such relative prices are not unusual."[28]

Dependence on price as *the* source of value contributes to the malaise of relativism and what Chesterton often described as a "catastrophe of contentment" where primary and secondary principles are inverted and values float about like commodities on an exchange. It also gives rise to consumerism, about which he issued a scathing indictment at the conclusion of his essay "Reflections on a Rotten Apple":

> Whether anything more solid can be built again upon a social philosophy of values, there is now no space to discuss at length here; but I am certain that nothing solid can be built on any other philosophy; certainly not upon the unphilosophical philosophy of blind buying and selling; of bullying people into purchasing what they do not want; of making it badly so that they may break it and imagine they want it again; of keeping rubbish in rapid circulation like a dust-storm in a desert; and pretending that you are teaching men to hope, because you do not leave them one intelligent instant in which to despair.[29]

Even at the dawn of industrial civilization, Chesterton recognized that the acceleration of commerce and the extension of the transaction into formerly sacred areas of life were crowding out essential human activities. Modernity leaves us no time to hope or despair, laugh or cry, love or hate; we are left merely to transact.

Chesterton also was undoubtedly right about how peculiar it is that the "modern" Christian is so sanguine about the prospects of modernity. Christian resistance to even contemplating deceleration of the economic machine in the attempt to synchronize material advance with moral development signals an abiding faith in the current direction of progress. In effect, most Christians have given in to Hayek's notion that we are "not only the creatures but the captives of progress."[30] Distributism dares to posit the unthinkable in an age of plenty—that a steady state or even regression in the material development of society can be a good thing, for "if we cannot go back, it hardly seems worthwhile to go forward." Chesterton reminds us that the proportion of our progress is a choice; we cannot retreat to survival as justification for some determinism that dictates our material and moral development. The proportionality of progress is an expression of our values; it is volitional not determinative. We can opt for a slower pace to cultural advance if it is deemed necessary to preserve our basic values.

For Hayek and others in the Austrian liberal tradition, such normative assessments of economic processes and outcomes are as futile as speculation on the proportion of progress or judgments concerning the moral consequences of human action. There is no transcendent standard that makes one society's proportion "right" and another's "wrong," one culture's progress "moral" and another's "immoral." Religious and other traditional values serve either to shape behavior in the direction of institutional survival, or they cease to exist. They cannot establish limits to development by claim to being moral absolutes, for the reason that all values are subject to alteration or eradication based on the institutional imperative of self-preservation. In this regard, Hayek may be categorized with the group of social thinkers that Chesterton labeled "evolutionary progressives," for whom "things are always getting better because there is one very simple form of good. It can only be expressed in very simple and crude images."[31] The simple and crude image that represented the good for Hayek was the persistence and material improvement of those institutions that survive the evolutionary gauntlet.

Christianity was, for Chesterton, the principal remedy to this pervasive problem of proportion. Margaret Canovan notes that the faith's erosion in industrial England "seemed to Chesterton to lead insidiously, through devious routes of well-intentioned ideas, to the denial of human equality, the denial of human freedom, and the belief that men are helpless victims of fate." This "travesty of the human situation" denied that men are "immortal souls, each of them a priceless individual who was the center of his own world, each capable of making earth-shaking choices and changing the course of history."[32] Canovan believes that Chesterton understood Christianity as embodying two essential values that gave the power to overcome such fatalism: "first, the sacredness of every man, woman, and child, regardless of their class, education, or 'eugenic fitness'; second, the goodness of human nature and the world in spite of their faults, mysteries, and contradictions."[33] These values, if allowed to flourish, have the potential to transform human culture; they also reflect the need to reproportion progress to match the essential nature of the person. History can serve as a critical guide in this conscious revaluation, for the medieval Christian valued the cathedral, the industrial landlord valued the "ruinous cottages of the poor," and the modern man values a valueless progress. Thus, it was the spiritual ethos of the Middle Ages and not the materialism of modernity that represents a more advanced cultural epoch for the Christian.

Vast differences separating ideals of progress result from the inability to understand that progress will inevitably assume some proportion that more or less *fits* the culture that is "progressing." In Chesterton's day, it also resulted in false accusations by those who failed to understand this fundamental sense of progress and the appropriate means to attain it. As Chesterton noted, "Those of us who have the cult of proportion are at perpetual cross-purposes with those who have merely the cult of progress. Because we do not believe in indefinite extension of anarchy, they imagine that we must believe in an indefinite extension of authority."[34] This charge that the distributists' dream was no less coercive than that of the collectivists they criticized would forever stick in the minds of many. Chesterton responded to those who insisted that distributism was merely another perfectionist ideal like socialism that would impose a lifeless uniformity,

> We do not offer perfection; what we offer is proportion. We wish to correct the proportions of the modern state; but proportion is between *varied* things; and a proportion is hardly ever a pattern. . . . We do not propose that in a healthy society all land should be held in the same way; or that all property should be owned on the same conditions; or that all citizens should have the same relation to the city. It is our whole point that the central power needs lesser powers to balance and check it, and these must be of many kinds: some individual, some communal, some official and so on.[35]

Chesterton's essential admission that distributism could not be systematized presaged its decline. He never claimed that achieving a distributist vision of progress would be easy, only that it was greatly preferred and certainly more fitting for a Christian society than the undirected and morally ungrounded form of progress advanced by progressives. He conceded that "it will be a much longer and more laborious business to find the right proportions than to float on a mere fatalistic tide that is called progress."[36] Hayek had not yet penned his theories of the spontaneous order and unintended consequences of human action by the time of "Progress and Proportion," yet the absence of teleology in Hayek's theory of cultural development suggests that his was the type of evolutionary progressivism Chesterton had in mind. Hayek's philosophical dominance of the latter half of the twentieth century ensured that the future of values would be indeterminate, and his prominence among Christian social thinkers insisted that transcendent ideals would suffer as a result.

EVOLUTIONARY PROGRESSIVISM AND THE ETHOS OF MATERIALISM

What we have gained by relinquishing moral direction is material affluence; what we have lost is poetry, imagination, and romance—in short, the spirit of life. This devil's bargain was so unimaginable that Chesterton often could not contain his anger in having to write against it. Chesterton was insistent that humankind's basic assumptions about "progress" were unfounded and often inconsistent with the fundamentals of their religious convictions and national traditions. Capitalism, of the form inspired by the Industrial Revolution, was indeed an obscenity for Chesterton; he perceived an endless concentration of wealth accompanied by a systematic erosion of individual self-sufficiency and communal values. Yet he may not have realized that a creeping evolutionary progressivism is more insidious and ultimately more intransigent than the dominant scientific progressivism of his day. The latter was so obviously flawed that it was destined to extinction by its own pretension. Evolutionary progressivism built on a spontaneous order of ostensibly unlimited human freedom has the allure of liberty where individuals can be as religious, as artistic, and as "peasantlike" as they desire. Yet in the end, minus a transcendent point of reference in an age of declining tradition, evolutionary progressivism exhibits much the same deterministic character as the more scientific and explicitly deterministic philosophy over which it triumphed.

Crude images are the reflections of disfigured cultures. American society, in particular, would be wise to heed Chesterton's insights on the proportion of progress. Our economic engine has accelerated material development beyond the ability of our religious and moral institutions to ingest and respond to the implications of that change. Our nation is like a bodybuilder on steroids who is infatuated with a mirror, but one that reflects only the torso. Thus, the upper body is overdeveloped at the expense of the lower. We are a Goliath on bird legs, disproportioned in our economic vis-à-vis our social and moral development; moreover, we are approaching a thoroughgoing subjectivism destined to vindicate Hayek and the Austrian tradition. In a world that functions remarkably as Hayek described, we are likely to continue getting "more"—the question is, "More of what?"

Property—Reconceived and Redistributed

Distributism's most controversial proposition was the idea that large landholders and business magnates could be persuaded through tax and other incentives to voluntarily divest their holdings for the common good. Chesterton could see nothing of the nature of progress in his time but "the increasing loss of property by everybody, as something swallowed up into a system equally impersonal and inhuman, whether we call it Communism or Capitalism."[37] He envisioned the redistribution of property as an ally to Christianity in the reformation of industrial society. This seemingly absurd possibility was part of the grander absurdity—that "modern man," and in particular modern Christians, should be able to envision material regression as well as progression.

One must remember, however, that Chesterton's social theories were fashioned from the vantage of the Industrial Revolution. History seemingly has invalidated his prediction of an "increasing loss of property by everybody." Ownership is more widely distributed than at any point in the history of Western culture. In the United States, sales clerks, construction workers, and schoolteachers own shares of the most prestigious American corporations. Home ownership extends to all but the lowest rungs of the socioeconomic ladder. But Chesterton's concept of ownership differed greatly from the modern notion. Property in the distributist paradigm is an "experience," not the mere fact of possession, and possessing "tokens" of ownership is in no way conducive to the experience of property. A true "owner" is a steward over something small enough that it can be understood in its entirety, simple enough that it can be known in its essence, concrete enough that it can be described without contradiction, and personal enough that it becomes fundamental to one's identity. Shares of a large corporation can never equal the acres of a small farm or the commodities of a small shop for the reason that shares represent, for the masses of modern owners, a form of ownership in which they have little or no control. Thus, the care and development of those assets can never serve as expressions of the owners' values.[38]

The most pressing need in English society at the turn of the twentieth century was "to create the experience of small property, the psychology of small property." Absent that experience, people would acquiesce to the psychology of big property, big shops, and big institutions of all kinds with limited purposes that promote inhumanity and indirection. Bigness in everything meant the loss of social idealism—not the utopian variety of the socialists but the type aligned with the values of the common man. Acquiescence to a hardened industrial realism meant the transition of control to "men with the largest of earthly fortunes and the smallest of earthly aims."[39]

Chesterton observed that ironies abound in the realm of property. He noted, for example, that those "who insist that roughly equalized ownership cannot exist, base their whole argument on the notion that it *has existed*. They have to suppose, in order to prove their point, that people in England, for instance, did begin as equal and rapidly reached inequality."[40] The argument against distributed property is exposed in its fullest contradiction with the observation that the naysayers "talk as if the first Rothschild was a peasant who patiently planted better cabbages than other peasants. The truth is that England became a capitalist country because it had long been an oligarchical country."[41] For Chesterton, the ideal of the self-made corporate mogul was a hoax, and a socially destructive one at that.

Technology is associated with property in Chesterton's thought for its potential to transform the concept of ownership and reshape social values.

Distributists were never content with the ability of technology to make things bigger and faster, and they were reluctant to concede that technology made things better. Every technological advance involved a concession, a trade-off with some previously established virtue or value that now seemed less important than it once did. In those rare instances where his writing reflects pessimism in the common man, it is usually in the context of the commoner's encounter with the machine. He worried that the extension of technology from work to leisure would only worsen its societal impact. Using an instrument "in the proper way" often meant that "man has used modern machinery to escape from modern society"; yet the "weaker brethren . . . are not content to trust Mr. Ford's car but also trust Mr. Ford's creed"—the reductionist ideal that "some men are born to make cars, or rather small bits of cars." In that case, "it will be far more worthy of a philosopher to say frankly that men never needed to have cars at all."[42] Chesterton was no Luddite; he even waxed poetic at times about the potential of technological invention to enhance the experience of property as he stated clearly in "The Free Man and the Ford Car":

> If possessing a Ford car means rejoicing in a Ford car, it is melancholy enough; it does not bring us much farther than Tooting or rejoicing in a Tooting tramcar. But if possessing a Ford car means rejoicing in a field of corn or clover, in a fresh landscape and a free atmosphere, it may be the beginning of many things—and even the end of many things. It may be, for instance, the end of the car and the beginning of the cottage. Thus we might almost say that the final triumph of Mr. Ford is not when the man gets into the car, but when he enthusiastically falls out of the car. It is when he finds somewhere, in remote and rural corners that he could not normally have reached, that perfect poise and combination of hedge and tree and meadow in the presence of which any modern machine seems suddenly to look like an absurdity; yes, even an antiquated absurdity.[43]

The distributist's fear of technology was the fear of technocracy—invention for invention's sake that "outstrips imagination." "Humanity has not got the good out of its own inventions," Chesterton noted, "and by making more and more inventions, it is only leaving its own power of happiness further and further behind."[44] Yet he refused to demonize technology as had Penty and others in the distributist movement for the reason that to do so implied the subjugation of human will to an inanimate force.[45]

The Internet explosion in the last two decades of the twentieth century serves both to reinforce and to challenge Chesterton's views on property and technology. On the one hand, the entrepreneurial expansion that accompanied this technological revolution had the effect of redistributing wealth. Property, albeit of a form Chesterton would not have recognized, was indeed dispersed, which led to the rise in prestige of an entirely new class of "techies," some of whom are now entering the realm of social theory and predicting our future. On the other hand, the Internet has greatly exacerbated indirection and contributed additional complexity and anonymity to the economy. The development of Internet-based "day trading" in the 1990s represents the quintessence of the ownership type against which Chesterton fought. That online entrepreneurs make instantaneous decisions involving ownership of companies about which they know little or nothing and either profit or lose thousands and even millions of dollars on those transactions would represent sheer obscenity to Chesterton. Moreover, the ubiquitous use of machinery in the form of PCs, laptops, cell phones, personal organizers, iPods, and other devices deemed necessary to "interface" with the global society has made an "unearthy" economy even more sterile.

The wealth-generation and dispersion characteristics of the Internet have been overwhelmed by its depersonalizing and obfuscating effects in relationships between producer and consumer, professional and client, owner and property. Today the need exists to reconnect owner and property, to restore self-reliance as fundamental to human dignity, and even to detechnologize areas of our lives if certain technologies are discovered to be harmful to our moral and spiritual well-being. In a world that conforms to Hayek's moral system, such value choices have no meaning; they do not exist. From a distributist perspective, however, we have "regressed" from the earthy, character-developing, and identity-reaffirming property of preindustrial civilization to the amorphous, tokenish, and identity-threatening forms of property in the Information Age. Thus, what we own is increasingly unable to express what we value.

This transition in the nature of property and ownership that Chesterton observed and that has continued to the present day has taken a significant toll on the ability of the market to accurately arbitrate social values. The loss of intimacy with and care for what we own has resulted in expressions of value that are inconsistent with fundamental beliefs. The complexity of modern ownership has resulted in Christians and other religious persons owning assets that do not reflect (and may fundamentally contradict) their values. Chesterton's answer to modernity's challenges was to sacralize small property. He noted, "The ground under the pioneer's feet can only be made solid by being made sacred. It is only religion that can thus rapidly give a sort of accumulated power of culture and legend to something that is crude or incomplete."[46] One of the principal obstacles to this sacralization of small property is what Chesterton referred to as the "catastrophe of contentment," where "men in large numbers have submitted to slavery."[47] Despotic government is tyrannical, but so too are corporate trusts and even the psychology of consumerism. Chesterton feared, in particular, the formation of a "business government" that would "combine everything that is bad into its plans for a better world. There will be no eccentricity; no humour; no noble disdain for the world."[48]

One wonders whether Chesterton would rethink his statement from "The Religion of Small Property" that "there cannot be a nation of millionaires, and there has never yet been a nation of utopian comrades; but there have been any number of nations of tolerably contented peasants." The United States is today a nation of millionaires, and the income of other nations has grown enormously in the milieu of a rapidly expanding global economy. It is ironic that Chesterton did not anticipate the paradox that a civilization founded on the principle of the equality of all before God could have emerged so unequal in structure and yet so prosperous. His point, however, was that "if we do not directly demand the religion of small property, we must at least demand the poetry of small property. It is a thing about which it is definitely and even urgently practical to be poetical."[49] He insisted that those who arrive at the experience of small property, the psychology of small property, and, yes, even the poetry of small property would be willing to sacrifice "the help of science to the hunger of possession."[50] For Chesterton, possession was the experience of responsibility, the charge of community to give oneself to stewardship for the sake of others.

Economic Indirection and Value Expression

Chesterton believed that modernity has contributed to a confusion of knowledge and causes that leads to a confusion of values. Absent understanding of cause and effect in a complex civilization, the moral foundation of society begins to erode, its basis for self-government declines, and the prospects for corruption increase, as he observed in "The Real Life of the Land":

> What is wrong with the man in the modern town is that he does not know the causes of things; and that is why, as the poet said, he can be too much dominated by despots and demagogues. He does not know where things come from; he is the type of cultivated Cockney who said

he liked his milk out of a clean shop and not a dirty cow. The more
elaborate is the town organization, the more elaborate even is the town
education, the less is he the happy man of Virgil who knows the causes
of things. The town civilization simply means the number of shops
through which the milk does pass from the cow to the man; in other
words, it means the number of opportunities of wasting the milk, of
watering the milk, of poisoning the milk, and of swindling the man.[51]

Today, vast networks of holding companies, online retailers, and financial intermediaries like mutual and pension funds contribute to this
phenomenon that Chesterton described as economic "indirection." Americans, in particular, transact across the Internet with anonymous persons,
donate their money to misunderstood or misrepresented causes, and engage a mass bureaucracy in even the simplest of economic functions.
Moreover, they are often unaware of their holdings in companies that may
or may not espouse values consistent with their own. The development of
"green" mutual funds, Lutheran funds, and even a Dow Jones Islamic Market Index that tracks the stock prices of halal companies[52] is a positive response to the realization that investment is the principal form of value expression in contemporary society, regardless of whether we are cognizant
of the values expressed. The question remains, however, whether these developments can effect institutional change in the economic mainstream,
not simply on the margins.

Conventional forms of ownership today exacerbate indirection
through myriad layers of complexity. The quest for innovation in investment leads to the development of instruments such as derivatives and hedge
funds that make a mockery of the concept of a "directed" economy. Financial managers are themselves often at a loss in explaining to investors
how these instruments increase or decrease in value; that duty is reserved
for the specialists and their computer models that perform the calculus necessary to derive value from disparate and ostensibly unrelated phenomena.
The investor, relieved from responsibility as caretaker for what she owns,
merely awaits the monthly statement and the crude acknowledgment of
profit or loss.

The bifurcation of moral and economic life in the United States contributes to economic indirection and the unintended consequences of value
expression through investment. Americans participating in the increasingly
complex global economy have achieved the ability to separate their economic behavior from their moral convictions. The introduction described
the 2004 senatorial campaign of Peter Coors, president of the Coors

Brewing Company of Colorado, as an example of this bifurcation of moral responsibility and economic behavior. Coors' run for the Senate as a "family values" candidate coincided with his family-owned company's sponsorship of the "Black & Blue 2004 Festival in Montreal," a weeklong gay benefit that included a "Raunch Fetish Night and a male nude revue."[53] Tim Russert, host of NBC's *Meet the Press* interviewed Coors and observed that his campaign had distributed a brochure that contained the statement, "Our company's values are our family's values." When Coors was asked whether he could see inconsistencies in his company's sponsorship of "male nude revues and fetish balls" and his campaigning as a "family values" candidate, he replied that he did not.[54] The pervasiveness of such attitudes in American culture respecting conduct in the economic realm is, as noted previously, aptly represented by the popular advertising slogan for the city of Las Vegas: "What happens here, stays here."

But neither Chesterton nor Hayek could have accepted such a maxim. Both recognized the porous borders between political, commercial, religious, and other institutions. Hayek granted preeminence to the economic realm, concluding, "Economic control is not merely control of a sector of human life which can be separated from the rest; it is the control of the means for all our ends."[55] Chesterton acknowledged that commercial values were rapidly displacing those of storied traditions, but he was unwilling to concede a purely material realm in which spirit and tradition were irrelevant, for "even what we call our material desires are spiritual, because they are human. Science can analyze a pork-chop and say how much of it is phosphorus and how much is protein; but science cannot analyze any man's wish for a pork-chop, and say how much of it is hunger, how much is custom, how much nervous fancy, how much a haunting love of the beautiful. The man's desire for the pork-chop remains literally as mystical and ethereal as his desire for heaven."[56] Modernity eradicates mystery and reduces life to endless calculations of utility.

Chesterton feared the allure of such a system and the materialistic ethos it fostered. He cautioned that materialism generally "leads men to complete fatalism," which, in turn, commits them to some deterministic scheme that claims to advance liberty but in fact destroys free will. "The determinists come to bind, not to loose."[57] While it is true that the principal object of his scorn was the scientific rationalism of Spencer, Wells, and the like, evolutionary determinism (as later espoused by Hayek and Mises) was also the object of Chesterton's ire. He could not stomach the social and moral erosion that accompanied indirection in "progress." His revulsion for all forms of determinism prompted a desperate appeal in his book *Ortho-doxy* to reclaim direction over progress:

> Reform implies form. It implies that we are trying to shape the world in a particular image; to make it something that we see already in our minds. Evolution is a metaphor for mere automatic unrolling. Progress is a metaphor from merely walking along a road—very likely the wrong road. But reform is a metaphor for reasonable and determined men: it means that we see a certain thing out of shape and we mean to put it into shape. And we know what shape.[58]

For Hayek, the impossibility of knowing "what shape" relegates free societies to the moral flux spawned by an evolutionary determinism. Attempts to apply moral boundaries to this process are merely defenses of the "old principles" by those "indignant moralists" of religious traditions, which inevitably result in their disappointment.[59]

Evidence of wide separation between economic behavior and religious and moral traditions substantially vindicates the Austrian economic tradition and, in particular, Hayek's views of the dominance of subjective to collective expressions of value. Moreover, it suggests truth in Hayek's statement that "the peace of the world and, with it, civilization itself thus depend on continued progress at a fast rate. At this juncture we are therefore not only the creatures but the captives of progress."[60] Western capitalists, including many Christians, have convinced themselves that they are powerless to interrupt or even redirect progress from the unknowable path established by an economic order of ever-increasing complexity.

Chesterton recognized, however, that the "materialist, like the madman, is in prison; in the prison of one thought." The materialist's consolation is in thinking it "singularly inspiring to keep on saying that the prison was very large."[61] Hayek's "one thought" was that the aggregate of subjective choice in the interplay of a free society inevitably works toward the material improvement of those groups that survive. Indeed, he was inspired by the conviction that a social order built on this philosophy (and on an ethos of subjectivism) was inevitably more productive than those based on collectivist principles. The material generation and value-shaping power of the spontaneous order determines the good without need for appeals to religious or other traditions, and it has produced a global economy of immense proportion. It is the immensity and productivity of the world economy (more so than its morality) that has drawn Christian and other religious thinkers to Hayek's conclusions.

CONCLUDING REMARKS

Many would argue that Chesterton's distributism was an eloquent though idiosyncratic response to a now nonexistent problem. He was indeed guilty, just as the youthful Reinhold Niebuhr, of miscalculating the effects of the distribution of property on social justice. In the gross disparities of ownership during the Industrial Revolution, redistribution was, for many who were resistant to socialization, an irresistible panacea. Yet acknowledging the claims of Chesterton's critics does not denigrate his social commentary. Despite the fact that liberal capitalism supplies sufficient freedom to enable an infinite variety of lifestyle choices, we are indeed distracted by an endless stream of life-encumbering activities, commodities, and superfluities. But distraction is not coercion, and it is certainly not oppression. The danger is that we will gravitate toward Hayek's form of materialistic determinism for the absence of a grander vision and for the lack of a sense of proportion.

The Austrian revolution that was significant in helping to defeat collectivist theories of social order also succeeded in conquering romantic, poetic, and religious ideals of cultural development. It suggested that free societies are open to all these possibilities as individuals express their values in free exchange with others, yet it dogmatically pronounced the futility of *collective* vision in directing progress. We are now discovering that collective vision is necessary for the sustenance of collective morality. Distributism's idyllic vision posits something remarkable—that a society of stable or even declining material affluence can be a good thing if it serves to properly proportion progress to conform to its cultural values. It calls for a redefinition of progress that draws on the sources of Christianity and other traditions to prevent an evolutionary determinism from monopolizing development.

It is likely that, at least in the West, the material component of human happiness will soon exhibit diminishing returns. Our prosperity has already begun to test one of the fundamental tenets of classical economics—the principle of the insatiability of human wants. As material goods become increasingly unsatisfying vis-à-vis spiritual needs, the market will become an even less accurate arbiter of social values for the reason that spiritual satisfactions are less commodifiable. The mystery of the pork chop is slowly coming to light. One answer to the dilemma we are facing is, in Chesterton's terms, to reapportion our progress such that it corresponds to the full range of values—individual and collective, immanent and transcendent—that make up humanity's marvelous diversity. To even approach the distributist vision of a "third way" that offers a Christian approach to economic life, we will have to prove ourselves capable of reenvisioning progress, which entails proving ourselves capable of much more—of greater vulnerability, of technological self-denial, of spiritual reformation. We will have to prove ourselves capable of altering our consumption patterns in ways consistent with our religious traditions. The fallacy today that consumers are "selective," when in fact they are often driven by a herd mentality into conspicuous and, worse, habitual consumption, must be exposed for what it is: the self-denial of a consumption-driven culture that lacks the imagination to live any other way.

The "future of values" lies somewhere between the philosophies of Chesterton and Hayek. That statement, however, erects a rather vast continuum in the imagination from a pastoral life of stable traditions and self-reliance to an economically interdependent and deterministic existence where the competition for survival dynamically reforms traditions. Chesterton's value as a social thinker is in reminding us that where we fall along that continuum is a choice. For Hayek, choice belongs only to increasingly traditionless individuals, the independent variables in a complex equation forged by a spontaneous order in which institutions, including religious traditions, are the dependent variables. Without a healthy dose of idealism, Western culture is likely to continue down the road to an evolutionary and deterministic order of the type Hayek so aptly described and against which Chesterton persistently warned. If we are to avoid Hayek's determinism and accept responsibility for the proportion of our progress, then there must be some ideal worthy of denying ourselves the benefits of our economic and technological prowess for the sake of our moral survival. Mises' statement that no theologian can advocate a system in which output per unit of input is lower than one in which it is higher must be challenged, or a thoroughly subjectivist and materially deterministic culture becomes a real possibility. Given the marginalization of religious traditions and the absence of teleological thinking today, it would appear that in the twenty-first century, the game is Hayek's to lose.

NOTES

1. Friedrich Hayek, *The Road to Serfdom*, Fiftieth Anniversary Edition (Chicago: University of Chicago Press, 1994), 181–82.

2. Thomas H. Naylor and Lawrence C. Smith are among the scholars who find in distributism a salient critique of modernity and globalization. See Naylor's "Averting

Self-Destruction: A Twenty-first Century Appraisal of Distributism" and Smith's introduction in *Distributist Perspectives*, vol. 1, *Essays on the Economics of Justice and Charity*
(Norfolk, VA: IHS Press, 2004).

3. Chesterton explains that this is a "sketch of the first principles of Distributism
and not the last details, about which even Distributists might dispute." G. K. Chesterton
(hereafter GK), "A Misunderstanding about Method," in *The Outline of Sanity* in *The
Collected Works of G. K. Chesterton*, vol. 5, *Family, Society, Politics* (San Francisco: Ignatius
Press, 1987), 98.

4. Chesterton continues his characterization of the modern man's position, noting
his particular dependence on education as a substitute for discussions of the good: "He
says, 'Neither in religion nor morality, my friend, lie the hopes of the race, but in education.' This, clearly expressed, means, 'We cannot decide what is good, but let us give
it to our children.'" GK, *Heretics*, in *The Collected Works of G. K. Chesterton*, vol. 1 (San
Francisco: Ignatius Press, 1986), 51.

5. Hayek, *The Road to Serfdom*, 97.

6. Friedrich A. Hayek, "Scientism and the Study of Society: Part III," *Economica*,
n.s., 11 (February 1944): 33.

7. Ludwig von Mises, "Economic Freedom in the Present-Day World," in *Economic
Freedom and Interventionism: An Anthology of Articles and Essays by Ludwig von Mises*, ed.
Bettina Bien Greaves (Irvington-on-Hudson, NY: The Foundation for Economic Edu-
cation, 1990), 238.

8. GK, "On a Sense of Proportion," in *The Collected Works of G. K. Chesterton*, vol. 5,
Family, Society, Politics, ed. George J. Marlin et al., 74–84 (San Francisco: Ignatius Press,
1986), 74–75. Chesterton noted another contradiction in capitalism that is somewhat
analogous to the contemporary "Wal-Mart phenomenon" and its perceived effect of reducing wages and benefits: "Capitalism is contradictory as soon as it is complete; because
it is dealing with the mass of men in two opposite ways at once. When most men are wage
earners, it is more and more difficult for most men to be customers. For the capitalist is
always trying to cut down what his servant demands, and in doing so is cutting down what
his customer can spend. . . . He is wanting the same man to be rich and poor at the same
time." GK, "The Peril of the Hour," in *The Collected Works of G. K. Chesterton*, vol. 5, edited by George J. Marlin et al., 54–64 (San Francisco: Ignatius Press, 1986), 59.

9. GK, "On a Sense of Proportion," 75.

10. GK, "On a Sense of Proportion," 78.

11. GK, "The Free Man and the Ford Car," in *The Collected Works of G. K. Chesterton*, vol. 5, edited by George J. Marlin et al., 165–72 (San Francisco: Ignatius Press,
1986), 170.

12. Michael Novak, introduction to *The Collected Works of G. K. Chesterton*, vol. 5,
Family, Society, Politics, ed. George J. Marlin et al. (San Francisco: Ignatius Press, 1987), 29.

13. GK, *Heretics*, 52.

14. GK, *Heretics*, 52. Chesterton went so far as to suggest that "nobody has any business to use the word 'progress' unless he has a definite creed and a cast-iron code of
morals. Nobody can be progressive without being doctrinal." GK, *Heretics*, 53. Chesterton's comments on progress can be seen as recognition of the "cultural lag" problem that
accompanied industrialization and preoccupied social science in its formative period as
has been discussed in previous chapters. Not only traditional conservatives but social
thinkers like Karl Marx, John Dewey, and William Ogburn were concerned that estab-

lished institutions might be on a collision course with the values spawned by an all-too-technical "progress."

15. GK, *Heretics*, 77. Discounting the Christian doctrine of "original sin" led moderns like Shaw and Wells to exaggerate the possibilities of sociological solutions to the problems of humankind. Were they to acknowledge the influence of the soul, they would discover that "a permanent possibility of selfishness arises from the mere fact of having a self, and not from any accidents of education or ill-treatment."

16. GK, "The Wheel of Fate," in *The Collected Works of G. K. Chesterton*, vol. 5, edited by George J. Marlin et al., 143–50 (San Francisco: Ignatius Press, 1986), 145–46.

17. GK, "A Misunderstanding about Method," 93.

18. GK, *Orthodoxy*, in *The Collected Works of G. K. Chesterton*, 1:230. San Francisco: Ignatius Press, 1986.

19. GK, *Heretics*, 164.

20. GK, *Heretics*, 203.

21. Chesterton suggested that the "threat" posed by ideas is contingent upon the recipient: "Ideas are dangerous, but the man to whom they are most dangerous is the man of no ideas. The man of no ideas will find the first idea fly into his head like wine to the head of a teetotaller [*sic*]." *Heretics*, 202–3. Not simply the "idea" but the concept of the thinking man threatens the capitalist and creates a "horror of holidays" that is "very largely a horror of the vision of a whole human being: something that is not a 'hand' or a 'head for figures.' But an awful creature that has met himself in the wilderness. The employers will give time to eat, time to sleep; they are in terror of a time to think." GK, "The War on Holidays," in *The Collected Works of G. K. Chesterton*, vol. 5, edited by George J. Marlin et al., 417–20 (San Francisco: Ignatius Press, 1986), 419.

22. Hayek reinforces this idea with examples that suggest he could have had Chesterton in mind: "The lover of the countryside who wants above all that its traditional appearance should be preserved . . . , no less than the health enthusiast who wants all the picturesque but insanitary old cottages cleared away, or the motorist who wishes the country cut up by big motor roads, the efficiency fanatic who desires the maximum of specialization and mechanization no less than the idealist who for the development of personality wants to preserve as many independent craftsmen as possible, all know that their aim can be fully achieved only by planning." Yet, "the adoption of the social planning for which they clamor can only bring out the concealed conflict between their aims." See Hayek, *The Road to Serfdom*, 61.

23. GK, *Heretics*, 197.

24. GK, "Reflections on a Rotten Apple," The American Chesterton Society website, at www.chesterton.org/gkc/Distributist/rottenapple.html (accessed July 15, 2005).

25. GK, "Reflections on a Rotten Apple." Chesterton follows with his traditional reinforcement of wit to drive the point home: "The moderns, mad upon mere multiplication, have even made a plural out of what is eternally singular, in the sense of a single. They have taken what all ancient philosophers called the Good, and translated it as the Goods."

26. GK, "Reflections on a Rotten Apple." Chesterton described traders as individuals "whose only hope is that Trade is Good or whose only secret terror is that Trade is Bad." He also offers the ironic observation that "the complexity of commercial society has become intolerable, because that society is commercial and nothing else."

27. GK, "Reflections on a Rotten Apple."

28. Frank Hyneman Knight, "The Ethics of Competition," in *The Ethics of Competition* (New Brunswick, NJ: Transaction Publishers, 1997), 47.

29. GK, "Reflections on a Rotten Apple."

30. Hayek, *The Constitution of Liberty* (London: Routledge and Kegan Paul, 1960), 52.

31. GK, "Progress and Proportion," in *The Collected Works of G. K. Chesterton*, vol. 33, *The Illustrated London News (1923–1925)*, ed. Lawrence J. Clipper (San Francisco: Ignatius Press, 1986), 339–40.

32. Margaret Canovan, *G. K. Chesterton: Radical Populist* (New York: Harcourt Brace, 1977), 122.

33. Canovan, *G. K. Chesterton: Radical Populist*, 63.

34. GK, "Progress and Proportion," 340.

35. GK, "On a Sense of Proportion," 63.

36. GK, "Progress and Proportion," 342. Chesterton even admitted that the distributist vision was utopian "in the sense that our task is possibly more distant and certainly more difficult [than that of Communism or capitalism]. We are more revolutionary in the sense that a revolution means a reversal: a reversal of direction, even if it were accompanied by a restraint upon pace. The world we want is much more different from the existing world than the existing world is different from the world of Socialism." GK, "On a Sense of Proportion," 61.

37. GK, "The Beginning of the Quarrel," in *The Collected Works of G. K. Chesterton*, vol. 5, edited by George J. Marlin et al., 41–53 (San Francisco: Ignatius Press, 1986), 52.

38. Chesterton glorified genuine property "as a point of honour." "The true contrary of the word 'property,'" he said, "is the word 'prostitution.'" See GK, "The Beginning of the Quarrel."

39. GK, *A Miscellany of Men*, 6th ed. (1912; London: Methuen, 1930), 141–42; quoted in Canovan, *G. K. Chesterton: Radical Populist*, 132.

40. GK, "The Beginning of the Quarrel," 51 (emphasis added).

41. GK, "The Beginning of the Quarrel," 51.

42. GK, "The Free Man and the Ford Car," 171. Chesterton placed infinite value on the variety of experience that has some affinity with John Paul II's conception of Christian personalism. The worker must be valued above capital and process—it is an essential Christian doctrine that human beings are valued above machines. Chesterton finds exemplars for his vision in peasantry and burghers, noting, "The peasant almost always runs two or three side-shows and lives on a variety of crafts and expedients. The village shopkeeper will shave travelers and stuff weasels and grow cabbages and do half a dozen such things, keeping a sort of balance in his life like the balance of sanity in the soul. The method is not perfect; but it is more intelligent than turning him into a machine in order to find out whether he has a soul above machinery." GK, "The Free Man and the Ford Car," 170.

43. GK, "The Free Man and the Ford Car," 171.

44. GK, "The Romance of Machinery," in *The Collected Works of G. K. Chesterton*, vol. 5, edited by George J. Marlin et al. (San Francisco: Ignatius Press, 1986), 154.

45. He stated, "It seems to me quite as idolatrous to blaspheme [machinery] as to worship it." See GK, "The Romance of Machinery," 152.

46. GK, "The Religion of Small Property," in *The Outline of Sanity* in *The Collected Works of G. K. Chesterton*, vol. 5, edited by George J. Marlin et al. (San Francisco: Ignatius Press, 1986), 165.

47. GK, "Summary," in *The Outline of Sanity* in *The Collected Works of G. K. Chesterton*, vol. 5, edited by George J. Marlin et al. (San Francisco: Ignatius Press, 1986), 199.

48. GK, "Summary," 201.

49. GK, "The Religion of Small Property," 167.

50. GK, "The Religion of Small Property," 143.

51. GK, "The Real Life of the Land," in *The Collected Works of G. K. Chesterton*, vol. 5, edited by George J. Marlin et al., 134–40 (San Francisco: Ignatius Press, 1986), 137.

52. "Halal" is an Arabic term that denotes the compliance of a good, service, or human activity with *Shariah* (Islamic Law). Institutions have begun to form that track business concerns in Islamic society and rate their compliance with *Shariah* respecting the products and services they produce, their methods of financial investment (acknowledging *Shariah*'s prohibition on interest-based investment), and other measures. For more, see Timur Kuran, "The Genesis of Islamic Economics: A Chapter in the Politics of Muslim Identity," *Social Research* 64 (Summer 1997).

53. NBC News, *Meet the Press*, October 10, 2004. A transcript of this show is available at www.msnbc.com/id/6200928.

54. NBC News, *Meet the Press*, October 10, 2004.

55. Hayek, *The Road to Serfdom*, 101.

56. GK, *Heretics*, 117. Chesterton witnessed the emergence of the behavioral sciences under the leadership of intellectuals like Herbert Spencer, but he characterized the attempt to erect sciences of history, sociology, and "folklore" as "not merely hopeless, but crazy" (117).

57. GK, *Orthodoxy*, 227. Chesterton states that "the materialist is sure that history has been simply and solely a chain of causation"; moreover, both "materialists and madmen never have doubts" (27).

58. GK, *Orthodoxy*, 310.

59. Friedrich Hayek, *Law, Legislation and Liberty*, vol. 3, *The Political Order of a Free People*, 2nd ed. (Chicago: University of Chicago Press, 1981), 165–66.

60. He continues, stating, "Even if we wished to, we could not sit back and enjoy at leisure what we have achieved." See Hayek, *The Constitution of Liberty* (London: Routledge and Kegan Paul, 1960), 52.

61. GK, Orthodoxy, 265.

8

JOHN PAUL II'S
ECONOMIC PERSONALISM

One may be excused for confusing Pope John Paul II with Milton Friedman or Robert Nozick after reading descriptions of his economic thought by Catholic social thinkers like Robert Sirico or Richard John Neuhaus. Libertarians and neoconservatives do their best to fully ground John Paul's economic ideas in the tradition of free market liberalism. Conversely, they often portray the social philosophy of his predecessors (notably Paul VI) as "left leaning," having been influenced by the rise of European socialism in the early twentieth century. According to these pundits, the socialist predilections of past pontiffs have been corrected in John Paul's newfound appreciation for the virtues of democratic capitalism.[1]

Such simplifications, however, do a great disservice to a tradition that has exhibited an unwavering commitment to core social principles and to a man whose economic ideas demonstrate remarkable balance. Perhaps I have some medical condition that renders me unable to detect philosophical nuance, but I have always been amazed by the remarkable *consistency* of the encyclicals, in particular regarding economic philosophy. When hearing the charge of inconsistency in papal economic thought, my response has been, relative to what? To Protestantism's "pink fringe" of the early twentieth century that morphed into evangelical zeal for the market and helped place Ronald Reagan in the White House in 1980? In the twentieth century alone, American Protestantism covered almost every conceivable point along the continuum of political economy from libertarianism to Marxism. By that standard and in that same period, Catholic economic thought, at least that articulated by the popes and their curia, demonstrated remarkable uniformity.

What is the motivation behind attempts to portray papal economics as unenlightened and in desperate need of John Paul's liberalizing influence?

Why enlist his social philosophy in an anachronistic campaign to eradicate socialism well after its ideological defeat? Why do many of John Paul's supporters extract the most positive of his comments regarding capitalism while minimizing his insights into the actual and potential abuses of the emerging global order? Did John Paul, as Sirico claims in describing the encyclical *Centesimus Annus*, actually reread Leo XIII's *Rerum Novarum* through the insights of Austrian liberalism and arrive at a greater appreciation for the virtues of capitalism than his predecessors or than he himself previously acknowledged?

The answers to these questions are not easily discerned. Explanations are undoubtedly clouded by a Cold War hangover and the persistence of political rancor even as the most fundamental questions of politics and economics have been resolved. Thankfully, there is one conclusion that will become apparent as this chapter unfolds: John Paul's economic ideas are far more balanced than many of his Catholic supporters are willing to admit. Part of the reason for his economic evenhandedness is the obvious value he places on the integrity and constancy of the Catholic social tradition, as reflected in myriad references to the letters of his predecessors. Another hint as to the source of balance in his economic philosophy is found in a comment by George Weigel: "John Paul II is arguably *the* iconic figure of the twentieth century because his life has embodied, personally and spiritually, the human crises with which Churchill, Lenin, Stalin, Mao, FDR, and Reagan (not to mention Watson and Crick, Heisenberg, Fermi, and Freud) were all engaged in their distinctive ways."[2] John Paul, just as Reinhold Niebuhr and G. K. Chesterton, witnessed philosophically inspired tragedy in the rise of collectivist totalitarianism as well as the promise of economic deliverance in the utopian ideals of Christian socialists and those who advanced a "Gospel of Wealth." Also in concert with Niebuhr and Chesterton, he recognized a common materialistic ethos as the sole source of happiness in these movements, and he insisted that Christians must maintain an appropriate distance from systems with such dependencies.

Still, some Catholics see the need to reach beyond the encyclicals to provide legitimacy to Catholic social philosophy. Sirico, for example, sees the influence of Hayek and other economic thinkers of the classical tradition in *Centesimus Annus*, noting that "Austrian methods, approaches, and insights pervade the document." The significance of the hundredth-anniversary encyclical of *Rerum Novarum* "is that it has enlarged the scope of social teaching, made it more sophisticated in light of contemporary economic science, and pronounced on the Church's overall vision of what constitutes a humane economy."[3] It is true that John Paul proposes a rereading of *Rerum Novarum*, but that endeavor does not rely on the principles of Austrian liberalism or any other secular philosophy; rather, its primary trust is in the superior insights into human nature and institutions passed down through millennia of Christian tradition. John Paul's proposal to reread this seminal document is largely a response to changing conditions: the rise of technology, the triumph of capitalism, and the emergence of a global economic system. *Rerum Novarum* gave the church what John Paul describes as "'citizenship status' . . . amid the changing realities of public life."[4] John Paul merely lends his own perspective as the leader of one of Christianity's largest and most revered traditions to the challenges of religious and economic life.

SUBSIDIARITY AND THE
PERSONALIST APPROACH TO ECONOMICS

What is most salient to Christian libertarians and neoconservatives in John Paul II's economic thought is his greater receptivity to principles of a market economy than his predecessors. They note John Paul's clear rejection of a "middle way" between capitalism and socialism—a recurrent theme among Christian social thinkers that is, for conservative Christians, an inevitable step out onto the slippery slope toward communism. Father Sirico offers an emphatic statement of what he considers to be John Paul's economic legacy:

> Where did Pope John Paul II stand on economic issues? The same place he stood on all other issues involving the well-being of the human person. He favored the rights and dignity of all people, freedom to work and to create, an environment of security that permits the flourishing of faith. He had faith in freedom and no love for the grand secular state. Thus did this pope understand that human dignity implies non-socialist political and economic structures, which are commonly known as the business economy.[5]

Certainly John Paul was a champion in the campaign to eradicate socialism. He recognized the "inherent" lack of personal dignity in all systems that render the individual a mere cog in some social or economic machine. One question, however, is to what extent he associated the dehumanizing influences of economic systems *exclusively* with socialism. Another question is to what extent he located the fountain of freedom in the institutions of the "business economy."

Sirico continues by quoting John Paul from *Centesimus Annus* that the "modern business economy has positive aspects." John Paul states, "Its basis is human freedom exercised in the economic field, just as it is exercised in many other fields. Economic activity is indeed but one sector in a great variety of human activities, and like every other sector, it includes the right to freedom." Moreover, John Paul agrees that "the free market is the most efficient instrument for utilizing resources and effectively responding to needs."[6] Positive comments, no doubt, but they are hardly a glowing endorsement of capitalism. If John Paul envisions the business economy as inherently dignifying and liberating as Sirico implies, one would think that he could locate more inspiring and convincing quotations of John Paul's promarket position.

The reason for Sirico's choice of quotations is simple. The words that he extracted from the encyclical *are* the most glowing endorsements for the free market system that John Paul offers. Not that John Paul is antagonistic to capitalism; rather, he maintains an even keel in contrasting the *inherently* dehumanizing qualities of collectivism with the virtues and *potentially* dehumanizing aspects of capitalism. Sirico notes that *Centesimus Annus* "reaffirms the autonomy of economics as a legitimate and positive discipline."[7] In places, John Paul recognizes the need for monetary and financial specialists to help analyze and guide complex modern economies. However, at other points in the encyclical, John Paul appears to challenge the autonomy of economics and suggests that its separation from other aspects of life has contributed to the diminution of the person, to the inappropriate elevation of capital over labor, and to the materialism that forms the core of contemporary Western society.

Far from distancing himself from the economic thought of his predecessors, John Paul compliments the prescience of past encyclicals and offers his own words in furthering the highly consistent voice of Catholic social thought. Specifically referencing Pope Leo XIII's *Rerum Novarum*, John Paul notes its "surprisingly accurate" prognosis of the events of 1989 and 1990 that resulted in the fall of Communism and observes, "The radical transformations which followed, can only be explained by the preceding situations which, to a certain extent, crystallized or institutionalized Leo XIII's predictions and the increasingly disturbing signs noted by his Successors."[8] These statements reflect the typical esteem of John Paul for the economic insights of twentieth-century popes.

Two concepts of Catholic social thought are critical to this consistency and to the continuance of the tradition: subsidiarity and Christian personalism. The bottom-up social structure of subsidiarity that John Paul outlines has become fundamental to the Catholic social tradition. No single ideal is as important in constructing a Catholic conception of society as the understanding that, in the words of Pius XI from *Quadragesimo Anno*, "It is an injustice and at the same time a grave evil and disturbance of right order to assign to a greater and higher association what lesser and subordinate organizations can do."[9] Political and economic structures that marginalize "lower-order" associations damage both individual and collective freedoms. Subsidiarity is critical to all social systems, which must enable freedom at the lowest levels or fail; such was the truth behind the revolution of 1989. And that truth has enabled recognition of the "relative" superiority of democratic capitalism to socialism. This distinction is grounded in an optimistic view of human nature as tending toward good but being "capable of evil."

The concept of subsidiarity compliments the notion of Christian personalism that has become increasingly integral to Catholic perspectives on the social order. Christian personalism focuses on the dignity of the individual in action with others as central to the Christian conception of the human person. John Paul views the individual as being able to "transcend his immediate interest and still remain bound to it"[10] with the aid of institutions extending from the family to the higher but less personal order of the state. Human associations are the critical link in establishing social and moral connections that are fundamental to Christian personalism. The truths that emanate from subsidiarity and personalism are essential in crafting systems of governance, for "the social order will be all the more stable, the more it takes this fact into account and does not place in opposition personal interest and the interests of society."[11] In other words, a Christian personalist view of society that embraces subsidiarity in the accomplishment of social goals is key to the material and moral sustainability of any system of social order.

The Acting Person

Like many of his supporters, John Paul sees a need for synthesis, but the synthesis he envisions is not between theology and philosophy but rather one that must occur *within the person*. Just as for Niebuhr, the transcendent human person is key to all motivations that enable the individual to rise above the contingencies of nature and history for the purpose of moral action. In *The Acting Person*, which he wrote while serving the Catholic Church as Cardinal Wojtyla in 1979, John Paul observes that the "basic intuition of the transcendence of the person in action allows us to perceive simultaneously that moment of integration of the person in action which is complementary in relation to transcendence."[12] This moral integration of the person at the point of action is far superior in its moral and social effects to the attempts to meld the metaphysical and ethical bases of theologies and philosophies.

Many scholars have noted John Paul's emphasis on human freedom and the importance of the ego in economic and other activity. Ego provides the drive to human action that derives from freedom, for the "person is dynamized in his own manner only when in the dynamization he depends on his ego."[13] But the exercise of free will depends on man's "autodeterminism," an innate orientation toward God, and it cannot be relegated to some *indeterminism* shaped only by a spontaneous order in the evolution of culture. "Choice and decision are obviously no substitute for the drive toward good that is appropriate to will and constitutive of the multifarious dynamism of the human person."[14] The drive toward good distinguishes acting "from any submission to action," a trait unique to human beings and one that differentiates John Paul's conception of action from that of Hayek and the Austrians with their overriding principle of institutional determinism:

> The essential condition of choice and of the ability to make a choice as such, seems to lie in the specific reference of will to truth, the reference that permeates the intentionality of willing and constitutes what is somehow the inner principle of volition. To "choose" does not mean to turn toward one value and away from others (this would be a purely "material" notion of choice). It does mean to make a decision, according to the principle of truth, upon selecting between possible objects that have been presented to the will.[15]

The turn toward one value and away from others is a perfect definition of individual choice in Austrian theory. Any reference to "truth" in this process is not only unessential but self-delusional for theorists like Hayek and Mises. Truth is found only in the "outcomes" of human decision making; it can be an input only in the sense of existing as a "temporal" value that informs the immediate choice but which is subject to change or elimination altogether.

The Acting Person addresses the complex relationship of value and action. Actions leave imprints and "once performed [do] not vanish without a trace: they leave their moral value, which constitutes an objective reality intrinsically cohesive with the person, and thus a reality also profoundly subjective." This statement is consistent with the moral theory of Hayek. However, John Paul follows this comment with one that shatters that harmony: "Being a person man is 'somebody' and being somebody he may be either good or bad."[16] Here John Paul refers to a quality of good or bad that "informs" the individual decision, not simply a posteriori assessments of decisions that have contributed to the survival of some social groups and to the extinction of others. In contrast to Austrian thought, John Paul insists that "action by the person should not be seen as having a purely ontological significance; on the contrary, we should attribute to it also an axiological significance." For personal action to have axiological significance, it must enable the "acting person" to "fulfill" himself in the action. The opposite of such self-fulfilling activity is what John Paul describes as "moral evil."[17] Thus, the personalism articulated by John Paul is "truly" subjective in a way that the subjectivism of Austrian liberal philosophy is not.

John Paul identifies the "fluid" concept of necessity in modern economic thinking as infringing upon the dynamic and inherent freedom of the human person in the Christian tradition and preventing her "true" self-fulfillment. Materialism has created a society in which necessity is perceived at every turn. Things once superfluous to human existence are now seen as necessary for survival. Things we must have now greatly eclipse mere human needs. This materialistic anthropology leads to an error in the basic conception of the person in which "the essence of freedom then becomes self-love carried to the point of contempt for God and neighbor, a self-love which leads to an unbridled affirmation of self-interest and which refuses to be limited by any demand of justice."[18] John Paul's use of quintessentially Niebuhrian language to describe the devolution of freedom into libertinism via "self-love" demonstrates his recognition of social principles quite similar to those of Christian Realism.

Intermediate communities are crucial for John Paul in avoiding the reduction of the human person in the interest of efficiency and material gain. They provide a critical identity to counter the influence of government and economy: "The individual today is often suffocated between two poles represented by the State and the marketplace. At times it seems as though he exists only as a producer and consumer of goods, or as an object of State administration."[19] Involvement in charitable organizations and various forms of volunteer work help to elevate the individual above these callous distinctions. Development begins with the family, for in a real sense "the family too can be called a community of work and solidarity."[20]

Some Christians have taken John Paul's priority for personalism and subsidiarity in economic affairs as a call for crafting a synthesis of philosophy and moral theology. Acton Institute scholar Gregory Gronbacher states that the "genesis of economic personalism is rightfully understood as a synthesis of Christian social teaching and economic science that affirms the centrality of the free human person."[21] Moreover, he insists that, "without a genuine synthesis of economic science and moral science, the enterprise of a humane economy drifts either into pious sentiments without practical use, or into economic ideology masquerading as legitimate moral theory."[22] History, however, confirms what John Paul understands—that the level at which synthesis is attempted is critical to success or failure. Past attempts to synthesize theology and philosophy, as in Christian socialism, the Social Gospel, liberation theology, and various abundance theologies, all failed due to the fact that they were largely economic ideologies masquerading as theology or moral philosophy. Moreover, these attempts to synthesize economic theory with Christian theology resulted in Christianity giving over too much to secular institutions: central planning committees, government bureaucracies, and the market, to name a few. All hope is placed in some secular theory or institution with the idea that its outcomes will be highly (if not perfectly) consistent with Christian theology and morality.

One reason for the failure of these efforts and for divergence in Christian and Austrian conceptions of action and morality might be discerned in Reinhold Niebuhr's observation that Christianity "transvalues history." There can be no synthesis of systems—in this case, economic philosophy and moral theology—where foundational values are largely at odds. The beatitudes will not work as value theory for either capitalist or socialist economic systems. We are suspended in a marvelous tension that brings out the good and bad in all of us as we pursue our spiritual and material ends. Pope John Paul recognizes this tension despite his adherence to natural law principles that illuminate certain harmonies between creation and the human spirit. Natural law informs basic human decision making, but John Paul understands that the greatest choices result from confronting the paradoxes, not discerning the harmonies. John Paul, just as Niebuhr and Chesterton, was aware of this truth and its importance to the construction of society.

Acknowledging an inherent tension between Christianity and all forms of political economy does not damn capitalism or even denigrate it as economic philosophy. It merely recognizes that Christian and secular teleologies will at times conflict and compete for our attention. That competition between value systems might be seen as a terrible burden or a gift of God who enables human free will in a universe of competing desires and motivations—some moral, some immoral, and, perhaps more problematic, some which are perceived as amoral. But to suggest such a tight coupling between Christianity and any social order is to necessarily relativize and minimize the value of Christian principles in informing individual and social behavior.

John Paul does not disregard the needs of an increasingly complex and global economy. Indeed, he calls for a critical analysis of the economic order by economists and monetary experts with the admonishment that it should favor a more "integral and concerted development of individuals and peoples."[23] There should be no central standard by which to measure the efforts of experts; however, he insists that the subjective element of the human person must be preserved along with the moral autonomy of institutions. Most important is that all such efforts should be conducted with an attitude of humility, for "when people think they possess the secret of a perfect social organization which makes evil impossible, they also think that they can use any means, including violence and deceit, in order to bring that organization into being."[24]

Squaring the Circle: The Quest for Christian Capitalism

Despite John Paul's caveats, some Christian theorists insist that their tradition's moral and social principles be reconciled with secular theories of human behavior or political and economic principles, or, at the very least, that tensions between them should be attenuated. Neuhaus, for example, takes exception with those who posit an inherent tension between the individualism of modern culture and Catholic teaching on community:

> It is a mistake to pit, as some do pit, modern individualism against a more organic Catholic understanding of community. Rather should we enter into a sympathetic liaison with the modern achievement of the idea of the individual, grounding it more firmly and richly in the understanding of the person destined from eternity to eternity for communion with God. The danger of rejecting individualism is that the real-world alternative is not a Catholic understanding of communion but a falling back into the collectivisms that are the great enemy of the freedom to which we are called.[25]

Thus, we discover one reason for the push toward *systematic synthesis* for many Christians: a dichotomous worldview that inspires fear of regression to the only "real-world" alternative to the individualism of modern culture: collectivism. Neuhaus finds support for attempts to harmonize individualism with the Catholic conception of community in a quotation taken from *Redemptor Hominis* and employed again by John Paul in *Centesimus Annus*: "This human person is the primary route that the Church must travel in fulfilling her mission"; moreover, "This, and this alone, is the principle which inspires the Church's social doctrine."[26] What Neuhaus fails to adequately explore are the frequent cautions against excessive individualism and consumerism that John Paul offers in the same encyclical. Only two paragraphs after the one from which Neuhaus takes his quotation, John Paul warns of "permissive and consumerist solutions, which under various pretexts seek to convince man that he is free from every law and from God himself, thus imprisoning him within a selfishness which ultimately harms both him and others."[27] This and other statements balance *Centesimus Annus* in a way that makes clear that John Paul is in no way christening the subjectivist ethos of modern capitalism.

Gronbacher uses the economic ideas of John Paul to attempt a wider synthesis between the Austrian, Chicago, and Virginia schools of economics (generally thought of as the most "free market" economic schools) with Christianity. Gronbacher's synthesis is based on another critical assumption that libertarians and neoconservatives often use to harmonize Christianity with market capitalism: "that methodological individualism properly understood is completely within the tradition of Christian social teaching and not morally suspect."[28] This *assumption* leads to the conclusion that "accepting the ontological priority of the individual human person does not inevitably lead to moral individualism. In fact, the ontological priority of the individual leads to a proper understanding of the methodologies of various social sciences, including moral theology."[29] Gronbacher recognizes that Hayek and other champions of liberalism tend to assert a form of "freedom as self-initiation." However, he distances Christian personalists from the secular liberals by noting that the former "want to preserve the fuller Christian understanding of freedom as ordained to the truth of the human person and to God. Without anchoring freedom in a transcendent foundation, it quickly degenerates into license."[30] The question is how to anchor freedom in a transcendent foundation in a culture where a growing number of individual activities take place in markets that are generally beyond the purview of our moral communities.

Neuhaus insists that "foes of the market economy" ignore the positive attitude toward capitalism displayed in *Centesimus Annus* and other encyclicals. Instead, they pounce on select statements such as the one John Paul issued at an address to the United Nations' Food and Agriculture Organization (FAO). In that address, John Paul referred to a "world divided" and stated that "often the selfishness of a few will not permit the weaker ones to benefit fully from resources and other goods, from commerce, scientific discoveries, the benefits of new technology; all this can help to negate the equal right of every people to be seated at the table of the common banquet."[31] Neuhaus portrays this statement by John Paul as isolated and atypical, something misconstrued and manipulated by those with an ulterior agenda—to subvert democratic capitalism. As evidence for John Paul's support of free trade, Neuhaus uses another statement from the FAO address that "the movement towards a new world order of trade which does not penalize agricultural progress in developing countries should be put into operation as quickly as possible, thus *fostering the integration of their potential into the economies of the rich countries*."[32] Neuhaus sees particular significance in the last phrase, adding italics for emphasis and noting that John Paul makes clear that "the economies of the rich countries are not the problem but the solution for development of the poor ones."[33]

In fact, both statements—the one Neuhaus references and the one he believes to be exaggerated by critics of capitalism—reflect the balance typically displayed in Pope John Paul II's economic writings. One statement demonstrates recognition of the "relative" superiority of democratic capitalism to socialism in its orientation toward human liberty and its potential to raise living standards. The other is typical of John Paul's concern for those less fortunate and his insistence that the developed world acknowledge its responsibility for poor nations and peoples. In representing the economic thought of John Paul, it is unfair to advance either position without recognition of the other.

Elevating Labor above Capital

For the Christian, the possibility of a durable tension in which Christian values inform economic decision making, both individual and collective, is a more realistic goal than the advancement of synthesis between theology and philosophy. Such an approach is also more compatible with "economic reality" in which irresolvable tensions are ever present: wealth and poverty, First World and Third World, localism and globalization. Historically, abuses have resulted from attempts at oncefor-all resolution of these tensions. Progressivism went too far in absolving individuals of responsibility and in targeting institutions for the social and moral reform of society. The subjectivism of modern liberal society has gone too far in the other direction, placing the burdens of sustainability largely on the individual and discounting the roles and contributions of collectives.

One of the most historically formative economic relationships is the inherent tension between labor and capital. The inability to maintain an appropriate balance in this relationship contributed to the injustices of the

Industrial Revolution that witnessed the rebellion of socialism and an intellectual reaction in the distributism of Chesterton and Belloc. Today, technological advances and competitive pressures exacerbate the labor-capital tension by adding pressure to take the path perceived as most contributory to the bottom line in the immediate term. Such decisions increasingly involve workforce downsizings, reductions in benefits, and outsourcing of labor-intensive business functions. Work in any economic system is more than its material product; it has social and moral components that must be accounted for.

John Paul II emerged as a champion of workers' rights and a holistic conception of human labor. In *Laborem Exercens*, he observes, "Man's life is built up every day from work, from work it derives its specific dignity, but at the same time work contains the unceasing measure of human toil and suffering, and also of the harm and injustice which penetrate deeply into social life within individual nations and on the international level."[34] The very nature of work "bears a particular mark of man and humanity"; it distinguishes human beings from the rest of creation because it is a call to exercise dominion and apply human creativity in participating at a higher level in the created order. The impossibility of overstating the importance of work in the economic thought of John Paul is reflected in his statement, "Human work is a key, probably the essential key, to the whole social question."[35]

John Paul describes work as a "transitive activity" in that it begins with the human person as subject and extends to external objects; moreover, it "presupposes a specific dominion by man over 'the earth.'"[36] This elevation of humanity to its proper status in the created order necessarily involves elevating human activity. But the call to dominion has often contributed to the problem of "proportion" in economic growth that Chesterton recognized. For John Paul, the elevation of labor "is not only a question of raising all peoples to the level currently enjoyed by the richest countries, but rather of building up a more decent life through united labor, of concretely enhancing every individual's dignity and creativity, as well as his capacity to respond to his personal vocation, and thus to God's call."[37] Such statements beg the question of how Christian libertarians and neoconservatives can be committed to John Paul's Christian personalism and yet unwilling to genuinely question the often depersonalizing working conditions dictated by the industrial structures of an increasingly global economic system.

Elevation of the individual laborer can itself become problematic when it results in a radical individualism that divorces the individual from community. The exaggeration of human freedom is potentially as damaging as the radical diminution of the individual in collectivist societies. Consistent with both Niebuhr and Chesterton, John Paul sees dangers at both extremes of the individualism-collectivism continuum in that "individualism sees in the individual the supreme and fundamental good, to which all interests of the community or the society have to be subordinated, while objective totalism relies on the opposite principle and unconditionally subordinates the individual to the community or society."[38]

Arriving at an appropriate "Christian" understanding of the individual necessitates an equally appropriate perspective on work as a Christian vocation. Work has a dual nature, both objective and subjective, which forces human beings into decisions and often trade-offs between work as the transformation of nature and the production of "things" (its objective nature) and work as fulfillment of the worker (its subjective nature).[39] Achieving the appropriate balance in a world of specialization requires insights of both Old and New Testaments to enable human decision making that extends beyond the immediate context to the whole of existence. Such an understanding "constitutes in itself the most eloquent 'Gospel of work,' showing that the basis for determining the value of human work is not primarily the kind of work being done, but the fact that the one who is doing it is a person. The sources of the dignity of work are to be sought primarily in the subjective dimension, not in the objective one."[40]

John Paul recognizes that various forms of work will have "greater or lesser objective value"; still, the principal criterion for assessing the value of work must be "judged above all by the *measure of the dignity* of the subject of work, that is to say the person, *the individual who carries it out*."[41] For John Paul, the individual must remain the "purpose" of work; thus, his primary reference throughout *Laborem Exercens* is to the person as worker, not as consumer. Indeed, the idea that human beings achieve their *dignity* principally as consumers is a major force driving the practical materialism that is consuming modern society. This distortion of the means by which dignity is achieved in the economic realm also makes hypocrites of those who are disillusioned by the moral compromises required by certain occupations but who choose to remain in those positions out of fear for their economic survival.

The subjective-objective distinction is critical in understanding John Paul's view of human labor, for all methods and systems for investigating economic life have an inherent bias, being "marked by the premises of materialistic economism." John Paul is cognizant of advances in working conditions and the inherent elevation of the individual worker in capitalist vis-à-vis collectivist societies. Human dignity has greater *potential* for

272   *Chapter 8*

sustainability in societies of democratic capitalism, but even in the most
affluent, market-based societies, there is the ever-present danger of "treating work as a special kind of 'merchandise' or as an impersonal 'force'
needed for production."[42] There is also danger in complacency with gains
already achieved and the idea that the advancement of personalism in
working relationships is a natural product of capitalism.

The net of the subjective-objective distinction for the relationship
between capital and labor is that the latter must retain priority in any system of political economy. Some systems are more favorably disposed to
the appropriate relationship than others. The priority of labor over capital results from the fact that "labor is always a primary *efficient cause*, while
capital, the whole collection of the means of production, remains a mere
instrument or instrumental cause."[43] This relationship should be self-evident; it is "natural" for the reason that capital—including not only natural resources but all means of production—is "the result of work and bears
the signs of human labor."[44] Capital is thus naturally subordinate to labor
in the order of creation.

Emphasis on labor and on maintaining human dignity in work can
help soften the blows of the economic cycle and must be considered in the
redistribution of resources that accompanies globalization. In *Laborem Exercens,* John Paul observes the force of creative destruction and the possibility that displacement of skilled workers due to technological and other advances can lead to unemployment and a lowered standard of living. Yet he
speaks favorably of the potential consequences of shifting production from
the West to developing countries in order to lower the cost of production:

> These changes may perhaps mean unemployment, at least for a time, or
> the need for retraining. They will very probably involve a reduction or
> a less rapid increase in material well-being for the more developed coun-
> tries. But they can also bring relief and hope to the millions who today
> live in conditions of shameful and unworthy poverty.[45]

The possibility of a "less rapid increase in material well-being for the
developed countries" causes no particular alarm for John Paul, who at times
evinces a distributist-like concern with the frenetic pace of material advance. He seems more focused on continuing the Catholic social tradition's
concern for "just remuneration" that is centered on the priority of the family. For a family breadwinner, this "means remuneration which will suffice
for establishing and properly maintaining a family and for providing security for its future," and a just wage also has symbolic significance in reaf-

firming that the "whole socioeconomic system" is operating in a way that is just. Popes from Leo XIII to the present have articulated the principles of just wages and working conditions. In the words of *Rerum Novarum*, "If through necessity or fear of a worse evil the workman accepts harder conditions because an employer or contractor will afford no better, he is made the victim of force and injustice."[46] The market can aid in determinations of justice in labor-management relationships, but it is no substitute for the transcendent moral perspective of the individual employer who wields economic power over others.

Much like Chesterton, John Paul perceives unions as roughly equivalent to the "medieval guilds of artisans" in bringing together people who practice the same craft. Yet unions differ from guilds in that the former rose up in defense of workers' rights, which John Paul describes as "indispensable" to social life. John Paul's experience with the solidarity movement in Poland undoubtedly conditions his views on the role of unions. The unionizing of workers often takes on characteristics of a struggle for rights, but it should not be a struggle with the objective of eliminating the opposition. The principal contribution of work is that it unites people and serves the all-important role of community building. Nevertheless, the defense of worker rights may necessitate stern action. Catholic social teaching recognizes the legitimacy of worker strikes "in the proper conditions and within just limits." But a strike must always be recognized as an "extreme means" of achieving justice; employing this instrument for political or other purposes "can lead to the paralysis of the whole of socioeconomic life."[47]

John Paul's emphasis on the role of labor is conditioned by his understanding of two related concepts: the notions of the "direct" and "indirect" employer. The direct employer is the person who hires, compensates, and may terminate an employee. In contrast, John Paul describes the indirect employer as "all the agents at the national and international level that are responsible for the whole orientation of labor policy."[48] These agencies have a significant role to play: they "must make provision for overall planning with regard to the different kinds of work by which not only the economic life, but also the cultural life of a given society is shaped."[49] Again, he is alluding to the subjective and holistic character of human labor, and he demonstrates no aversion to the term "planning." Thus, John Paul understands what many of his supporters do not: there are "collective and qualitative needs which cannot be satisfied by market mechanisms." Indeed, he identifies the "frequent lack of planning" in urbanization as a "source of many evils."[50]

Again echoing a concern of distributism, John Paul fears the influence of complexity and the depersonalization of a mass economy on the individual worker. Some have no means "of entering the network of knowledge and intercommunication which would enable them to see their qualities appreciated and utilized. Thus, if not actually exploited, they are to a great extent marginalized; economic development takes place over their heads, so to speak."[51] He sees these classes as especially prevalent in developing nations, but he also recognizes large segments of workers in developed countries that are relegated to the peripheral economy and the struggle for mere subsistence.

John Paul posits something of a moral hierarchy of occupations and industries based on their respective contributions to both society and the individuals who hold those positions or work in those industries. Agricultural work has an inherent dignity and special role in society. He notes that even in developed countries, agricultural labor is often exposed to the "land hunger" of the powerful; moreover, agricultural laborers are especially susceptible to the vicissitudes of creative destruction.[52] However, the vital connection to the land found in agriculture enables the spiritual development of the person in ways that are more difficult to achieve or maintain in other occupations.

The rights of disabled and migrant workers are a prominent theme in *Laborem Exercens*, written in 1981 at a time when many national and international organizations were addressing these issues. He notes, "Since disabled people are subjects with all their rights, they should be helped to participate in the life of society in all its aspects and at all the levels accessible to their capacities."[53] Emigrant workers are exposed in unique ways to changes in the market order. Again, John Paul emphasizes the importance of coordination and planning involving not only the market but also public authorities, intermediary institutions, and individuals, including employers and even the emigrants themselves. Care should be taken such "that the person working away from his native land, whether as a permanent emigrant or as a seasonal worker, should not be placed at a disadvantage in comparison with the other workers in that society in the matter of worker rights." Emigration to pursue one's livelihood must not be exploited by those who wield economic power. John Paul reiterates that the protection of disabled and emigrant worker rights is simply another contribution to the more fundamental principle that the "hierarchy of values and the profound meaning of work itself require that capital should be at the service of labor and not labor at the service of capital."[54]

Finally, again following the prescription of Leo XIII, the rights of workers extend beyond their material well-being and include the right to attend to their religious duties. Employers, in particular Catholic ones, have a critical role to play in ensuring that their workers have ample time and opportunity to worship. Carving out space for spiritual development in a frenetic, market-based culture is not easily achieved, yet it is essential not only to the spiritual development of the person but also to enable society to arrive at a Christian concept of development. Employers must not use the competitive pressures of the marketplace or the demands of their own economic survival as excuses for denying their workers ample opportunity to pursue a spiritual life beyond the workplace.

John Paul says it is legitimate to speak of a "struggle against an economic system" if that system upholds the "absolute predominance of capital" vis-à-vis "the free and personal nature of human work."[55] He insists that use of the term "struggle" in describing economic systems that inappropriately raise capital above labor does not mean that socialist philosophy is being resurrected as the alternative, but rather it calls for the promotion of "*a society of free work, of enterprise and of participation*."[56] This concept of "struggle" against the abuses of impersonal economic systems is one that alarms many Christian libertarians and neoconservatives. They are, unlike John Paul, quick to label those who criticize what they consider to be un-Christian characteristics of contemporary capitalism. They claim to defend capitalism against its enemies, when in fact they jeopardize its existence by refusing to acknowledge abuses. They seem intent on killing capitalism with kindness and refuse to accept the possibility that the gravest threats to capitalism today are not Marxist philosophy or radical environmentalists but rather the continued growth in income disparities, injustice in the allocation of scarce resources, inequities in health care and legal services, corruption in government and private corporations, and the acquiescence to such injustices as simple "realities" of market economics. Such "friends" of capitalism have the potential to become its greatest enemies if they continue to ignore their own tradition's insightful pronouncements on economic life.

ENABLING A "UNIVERSAL DESTINATION OF GOODS"

In describing Leo XIII's attitude toward property, John Paul states that he was "well aware that private property is not an absolute value, nor does he fail to proclaim the necessary complementary principles, such as the *universal destination of goods*."[57] The concept of a universal destination of goods in Catholic social thought asserts that Christian teaching prioritizes material goods as belonging to all, above private claims to possession and their private use by individuals. Individual property rights are acknowledged and even lauded as necessary for the proper functioning of a modern economy. However, private property rights are circumscribed by recognition of their social consequences and realization that gross inequities violate Christian principles of fairness and brotherhood, irrespective of their worldly justification. This idea of a universal destination of goods is one that has long concerned economically conservative Catholics who fear that some Christians misinterpret the term to mean the promotion of "one form of socialism or another, including government redistribution of wealth."[58] What the popes have in fact done is to provide an important contextualizing principle for the Christian treatment of property. Popes from Leo to John Paul have affirmed the right to private property, yet they have insisted that the proper use of goods remains subordinate to their original destination as goods intended for all.

John Paul II described the universal declaration of goods as a "characteristic principle of Christian social doctrine," recognizing both the right to private property as well as its "intrinsically social function."[59] Christian advocates of highly privatized conceptions of property have insisted that this concept of goods as originally intended for all not be misconstrued or taken too literally. They rightly employ John Paul's steadfast criticism of collectivist principles in defense of their position. But it should be equally obvious from its ubiquity in Catholic social teaching that the "universal destination" is no mere pipe dream of some idyllic Christian society. It has a real purpose in reminding Christians that ownership of property is not an "absolute" right; thus, conceptions of property will necessarily change along with developments in cultural and historical conditions.

John Paul is convinced that the universal destination is just as appropriate a conceptual reference for contemporary investigations of property rights and, in particular, for nations formerly dominated by collectivist systems, as it was in fending off the threat of communism. He utilizes the universal destination concept in particular for criticism of the international trade system, "which is mortgaged to protectionism and increasing bilateralism," and he insists on the reform of trade to eradicate discrimination against the inchoate industries of developing countries and to correct the inherent inequities in the exchange of technology.[60] Markets are the most efficient instrument for allocating the world's resources, but they are limited to the satisfaction of needs "which are 'solvent,' insofar as they are endowed with purchasing power, and for those resources which are 'marketable,' insofar as they are capable of obtaining a satisfactory price."[61] Thus, John Paul recognizes a hierarchy of needs in terms of their ability to be satisfied by the market, from the most basic and commodifiable to the most spiritual and unmarketable. Some human needs evade fulfillment through the instrument of the market altogether; thus, other institutions and means must be available for their satisfaction.

Despite the market's limitations, consumerism has spread with the idea that our most intimate and spiritual needs can be fulfilled through the exchange of material goods. Producers, too, inhibit the understanding of goods as meant for all through an "all-consuming desire for profit" and "the thirst for power with the intention of imposing one's will on others."[62] Fear is another obstacle. Our recognized interdependence tempts the individual participant in the capitalist economy to "go it alone" in making decisions that she believes are in the best interests of herself and her immediate family. In some utopian instantiation of liberalism, such decisions pose no problem. However, John Paul recognized that harmonizing the individual decision with a universal common good in the spontaneous order of a complex society is not easily achieved. Some degree of planning is required, as is government intervention in cases where individuals or groups seek to force that universal destination to conform to their own self-interest.

Reflecting on John Paul's attitude toward the consumerist culture, Gronbacher states, "Clearly consumerism is a problematic reality, yet its existence cannot be fully credited to the market." For Gronbacher, consumerism is more a "moral malfunction" than a "market failure."[63] Similarly, Sirico recites a commonplace criticism of the market, "that we live in an age in which everything is for sale, including many things—such as the human body—that should not be." But according to Sirico, this condition "does not arise out of the nature of the market but out of our particular cultural and historical situation."[64] There is little doubt that the market is not singularly at fault for capitalist culture's moral failings. However, the assumption that the market is a morally neutral arbiter of social values is one made far too casually by libertarians and neoconservatives. The ramifications of their being wrong in this assumption in a society in which markets are expanding into all areas of life are dire indeed. There is sufficient anecdotal evidence to suggest that the assumption of market neutrality should at least be open to question. At the very least, the market appears to force the commodification of those goods that enter its domain. Rational behavior is rewarded, immediate human wants are satisfied, and spiritual values associated with deferred gratification are gradually eroded.

Pope John Paul is thankfully more equitable than many of his supporters in his approach to the moral determinants of modern society. He makes no assumptions that the market itself is neutral, while he simultaneously acknowledges democratic capitalism as morally superior to forms of political economy that have gone before. The marvelous balance in John Paul's economic thought is evident in a passage from *Centesimus Annus* in which he reflects on various efforts to construct democratic societies in the aftermath of the Second World War:

> In general, such attempts endeavor to preserve free market mechanisms, ensuring, by means of a stable currency and the harmony of social relations, the conditions for steady and healthy economic growth in which people through their own work can build a better future for themselves and their families. At the same time, these attempts try to avoid making market mechanisms the only point of reference for social life, and they tend to subject them to public control which upholds the principle of the common destination of material goods.[65]

John Paul appears to express a preference for European systems of democracy that exhibit greater measures of "public control" and less dependence on the market than the American system of "less fettered" capitalism, where markets are more exclusive guides to the good. He follows this statement with criticism of what he terms the "affluent society or the consumer society," which "seeks to defeat Marxism on the level of pure materialism by showing how a free-market society can achieve a greater satisfaction of material human needs than Communism, while equally excluding spiritual values."[66] The consumer society "denies an autonomous existence and value to morality, law, culture, and religion" and in this way is consonant with the philosophical materialism of Marxist theory.[67] This was a critical insight of Reinhold Niebuhr's *The Children of Light and the Children of Darkness*: both Marxist and capitalist societies depend on a material foundation for the pursuit of human happiness and deny the spiritual element of the person. The consumer society arrives at a similar denial of the spiritual aspect of life via a different route from that of communism; however, the consequences are largely the same.

Critical for John Paul in the restraint of consumerism is recognition of the difference between "being" and "having." This problem of being and having is one of priority. He states that "there are some people—the few who possess much—who do not really succeed in 'being' because, through a reversal of the hierarchy of values, they are hindered by the cult of 'having.'"⁶⁸ John Paul also recognizes the phenomenon of conspicuous consumption that results in the construction of artificial needs. Any Christian notion of consumption must recognize the "interior dimension" of the human person and enable a hierarchical ordering of goods that prioritizes that interior dimension. Much as with individual choices in consumption, John Paul is cognizant of the moral implications of the economic principle of opportunity cost with respect to investment, stating, "The decision to invest in one place rather than another, in one productive sector rather than another, is always *a moral and cultural choice*."⁶⁹ Christian involvement in consumption and investment necessitates the expression of moral values, and those expressions must always recognize the universal destination of goods that is superior to personal preferences.

Complicating the determination of a universal destination of goods is the "acceleration" of economic activity through progress in science and technology. John Paul is sensitive to this condition, but he insists "that none of these phenomena of 'acceleration' exceeds the essential content of what was said in the most ancient of biblical texts." Christianity aids in keeping technological achievements in proper perspective. Irrespective of how advanced civilization becomes, the person in his work "remains in every case and at every phase of this process within the Creator's original ordering."⁷⁰ Biblical principles still apply regardless of the level of technology achieved in particular cultures. John Paul does recognize, however, that technology has altered the landscape of property; the possession of technical skills and know-how has become no less important than the possession of land during the time of Leo XIII. Technology can be a great ally in the perfection of human activity, yet it can turn inimical in those contexts where the human person is supplanted by the machine.

The difficulty in achieving a universal destination of goods and appropriately maintaining the capital-labor relationship in a highly technical society results from what John Paul describes as an "error of materialism," which he perceives to follow from the "error of economism":

> This fundamental error of thought can and must be called an *error of materialism*, in that economism directly or indirectly includes a conviction of the primacy and superiority of the material, and directly or indirectly places the spiritual and the personal (man's activity, moral values and such matters) in a position of subordination to material reality. This is not *theoretical materialism* in the full sense of the term, but it is certainly *practical materialism*, a materialism judged capable of satisfying man's needs not so much on the grounds of premises derived from the materialist theory as

on the grounds of a particular way of evaluating things and so on the grounds of a certain hierarchy of goods based on the greater immediate attractiveness of what is material.[71]

It obviously matters little to John Paul whether the source of materialism involves a philosophical change in the foundations of a society or results from infinite calculations and actions toward what is perceived as practical necessity. Materialism's consequences are equally erroneous regardless of their basis, in that they deny the person's spiritual nature and result in an inappropriate ordering of goods for the satisfaction of human needs.

While the concept of a universal destination of goods has often been criticized for its collectivist connotation, according to John Paul it was the anti-Communist revolution that "highlighted the reality of interdependence among peoples."[72] Both nations and the individuals and institutions they comprise cannot retreat so easily into isolationism and self-interest due to their recognized dependence upon others. Certain fundamental goods such as peace and prosperity "belong to the whole human race: it is not possible to enjoy them in a proper and lasting way if they are achieved and maintained at the cost of other peoples and nations."[73] But what is the potential of this concept in shaping the global economic order? Is a universal destination achievable beyond the boundaries of religious or, more specifically, Christian communities? Can this principle influence the attitudes of international financial institutions in their relationships with developing (and developed) nations? For now, the universal destination of goods exists as a prophetic Catholic utterance to the world, highlighting the impossibility of retreat by nations and persons into themselves.

Transitioning to Social Subjectivity

Scholars who have studied Pope John Paul II's social thought are often struck by the priority he assigns to the individual as the appropriate subject for the analysis of human action. They commonly contrast John Paul's priority for the person with the ostensibly higher status assigned collectives in the encyclicals of his predecessors. Some take this as a sign of John Paul's affinity for principles of the liberal tradition and even go so far as to associate his social philosophy with that of Austrian philosophers like Hayek and Mises.[74] However, whereas John Paul states that "even when the being and acting is realized together with others it is a *man-person who is always the proper subject*,"[75] he is also careful to circumscribe the subjectivity of the human person in ways the Austrians do not. Subjective valuation and action in John Paul's philosophy never escapes the social context, for that would make determination of the common good impossible:

> It is impossible to define the common good without simultaneously tak-
> ing into account the subjective moment, that is, the moment of acting
> in relation to the acting persons. When we consider this moment we see
> that the common good does not exist solely in the goal of the common
> acting performed by a community or group; indeed, it also, or even pri-
> marily, consists in that which conditions and somehow initiates in the
> persons acting together their participation, and thereby develops and
> shapes in them a subjective community of acting.[76]

Analogous to his recognition of the interdependency of nations, Pope John Paul insists that the subjectivity of the human person cannot be isolated from her interaction with social groups or from the "intersubjectivity" of individuals and institutions in society. In *The Acting Person*, he states, "It is the person's transcendence in the action when the action is being performed 'together with others'—transcendence which manifests that the person has not become altogether absorbed by social interplay and thus 'conditioned,' but stands out as having retained his very own freedom of choice and direction—which is the basis as well as the condition of his participation."[77] Thus, despite the prevalence of methodological individualism as the basis of many systems of human behavior, the social aspect of human subjectivity must be accounted for in any system if it is to accurately portray the acting subject. This serves not only as a precondition for determination of the good but also as an a priori condition of John Paul's personalism.

The inherent sociality of subjectiveness in the thought of John Paul contrasts markedly with the unbounded subjectivity of the person in Hayek's philosophy. Hayek dismisses altogether the notion of common good where it is collectively defined, suggesting that terms like common good, general welfare, or general interest "have no sufficiently definite meaning to determine a particular course of action."[78] Social groups cannot be defined according to their collective goals, morals, or values; rather, they are derived from the aggregation of values that make up their membership. For Hayek, social groups are collections of individuals that provide a representation of order for what is, in essence, a thoroughly subjective civilization. Institutions like the church exist merely as placeholders for social norms and practices, the transitory and evolutionary result of millennia of individual decisions.

Thus, while John Paul and Hayek both recognize the indispensability of subjective assessment and action to human progress, there are stark differences in their respective views on subjectivity. For John Paul, the omnipresent influence of community on the person and the inseparability of one with the other are critical. He states that the "'community of being' always conditions the 'community of acting,' and so the latter cannot be considered apart from the former."[79] Moreover, he insists that the crux of the problem is to be found "in that *membership in any of these communities is not to be identified with participation.*"[80] John Paul offers two examples to make his point: citing a team of laborers digging a trench and a group of students attending a lecture. While individual laborers and students seek to fulfill themselves in activity through a "definite community of acting," the communities of which they are a part have an "objective unity of goals" that defines each community as a distinct entity. In this case, the community of acting "may be defined according to the aim that brings men to act together; each of them is then a member of an objective community"[81] that has its own unique values and norms that exist in something like a dialectical tension with the individuals who constitute it.

For Hayek, such an objective reality of social groups is illusory. They may appear to have objective values apart from the individuals that make them up, but in fact they are merely collections of individuals. Regarding the aforementioned and, according to Hayek, ambiguously applied term "general welfare," he states that it must not be viewed as a single end; rather, the welfare of a people can only exist "as a hierarchy of ends, a comprehensive scale of values in which every need of every person is given its place." To view the general welfare as a single end is to presuppose "the existence of a single ethical code in which all the different human values are allotted their due place."[82] Because he can perceive no transcendent value or set of values capable of binding people together beyond the machinations of human culture, and because no rational power can accurately assess the full range of values and appropriate priorities for those values within communities, the concept of a single ethical code is, for Hayek, an impossibility, or perhaps more accurately an absurdity.

Having witnessed the great tragedies of the twentieth century, John Paul recognizes the danger of too fully socializing the individual and thus making her a mere product of institutions. That danger was articulated in *Rerum Novarum* and has been voiced consistently in Catholic social doctrine. In *Centesimus Annus*, John Paul states, "The social nature of man is not completely fulfilled in the State, but is realized in various intermediary groups, beginning with the family and including economic, social, political and cultural groups which stem from human nature itself and have their own autonomy, always with a view to the common good."[83] He observes that the error of "Real Socialism" was anthropological in not realizing this "true" and essential social structure of the human person.

Conversely, Hayek's error was the failure to recognize that cultural groups "have their own autonomy" and will invariably articulate conceptions of the good that are not merely the evolved and aggregate expressions of their memberships in response to survival decisions. Transcendent beliefs and values matter. Awareness of the transcendent dignity of the person is the apex of humanity for John Paul, "and no social mechanism or collective subject can substitute for it."[84] John Paul's concept of "social subjectivity" aims to prevent abuses found in extreme views on the role of the subjective in society. Ironically, both Marxists and radical anticollectivists end up portraying a dichotomous economic world in which choices among economic systems narrow to two: communism and an intensely individualistic capitalism. They envision a world in which everyone is required to choose between two extremes and endure the injustice resulting from their decisions. John Paul notes how Marxists blamed bourgeois capitalism for the "commercialization and alienation" found in the human condition: "Marxism thus ends up by affirming that only in a collective society can alienation be eliminated." But collectivism has proven only to exacerbate alienation, "adding to it a lack of basic necessities and economic inefficiency." Similarly, alienation exists in Western capitalist societies in the form of consumerism, "when people are ensnared in a web of false and superficial gratifications rather than being helped to experience their personhood in an authentic and concrete way."[85] Thus, both systems have common tendencies that work against Christian teaching on the appropriate subjectivity of the person in economic life.

Just as Niebuhr and Chesterton, John Paul rejects socialism, with its elevation of the state over the family and all other social institutions as inherently depersonalizing and dehumanizing. Yet certain structures within democratic capitalism also work toward an inappropriate subjectiveness, which results in moral and spiritual damage. He expresses concern, for example, that human interdependence in the emerging global village has placed too great a reliance on rational vis-à-vis moral criteria in establishing relationships between individuals and institutions. He speaks of "radical interdependence" that necessitates "a solidarity which will take up interdependence and transfer it to a moral plane."[86] The interconnectedness of modern capitalism and the frenetic pace of economic development conspire to form relationships at the most basic level; the church must advocate the elevation of economic relations to a higher moral and spiritual level.

Arriving at an appropriate social subjectivity will require redefinition
of fundamental institutions. There is an essential social nature to property,
for example, that was radically exaggerated within collectivist philosophy
at the expense of personal property rights, but capitalist societies tend to
minimize the collective aspects of ownership. The social nature of property cannot be expressed by nationalization but only by an enlightened
form of "socialization," which does not involve conversion of capital to
"state property" but construction of means to acknowledge our interdependence only after the "subject character of society is ensured, that is to
say, when on the basis of his work each person is fully entitled to consider
himself a part owner of the great workbench at which he is working with
everyone else."[87] John Paul does not avoid use of the term "socialization"
because of its past association with socialism; rather, he is concerned that
it reflect the appropriate social dimension of human activity and that
whatever system is employed, "the human person can preserve his awareness of working 'for himself.'"[88]

The "indirect employer" can be a means of achieving social subjectivity by enabling institutions that are able to promote values that are not easily arbitrated through the market. Establishment of labor policies and the
setting of minimal objective standards for working conditions such as a
minimum wage are necessary to counter forces within the global economy
that work against the attainment of justice. The gap between rich and poor
is growing wider; this will have an obvious "effect on local labor policy and
on the worker's situation in the economically disadvantaged societies."[89]
The direct employer who finds himself in a position of advantage vis-à-vis
his workers will attempt to maximize profits, and thus he often "fixes working conditions below the objective requirements of workers."[90] The indirect employer can serve to counteract the inappropriately subjective quest
for profit when it neglects the rights of those who are weakest.

That many Christian libertarians and neoconservatives have warmed
to the limitless subjectivism of Friedrich Hayek is perhaps the most baf-
fling aspect of their social thought. The fact that many of these Christian
social thinkers (both Catholic and Protestant) have studied the economic
thought of John Paul II makes this attraction all the more puzzling. The
major difference between John Paul's view of social subjectivity and the
subjectivism advanced by Christian advocates of Austrian economics is
primarily one of emphasis. The latter emphasize the subjective autonomy
of the individual as an economic decision maker, while John Paul focuses
more on the person as a worker in a system where a network of institutions illuminates the truly social nature of subjectivity. John Paul's view of

human subjectiveness as circumscribed by the ubiquitous interactions of individuals and institutions and by the transcendent dignity that results from a theistic worldview serves as a caution against an unbounded subjectivism that inspires methodological individualism. It can also serve as a model for Christian social thinkers seeking the appropriate social subjectivity for a Christian economic order.

AN APPROPRIATE JURIDICAL
ORDER FOR ECONOMIC JUSTICE

In *Sollicitudo Rei Socialis* (1987), John Paul assesses the difficulties in attempting to affix boundaries for the determination of social justice in an expanding global economy. He notes that with the advent of globalization, problems in industry and in workers' movements can no longer be isolated to a particular country or region. On the contrary, "they depend more and more on the influence of factors beyond regional boundaries and national frontiers."[91] The church's role in this transformation is in maintaining consistent adherence to basic principles and using its voice to speak out against injustice, which requires neither a liberal nor a conservative paradigm.

Encyclicals in the Catholic social tradition are key to the church's constancy respecting social issues. John Paul insists that a rereading of *Rerum Novarum* engenders appreciation for "*the Church's constant concern for and dedication to* categories of people who are especially beloved to the Lord Jesus." This commitment includes its "preferential option for the poor," as well as concern for working conditions and a priority for the exercise of Christian charity.[92] To those developed nations that might choose to ignore the problems of the developing world, John Paul underscores the "impossibility" of that approach in the new economic order. Interestingly, John Paul broaches the subject of violence between developed and developing nations and the possibility that "peoples excluded from the fair distribution of goods originally destined for all could ask themselves: why not respond with violence to those who first treat us with violence?"[93]

Sollicitudo Rei Socialis was written on the twentieth anniversary of Paul VI's *Populorum Progressio* and is respectful of Paul VI's concern with rising inequalities in income and economic power and, in particular, with militarization that has undermined essential priorities:

> How can one justify the fact that huge sums of money, which could and should be used for increasing the development of peoples, are instead

utilized for the enrichment of individuals or groups, or assigned to the increase of stockpiles of weapons, both in developed countries and developing ones, thereby upsetting real priorities?[94]

One can infer that John Paul is no fan of trickle-down economics or the military-industrial complex. He is economically iconoclastic in a Christian way, promoting the notion of economic fairness on a world stage in which some countries are fabulously wealthy while others are mired in abject poverty, and where many have come to accept this condition as "reality." He abhors the fact that so much of the world's limited resources are applied to the preparation for and conduct of war. "If development is the new name for peace," he writes, "war and military preparations are the major enemy of the integral development of peoples."[95]

John Paul also expresses concern that self-determination be seen as a fundamental freedom of peoples. Self-determination has an unavoidably economic component that must be respected, and he is disturbed that "developing countries, instead of becoming autonomous nations concerned with their own progress towards a just sharing in the goods and services meant for all, become parts of a machine, cogs on a gigantic wheel."[96] Yet the international network of economic and financial institutions that was established to aid developing nations often has neglected its duties. It claims to promote fairness in opportunity when in fact these organizations "often function almost automatically, thus accentuating the situation of wealth for some and poverty for the rest."[97] Developed countries use these mechanisms to their own advantage, enhancing their positions of power vis-à-vis the developing world and favoring "the interests of the people manipulating them." Paul VI's *Populorum Progressio* was prescient in observing these developments. *Centesimus Annus* merely expands the dialogue with new historical awareness, being written at the time of the anti-Communist revolution of 1989.

Despite these perceived injustices and the inability of international institutions to tame the new order, John Paul is not averse to forces of globalization. It has both positive and negative consequences. Globalization can aid developing nations by enhancing efficiency in production and enabling links between nations that "can help bring greater unity among peoples and make possible a better service to the human family." But John Paul, in his encyclical *Ecclesia in America*, states that "if globalization is ruled merely by the laws of the market applied to suit the powerful, the consequences cannot be but negative."[98] In contexts both of domestic and international economies, John Paul seems more reticent to embrace the moral and social consequences of expanding markets than many of his Catholic supporters. Markets are not monolithic institutions; they vary according to complexity of commodities, concentrations of economic power, and legal and other institutional influences. He does not simplistically assume a neutral system of exchange that arbitrates the resources and values of its participants without bias. Moreover, John Paul is savvy to the fact that market participants will inevitably attempt to gain control by using the political and legal (as well as economic) resources at their disposal.

Recognition of the market's imperfections necessitates some form of planning and control. He rejects the notion that social and economic planning is evil or even inherently inept. It is a necessary complement to the market in determining resource allocations and in constructing a society with some teleological orientation. Planning is especially appropriate to help smooth over the bumps associated with the economic cycle and the resultant effects of unemployment and misemployment that depreciate the quality of human existence:

> Rational planning and the proper organization of human labor in keeping with individual societies and states should also facilitate the discovery of the right proportions between the different kinds of employment: work on the land, in industry, in various services, white-collar work and artistic work, in accordance with the capacities of individuals and for the common good of each society and the whole of mankind.[99]

John Paul affirms the necessity of rational human planning and conscious orientation toward the good while coequally affirming the values of democracy. The church advocates political systems in which political and economic power are distributed across society rather than concentrated narrowly "for individual interests or for ideological ends." He believes that "authentic democracy" requires the rule of law to complement an accurate conception of the human person. He is especially concerned that the church's political and economic principles remain independent from any secular philosophy, for "*Christian truth* is not of this kind. Since it is not an ideology, the Christian faith does not presume to imprison changing sociopolitical realities in a rigid schema, and it recognizes that human life is realized in history in conditions that are diverse and imperfect."[100] Thus, Christianity resists alignment with any system of political economy, regardless of its material or moral superiority to other systems.

The problem is that the rightful turn of the world against socialism has resulted in an overemphasis on material development at the expense of other forms. *Populorum Progressio* was farsighted in this regard according to John Paul; the difficulty for economists and popes alike has been in locating the proper role of the state in economic affairs. John Paul, like Paul VI, acknowledges the state's right to regulate monopolies, to harmonize and guide development, and even to "exercise *a substitute function,* when social sectors or business systems are too weak or are just getting under way."[101] But at this point, John Paul's commitment to subsidiarity is evidenced by recognition that the *substitute function* of the state should not become permanent and absorb functions that are appropriately the domain of the private sector. He is aware of the abuses of the welfare state that result from the state's inadequate understanding of its own role, which inevitably results in a "loss of human energies and an inordinate increase of public agencies, which are dominated more by bureaucratic ways of thinking . . . and which are accompanied by an enormous increase in spending."[102]

Globalization has expanded the prophetic role of the church regarding economic life. The goals and virtues that it is called to promote must extend beyond particular states to the international community:

> Just as there is a collective responsibility for avoiding war, so too there is a collective responsibility for promoting development. Just as within individual societies it is possible and right to organize a solid economy which will direct the functioning of the market to the common good, so too there is a similar need for adequate interventions on the international level. For this to happen, *a great effort must be made to enhance mutual understanding and knowledge, and to increase the sensitivity of consciences.*[103]

Contrary to Hayek's assessment that morals are associated strictly with individual conduct, John Paul suggests an inherent moral component among institutions in international relations. He is accepting of the notion of "structural sin" to some extent and thus believes that the global economy must be evaluated with respect to principles of social justice, a preferential option for the poor, and even a notion of the international common good. Moreover, that good cannot overlook the rights of traditional societies. According to John Paul, the world is at risk of losing the values of indigenous cultures to a "misconstrued homogenization."[104] The stifling debt load on developing nations adds to the pressures toward homogeneity and must be reappraised by the West in the context of an international norm of justice. International institutions have an indispensable role in this process; therefore, reform of these institutions is an immediate priority.

An appropriate juridical order must work to guarantee fairness in economic relationships in order to prevent the economic dominance of certain individuals or groups by others. That right in some cases dovetails with other natural rights such as the freedom of association. The right to form professional associations like trade unions exists "not because of ideological prejudices or in order to surrender to a class mentality" but because the "right of association is a natural right of the human being, which therefore precedes his or her incorporation into political society."[105] Just as the transcendent conscience of the direct employer must uphold the rights of his workers, so too the indirect employer—the vast network of institutions designed to ensure justice—must recognize worker rights, including the right to associate with members of one's trade or occupation. John Paul specifically targets the "neoliberalism" of America that is based on a purely economic conception of the individual as uniquely offensive to these rights.[106]

Consistent with Niebuhr, John Paul understands that "rigid" capitalism, as all necessarily flawed systems of political economy, "must undergo continual revision in order to be reformed from the point of view of human rights."[107] Interestingly, given a mixed Catholic history with respect to liberty, religious freedom becomes a wellspring of all other freedoms for John Paul that contributes to the transcendent dignity of the person. In promoting the right to apply one's intellect in pursuit of truth, to share in the earth's resources, and to establish a family and exercise familial responsibility, John Paul sees that "the source and synthesis of these rights is religious freedom."[108] The right to "seek God" is the underpinning of all human activity; thus, recognition of this right has economic significance. No economic system can make claims to justice without due consideration for the religious rights of the individual. Religious freedom thus becomes the critical link in establishing an appropriate juridical order for economic justice.

A CATHOLIC CONCEPTION OF DEVELOPMENT

John Paul's encyclicals are consistently critical of the shrinking dimensionality in both individual and social development in a way quite similar to Chesterton's comments on "progress and proportion." John Paul cautions against one-sided notions of progress—the exaggeration of material vis-à-vis spiritual and moral growth—for "collaboration in the development of the whole person and of every human being is in fact a duty of all towards all."[109] Any Catholic understanding of development must be inclusive of the transcendent element of the human person and the particularities of traditional cultures. Catholics must come together to promote the "moral character" of progress; more limited conceptions are permeated by what he describes as "intrinsic contradiction":

> When individuals and communities do not see a rigorous respect for the moral, cultural and spiritual requirements, based on the dignity of the person and on the proper identity of each community, beginning with the family and religious societies, then all the rest—availability of goods, abundance of technical resources applied to daily life, a certain level of material well-being—will prove unsatisfying and in the end contemptible.[110]

Expansion of goods and availability of technical resources will prove "contemptible" without consideration of the cultural and spiritual requirements of development. Again, the teleological emphasis of John Paul's words is unmistakable. Moral character does not arise from mere participation in a market-based economy; it must be nurtured through a harmony of institutions, engendering an appropriate social subjectivity such that the dignity of the person can be preserved. For the Christian, maintaining teleology in development, considered both individually and socially, is an inescapable duty in order to counter conceptions of progress that are purely economic. Moreover, Christians who are taught to see that "man is the image of God" cannot understand forms of development that disregard or disrespect this "unique dignity." Thus, the only true form of development for the Christian "must be based on the love of God and neighbor" and must actively promote relationships between individuals and society, a condition Pope Paul VI often referred to as the "civilization of love."[111]

The essence of John Paul's social encyclicals calls for "Catholicizing" development in a way consistent with the foundations of the Catholic social tradition. This process involves redefinition of various economic terms— poverty, profit, investment, consumption, and others—in ways more consistent with Catholic thought:

> In today's world there are many other forms of poverty. For are there not certain privations or deprivations which deserve this name? The denial or the limitation of human rights—as for example the right to religious freedom, the right to share in the building of society, the freedom to organize and to form unions, or to take initiatives in economic matters— do these not impoverish the human person as much as, if not more than, the deprivation of material goods? And is development which does not

take into account the full affirmation of these rights really development on the human level?[112]

The holistic concept of development that John Paul advances is much like that articulated by Chesterton and the distributists; moreover, it has similarities to secular visions, as well, like Amartya Sen's promotion of "development as freedom."[113] John Paul accepts the basic instruments of capitalism, and he also accepts that inequalities among individuals create differences in wealth and income. What he does not accept are gross disparities in income and resources that enable fabulous wealth among some countries while relegating others to destitution. Such disparities reflect neither our common humanity nor our capabilities as persons; rather, they are conditioned by structural forces that favor the rights and opportunities of some over others.

Domination of the material concept of development leads to what John Paul terms "super-development," the idea of "an excessive availability of every kind of material goods for the benefit of certain social groups" that "easily makes people slaves of 'possession' and of immediate gratification, with no other horizon than the multiplication or continual replacement of the things already owned with others better still."[114] Christians are often troubled by their own inability to "progress" in such a system because they have bought into this intensely secular notion of progress. The world has progressed in certain ways but regressed in others. There is hope, however, in that there is a "better understanding today that the mere accumulation of goods and services, even for the benefit of the majority, is not enough for the realization of human happiness."[115] Again, recognition of a universal destination of goods is key to understanding the inherent limitations of the material world for the satisfaction of ultimate human needs.

For Hayek and others in the Austrian liberal tradition, there is no "original intention" behind the world's resources; nor is there a central set of values to guide their utilization. The "proper" allocation of resources is subject only to a spontaneous order in which individuals and their associated institutions jockey for position in order to ensure their survival and enhance their power. This thoroughly materialistic understanding of development leads, in the end, to a form of evolutionary determinism that insinuates the "moral" value of religion while undermining any theological premises that defy the natural theology of the market.

John Paul envisions a mode of social development that differs radically from that of Hayek. John Paul is refreshingly straightforward in advancing ideas of "Catholic economics," yet he is honest in admitting the church's limitations in that endeavor. His words are often reminiscent of Niebuhr's comment that there is no Christian political or economic system, but "there is a Christian attitude toward all systems and schemes of justice":

> The Church has no models to present; models that are real and truly effective can only arise within the framework of different historical situations, through the efforts of all those who responsibly confront concrete problems in all their social, economic, political and cultural aspects, as these interact with one another.[116] For such a task the Church offers her social teaching as an indispensable and ideal orientation, a teaching which, as already mentioned, recognizes the positive value of the market and of enterprise, but which at the same time points out that these need to be oriented towards the common good.[117]

The church's orientation inevitably will encounter a material reality. What are the implications of John Paul's thought for a Catholic middle manager in a Fortune 500 corporation? Is she required to promote an environment that supports a more elevated conception of "fulfillment" for her employees vis-à-vis her non-Catholic colleagues even when her bosses insist that such activity is uneconomic or beyond the scope of her duties? What is the Catholic laborer's responsibility to the bottom line when his work activities conflict in some way with Catholic moral or social teaching? Does it "raise the bar" for Christians in general competing in a market economy, and if so, could such a conception of development adversely affect the competitiveness of Christians in a capitalist society? Does it place an undue burden on Christian consumers to avoid participation in certain markets that tend to denigrate Christian values?

The exceptional balance of John Paul's economic thought engenders expansive and insightful answers to these difficult questions. While understanding the influence that producers can have on consumers, he avoids simplistic conclusions concerning the source of immorality in capitalist cultures. He recognizes that "a given culture reveals its overall understanding of life through the choices it makes in production *and* consumption."[118] Producers are responsible more for meeting needs than manufacturing them, although they can influence consumer behavior by appealing to "base instincts." Another common insight among John Paul, Niebuhr, and Chesterton is that, "of itself, an economic system does not possess criteria for correctly distinguishing new and higher forms of satisfying human needs from artificial new needs which hinder the formation of a mature personality."[119] This reality implies the need for "*educational and cultural work*" that includes "education of consumers in the responsible use of their power of choice" as well as forming "a strong sense of responsibility among producers and among people in the mass media in particular, as well as the necessary intervention by public authorities."[120]

The systemic flaw of the market economy that John Paul observes— its inability to distinguish higher from lower human needs—makes attainment of these goals difficult but not impossible. The market's limitations result in an orientation toward the satisfaction of instinctual wants over aesthetic goals, and this predisposition must be countered by a diverse set of educational and cultural measures:

> It is not wrong to want to live better; what is wrong is a style of life which is presumed to be better when it is directed towards "having" rather than "being," and which wants to have more, not in order to be more but in order to spend life in enjoyment as an end in itself.[121] It is therefore necessary to create life-styles in which the quest for truth, beauty, goodness and communion with others for the sake of common growth are the factors which determine consumer choices, savings and investments.[122]

Does this imply that Christian tradition establishes "transcendent blocks" to economic progress? John Paul does not shy away from the possibility, noting that "because of the essentially moral character of development, it is clear that obstacles to development likewise have a moral character."[123] But this observation is balanced by his recognition of *material blocks to spiritual development*. What hinders a fuller, more Christian conception of development than the one that exists in the West today is the all-consuming "desire for profit" and an equally obsessive "thirst for power." Achieving a Catholic, or more generally Christian, understanding of economic progress necessarily involves recognizing the limits of material development in contributing to spiritual and moral progress.

CONCLUDING REMARKS

Robert Sirico's contention that Pope John Paul II reread *Rerum Novarum* with insights gleaned from the Austrian liberal tradition diminishes the value of Christian insights into economic life. If John Paul had reread previous encyclicals through a liberal lens, then the result would be to narrow his focus, not to widen it, because Christianity embraces the fuller dimensionality of the human person as well as the moral autonomy of his institutions. Widening that lens does indeed force decisions on Christian participants in a capitalist economy that may well affect their competitiveness. Morally thin liberals may well have an economic advantage absent allegiance to transcendent moral principles like those of Christianity. Christians cannot avoid this fact, because of its potential to dampen optimal efficiency, limit the range of technological development, or reduce the number of prospective occupations for the Christian. Niebuhr recognized that moral cynicism has had a historical advantage over moral sentimentality not only for its "lack of moral scruple but also in its shrewd assessment of the power of self-interest."[124] Similarly, morality erected upon the "mere" foundation of human culture like that described by Hayek has an "immediate" economic advantage over that constructed upon the transcendent moral core of long-standing religious traditions.

One might hope instead that the Austrian economic tradition could be reshaped through insights gleaned from Catholic social thought. The fuller dimensionality of both person and institution in the latter could help stave off the gloom of a fully materialistic existence that led to Hayek's statement, "The peace of the world and, with it, civilization itself thus depend on continued progress at a fast rate. At this juncture we are therefore not only the creatures but the captives of progress."[125] Moreover, recognition that the physical persistence of social groups must be balanced against the imperative of moral persistence for Christians and others who adhere to transcendent values could serve as a means to throttle down our economic machine in a way that is materially as well as morally sustainable.

Restating the words of Pope Paul VI, John Paul recognizes that it is the church that is an "expert in humanity."[126] This critical insight is lost by Christian libertarians and neoconservatives who at times seem embarrassed by the church's particularity in moral discourse and focus more on its limitations than its assets. A more complex view of the person indeed muddies the water; the black and white of secular measures of economic development are illuminated in vivid color by consideration of the spiritual character of human progress. Such is the lot of the Christian social thinker. Yet the rewards of embracing this more complex view of human nature and institutions more than compensate for the difficulty. That is the reason why the social thought of Niebuhr, Chesterton, and Pope John Paul reaches a level not attainable for John Dewey, Milton Friedman, and Friedrich Hayek. These secular thinkers minimize the most crucial aspect of the human person—her moral and spiritual development—in favor or her material well-being. Thus, the systems they describe are limited as well.

In *Centesimus Annus*, John Paul ventures the question of whether capitalism should be the "goal" of developing nations, in particular, those that are rebuilding after failed experiments with collectivism. He describes the answer as "obviously complex" and suggests that the term "capitalism" must be qualified before an answer can be given. He states that if by capitalism "is meant an economic system which recognizes the fundamental and positive role of business, the market, private property, and the resulting responsibility for the means of production, as well as free human creativity in the economic sector, then the answer is certainly affirmative."[127] But if by capitalism "is meant a system in which freedom in the economic sector is not circumscribed within a strong juridical framework which places it at the service of human freedom in its totality, and which sees it as a particular aspect of that freedom, the core of which is ethical and religious, then the reply is certainly negative."[128] John Paul thus bequeaths to us a test for the Christianness of our economic system. These are not mere platitudes for the assessment of capitalism's virtues, but hard criteria for investigation of an expanding and immensely complex global economy.

NOTES

1. Maciej Zieba, in an Acton Institute journalist, notes that Paul VI's encyclical *Populorum Progressio* "shifts in the direction of centrally planning social life while the areas of State intervention are clearly expanded. The meaning of this role for the state and the view of central planning are again clearly halted in John Paul II." See Zieba, "From Leo XIII's *Rerum Novarum* to John Paul II's *Centesimus Annus*," *Journal of Markets and Morality* 5 (Spring 2002).

2. George Weigel, "John Paul II and the Crisis of Humanism," *First Things* 98 (December 1999): 31–32.

3. Robert Sirico, "The Late-Scholastic and Austrian Link to Modern Catholic Social Thought," *Journal of Markets and Morality* 2 (October 1998); available at www.acton.org/publicat/m_and_m/1998_oct/sirico.html (accessed May 12, 2003). Sirico states that *Centesimus Annus* witnessed the "fruition of the 'Personalist Revolution' in theology, begun with *Redemptor Hominis*." See Sirico, "The Late-Scholastic and Austrian Link."

4. John Paul II, *Centesimus Annus* [On the Hundredth Anniversary of *Rerum Novarum*] (May 1, 1991), no. 5; available at www.vatican.va/holy_father/john_paul_ii/encyclicals/documents/hf_jp_ii_enc_01051991_centesimus-annus_fr.html.

5. Sirico is quoting from paragraphs 32 and 34 of *Centesimus Annus*. See Robert A. Sirico, "Papal Economics 101: Freedom and Truth," *Religion and Liberty*; available at www.acton.org/publicat/randl/article.php?=523 (accessed November 21, 2005).

6. John Paul II, *Centesimus Annus*, no. 34; quoted in Sirico, "Papal Economics 101."

7. Sirico, "Reading *Centesimus Annus*," *Religion and Liberty* 11 (May–June 2001); available at www.acton.org/publicat/randl/article.php?id=384 (accessed January 12, 2005).

8. John Paul II, *Centesimus Annus*, no. 12.

9. Pius XI, *Quadragesimo Anno: On Constructing the Social Order*, 1931, no. 79.

10. John Paul II, *Centesimus Annus*, no. 25.

11. John Paul II, *Centesimus Annus*, no. 25.

12. Karol Wojtyla [Pope John Paul II], *The Acting Person*, trans. Andrzej Potocki (Boston: D. Reidel Publishing Company, 1979), 20. The future pope does not minimize the difficulty or significance of this synthesis: "Perhaps the problem consists of the fact that man is still awaiting a new and profound analysis of himself, or rather, what is more important, an ever-new synthesis, and this is not easy to attain" (21).

13. Wojtyla, *The Acting Person*, 117.

14. Wojtyla states that "any interpretation of the free will, if it is to conform to reality, must rely on man's autodeterminism instead of floating in the air by stressing merely indeterminism." See Wojtyla, *The Acting Person*, 121, 127.

15. Wojtyla, *The Acting Person*, 137.

16. Wojtyla, *The Acting Person*, 151.

17. Wojtyla, *The Acting Person*, 265.

18. *Centesimus Annus*, no. 17. Here John Paul cites Leo XIII's encyclical letter *Libertas Praestantissimum*, no. 10.

19. *Centesimus Annus*, no. 49. The pope observes that "people lose sight of the fact that life in society has neither the market nor the State as its final purpose." *Centesimus Annus*, no. 49.

20. *Centesimus Annus*, no. 49.

21. Gregory M. A. Gronbacher, "The Humane Economy: Neither Right Nor Left; a Response to Daniel Rush Finn," *Journal of Markets and Morality* 2 (Fall 1999); available at www.acton.org/publicat/m_and_m/1999_fall/gronbacher.html (accessed November 15, 2005). Gronbacher is the director of the Center for Economic Personalism at the Acton Institute for the Study of Religion and Liberty.

22. Gronbacher, "The Humane Economy."

23. *Ecclesia in America* [The Way to Conversion, Communion and Solidarity in America], (January 22, 1999), no. 59. The pope references *Propositio* 75.

24. *Centesimus Annus*, no. 25.

25. Richard John Neuhaus, "The Liberalism of John Paul II," *First Things* 73 (May 1997): 19.

26. The actual quotation reads "this man person" and is taken from *Redemptor Hominis*, no. 14. The second part of the quotation is an original statement from *Centesimus Annus*, no. 53. See Neuhaus, "The Liberalism of John Paul II," 18.

27. *Centesimus Annus*, no. 55.

28. Gronbacher, "The Humane Economy." See also Gronbacher's article, "The Need For Economic Personalism," *Journal of Markets and Morality* 1 (March 1998); available at www.acton.org/publicat/m_and_m/1998_mar/gronbach.html (accessed May 12, 2005).

29. Gronbacher, "The Humane Economy."

30. Gronbacher, "The Humane Economy."

31. Quoted in Neuhaus, "John Paul's 'Second Thoughts' on Capitalism," *First Things* 41 (March 1994): 66.

32. John Paul II quoted in Neuhaus, "John Paul's 'Second Thoughts' on Capitalism."

33. Neuhaus, "John Paul's 'Second Thoughts' on Capitalism," 66.

34. John Paul II, *Laborem Exercens* [On Human Work], (September 14, 1981), no. 3; available at www.vatican.va/holy_father/john_paul_ii/encyclicals/documents/hf_jp_ii_enc_14091981_laborem-exercens_fr.html.

35. John Paul II, *Laborem Exercens*, introduction and no. 11.

36. The pope says that the biblical understanding of the earth is taken to be a "fragment of the visible universe that man inhabits." But it also "can be understood as the whole of the visible universe that man inhabits." See John Paul II, *Laborem Exercens*, no. 14.

37. John Paul II, *Centesimus Annus*, no. 29.

38. Wojtyla, *The Acting Person*, 273.

39. Pope John Paul II states, "Work is a good thing for man—a good thing for his humanity—because through work man *not only transforms nature*, adapting it to his own needs, but he also *achieves fulfillment* as a human being and, indeed, in a sense, becomes 'more a human being.'" *Laborem Exercens*, no. 9 (emphasis author's).

40. John Paul II, *Laborem Exercens*, no. 6.

41. John Paul II, *Laborem Exercens*, no. 6 (emphasis author's).

42. John Paul II, *Laborem Exercens*, no. 7.

43. John Paul II, *Laborem Exercens*, no. 12 (emphasis author's).

44. John Paul II, *Laborem Exercens*, no. 12.

45. John Paul II, *Laborem Exercens*, no. 1.

46. John Paul quotes Leo XIII from *Rerum Novarum*, no. 45; quoted in *Centesimus Annus*, no. 8, note 25. John Paul also suggests that work should be evaluated and structured so as to accommodate the gender and age of the worker. Occupations for female laborers, for example, must not be ordered such that women "have to pay for their advancement by abandoning what is specific to them and at the expense of the family, in which women as mothers have an irreplaceable role." Thus, structuring work environments to the needs of the individual is a significant component of the pope's personalism. See *Laborem Exercens*, no. 19.

47. *Laborem Exercens*, no. 20.

48. *Laborem Exercens*, no. 18.

49. *Laborem Exercens*, no. 18. He notes that ultimate responsibility for this indirect employer function must rest with the state, but that concern "cannot mean a one-sided centralization by the public authorities. Instead, what is in question is a just and rational coordination, within the framework of which the initiative of individuals, free groups and local work centers and complexes must be safeguarded, keeping in mind what has been said above with regard to the subject character of human labor." See *Laborem Exercens*, no. 18.

50. John Paul II, *Ecclesia in America: The Way to Conversion, Communion and Solidarity in America* (January 22, 1999), no. 21.

51. John Paul II, *Centesimus Annus*, no. 33.

52. John Paul II, *Laborem Exercens*, no. 21. The pope calls for "radical and urgent changes" in order "to restore to agriculture—and to rural people—its just value as the basis for a healthy economy, within the social community as a whole. Thus it is necessary to proclaim and promote the dignity of work, of all work, but especially of agricultural work in which man so eloquently 'subdues' the earth he has received as a gift from God and affirms his 'dominion' in the visible world." See John Paul II, *Laborem Exercens*, no. 21.

53. John Paul II, *Laborem Exercens*, no. 22.

54. John Paul II, *Laborem Exercens*, no. 23.

55. John Paul II, *Centesimus Annus*, no. 35. He references is own encyclical *Laborem Exercens*, no. 7.

56. John Paul II, *Centesimus Annus*, no. 35 (emphasis author's).

57. John Paul II, *Centesimus Annus*, no. 6.

58. John S. Barry, "On the Universal Destination of Material Goods," *Religion and Liberty* 10 (January–February 2000); available at www.acton.org/publicat/randl/article .php?id=332 (accessed December 15, 2005).

59. John Paul II, *Sollicitudo Rei Socialis* [On Social Concern] (1987), no. 42. The pope's footnote here references Second Vatican Ecumenical Council, Pastoral Constitution on the Church in the Modern World *Gaudium et Spes*, 69, Paul VI, encyclical letter *Populorum Progressio*, 22: loc. cit., 268; Congregation for the Doctrine of the Faith, Instruction on Christian Freedom and Liberation *Libertatis Conscientia* (March 22, 1986), 90: AAS 79 (1987), 594; St. Thomas Aquinas, *Summa Theologica* IIa IIae, q. 66, art. 2.

60. John Paul II, *Sollicitudo Rei Socialis*, no. 43.

61. John Paul II, *Centesimus Annus*, no. 34.

62. John Paul II, *Sollicitudo Rei Socialis*, no. 37.

63. Gronbacher, "The Humane Economy."

64. Sirico, "The Mystery and Morality of Markets—Explained!" *Acton Commentary* (October 17, 2001); available at www.acton.org/ppolicy/comment/article.php?id=56 (accessed January 13, 2006).

65. John Paul II, *Centesimus Annus*, no. 19. The pope states that one of the objectives of these attempts is to "deliver work from the mere condition of 'a commodity,' and guarantee its dignity." See John Paul II, *Centesimus Annus*, no. 19.

66. John Paul II, *Centesimus Annus*, no. 19.

67. John Paul II, *Centesimus Annus*, no. 19.

68. John Paul II, *Sollicitudo Rei Socialis*, no. 28.

69. John Paul II, *Centesimus Annus*, no. 36.

70. John Paul II, *Laborem Exercens*, no. 4.

71. John Paul II, *Laborem Exercens*, no. 13 (emphasis author's).

72. John Paul II, *Centesimus Annus*, no. 27.

73. John Paul II, *Centesimus Annus*, no. 27.

74. See, for example, Robert Sirico's article "The Late-Scholastic and Austrian Link to Modern Catholic Social Thought," *Journal of Markets and Morality* 2 (October 1998); accessible via the Acton Institute at www.acton.org/publicat/m_and_m/1998_oct/ sirico.html.

75. Wojtyla, *The Acting Person*, 277 (emphasis author's).

76. Wojtyla, *The Acting Person*, 281.

77. Wojtyla, *The Acting Person*, 269.

78. Friedrich Hayek, *The Road to Serfdom*, Fiftieth Anniversary Edition (Chicago: University of Chicago Press, 1994), 64.

79. Wojtyla, *The Acting Person*, 279.

80. Wojtyla, *The Acting Person*, 279 (emphasis author's).

81. Wojtyla, *The Acting Person*, 279.

82. Hayek, *The Road to Serfdom*, 64.

83. John Paul II, *Centesimus Annus*, no. 13.

84. John Paul II, *Centesimus Annus*, no. 13.

85. He also notes that "alienation is to be found in work, when it is organized so as to ensure maximum returns and profits with no concern whether the worker, through his own labor, grows or diminishes as a person, either through increased sharing in a

genuinely supportive community or through increased isolation in a maze of relationships marked by destructive competitiveness and estrangement, in which he is considered only a means and not an end." See John Paul II, *Centesimus Annus*, no. 41.

86. John Paul II, *Sollicitudo Rei Socialis*, no. 26.

87. John Paul II, *Laborem Exercens*, no. 14.

88. John Paul II, *Laborem Exercens*, no. 15.

89. John Paul II, *Laborem Exercens*, no. 17.

90. John Paul II, *Laborem Exercens*, no. 17.

91. John Paul II, *Sollicitudo Rei Socialis*, no. 9.

92. *Centesimus Annus*, no. 11 (emphasis author's). John Paul II here references his own encyclical letter *Sollicitudo Rei Socialis*, no. 42.

93. John Paul II, *Sollicitudo Rei Socialis*, no. 10.

94. John Paul II, *Sollicitudo Rei Socialis*, no. 10.

95. John Paul II, *Sollicitudo Rei Socialis*, no. 10.

96. John Paul II, *Sollicitudo Rei Socialis*, no. 10, 22. The pope's language is interesting since he uses virtually the same words in *Laborem Exercens* to describe the atomism of the modern workplace where laborers feel (and are treated) like mere cogs in some enormous machine that cranks out impersonal products. The language he employs to describe this condition is much like that used by Chesterton and Niebuhr to describe the depersonalizing effects of the Industrial Revolution.

97. John Paul II, *Sollicitudo Rei Socialis*, no. 16.

98. John Paul II, *Ecclesia in America*, no. 20.

99. The pope follows by stating, "The organization of human life in accordance with the many possibilities of labor should be matched by a suitable system of instruction and education aimed first of all at developing mature human beings, but also aimed at preparing people specifically for assuming to good advantage an appropriate place in the vast and socially differentiated world of work." John Paul II, *Laborem Exercens*, no. 18.

100. John Paul II, *Centesimus Annus*, no. 46.

101. John Paul II, *Centesimus Annus*, no. 48.

102. John Paul II, *Centesimus Annus*, no. 48.

103. John Paul II, *Centesimus Annus*, no. 52 (emphasis author's).

104. John Paul II, *Ecclesia in America*, no. 55.

105. John Paul quotes Leo XIII that the right to form unions "cannot . . . be prohibited by the State" because "the State is bound to protect natural rights, not to destroy them; and if it forbids its citizens to form associations, it contradicts the very principle of its own existence." *Rerum Novarum* from paragraph 51; quoted in *Centesimus Annus*, no. 7, note 20.

106. John Paul II, *Ecclesia in America*, no. 56.

107. John Paul II, *Laborem Exercens*, no. 14.

108. John Paul II, *Centesimus Annus*, no. 47.

109. John Paul II, *Sollicitudo Rei Socialis*, no. 32.

110. John Paul notes that "the true elevation of man, in conformity with the natural and historical vocation of each individual, is not attained only by exploiting the abundance of goods and services, or by having perfect infrastructures." Rather, it also includes political rights, human rights, and "rights based on the transcendent vocation of the human being, beginning with the right of freedom to profess and practice one's own religious belief." John Paul II, *Sollicitudo Rei Socialis*, no. 33.

111. John Paul II, *Sollicitudo Rei Socialis*, no. 33.

112. John Paul II, *Sollicitudo Rei Socialis*, no. 15.

113. Sen has advanced the idea that rather than purely material measures like gross domestic product and national income, development should be measured in terms of the expansion of freedom, which would become both "the primary end and principal means of development." This accounts for the removal of what Sen terms "unfreedoms" to social progress. In Sen's view, development should focus "particularly on the roles and interconnections between certain crucial instrumental freedoms, including *economic opportunities, political freedoms, social facilities, transparency guarantees, and protective security.*" Sen won the Nobel Prize in economic science in 1998 for his contribution. See Amartya Sen, *Development as Freedom* (New York: Alfred A. Knopf, 1999). Quotations taken from pages xii and xiii (emphasis author's).

114. John Paul II, *Sollicitudo Rei Socialis*, no. 28.

115. John Paul follows that comment by noting, "Nor, in consequence, does the availability of the many real benefits provided in recent times by science and technology, including the computer sciences, bring freedom from every form of slavery. On the contrary, the experience of recent years shows that unless all the considerable body of resources and potential at man's disposal is guided by a moral understanding and by an orientation towards the true good of the human race, it easily turns against man to oppress him." See *Sollicitudo Rei Socialis*, no. 27.

116. Second Vatican Ecumenical Council, Pastoral Constitution on the Church in the World of Today *Gaudium et Spes*, no. 36; Paul VI, Apostolic Epistle *Octogesima Adveniens*, nos. 2–5.

117. John Paul II, *Centesimus Annus*, no. 43.

118. John Paul II, *Centesimus Annus*, no. 36 (emphasis added). Later in the encyclical, John Paul notes how the maturation of the person "can be hindered as a result of manipulation by the means of mass communication, which impose fashions and trends of opinion through carefully orchestrated repetition, without it being possible to subject to critical scrutiny the premises on which these fashions and trends are based." See *Centesimus Annus*, no. 41.

119. John Paul II, *Centesimus Annus*, no. 36.

120. John Paul II, *Centesimus Annus*, no. 36.

121. John Paul references Second Vatican Ecumenical Council, Pastoral Constitution on the Church in the World of Today, *Gaudium et Spes*, no. 35 and Paul VI, Encyclical Letter *Populorum Progressio*, no. 19.

122. John Paul II, *Centesimus Annus*, no. 36.

123. John Paul II, *Sollicitudo Rei Socialis*, no. 35.

124. Niebuhr, *The Children of Light and the Children of Darkness*, 12.

125. Friedrich A. Hayek, *The Constitution of Liberty* (London: Routledge and Kegan Paul, 1960), 52, 50; quoted in Koyzis, "Progress as an Object of Faith in the Thought of Friedrich A. von Hayek," *Christian Scholars Review* 12 (1983): 147, 146.

126. He cites Paul VI, *Populorum Progressio* (March 26, 1967), no. 13; in *Sollicitudo Rei Socialis*, no. 7.

127. John Paul II, *Centesimus Annus*, no. 42.

128. John Paul II, *Centesimus Annus*, no. 42.

9

CONCLUSION

The danger to Christianity's moral foundation and its conception of the person that has been posited in this book does not result from the faith's possible relegation to obscurity in the procession of modernity or in any competition between warring secular philosophies. Such ideological battles have raged throughout history, yet Christianity has maintained its spiritual and institutional vigor in the face of radical changes in theories of social order. Moreover, it has been shown that no period in Western (and, in particular, American) history has witnessed a greater consensus on the means by which society attains the good. Rather, the immediate threat results from a growing consensus that Christian morality conforms to market ethics—specifically, that the naturalistic and evolutionary moral system of Friedrich Hayek, which aptly describes the ethical flux of modern capitalism, is harmonious with the transcendent moral foundation of Christianity.

While this synthesis that Christian libertarians and neoconservatives have attempted to forge between the moral basis of their faith tradition and that of Austrian liberalism is only the most recent in a long history of similar projects, it is more threatening for three reasons. First, the "hypotheticality" of cultural evolution has rendered the consequences of economic and technological change less comprehensible and thus less predictable than ever before. Hayek saw no problem with such developments, for in his system, we are at the mercy of an incomprehensible and unpredictable competition for survival that cannot be circumscribed by the beliefs of any faith tradition. Second, the widespread belief that civilization has arrived at the "end of history" is dashing all hope to seek something better—specifically more holistic forms of progress capable of maintaining material development while better attending to spiritual and aesthetic needs. The death of constructivist theories of social organization and the cessation of discourse

301

concerning the "good" are evidence of this consensus. Finally, obsession with economic growth is fast displacing other values by extending the reach of the market into the most sacred areas of life. The silence of the church on emerging markets and technologies of "high moral content" is perhaps the most ominous sign for our future.

Rising economic conservatism among American Christians and their reliance on the market as a moral instrument has promoted complacency among religious communities regarding the moral sustainability of capitalism. The natural theology of the market serves today as an extension of the Christian faith and results from an amalgamation of Christian and capitalist values. Reinforcing this union has been the remarkable freedom and affluence enabled by the global proliferation of markets for an inconceivable array of products and services, some of which touch upon the very defining characteristics of the human person. These new threats to Christianity have materialized in a triumphal spirit where a highly subjectivist capitalism has emerged not simply as the superior but as the only form of social organization for an increasingly complex and technological world. Thus, civilization conceives of ultimate possibilities on this side of both telos and finis.[1]

Reinhold Niebuhr's economic realism, G. K. Chesterton's distributism, and John Paul II's Christian personalism are critical guides that demonstrate that there is no easy synthesis in history that enables Christians to avoid the hard choices of a highly interdependent and technological civilization. Individual Christians as well as their religious associations are called to engage the creative center where values and aspirations converge. Not only reason, but also spirituality, artistry, and intuition are required to deal with the complexity spawned by "progress." No single institution—government, market, or even church—is capable of going it alone. Niebuhr's realism and indeed even his pessimism emerge as critical barriers to the implicitly utopian aspirations of those who place all hope in some theory or institution. Niebuhr recognized the temptation of every society to assert its own preeminence:

> Thus every civilization contemplates the ruin of social orders which preceded it and dreams of its own indestructibility. There is no emancipation from these illusions in any philosophy; for every philosophy is under the illusion that it has no illusions because it has discovered the illusions of its predecessors.[2]

No other comment could better describe the attitudes among those who have contributed to the succession of subjectivist and collectivist social philosophies that have risen and fallen throughout the modern period of human history. Devotees of various theories of social organization have believed that they have discovered past errors in the structures of societies that resulted in social disintegration, economic privation, revolution, war, despair, and countless other social maladies. Yet they have remained habitually ignorant of the shortcomings of their favored "systems"; thus, they are destined to discover new errors that will inevitably precipitate new tragedies. "Prophetic Christianity" is uniquely able to discern flaws in the idealisms of all political and economic orders, for its emphasis on the abstraction of religious meaning from historical contingency. But truly prophetic religion requires distance from those human institutions that it seeks to inform. For, as Niebuhr noted, "if we seek to justify Christianity because it preserves democracy, or inspires hatred of dictatorship, or makes a 'free enterprise system' possible, . . . our utilitarian attitude debases the Christian faith to the status of a mere instrument of the warring creeds from which the world suffers."[3]

Friedrich Hayek and Ludwig Mises had no reservations in this purely utilitarian application of Christianity and other religions to social order. Christian libertarians, neoconservatives, reconstructionists, and others who embrace Austrian principles must at least acknowledge the role of religion in that system. Niebuhr, Chesterton, and John Paul warned against attempts to "use" Christianity to support what ultimately are political and philosophical positions, and Niebuhr insisted that tension among the social philosophies of various Christian groups is preferable to dominance by any particular group. He stated, "Even now many contradictory testimonies of various types of Christians in our nation tend to be either so irrelevant or so dangerous that a wise statesman will do well to ignore most of them; and he may well thank God that they cancel each other out sufficiently to make this indifference politically expedient."[4] Rising consensus by Christians on the morality of the market suggests that political and economic differences between Christians no longer "cancel each other out." Thus, new dangers lurk behind unmarked doors. John Paul's Christian personalism, Niebuhr's Christian realism, and Chesterton's distributism exist as vital resources for that task in their recognition that theological and philosophical meanings often are distorted by the immediate historical context. Ironically, this critical need for abstraction beyond the petty squabbles of politics and economics is articulated beautifully by the Austrian social theorist Wilhelm Röpke:

> Behind all of these perils we always encounter one predominant problem which we must face whenever we stop to think about the fate

awaiting the industrial nations that are built upon the principle of economic freedom, a fate which these nations approach with alarming complacency or even with pride in something they call progress. This all pervading problem is the process of growing concentration in the widest sense and in all spheres: concentration of the power of government and administration; concentration of economic and social power beside and under the state; concentration of decision and responsibility, which thereby become more and more anonymous, unchallengeable, and inscrutable; and concentration of people in organizations, towns and industrial centers, and firms and factories. If we want to name a common denominator for the social disease of our times, then it is concentration, and collectivism and totalitarianism are merely the extreme and lethal stages of the disease.[5]

The three Christian thinkers reviewed here, too, recognized these "concentrations" in modern culture and understood that the abuses of totalitarian governments are merely extreme manifestations of the sin that infects all human institutions. But these insights coequally suggest that the very idea of progress is at the heart of the economic problem for the Christian. Recognition by Niebuhr, Chesterton, and John Paul, and by secular theorists like Nicholas Boyle, Joseph Schumpeter, and John Kenneth Galbraith, that "concentrations" form naturally in technical societies and that such concentrations distort values, implies the need for a redefinition of progress just as Chesterton called for a century ago. However, the tendency for economic philosophy to swing wildly between the extremes of constructivist rationalism and subjectivist naturalism makes attempts to redefine progress all the more difficult. Christian thinkers too often have been caught up in these waves of political and economic ideas and their panaceas, to the detriment of the church's prophetic voice.

The economic ideas of Niebuhr, Chesterton, and John Paul provide a critical ballast to stabilize Christian social thought in such a way as to offer a more persistent and consistent guide to a morally sustainable society. Moreover, they offer a consistent model by which Christians may approach economic questions in a way that suggests no Christian system but a definite Christian "attitude" toward economic life. Four principal ideals emerge as critical in a Christian approach to economics: that "true" value can be discerned only by relating the worth of that which is valued to the totality of existence in the context of a personalized universe; that human beings are both spirit and creature, capable of both self-seeking and self-giving; that social groups are inherently more self-interested than individuals and progressively more so as they grow in size and power, and thus institutional balance is the key to justice; and, finally, that the technical advances of human progress are socially and morally indeterminate, and thus Christians must be involved in a continual process of assessing the moral outcomes of technological achievements.

While these admittedly broad principles do not by themselves offer a guidebook to a morally sustainable society, they do establish a foundation for the construction of economic ideas and institutional structures capable of mitigating the intense self-interestedness of individuals and the will to power inherent in all social groups. Moreover, they reaffirm Niebuhr's understanding of the critical need for balance in progress. It was this intense emphasis on social balance that illustrated both the nature of Niebuhr's liberalism and his confidence in the virtues of pluralism. These convictions are reflected in his statement concerning religious activism that Christians must make hard choices while recognizing that "others equally devoted to the common good may arrive at contrary conclusions. They will be less affronted and baffled by the different conclusions if they have some humble recognition of the taint of individual and collective self-interest which colors even our purest political and moral ideals."[6] Our confidence in the ability of collectives to contribute to the good has been denigrated by the overwhelming triumph of capitalism in the twentieth century. The isolated individual is becoming the sole guide to material prosperity and moral sustenance. "Social fabric" is an archaic term; telos, as that inspired by a marvelous tapestry of social institutions in a culture of pluralism, has lost out to the market transaction in seeking our collective good. The consumer, not the Christian, Jew, or Muslim, is now the measure of success.

Those who retain belief in Christianity's ultimate truths must not use that belief as an excuse for fatalism regarding the future of civilization. The remarkable energy of Niebuhr, Chesterton, and John Paul in fleshing out the most intricate social problems serves as an example to all Christians of their obligations as stewards of nature and their responsibilities to all human beings. That responsibility includes the physical and material well-being of the earth and its inhabitants, yet, more importantly for the Christian, it is also a moral responsibility. Thus, the critical difference between the moral systems of the three eminent Christian social thinkers referenced here and that of Hayek is the recognition by the former that, in the words of Niebuhr, for the Christian faith, "the final pinnacle of meaning transcends all possibilities of history. It is recognized that physical survival may be bought at too high a price."[7] That "moral" price to which Niebuhr was referring and with which Chesterton and John Paul undoubtedly would agree is never too high in Hayek's evolutionary system, in which decisions that contribute to the survival of civilization are "moral" by definition. Hayek's belief that ultimate sacrifices are often necessary for the preservation of the greater good is nowhere more evident than in his statement, "However much we dislike it, we are again and again forced to recognize that there are no truly absolute values whatever. Not even human life itself."[8] The advent of new technologies that impinge directly on the religious meaning of human life suggests that such sacrifices may well become commonplace in the brave new world of the twenty-first century.

A redemptive economy requires that the ideas, institutions, and instruments that contribute to human survival must be evaluated by their moral consequences. We must be mindful that there are "morally ambiguous elements in human history on every level of achievement."[9] Importantly, Niebuhr, Chesterton, and John Paul provided contemporary culture with two critical guides for the determination of the morality of progress. First, they recognized that determinations of the market and other human institutions must be assessed by their impacts on the collective understanding of human personality. The "person" becomes the perfect locus for assessing the prophetic role of Christian churches. As a counterweight to the dominant emphasis on economic utility, the Christian conception of personality can be concisely articulated, agreed to by many religious groups (even those beyond the Christian community), and communicated with considerable clarity to their respective memberships. Second, their insistence that a transcendently grounded sense of justice must exist as a critical ideal to prevent cultural drift into naturalism establishes a critical base for the morally redemptive economy.

Some have disavowed notions such as justice that drift too far, in their view, toward emotional or intuitional assessments of "what is just" at the expense of market logic and other determinants. In his essay "Defining Social Justice," Michael Novak defends Friedrich Hayek as a social theorist whose life exemplified "the virtue [justice] whose common misuse he so deplored."[10] Novak suggests that for Hayek, justice could only be understood in an individual context; thus, "social justice is either a virtue or it is not. If it is, it can properly be ascribed only to the reflective and deliberate acts of individual persons."[11] Ironically, given Novak's emphasis on the moral-cultural sector of his tripartite system, his radical individualizing of justice would seem to minimize the responsibility of collectives for society's moral fabric. Moreover, he states from the vantage

of Hayek's conception of justice that "the minute one begins to define social justice, one runs into embarrassing intellectual difficulties."[12] But it
was Hayek's inability to acknowledge the transcendence of the human
person that led him to such a conclusion. Novak's explanation for Hayek's
notion of justice illustrates the depth of Hayek's trust in the spontaneous
order of a free civilization:

> We are not wrong, Hayek concedes, in perceiving that the effects of the
> individual choices and open processes of a free society are not distrib-
> uted according to a recognizable principle of justice. The meritorious
> are sometimes tragically unlucky; the evil prosper; good ideas don't pan
> out, and sometimes those who backed them, however noble their vi-
> sions, lose their shirts. But a system that values both trial-and-error and
> free choice is in no position to guarantee outcomes in advance. Fur-
> thermore, no one individual (and certainly no politburo or congressional
> committee or political party) can design rules that would treat each per-
> son according to his merit or even his need.[13]

Niebuhr, Chesterton, and John Paul likely would agree with much
of the substance of Novak's interpretation of Hayek. Where they would
almost certainly disagree is with Novak's conclusion from the same essay
that "we must rule out any use of 'social justice' that does not attach to
the habits (that is, virtues) of individuals. Social justice is a virtue, an attribute of individuals, or it is a fraud."[14] Novak's (and Hayek's) dogmatism
suggesting that justice is an appropriate "attribute" almost exclusively at
the level of the individual goes too far for Christian realism, Christian
personalism, or distributism. It denies the reality that collectives inevitably
will articulate their own conceptions of justice and that individuals often
voice more reflective expressions of what is just in the context of social
groups than in the intensely self-interested context of the market.
Churches, schools, political parties, trade unions, and other institutions
will express their unique ideas on justice from unique vantages and in the
appropriate forums. The need for institutional expressions of justice and
morality is radically heightened in a world where complexity overwhelms
the individual. These groups must risk "intellectual embarrassment" in the
articulation of those principles of justice that are derived from insights of
their respective traditions.

The common dismissal of institutional expressions of justice by conservatives might be seen as emanating from their often-voiced fear of the

"middle way" to human progress. However, this fear might be seen more as confusion of a secularly confined middle way with the more expansive and inclusive conception of the "third way" that embraces religious and other conceptions of the good. Samuel Gregg, director of research for the Acton Institute, in his fine article on Wilhelm Röpke, offers an explanation for Röpke's characterization of the "third way" that has much in common with the thought of Niebuhr, Chesterton, and John Paul. While the "middle way" implies a rationally attained middle ground between laissez-faire capitalism and totalitarian collectivism, the third way exists as the point of confluence among many religious and philosophical ideals and rational systems of thought:

> When Röpke used the expression "third way," he was emphasizing the need for a free society to complement the market economy and a limited state with both a flourishing range of intermediate associations as well as a moral culture that recognized what Christians understand as the objective hierarchy of values. Concerning intermediate associations, Röpke was clearly influenced by his observations of how such organizations prevented freedom from degenerating into anarchy in economically and politically decentralized Switzerland. Regarding issues of moral culture, Röpke was deeply disturbed by what he described as Western society's "proletarianization"—that is, a growing sameness and monotony of social and cultural conditions.[15]

Gregg continues his description of Röpke's philosophy, stating that Röpke was quick to point out the "romantic delusions of Enlightenment rationalists and their modern heirs." It was Röpke the Christian humanist who "accepted the insight of revelation" and recognized "that atheistic and agnostic anthropologies of man were inadequate foundations for a truly free society."[16]

Gregg's description of Röpke's philosophy hints at the common confusion among Christian and other social theorists between the "middle way" and the "third way" that has been a principal catalyst for the slippery slope theory. The middle way as some common ground between democratic capitalism and collectivism is indeed a dead end that contributes to the vacillations between purely secular ideals of society to which Christians have been vulnerable. However, the third way is an absolute necessity for a Christian definition of progress, for it employs all resources at the disposal of Christian social thinkers, and its myriad influences greatly lessen the tendency to absolutize elements of social philosophy.[17] The third way is *the* way to a redemptive economy, and it conforms to Christian realism's emphasis on balance for the attainment of the social good, to Christian personalism's insistence on subsidiarity in economic relationships, and to distributism's holistic conception of progress. The third way is consistent with a continual reassessment of property and ownership and its institutional forms like "stakeholders" and "consensus conferences." These concepts account for the true breadth of ownership in modern capitalism, and they offer structures capable of averting "concentrations" and distributing accountability to those most impacted by economic action, consistent with subsidiarity. These ideas also suggest the need for supplementary expressions to market determinations of value in the implementation of technologies that weigh so heavily on the definition of the human person and that greatly impact the value system of the wider community. Moreover, these and other ideas like the "enabling state" embody more holistic conceptions of the role of government in economic progress that break down traditional distinctions between "public" and "private" that have become increasingly divisive in the individualist culture of modern capitalism.[18]

The market is an important component to a redemptive economy for the arbitration of social values that cannot be accomplished by other institutions. Yet there are other sources of values and means of distilling them that offer a different perspective from the market. The intensely individual and material character of the market order suggests that participants are in less reflective (and thus less moral) states of mind when they transact than when they worship, vote, pursue education, act altruistically, or any number of other functions that are also critical to the determination of the good. Yet the ubiquitous reach of the market suggests that it has become an inordinate measure of human values and desires.

The timing is right for Christian churches to articulate economic policies derived from the insights of their faith that promote a morally redemptive economy. The American public is clamoring for greater accountability among its institutions, and the economic principles advanced in Christian realism, Christian personalism, and distributism are capable of contributing to a redefinition of progress that would draw values from a wider cross-section of society and spread responsibility across both individuals and institutions. Moreover, if the thesis articulated by Nicholas Boyle is correct that governments can serve to empower themselves by breaking down intermediate institutions, then enabling a more collective voice should have the effect of curbing government power.

Most importantly, these ideas are consistent with Reinhold Niebuhr's caution that society must remain vigilant against the tendency to absolutize what are necessarily flawed human contrivances designed for the attainment of what will always be an imprecise and near inexpressible ideal—justice:

> But the whole capital of religious sanctity must not be invested in these norms. For these systems and structures of justice are not eternal norms to which life must perennially conform but rather ad hoc efforts to strike a balance between the final moral possibilities of life and the immediate and given realities. If certain moral, social, and economic traditions have become firmly established, they will not be lightly cast aside. The more it is recognized that there is not one single rational and just method of organizing the life of the community, the more will an established historic method be given due reverence, the more so if there is no illusion that some other method will overcome every past evil or be immune to opposite evils. A proper understanding of the historical and contingent nature of these various structures of justice will discourage both the revolutionary ardor which is always informed by some illusions and the conservatism which pretends that established norms are absolute.[19]

It is not capitalism per se but rather the intensely individualistic and rationalistic character of modern capitalism that threatens Christianity's moral system and its conception of the person. The radical elevation of subjective judgments over collective assessments of the good has had the affect of denigrating the contributions of all institutions, including the church. A redemptive economy requires the vital contribution of intermediate associations of all kinds to enable expressions of the good (both individual and collective) from a variety of perspectives.

The attempt to conceptualize a redemptive economy cannot exceed our imagination because it is part of our history. It is the lack of moral consideration of our social structures that is today an aberration of our heritage. The moral consequences of capitalism have been an essential element of social discourse in the West from the treatises of Scholastic theologians to the "table talk" of Reformers to the musings of the American Founding Fathers. That vital tradition must be relocated and revitalized if we are to balance the need for moral sustenance with our material progress. The redemptive economy insists that economic truth, as all other truths, can only be approximated by locating the intersection of seemingly contradictory human ideals, values, and beliefs, as best illuminated by the paradox of the Cross.

NOTES

1. Reinhold Niebuhr stated, "The problem is that the end as *finis* is a threat to the end as *telos*. Life is in peril of meaninglessness because *finis* is a seemingly abrupt and capricious termination of the development of life before it has reached its true end or *telos*. The Christian faith understands this aspect of the human situation" for it "asserts that it is not within man's power to solve the vexing problem of his subjection to, and partial freedom from, the flux of time. It holds, furthermore, that evil is introduced into history by the very effort of men to solve this problem by their own resources." See Reinhold Niebuhr (hereafter RN), *The Nature and Destiny of Man*, vol. 2, *Human Destiny*, one-volume ed. (New York: Charles Scribner's Sons, 1949 [orig. pub. 1941]), 287.

2. Niebuhr further noted, "What no civilization or culture has ever done, . . . , is to admit that the force of a new condition, necessity or power in history, incompatible with its own established presuppositions and privileges, had an equal or superior right to existence with itself. Civilizations meet such a situation with instinctive reactions derived from the impulse of survival." See RN, *Beyond Tragedy: Essays on the Christian Interpretation of History*, Essay Index Reprint Series (New York: Charles Scribner's Sons, 1937; reprint, Freeport, NY: Books for Libraries Press, 1971), 223, 225.

3. RN, "Utilitarian Christianity and the World Crisis," *Christianity and Crisis* 10 (May 29, 1950): 66.

4. RN, "Utilitarian Christianity and the World Crisis." See also Charles McDaniel, "Friedrich Hayek and Reinhold Niebuhr on the Moral Persistence of Liberal Society," *Journal of Interdisciplinary Studies* 16, nos. 1–2 (2004): 153.

5. Wilhelm Röpke, *A Humane Economy: The Social Framework of the Free Economy*, trans. Elizabeth Henderson (Chicago: Henry Regnery Company, 1960), 32.

6. RN, "Christian Faith and Political Controversy," in *Love and Justice: Selections from the Shorter Writings of Reinhold Niebuhr*, ed. D. B. Robertson (Louisville, KY: Westminster/John Knox Press, 1957), 61 (originally published in *Christianity and Crisis* [July 21, 1952]).

7. Reinhold Niebuhr, "The Christian Faith and the Economic Life," in *Goals of Economic Life*, ed. A. Dudley Ward (New York: Harper & Brothers, 1953), 452.

8. Hayek, *New Studies in Philosophy, Politics, Economics and the History of Ideas* (London: Routledge and Kegan Paul, 1979), 298; quoted in Graham Walker, *The Ethics of F. A. Hayek* (Lanham, MD: University Press of America, 1986), 58n78.

9. RN, "A Faith for History's Greatest Crisis," in *A Reinhold Niebuhr Reader: Selected Essays, Articles, and Book Reviews*, comp. and ed. Charles C. Brown (Philadelphia: Trinity Press International, 1992), 12.

10. Michael Novak, "Defining Social Justice," *First Things* 108 (December 2000): 11.

11. Novak, "Defining Social Justice." Hayek was even more defiant in his rejection of *any* conception of justice in his essay "The Fatal Conceit." He stated, "Demands for justice are simply inappropriate to a naturalistic evolutionary process—inappropriate not just to what has happened in the past, but to what is going on in the present." See Hayek, "The Fatal Conceit," in *The Collected Works of F. A. Hayek*, ed. W. W. Bartley III, vol. 1, *The Fatal Conceit: The Errors of Socialism* (Chicago: The University of Chicago Press, 1988), 74.

12. Novak observes Hayek's criticism of the tomes that have been written on justice "without ever offering a definition of it." Justice is, in Novak's interpretation of Hayek, "allowed to float in the air as if everyone will recognize an instance of it when it appears." See Novak, "Defining Social Justice," 11.

13. Novak, "Defining Social Justice," 12.

14. Novak, "Defining Social Justice."

15. Samuel Gregg, "A Humanist for Our Time," *Religion & Liberty* 12 (March and April 2002): 11.

16. Samuel Gregg, "A Humanist for Our Time," 11.

17. Christian economist Robert Nelson states, "Economic progress, many have concluded, has not turned out to be all it was cracked up to be. Indeed, it is significant that a number of economists and organizations are attempting to determine once again how to put economic knowledge at the service of Christian values. It is, in part, a reflection of a growing recognition in American society that the past attempt to separate technical economics from value considerations has not worked as expected. If Christian values are not explicitly incorporated into the practice of economics, it may simply create a vacuum in which other types of values—perhaps at odds with Christianity—dominate the field." See Robert H. Nelson, "Economic Religion versus Christian Values," *Journal of Markets and Morality* 1 (October 1998); available from the Acton Institute website www.acton.org/publicat/m_and_m/1998_Oct/nelson.htm.

18. The Gilberts' idea of the "enabling state" suggests that government can serve best in a noncoercive role as facilitator rather than overseer or administrator of many forms of public works. See Neil Gilbert and Barbara Gilbert, *The Enabling State: Modern Welfare Capitalism in America* (New York: Oxford University Press, 1989).

19. RN, "The Christian Faith and the Economic Life," 451.

BIBLIOGRAPHY

PRIMARY SOURCES

Books

Ackerman, Bruce, and Anne Alstott. *The Stakeholder Society*. New Haven, CT: Yale University Press, 1999.

Acquaviva, S. S. *The Decline of the Sacred in Industrial Society*. Translated by Patricia Lipscomb. New York: Harper & Row, 1979.

Barbour, Ian. *Ethics in an Age of Technology: The Gifford Lectures*. San Francisco: Harper, 1992.

Barth, Karl. *Dogmatics in Outline*. New York: Harper & Row, 1959.

Bayer, Richard C. *Capitalism and Christianity: The Possibility of Christian Personalism*. Washington, DC: Georgetown University Press, 1999.

Becker, Gary. *A Treatise on the Family*. Cambridge, MA: Harvard University Press, 1981.

Bell, Daniel. *The Cultural Contradictions of Capitalism*. Twentieth Anniversary Edition. New York: Basic Books, 1976.

———. *The End of Ideology: On the Exhaustion of Political Ideas in the Fifties*. Glencoe, IL: The Free Press, 1960.

Bennett, John C. *Christian Ethics and Social Policy*. New York: Charles Scribner's Sons, 1950.

Berger, Peter. *The Sacred Canopy: Elements of a Sociological Theory of Religion*. Garden City, NY: Doubleday & Company, 1967.

———, ed. *The Capitalist Spirit: Toward a Religious Ethic of Wealth Creation*. San Francisco: Institute for Contemporary Studies, 1990.

Block, Walter. *The U.S. Bishops and Their Critics: An Economic and Ethical Perspective*. Vancouver, BC: Fraser Institute, 1986.

Block, Walter, Geoffrey Brennan, and Kenneth Elzinga, eds. *Morality of the Market: Religious and Economic Perspectives*. Vancouver, BC: Fraser Institute, 1985.

Bloom, Harold. *The American Religion: The Emergence of the Post-Christian Nation*. New York: Simon & Schuster, 1992.

Boyle, Nicholas. *Who Are We Now? Christian Humanism and the Global Market from Hegel to Heaney*. Notre Dame, IN: University of Notre Dame Press, 1998.

Catherwood, H. F. R. *The Christian in Industrial Society*. London: The Tyndale Press, 1964.

Chesterton, G. K. *Heretics*. In *The Collected Works of G. K. Chesterton*, vol. 1. San Francisco: Ignatius Press, 1986.

———. *The Collected Works of G. K. Chesterton*. Vol. 33, *The Illustrated London News (1923–1925)*. Edited by Lawrence J. Clipper. San Francisco: Ignatius Press, 1986.

———. *Orthodoxy*. In *The Collected Works of G. K. Chesterton*, vol. 1. San Francisco: Ignatius Press, 1986.

———. *The Outline of Sanity*. In *The Collected Works of G. K. Chesterton*, vol. 5, edited by George J. Marlin et al. San Francisco: Ignatius Press, 1986.

———. *Utopia of Usurers*. In *The Collected Works of G. K. Chesterton*, vol. 5, edited by George J. Marlin et al. San Francisco: Ignatius Press, 1986.

Clapp, Rodney, ed. *Consuming Passion: Christianity and the Consumer Culture*. Downers Grove, IL: InterVarsity Press, 1998.

Dempsey, Bernard. *The Functional Economy: The Bases of Economic Organization*. Englewood Cliffs, NJ: Prentice-Hall, 1958.

Dewey, John. *A Common Faith*. New Haven, CT: Yale University Press, 1934.

———. *The Public and Its Problems*. New York: Henry Holt & Company, 1927.

Ellul, Jacques. *The Technological Bluff*. Translated by Geoffrey W. Bromiley. Grand Rapids, MI: William B. Eerdmans, 1990.

Elshtain, Jean Bethke. *Who Are We? Critical Reflections and Hopeful Possibilities*. Grand Rapids, MI: William B. Eerdmans, 2000.

Ely, Richard T. *Social Aspects of Christianity and Other Essays*. New York: Thomas Y. Crowell & Co., 1889.

Engelhardt, H. Tristram, Jr. *Bioethics and Secular Humanism: The Search for Common Morality*. London: SCM Press, 1991.

Finke, Roger, and Rodney Stark. *The Churching of America, 1776–1990: Winners and Losers in Our Religious Economy*. New Brunswick, NJ: Rutgers University Press, 1992.

Fukuyama, Francis. *The End of History and the Last Man*. New York: The Free Press, 1992.

Gay, Craig M. *With Liberty and Justice for Whom? The Recent Evangelical Debate over Capitalism*. Grand Rapids, MI: William B. Eerdmans, 1991.

Galbraith, John Kenneth. *The Affluent Society*. Boston: Houghton Mifflin, 1976.

———. *American Capitalism: The Concept of Countervailing Power*. New Brunswick, NJ: Transaction Publishers, 1993. Originally published by Houghton Mifflin, 1952.

Gates, Jeff. *The Ownership Solution: Toward a Shared Capitalism for the Twenty-first Century*. Reading, MA: Addison-Wesley, 1998.

Giarini, Orio, and Henri Louberge. *The Diminishing Returns of Technology: An Essay on the Crisis in Economic Growth*. Translated by Maurice Chapman. New York: Pergamon Press, 1978.

Gilbert, Neil, and Barbara Gilbert. *The Enabling State: Modern Welfare Capitalism in America*. New York: Oxford University Press, 1989.

Gilder, George. *Life after Television*. New York: W. W. Norton, 1994.

———. *The Spirit of Enterprise*. New York: Simon & Schuster, 1984.

———. *Wealth and Poverty*. New York: Basic Books, 1981.

Gladden, Washington. *Social Salvation*. Boston: Houghton Mifflin, 1902.

Goudzwaard, Bob. *Capitalism and Progress: A Diagnosis of Western Society*. Translated and edited by Josina Van Nuis Zylstra. Grand Rapids, MI: William B. Eerdmans, 1979.

Hayek, Friedrich A. von. *The Collected Works of F. A. Hayek*. Edited by W. W. Bartley III. Vol. 1, *The Fatal Conceit: The Errors of Socialism*. Chicago: University of Chicago Press, 1988.

———. *The Constitution of Liberty*. London: Routledge and Kegan Paul, 1960.

———. *Law, Legislation and Liberty*. Vol. 1, *Rules and Order*. Chicago: University of Chicago Press, 1973.

———. *Law, Legislation and Liberty*. Vol. 3, *The Political Order of a Free People*, 2nd ed. Chicago: University of Chicago Press, 1981.

———. *New Studies in Philosophy, Politics, Economics and the History of Ideas*. London: Routledge and Kegan Paul, 1979.

———. *The Road to Serfdom*. London: George Routledge & Sons, 1944.

———. *Studies in Philosophy, Politics and Economics*. London: Routledge and Kegan Paul, 1967.

Henry, Carl F. H. *The Uneasy Conscience of Modern Fundamentalism*. Grand Rapids, MI: William B. Eerdmans, 1947.

Herberg, Will. *Protestant-Catholic-Jew: An Essay in American Religious Sociology*. Garden City, NY: Anchor Books, 1960.

Hirsch, Fred. *Social Limits to Growth*. Cambridge, MA: Harvard University Press, 1976.

Hirschmann, Albert O. *Morality and the Social Sciences: A Durable Tension*. Memphis, TN: P. K. Seidman Foundation, 1980.

Hudson, Winthrop S. *Religion in America: An Historical Account of the Development of American Religious Life*. 4th ed. New York: Macmillan Publishing Company, 1987.

Hutchison, William R. *The Modernist Impulse in American Protestantism*. Cambridge, MA: Harvard University Press, 1976.

John Paul II, Pope. *Centesimus Annus*. Washington, DC: Office for Publishing and Promotion Services, United States Catholic Conference, 1991.

———. *Ecclesia in America* [The Way to Conversion, Communion and Solidarity in America]. January 22, 1999. www.vatican.va/holy_father/john_paul_ii/apost_exhortations/documents/hr_jp-ii_exh_22011999_ecclesia-in-america_en.html.

———. *Laborem Exercens* [On Human Work]. September 14, 1981. www.vatican.va/holy_father/john_paul_ii/encyclicals/documents/hf_jp_ii_enc_14091981_laborem-exercens_fr.html.

———. *Sollicitudo Rei Socialis* [On Social Concern]. December 30, 1987. www.vatican.va/holy_father/john_paul_ii/encyclicals/documents/hf_jp_ii_enc_30121987_solicitudo-rei-socialis_en.html.

Knight, Frank Hyneman. *The Ethics of Competition*. New Brunswick, NJ: Transaction Publishers, 1997.

Khomiakov, Alexei. *The Church Is One*. Seattle, WA: St. Nectarios Press, 1979.

Linder, Staffan Burenstam. *The Harried Leisure Class*. New York: Columbia University Press, 1970.

Long, D. Stephen. *Divine Economy: Theology and the Market*. New York: Routledge, 2000.

MacIntyre, Alasdair. *After Virtue: A Study in Moral Theory*. 2nd ed. Notre Dame, IN: University of Notre Dame Press, 1984.

Maguire, Daniel C. *Sacred Choices: The Right to Contraception and Abortion in Ten World Religions.* Minneapolis: Fortress Press, 2001.

Marx, Karl. *The Communist Manifesto.* In *Karl Marx Selected Writings,* edited by Lawrence H. Simon. Indianapolis: Hackett Publishing, 1994.

Meilaender, Gilbert C. *Body, Soul, and Bioethics.* Notre Dame, IN: University of Notre Dame Press, 1995.

Miller, William Lee. *The First Liberty: Religion and the American Republic.* New York: Paragon House Publishers, 1985.

Mises, Ludwig von. *Economic Freedom and Interventionism: An Anthology of Articles and Essays by Ludwig von Mises.* Edited by Bettina Bien Greaves. Irvington-on-Hudson, NY: The Foundation for Economic Education, 1990.

———. *Epistemological Problems of Economics.* Translated by George Reisman. Princeton, NJ: D. Van Nostrand Company, 1960.

———. *Human Action: A Treatise on Economics.* 3rd rev. ed. Chicago: Henry Regnery Company, 1949.

———. *Liberalism in the Classical Tradition.* Translated by Ralph Raico. Irvington-on-Hudson, NY: Foundation for Economic Education, 1985.

———. *Planning for Freedom, and Sixteen Other Essays and Addresses.* South Holland, IL: Libertarian Press, 1980.

Moore, R. Laurence. *Selling God: American Religion in the Marketplace of Culture.* Oxford: Oxford University Press, 1994.

Munkirs, John R. *The Transformation of American Capitalism: From Competitive Market Structures to Centralized Private Sector Planning.* Armonk, NY: M. E. Sharpe, 1985.

Nash, Ronald, ed. *Liberation Theology.* Milford, MI: Mott Media, 1984.

Nash, Ronald H. *Poverty and Wealth: The Christian Debate over Capitalism.* Westchester, IL: Crossway Books, 1986.

———. *Social Justice and the Christian Church.* Milford, MI: Mott Media, 1983.

Nelson, Robert H. "Economic Religion versus Christian Value." *The Journal of Markets and Morality* 1 (October 1998). Available from the Acton Institute website at www.acton.org/publicat/m_and_m/1998_oct/nelson.html.Neuhaus, Richard John. *The Naked Public Square: Religion and Democracy in America.* Grand Rapids, MI: William B. Eerdmans, 1984.

Niebuhr, H. Richard. *Christ and Culture.* New York: Harper & Brothers, 1951.

———. *Radical Monotheism and Western Culture: With Supplementary Essays.* Library of Theological Ethics Series. Louisville, KY: Westminster/John Knox Press, 1960.

———. *The Social Sources of Denominationalism.* Hamden, CT: Shoestring Press, 1929.

Niebuhr, Reinhold. *Beyond Tragedy: Essays on the Christian Interpretation of History.* Essay Index Reprint Series. New York: Charles Scribner's Sons, 1937. Reprint, Freeport, NY: Books for Libraries Press, 1971.

———. *The Children of Light and the Children of Darkness: A Vindication of Democracy and a Critique of Its Traditional Defense.* New York: Charles Scribner's Sons, 1944.

———. *Christian Realism and Political Problems.* New York: Charles Scribner's Sons, 1953. Reprint, Fairfield, NJ: Augustus M. Kelley Publishers, 1977.

———. *Does Civilization Need Religion? A Study in the Social Resources and Limitations of Religion in Modern Life.* New York: The Macmillan Company, 1927.

———. *Faith and Politics: A Commentary on Religious, Social and Political Thought in a Technological Age.* Edited by Ronald H. Stone. New York: George Braziller, 1968.

———. *An Interpretation of Christian Ethics*. New York: Harper & Brothers, 1935. Reprint, New York: Meridian Books, 1956.

———. *The Irony of American History*. New York: Charles Scribner's Sons, 1952.

———. *Man's Nature and His Communities: Essays on the Dynamics and Enigmas of Man's Personal and Social Existence*. New York: Charles Scribner's Sons, 1965.

———. *Moral Man and Immoral Society*. New York: Charles Scribner's Sons, 1932.

———. *The Nature and Destiny of Man: A Christian Interpretation*. Vol. 1, *Human Nature*. One-volume edition. New York: Charles Scribner's Sons, 1949. Originally published in 1941.

———. *The Nature and Destiny of Man: A Christian Interpretation*. Vol. 2, *Human Destiny*. One-volume edition. New York: Charles Scribner's Sons, 1949. Originally published in 1941.

———. *Reflections on the End of an Era*. New York: Charles Scribner's Sons, 1934.

———. *The Self and the Dramas of History*. New York: Charles Scribner's Sons, 1955.

Niebuhr, Reinhold, and Alan Heimert. *A Nation So Conceived: Reflections on the History of America from Its Early Visions to Its Present Power*. New York: Scribner's, 1973.

Niebuhr, Reinhold, and Paul E. Sigmund. *The Democratic Experience: Past and Prospects*. New York: Frederick A. Praeger Publishers, 1969.

North, Gary. *An Introduction to Christian Economics*. Craig Press, 1976.

———. *Puritan Economic Experiments*. Tyler, TX: Institute for Christian Economics, 1988.

Novak, Michael. *Business as a Calling: Work and the Examined Life*. New York: The Free Press, 1996.

———. *The Catholic Ethic and the Spirit of Capitalism*. New York: The Free Press, 1993.

———. *Freedom with Justice: Catholic Social Thought and Liberal Institutions*. San Francisco: Harper & Row, 1984.

———. *Free Persons and the Common Good*. Lanham, MD: Madison Books, 1989.

———. *The Spirit of Democratic Capitalism*. New York: Simon & Schuster, 1982.

———. *Toward a Theology of the Corporation*. Washington, DC: The American Enterprise Institute Press, 1990.

Paul VI, Pope. *Humanae Vitae: Encyclical Letter of His Holiness Pope Paul VI on the Regulation of Births*. San Francisco: Ignatius Press, 1978. Originally published in 1968.

Peacocke, Arthur. *Theology for a Scientific Age: Being and Becoming—Natural and Divine*. Cambridge, MA: Basil Blackwell, 1990.

Pius XI, Pope. *Quadragesimo Anno: On Constructing the Social Order*. Washington, DC: United States Catholic Conference, 1991. Originally issued on May 15, 1931. Published by the Catholic Truth Society in 1939.

Rae, Scott B., and Paul M. Cox. *Bioethics: A Christian Approach in a Pluralistic Age*. Grand Rapids, MI: William B. Eerdmans, 1999.

Ramsey, Paul. *The Patient as Person: Explorations in Medical Ethics*. New Haven, CT: Yale University Press, 1970.

Rawls, John. *Political Liberalism*. The John Dewey Essays in Philosophy, no. 4. New York: Columbia University Press, 1993.

———. *A Theory of Justice*. Cambridge, MA: Belknap Press of Harvard University Press, 1971.

Röpke, Wilhelm. *A Humane Economy: The Social Framework of the Free Market*. Translated by Elizabeth Henderson. Chicago: Henry Regnery Company, 1960.

Sandel, Michael J. *Democracy's Discontent: America in Search of Public Philosophy*. Cambridge, MA: The Belknap Press of Harvard University Press, 1996.

Say, Jean-Baptiste. *A Treatise on Political Economy, or the Production, Distribution, and Consumption of Wealth*. Reprints of Economic Classics Series. New York: Augustus M. Kelley, 1964. Originally printed by Wells & Lilly, 1821.

Schaeffer, Francis A. *Back to Freedom and Dignity*. Downers Grove, IL: InterVarsity Press, 1979.

Schumpeter, Joseph A. *Capitalism, Socialism and Democracy*. 3rd ed. New York: Harper & Brothers, 1950.

———. *History of Economic Analysis*, ed. E. B. Schumpeter. New York: Oxford University Press, 1954.

Sen, Amartya. *Development as Freedom*. New York: Alfred A. Knopf, 1999.

Shinn, Roger Lincoln. *Forced Options: Social Decisions for the 21st Century*. Religious Perspectives, vol. 27. San Francisco: Harper & Row, 1982.

Smith, Adam. *An Inquiry into the Nature and Causes of the Wealth of Nations*. 5th ed., abridged. New York: Random House, 1985. Originally published in 1776.

———. *The Theory of Moral Sentiments*. Indianapolis: Liberty Class, 1976. Edition follows the text of the "New Edition." London: Henry G. Bohn, 1853.

Thielicke, Helmut. *Theological Ethics*. Vol. 1, *Foundations*. Edited by William H. Lazareth. Philadelphia: Fortress Press, 1966.

Tocqueville, Alexis de. *Democracy in America*. Translated by George Lawrence. Edited by J. P. Mayer. Garden City, NY: Doubleday & Company, 1969. Originally published in two parts in 1835 and 1840.

Veatch, Robert M. *Death, Dying and the Biological Revolution: Our Last Quest for Responsibility*. New Haven, CT: Yale University Press, 1989.

Veblen, Thorstein. *The Theory of the Leisure Class: An Economic Study of Institutions*. New York: B. W. Huebsch, 1912.

Ward, Harry F. *Our Economic Morality & the Ethic of Jesus*. New York: The Macmillan Company, 1929.

Wayland, Francis. *The Elements of Moral Science*. Boston: Gould & Lincoln, 1854.

Weber, Max. *The Protestant Ethic and the Spirit of Capitalism*. Translated by Talcott Parsons. Gloucester, MA: Peter Smith, 1988.

Whitehead, Alfred North. *Introduction to Mathematics*. London, 1911.

———. *Science and the Modern World*. New York: Macmillan, 1929.

Wilentz, Sean. *Chants Democratic: New York City & the Rise of the American Working Class, 1788–1850*. New York: Oxford University Press, 1984.

Wojtyla, Karol [Pope John Paul II]. *The Acting Person*. Translated by Andrzej Potocki. Boston: D. Reidel Publishing Company, 1979.

Wuthnow, Robert. *The Restructuring of American Religion: Society and Faith since World War II*. Princeton, NJ: Princeton University Press, 1988.

Yoder, John Howard. *The Politics of Jesus: Vicit Agnus Noster*. 2nd ed. Grand Rapids, MI: William B. Eerdmans, 1994.

Young, Jeffrey T. *Economics as a Moral Science: The Political Economy of Adam Smith*. Cheltenham, UK: Edward Elgar Publishing, 1997.

Young, Lawrence A., ed. *Rational Choice Theory and Religion: Summary and Assessment*. New York: Routledge, 1997.

Articles

Allen, John L., Jr. "Abortion Debates Rock Germany." *National Catholic Reporter* 35 (February 12, 1999): 5.

Babcock, Robert H. "The Decline of Artisan Republicanism in Portland, Maine, 1825–1850." *The New England Quarterly* 63 (March 1990): 3–34.

Block, Walter. "Private Property, Ethics, and Wealth Creation." In *The Capitalist Spirit: Toward a Religious Ethic of Wealth Creation*, edited by Peter Berger, 107–28. San Francisco: ICS Press.

Bork, Robert H. "Hard Truths about the Culture War." *First Things* 54 (June–July 1995): 18–23.

Boyle, Nicholas. "Understanding Thatcherism (1988)." In *Who Are We Now? Christian Humanism and the Global Market from Hegel to Heaney*. Notre Dame, IN: University of Notre Dame Press, 1998.

Brinkman, Richard L., and June E. Brinkman. "Cultural Lag: Conception and Theory." *International Journal of Social Economics* 24 (1997). alidoro.emeraldinsight.com/v.../cw/mcb/03068293/v24n6/s2/p609.html.

Carnegie, Andrew. "The Gospel of Wealth." In *The Responsibilities of Wealth*, edited by Dwight F. Burlingame, 1–31. Bloomington, IN: Indiana University Press, 1992.

Chesterton, G. K. "The Beginning of the Quarrel." In *The Collected Works of G. K. Chesterton*, vol. 5, edited by George J. Marlin et al., 41–53. San Francisco: Ignatius Press, 1986.

———. "Democracy and Industrialism." American Chesterton Society. www.chesterton.org/gkc/Distributist/industrial.htm (accessed December 21, 2004).

———. "The Free Man and the Ford Car." In *The Collected Works of G. K. Chesterton*, vol. 5, edited by George J. Marlin et al., 165–72. San Francisco: Ignatius Press, 1986.

———. "A Misunderstanding about Method." In *The Outline of Sanity*, in *The Collected Works of G. K. Chesterton*, vol. 5, *Family, Society, Politics*, edited by George J. Marlin et al. San Francisco: Ignatius Press, 1987.

———. "On a Sense of Proportion." In *The Collected Works of G. K. Chesterton*, vol. 5, *Family, Society, Politics*, edited by George J. Marlin et al., 74–84. San Francisco: Ignatius Press, 1986.

———. "The Peril of the Hour." In *The Collected Works of G. K. Chesterton*, vol. 5, edited by George J. Marlin et al., 54–64. San Francisco: Ignatius Press, 1986.

———. "Progress and Proportion." In *The Collected Works of G. K. Chesterton*, vol. 33, *The Illustrated London News (1923–1925)*. Edited by Lawrence J. Clipper. San Francisco: Ignatius Press, 1986.

———. "The Real Life of the Land." In *The Collected Works of G. K. Chesterton*, vol. 5, edited by George J. Marlin et al., 134–40. San Francisco: Ignatius Press, 1986.

———. "Reflections on a Rotten Apple." American Chesterton Society. www.chesterton.org/gkc/Distributist/rottenapple.html.

———. "The Religion of Small Property." In *The Collected Works of G. K. Chesterton*, vol. 5, edited by George J. Marlin et al., 184–93. San Francisco: Ignatius Press, 1986.

———. "The Romance of Machinery." In *The Collected Works of G. K. Chesterton*, vol. 5, edited by George J. Marlin et al. San Francisco: Ignatius Press, 1986.

———. "The War on Holidays." In *The Collected Works of G. K. Chesterton*, vol. 5, edited by George J. Marlin et al., 417–20. San Francisco: Ignatius Press, 1986.

——. "The Wheel of Fate." In *The Collected Works of G. K. Chesterton*, vol. 5, edited by George J. Marlin et al., 143–50. San Francisco: Ignatius Press, 1986.

Gay, Craig M. "The Technological Ethos and the Spirit of (Post) Modern Nihilism." *Christian Scholars Review* 28 (Fall 1998): 90–110.

Gray, John. "F. A. Hayek and the Rebirth of Classical Liberalism." *Literature of Liberty* 5 (Winter 1982).

Harris, Ralph. "The Plan to End Planning." *National Review* 49 (June 16, 1997): 23–24.

Hayek, Friedrich A. von. "Between Instinct and Reason." In *The Collected Works of F. A. Hayek*, vol. 1, *The Fatal Conceit: The Errors of Socialism*, edited by W. W. Bartley III, 11–28. Chicago: University of Chicago Press, 1988.

——. "The Fatal Conceit." In *The Collected Works of F. A. Hayek*, vol. 1, *The Fatal Conceit: The Errors of Socialism*, edited by W. W. Bartley III, 66–88. Chicago: University of Chicago Press, 1988.

——. "Religion and the Guardians of Tradition." In *The Collected Works of F. A. Hayek*, vol. 1, *The Fatal Conceit: The Errors of Socialism*, edited by W. W. Bartley III, 135–42. Chicago: University of Chicago Press, 1988.

——. "Scientism and the Study of Society: Part III," *Economica*, n.s., 11 (February 1944).

——. "Was Socialism a Mistake?" In *The Collected Works of F.A. Hayek*, vol. 1, *The Fatal Conceit: The Errors of Socialism*, edited by W. W. Bartley III, 6–10. Chicago: University of Chicago Press, 1988.

Heyne, Paul. "Clerical Laissez-Faire: A Study in Theological Economics." In *Religion, Economics and Social Thought*, edited by Walter Block and Irving Hexham, 125–52. Vancouver, BC: The Fraser Institute, 1986.

Hudspith, Robert. "Using a Consensus Conference to Learn about Public Participation in Policymaking in Areas of Technical Controversy." *Political Science & Politics* 34 (June 2001): 313–17.

Kaveny, M. Cathleen, and James F. Keenan, SJ. "Ethical Issues in Health-Care Restructuring." *Theological Studies* (March 1995): 136–50.

Knight, Frank Hyneman. "Ethics and Economic Interpretation." In *The Ethics of Competition*, 11–32. New Brunswick, NJ: Transaction Publishers, 1997. Originally published by Harper & Brothers and George Allen & Unwin, 1935.

——. "The Ethics of Competition." In *The Ethics of Competition*, 33–67. New Brunswick, N J: Transaction Publishers, 1997. Originally published by Harper & Brothers and George Allen & Unwin, 1935.

Long, D. Stephen. "A Global Market—A Catholic Church: The New Political (Ir)realism." *Theology Today* 52 (October 1995): 360.

Luther, Martin. "On Secular Authority." In *Luther and Calvin on Secular Authority*, edited by Harro Höpfl. Cambridge Text in the History of Political Thought Series. New York: Cambridge University Press, 1991.

Meilaender, Gilbert. "Begetting and Cloning." *First Things* 74 (June 1, 1997): 41–43.

Mises, Ludwig von. "Economic Freedom in the Present-Day World." In *Economic Freedom and Interventionism: An Anthology of Articles and Essays by Ludwig von Mises*, edited by Bettina Bien Greaves. Irvington-on-Hudson, NY: The Foundation for Economic Education, 1990.

———. "Liberty and Its Antithesis." In *Economic Freedom and Interventionism: An Anthology of Articles and Essays by Ludwig von Mises*, edited by Bettina Bien Greaves, 149–53. Irving-on-Hudson, NY: Foundation for Economic Education, 1990.

Mishan, Ezra J. "Religion, Culture, and Technology." In *Morality of the Market: Religious and Economic Perspectives*, edited by Walter Block, Geoffrey Brennan, and Kenneth Elzinga, 279–312. Vancouver, BC: Fraser Institute, 1985.

Matthews, J. B. "Reds and Our Churches." *American Mercury* (July 1953): 3–13.

Mays, Thomas D. "Biotech Incites Outcry: Public Policy Debates Arise over Human-Animal Hybrid Patents and Germline Gene Therapy." *The National Law Journal* 20 (June 22, 1998).

Mouw, Richard J. Foreword to *Catholics and Evangelicals: Do They Share a Common Future?* edited by Thomas P. Rausch. New York: Paulist Press, 2000.

Nash, Ronald H. "The Christian Choice between Capitalism and Socialism." In *Liberation Theology*, edited by Ronald Nash, 45–68. Milford, MI: Mott Media, 1984.

———. "The Economics of Justice: A Conservative's View." In *Economic Justice and the State: A Debate between Ronald H. Nash and Eric H. Beversluis*, edited by John A. Bernbaum. Grand Rapids, MI: Baker Book House, 1986.

———. "A Reply to Eric Beversluis." In *Economic Justice and the State: A Debate between Ronald H. Nash and Eric H. Beversluis*, edited by John A. Bernbaum, 49–65. Grand Rapids, MI: Baker Book House, 1986.

———. "The Subjective Theory of Economic Value." In *Biblical Principles and Economics: The Foundations*, edited by Richard C. Chewning, 80–96. Colorado Springs, CO: NavPress, 1989.

Nelson, Robert H. "Economic Religion versus Christian Values." *Journal of Markets and Morality* 1 (October 1998). Available from the Acton Institute website at www .acton.org/publicat/m_and_m/1998_Oct/nelson.html.

Neuhaus, Richard John. "John Paul's 'Second Thoughts' on Capitalism." *First Things* 41 (March 1994).

———. "The Liberalism of John Paul II." *First Things* 73 (May 1997).

Niebuhr, H. Richard. *Radical Monotheism and Western Culture: With Supplementary Essays*. Library of Theological Ethics Series. Ed. Robin W. Lovin, Douglas F. Ottati, and William Schweiker. Louisville, KY: Westminster/John Knox Press, 1993. Originally published in 1943.

Niebuhr, Reinhold. "Christian Faith and Political Controversy." In *Love and Justice: Selections from the Shorter Writings of Reinhold Niebuhr*, edited by D. B. Robertson, 59–61. Louisville, KY: Westminster/John Knox Press, 1957. Originally published in *Christianity and Crisis*, July 21, 1952.

———. "Christian Faith and Social Action." In *Christian Faith and Social Action*, edited by John A. Hutchison, 225–42. New York: Charles Scribner's Sons, 1953.

———. "The Christian Faith and the Economic Life of Liberal Society." In *Goals of Economic Life*, edited by A. Dudley Ward, 433–59. New York: Harper & Brothers, 1953.

———. "The Church and the Industrial Crisis." *The Biblical World* 54 (November 1920): 588–92.

———. "Coexistence under a Nuclear Stalemate." In *A Reinhold Niebuhr Reader: Selected Essays, Articles, and Book Reviews*, compiled and edited by Charles C. Brown, 103–5. Philadelphia: Trinity Press International, 1992.

———. "The Collectivist Bogey." *The Nation* 159 (October 21, 1944): 478, 480.

———. "The Cult of Freedom in America." *Christianity and Crisis* 9 (February 7, 1949): 4–7.

———. "Editorial: Politics and Economics." *Christianity and Society* (Autumn 1942): 7–8.

———. "Editorial: The Probable End of the New Deal." *Radical Religion* 8 (Winter 1942): 6–7.

———. "A Faith for History's Greatest Crisis." In *A Reinhold Niebuhr Reader: Selected Essays, Articles, and Book Reviews*, compiled and edited by Charles C. Brown, 3–15. Philadelphia: Trinity Press International, 1992.

———. "Ford's Five-day Week Shrinks." *Christian Century* 44 (June 9, 1927): 713–14.

———. "God's Design and the Present Disorder of Civilization." In *Faith and Politics: A Commentary on Religious, Social and Political Thought in a Technological Age*, edited by Ronald H. Stone, 103–18. New York: George Braziller, 1968.

———. "Halfway to What?" In *A Reinhold Niebuhr Reader: Selected Essays, Articles, and Book Reviews*, compiled and edited by Charles C. Brown, 72–75. Philadelphia: Trinity Press International, 1992. Philadelphia: Trinity Press International, 1992.

———. "How Philanthropic is Henry Ford?" *Christian Century* 43 (December 9, 1926): 1516–17.

———. "The Hydrogen Bomb." *Christianity and Society* 15 (Spring 1950): 5–7.

———. "Ideology and the Scientific Method." In *Christian Realism and Political Problems*, 75–94. New York: Charles Scribner's Sons, 1953. Reprint, Fairfield, NJ: Augustus M. Kelley Publishers, 1977.

———. "The Illusion of World Government." In *Christian Realism and Political Problems*, 15–32. New York: Charles Scribner's Sons, 1953. Reprint, Fairfield, NJ: Augustus M. Kelley Publishers, 1977.

———. "The Meaning of Labor Unity." In *A Reinhold Niebuhr Reader: Selected Essays, Articles, and Book Reviews*, compiled and edited by Charles C. Brown, 88–90. Philadelphia: Trinity Press International, 1992. Originally published in *The New Leader* 38 (March 28, 1955).

———. "The Negro Minority and Its Fate in a Self-Righteous Nation." In *A Reinhold Niebuhr Reader*, edited by Charles C. Brown, 118–24. Philadelphia: Trinity Press International, 1992. Originally published in *Social Action* 35 (October 1968).

———. "Our Country and Our Culture." *Partisan Review* 19 (May–June 1952): 282–326. Niebuhr's contribution to this symposium article is included in pages 301–3.

———. "Rationing and Democracy." In *Love and Justice: Selections from the Shorter Writings of Reinhold Niebuhr*, edited by D. B. Robertson, 61–63. Louisville, KY: Westminster/John Knox Press, 1957. Originally published in *Christianity and Crisis*, November 24, 1952.

———. "The Sickness of American Culture." *The Nation* 166 (March 6, 1948): 267–70.

———. "Socialism and Christianity." *Christian Century* 48 (August 19, 1931): 1038–40.

———. "Television's Peril to Culture." In *A Reinhold Niebuhr Reader: Selected Essays, Articles, and Book Reviews*, compiled and edited by Charles C. Brown, 77–80. Philadelphia: Trinity Press International, 1992.

———. "Theology and Political Thought in the Western World." In *Faith and Politics: A Commentary on Religious, Social and Political Thought in a Technological Age*, edited by Ronald H. Stone, 55–66. New York: George Braziller, 1968.

——. "Those 'Right to Work' Laws." *American Federationist* 64 (February 1957): 14.

——. "The Truth in Myths." In *Faith and Politics: A Commentary on Religious, Social and Political Thought in a Technological Age*, edited by Ronald H. Stone, 15–31. New York: George Braziller, 1968.

——. "The Tyranny of Science." *Theology Today* 10 (January 1954): 464–73.

——. "Utilitarian Christianity and the World Crisis." *Christianity and Crisis* (May 29, 1950): 66–69.

——. "Walter Rauschenbusch in Historical Perspective." In *Faith and Politics: A Commentary on Religious, Social and Political Thought in a Technological Age*, edited by Ronald H. Stone, 33–45. New York: George Braziller, 1968.

——. "Why Is Communism So Evil?" In *Christian Realism and Political Problems*, 33–42. New York: Charles Scribner's Sons, 1953. Reprint, Fairfield, NJ: Augustus M. Kelley Publishers, 1977.

——. "Why We Need a New Economic Order." *World Tomorrow* (October 1928): 395–98.

——. "Will Civilization Survive Technics?" In *A Reinhold Niebuhr Reader: Selected Essays, Articles, and Book Reviews*, compiled and edited by Charles C. Brown, 33–42. Philadelphia: Trinity Press International, 1992.

Novak, Michael. "Defining Social Justice." *First Things* 108 (December 2000): 11–13.

——. "Economics as Humanism." *First Things* 76 (October 1997): 18–19.

——. "Introduction." In *The Denigration of Capitalism: Six Points of View*, edited by Michael Novak, 1–6. Washington, DC: American Enterprise Institute for Public Policy Research, 1980.

——. "The Judeo-Christian Foundation of Human Dignity, Personal Liberty, and the Concept of the Person." *Journal of Markets and Morality* 1 (October 1998). Available from the Acton Institute website at www.acton.org/publicat/m_and_m/1998_Oct/novak.html.

——. "New Questions for Humanists." In *The Denigration of Capitalism*, edited by Michael Novak, 54–62. Washington, DC: American Enterprise Institute for Public Policy Research, 1980.

——. "Overview." In *Morality of the Market: Religious and Economic Perspectives*, edited by Walter Block, Geoffrey Brennan, and Kenneth Elzinga, 567–87. Vancouver, BC: Fraser Institute, 1985.

——. "Reinhold Niebuhr: Model for Neoconservatives." *Christian Century* 103 (January 22, 1986): 69–71.

——. "Wealth and Virtue: The Development of Christian Economic Thinking." In *The Capitalist Spirit: Toward a Religious Ethic of Wealth Creation*, edited by Peter Berger, 51–80. San Francisco: Institute for Contemporary Studies, 1990.

Sandel, Michael. *Democracy's Discontent: America in Search of a Public Philosophy.* Cambridge, MA: The Belknap Press of Harvard University Press, 1996.

Shinn, Roger L. "From Theology to Social Decisions—and Return." In *Morality of the Market: Religious and Economic Perspectives*, edited by Walter Block, Geoffrey Brennan, and Kenneth Elzinga, 279–312. Vancouver, BC: Fraser Institute, 1985.

Sirico, Robert A. "The Late-Scholastic and Austrian Link to Modern Catholic Economic Thought." *Journal of Markets and Morality* 1 (October 1998). Available from the Acton Institute website at www.acton.org/publicat/m_and_m/1998_Oct/sirico.html (accessed October 3, 2001).

———. "Free Markets and the Profit of Solidarity." Available from the Acton Institute website at www.acton.org/ppolicy/editorials/sirico/freemarkets.html.

———. "Of Markets and Morality." *Religion & Liberty* 7 (July–August 1997). Available from the Acton Institute website at www.acton.org/publicat/randl/97jul_aug/sirico.html.

———. "Mater et Magistra (1961)." In *A Century of Catholic Social Thought*, edited by George Weigel and Robert Royal, 45–59. Washington, DC: Ethics and Public Policy Center, 1991.

———. "The Mystery and Morality of Markets—Explained!" *Acton Commentary*. Available from the Acton Institute website at www.acton.org/research/comment/comment.html.

———. "Reading *Centesimus Annus*." *Religion & Liberty* 11 (May–June 2001). Available from the Acton Institute website at www.acton.org/publicat/randl/article.php?id=384.

———. "The Return of Faith on Film." *Religion & Liberty* 9 (January–February 1999). Available from the Acton Institute website at www.acton.org/publicat/randl/99jan_feb/sirico.html.

———. "Toward a New Liberty." *Religion & Liberty* 7 (September–October 1997). Available from the Acton Institute website at www.acton.org/publicat/randl/97sep_oct/sirico.html (accessed August 22, 2001).

Swain, Margaret S., and Randy W. Marusyk. "An Alternative to Property Rights in Human Tissue." In *Life Choices: A Hastings Center Introduction to Bioethics*, 2nd ed., edited by Joseph H. Howell and William Frederick Sale, 484–93. Washington, DC: Georgetown University Press, 2000.

Walter, James J. "Theological Studies in Genetics." *Theological Studies* 60 (1999): 124–34.

Weigel, George. "Camels and Needles, Talents and Treasure: American Catholicism and the Capitalist Ethic." In *The Capitalist Spirit: Toward a Religious Ethic of Wealth Creation*, edited by Peter Berger, 81–105. San Francisco: ICS Press, 1990.

Zanotti, Gabriel J. "Misesian Praxeology and Christian Philosophy." *Journal of Markets and Morality* 1 (March 1998): 3. Available from the Acton Institute website at www.acton.org/publicat/m_and_m/1998_Mar/zanotti.html (accessed March 11, 2002).

Zaratiegui, Jesus M. "The Imperialism of Economics over Ethics." *Journal of Markets and Morality* 2 (Fall 1999). Available from the Acton Institute website at www.acton.org/publicat/m_and_m/1999_fall/zaratiegui.html.

Zuniga, Gloria L. "Truth in Economic Subjectivism." *Journal of Markets and Morality* 1 (October 1998). Available from the Acton Institute website at www.acton.org/publicat/m_and_m/1998_Oct/zuniga.html.

SECONDARY SOURCES

Books

Aquinas, Thomas. *On the Governance of Rulers*. Translated by Gerald Phelan. New York: Sheed & Ward, 1938.

Balmer, Randall. *Religion in Twentieth Century America*. Oxford: Oxford University Press, 2001.

Beauchamp, Tom L., and LeRoy Walters, eds. *Contemporary Issues in Bioethics*. 5th ed. Belmont, CA: Wadsworth Publishers, 1999.

Bellah, Robert, et al. *Habits of the Heart: Individualism and Commitment in American Life.* New York: Harper & Row, 1985.

Berryman, Phillip. *Liberation Theology: Essential Facts about the Revolutionary Movement in Latin America and Beyond.* New York: Pantheon Books, 1987.

Bingham, June. *Courage to Change: An Introduction to the Life and Thought of Reinhold Niebuhr.* New York: Charles Scribner's Sons, 1972.

Brodie, Fawn M. *No Man Knows My History: The Life of Joseph Smith the Mormon Prophet.* New York: Alfred A. Knopf, 1966.

Brown, Charles C. *Niebuhr and His Age: Reinhold Niebuhr's Prophetic Role in the Twentieth Century.* Philadelphia: Trinity Press International, 1992.

———, comp. and ed. *A Reinhold Niebuhr Reader: Selected Essays, Articles, and Book Reviews.* Philadelphia: Trinity Press International, 1992.

Burlingame, Dwight F., ed. *The Responsibilities of Wealth.* Bloomington, IN: Indiana University Press, 1992.

Canovan, Margaret. *G. K. Chesterton: Radical Populist.* New York: Harcourt Brace, 1977.

Clark, Henry B. *Serenity, Courage, Wisdom: The Enduring Legacy of Reinhold Niebuhr.* Cleveland: The Pilgrim Press, 1994.

Conkin, Paul K. *When All the Gods Trembled: Darwinism, Scopes, and American Intellectuals.* Lanham, MD: Rowman & Littlefield Publishers, 1998.

Crowley, Brian Lee. *The Self, the Individual, and the Community: Liberalism in the Political Thought of F. A. Hayek and Sydney and Beatrice Webb.* Oxford: Clarendon Press, 1987.

Curtis, Susan. *A Consuming Faith: The Social Gospel and Modern American Culture.* Baltimore: Johns Hopkins University Press, 1991.

Desroche, Henri. *The American Shakers: From Neo-Christianity to Presocialism.* Translated and edited by John K. Savacool. Amherst, MA: University of Massachusetts Press, 1971.

Dorrien, Gary. *The Neoconservative Mind: Politics, Culture, and the War of Ideology.* Philadelphia: Temple University Press, 1993.

Ellwood, Robert S. *The Fifties Spiritual Marketplace: American Religion in a Decade of Conflict.* New Brunswick, NJ: Rutgers University Press, 1997.

Ferre, Frederick. *Hellfire and Lightning Rods: Liberating Science, Technology, and Religion.* Maryknoll, NY: Orbis Books, 1993.

Fisher, James T. *Catholics in America.* Oxford: Oxford University Press, 2000.

Fowler, Robert Booth. *The Greening of Protestant Thought.* Chapel Hill, NC: University of North Carolina Press, 1995.

Fox, Richard Wightman. *Reinhold Niebuhr: A Biography.* New York: Pantheon Books, 1985.

Gappert, Gary. *Post-Affluent America: The Social Economy of the Future.* New York: New Viewpoints, 1979.

Gilbert, James. *Redeeming Culture: American Religion in an Age of Science.* Chicago: University of Chicago Press, 1997.

Grassl, Wolfgang, and Barry Smith, eds. *Austrian Economics: Historical and Philosophical Background.* New York: New York University Press, 1986.

Gray, John. *Hayek on Liberty.* Oxford: Basil Blackwell Publishers, 1984.

Grelle, Bruce, and David A. Krueger. *Christianity and Capitalism: Perspectives on Religion, Liberalism and the Economy.* Chicago: Center for the Scientific Study of Religion, 1986.

Handy, Robert T. *The American Religious Depression, 1925–1935*. Facet Books Historical Series, no. 9, edited by Richard C. Wolf. Philadelphia: Fortress Press, 1968.

Hawkin, David J. *Christ and Modernity: Christian Self-Understanding in a Technological Age*. Waterloo, Ontario: Wilfrid Laurier University Press, 1985.

Hooper, J. Leon, SJ, ed. *Bridging the Sacred and the Secular: Selected Writings of John Courtney Murray, S.J.* Washington, DC: Georgetown University Press, 1994.

Hopper, David C. *Technology, Theology, and the Idea of Progress*. Louisville, KY: Westminster/John Knox Press, 1991.

Hunter, James Davison. *Culture Wars: The Struggle to Define America*. New York: Basic Books, 1991.

Innes, Stephen. *Creating the Commonwealth: The Economic Culture of Puritan New England*. New York: W. W. Norton, 1995.

Jones, Arthur. *Capitalism and Christians: Tough Gospel Challenges in a Troubled World Economy*. Mahwah, NJ: Paulist Press, 1992.

Kelley, George Armstrong. *Politics and Religious Consciousness in America*. New Brunswick, NJ: Transaction Books, 1984.

Landis, Benson Y., ed. *A Rauschenbusch Reader: The Kingdom of God and the Social Gospel*. New York: Harper & Brothers, 1957.

Linder, Robert D., and Richard V. Pierard. *Twilight of the Saints: Biblical Christianity and Civil Religion in America*. Downers Grove, IL: InterVarsity Press, 1978.

Long, Douglas G. *Bentham on Liberty: Jeremy Bentham's Idea of Liberty in Relation to His Utilitarianism*. Toronto: University of Toronto Press, 1977.

Lovin, Robin. *Reinhold Niebuhr and Christian Realism*. New York: Cambridge University Press, 1995.

Ludmerer, Kenneth M. *Genetics and American Society: A Historical Appraisal*. Baltimore: Johns Hopkins University Press, 1972.

Marsden, George. *The Soul of the American University: From Protestant Establishment to Established Nonbelief*. New York: Oxford University Press, 1994.

Marsden, George M. *Religion and American Culture*. New York: Harcourt Brace College Publishers, 1990.

Marty, Martin E. *The One and the Many: America's Struggle for the Common Good*. Cambridge, MA: Harvard University Press, 1997.

——, ed. *Modern American Protestantism and Its World*. Vol. 3, *Historical Articles on Protestantism in American Life*. Munich: K. G. Saur, 1992.

——, ed. *Modern American Protestantism and Its World*. Vol. 6, *Protestantism and Social Christianity*. Munich: K. G. Saur, 1992.

Maslow, Abraham. *The Farther Reaches of Human Nature*. New York: Viking Press, 1971.

——. *Toward a Psychology of Being*. Princeton, NJ: D. Van Nostrand Company, 1968.

McCann, Dennis P. *Christian Realism and Liberation Theology: Practical Theologies in Creative Conflict*. Maryknoll, NY: Orbis Books, 1981.

McCormick, Richard A. *Corrective Vision: Exploration in Moral Theology*. Kansas City: Sheed & Ward, 1994.

Menger, Carl. *Problems of Economics and Sociology*. Urbana: University of Illinois Press, 1963, 171. Quoted in Jeremy Shearmur, "The Austrian Connection: Hayek's Liberalism and the Thought of Carl Menger," in *Austrian Economics: Historical and Philosophical Background*, edited by Wolfgang Grassl and Barry Smith, 213 (New York: New York University Press, 1986).

Merkley, Paul. *Reinhold Niebuhr: A Political Account.* Montreal and London: McGill-Queens University Press, 1975.

Mounier, Emmanuel. *Personalism.* Notre Dame, IN: University of Notre Dame Press, 1950. Quoted in Richard C. Bayer, *Capitalism and Christianity: The Possibility of Christian Personalism*, 101–2 (Washington, DC: Georgetown University Press, 1999).

Neuhaus, Richard John, ed. *Reinhold Niebuhr Today.* Encounter Series. Grand Rapids, MI: William B. Eerdmans, 1989.

Noble, David F. *The Religion of Technology: The Divinity of Man and the Spirit of Invention.* New York: Alfred A. Knopf, 1997.

Noll, Mark A., and Carolyn Nystrom. *Is the Reformation Over? An Evangelical Assessment of Contemporary Roman Catholicism.* Grand Rapids, MI: Baker Academic, 2005.

Papandreou, Andreas. *Externality and Institutions.* Oxford: Clarendon Press, 1994.

Phillips, Paul T. *A Kingdom on Earth: Anglo-American Social Christianity, 1880–1940.* University Park, PA: Pennsylvania State University Press, 1996.

Pope John Center Staff, ed. *Technological Powers and the Person: Nuclear Energy and Reproductive Technologies.* St. Louis: The Pope John Center, 1983.

Preston, Robert H. *Religion and the Persistence of Capitalism.* London: SCM Press, 1979.

Reeves, Thomas C. *The Empty Church: The Suicide of Liberal Christianity.* New York: The Free Press, 1996.

Rice, Daniel F. *Reinhold Niebuhr and John Dewey: An American Odyssey.* Albany, NY: State University of New York Press, 1993.

Rich, David. *Myths of the Tribe: When Religion, Ethics, Government and Economics Converge.* Buffalo, NY: Prometheus Books, 1993.

Rockefeller, Steven C. *John Dewey: Religious Faith and Democratic Humanism.* New York: Columbia University Press, 1991.

Rodgers, Neal. "A Critical Analysis of Democratic Capitalism." PhD diss., Baylor University, 1985.

Ross, Robert J., and Kent C. Trachte. *Global Capitalism: The New Leviathan.* Albany, NY: State University of New York Press, 1990.

Schenkel, Albert F. *The Rich Man and the Kingdom: John D. Rockefeller, Jr., and the Protestant Establishment.* Minneapolis: Fortress Press, 1995.

Selden, Steven. *Inheriting Shame: The Story of Eugenics and Racism in America.* Advances in Contemporary Educational Thought Series. New York: Teachers College Press, 1999.

Shannon, Christopher. *Conspicuous Criticism: Tradition, the Individual, and Culture in American Social Thought, from Mills to Veblen.* Baltimore: Johns Hopkins University Press, 1996.

Sher, William, and Rudy Pinola. *Microeconomic Theory: A Synthesis of Classical Theory and the Modern Approach.* New York: North Holland, 1981.

Smith, Barry. *Austrian Philosophy.* Chicago: Open Court Publishing, 1994.

Southey, Robert. *The Life of Wesley.* London: Hutchison & Co., 1820.

Steinfels, Peter. *The Neoconservatives: The Men Who Are Changing America's Politics.* New York: Simon & Schuster, 1979.

Stone, Ronald H. *Reinhold Niebuhr: Prophet to Politicians.* Nashville: Abingdon Press, 1972.

Szasz, Ferenc Morton. *The Divided Mind of Protestant America, 1880–1930.* University, AL: University of Alabama Press, 1982.

Thomas, J. Mark, ed. *The Spiritual Situation in Our Technological Society.* Macon, GA: Mercer University Press, 1988.

Verhey, Allen. *Religion and Medical Ethics: Looking Back, Looking Forward.* Institute of Religion Series on Religion and Healthcare, no. 1. Grand Rapids, MI: William B. Eerdmans, 1996.

Walker, Graham. *The Ethics of F. A. Hayek.* Lanham, MD: University Press of America, 1986.

Wells, Harold. *A Future for Socialism? Political Theology and the "Triumph of Capitalism."* Valley Forge, PA: Trinity Press International, 1986.

West, Charles C. *Communism and the Theologians: Study of an Encounter.* Philadelphia: Westminster Press, 1958.

West, John G., and Sonja E. West, eds. *The Theology of Welfare: Protestants, Catholics, and Jews in Conversation about Welfare.* Lanham, MD: University Press of America, 2000.

White, Hugh C., Jr. ed. *Christians in a Technological Era.* New York: Seabury Press, 1964.

Wiser, James. *Political Theory: A Thematic Inquiry.* Chicago: Nelson-Hall, 1986.

Articles

Anderson, Brian C. "Capitalism and the Suicide of Culture." *First Things* 100 (February 2000): 23–30.

Barry, John S. "On the Universal Destination of Material Goods." *Religion & Liberty* 10 (January–February 2000). Available from the Acton Institute website at www.acton .org/publicat/randl/article.php?id=332.

Bayer, Richard C. "Do We Want a Christian Economics? The U.S. Bishops' Pastoral Letter." *Theological Studies* 51 (December 1990): 627–49.

Benne, Robert. "Capitalism with Fewer Tears." In *Christianity and Capitalism: Perspectives in Religion, Liberalism and the Economy,* edited by Bruce Grelle and David A. Krueger, 67–78. Chicago: Center for the Scientific Study of Religion, 1986.

Bonino, Jose Miguez. "Wesley's Doctrine of Sanctification from a Liberationist Perspective." In *Sanctification & Liberation: Liberation Theologies in Light of the Wesleyan Tradition,* edited by Theodore Runyan, 49–63. Nashville: Abingdon Press, 1981.

Braaten, Carl E. "Protestants and Natural Law." In Acton Institute, ed., *Toward a Free and Virtuous Society: A Conference for Future Religious Leaders,* January 2000.

Branson, Roy. "James Madison and the Scottish Enlightenment." *Journal of the History of Ideas* 40 (April–June, 1979): 235–50.

Brown, Robert McAfee. "Reinhold Niebuhr: His Theology in the 1980s." *Christian Century* 103 (January 22, 1986): 66–68.

Bucher, Glenn. "Christian Political Realism after Niebuhr: The Case of John C. Bennett." *Union Seminary Quarterly Review* 41 (1986): 43–58.

Clapp, Rodney. "Where Capitalism and Christianity Meet." *Christianity Today* 27 (February 4, 1983): 22–28.

Clouse, Robert G., and Rodney Clapp. "A Little Victory over Death." *Christianity Today* 32 (March 18, 1988): 17–23.

Coates, Dennis. "A Diagrammatic Demonstration of Public Crowding-Out of Private Contributions to Public Goods." *Journal of Economic Education* 27 (Winter 1996): 49–58.

Colson, Charles, and Richard John Neuhaus. Introduction to *Your Word Is Truth: A Project of Evangelicals and Catholics Working Together,* edited by Charles Colson and Richard John Neuhaus. Grand Rapids, MI: William B. Eerdmans, 2002.

Cooper, John W. "Markets, Freedom, and the State: Friedrich Hayek's Enduring Vision." *Brethren Life and Thought* 35 (Spring 1990): 154–59.

Craig, Robert H. "An Introduction to the Life and Thought of Harry F. Ward." In *Modern American Protestantism and Its World: Historical Articles on Protestantism in American Religious Life*, vol. 6, *Protestantism and Social Christianity*, edited by Martin E. Marty, 258–83. Munich: K. G. Saur, 1992.

———. "The Underside of History: American Methodism, Capitalism and Popular Struggle." *Methodist History* 27 (January 1989): 73–88.

Donohue-White, Patricia. "Controversy: Does the Free Market Undermine Culture? A Response to D. Eric Schansberg." *Journal of Markets and Morality* 2 (Spring 1999). Available from the Acton Institute website at www.acton.org/publicat/m_and_m/1999_spr/schanberg2.html.

Dulles, Avery, SJ. "Truth as the Ground of Freedom: A Theme from John Paul." In Acton Institute, ed., *Toward a Free and Virtuous Society: A Conference for Future Religious Leaders*, January 2000.

Finn, Daniel Rush. "Contributions of Orthodox Economics to Ethical Reflection." In *Christianity and Capitalism: Perspectives on Religion, Liberalism and the Economy*, edited by Bruce A. Grelle and David A. Krueger, 130–48. Chicago: Center for the Scientific Study of Religion, 1986.

———. "The Economic Personalism of John Paul II: Neither Right nor Left." *Journal of Markets and Morality* 2 (Spring 1999). Available from the Acton Institute website at www.acton.org/publicat/m_and_m/1999_spr/finn.html.

Fox, Richard Wightman. "Niebuhr's World and Ours." In *Reinhold Niebuhr Today*, Encounter Series, edited by Richard John Neuhaus, 1–18. Grand Rapids, MI: William B. Eerdmans, 1989.

George, Timothy. "Catholics and Evangelicals in the Trenches." *Christianity Today* (May 16, 1994).

Glasner, David. "Hayek and the Conservatives." *Commentary* (October 1992): 48–50.

Grassl, Wolfgang. "Markets and Morality: Austrian Perspectives on the Economic Approach to Human Behavior." In *Austrian Economics: Historical and Philosophical Background*, edited by Wolfgang Grassl and Barry Smith, 139–81. New York: New York University Press, 1986.

Greenberg, Herb. "Does Tyco Play Accounting Games?" *Fortune* 145 (April 1, 2002): 83–84, 86.

Gregg, Samuel. "A Humanist for Our Time." *Religion & Liberty* 12 (March–April 2002): 9–11.

Gronbacher, Gregory M. A. "Ethics and Economics: The Philosophical Foundations of the Austrian School of Economics." Paper prepared for McGill University, Faculty of Education, November 1995. Available from the "Center for Economic Personalism" section of the Acton Institute website at www.acton.org.

———. "The Humane Economy: Neither Right Nor Left; a Response to Daniel Rush Finn." *Journal of Markets and Morality* 2 (Fall 1999). Available from the Acton Institute website www.acton.org/publicat/ m_and_m/1999_fall/gronbacher.html on 15 November 2005.

———. "The Need for Economic Personalism." *Journal of Markets and Morality* 1 (March 1998). Available from the Acton Institute website at www.acton.org/publicat/m_and_m/1998_Mar/gronbach.html.

Handy, Robert T. "Christianity and Socialism in America, 1900–1920." In *Modern American Protestantism and Its World*, vol. 6, *Protestantism and Social Christianity*, edited by Martin E. Marty, 83–98. Munich: K. G. Saur, 1992.

Harrill, J. Albert. "The Use of the New Testament in the American Slave Controversy: A Case History in the Hermeneutical Tension between Biblical Criticism and Christian Moral Debate." *Religion and American Culture* 10 (Summer 2000): 149–86.

Hodgson, Geoffrey M. "The Political Economy of Utopia." *Review of Social Economy* 53 (Summer 1995).

Iannaccone, Laurence R. "Risk, Rationality, and Religious Portfolios." *Economic Inquiry* 33 (April 1995): 285–95.

Koyzis, David T. "Progress as an Object of Faith in the Thought of Friedrich A. von Hayek." *Christian Scholars Review* 12 (1983): 139–55.

Kuran, Timur. "The Genesis of Islamic Economics: A Chapter in the Politics of Muslim Identity." *Social Research* 64 (Summer 1997). www.mtholyoke.edu/acad/intrel/kuran.htm (accessed June 5, 2005).

Lewis, Marlo, Jr. "The Achilles Heel of F. A. Hayek." *National Review* 37 (May 17, 1985): 32–36.

Marsden, George. "The Gospel of Wealth, the Social Gospel, and the Salvation of Souls in Nineteenth-Century America." In *Modern American Protestantism and Its World*, vol. 6, *Protestantism and Social Christianity*, edited by Martin E. Marty, 3–14. Munich: K. G. Saur, 1992.

Marty, Martin E. "Comment." In *Religion, Economics and Social Thought*, edited by Walter Block and Irving Hexham, 153–59. Vancouver, BC: Fraser Institute, 1986.

Mayer, Jane. "Contract Sport: What Did the Vice-President Do for Halliburton?" *New Yorker*, "Fact: Letter from Washington," November 23, 2004. www.newyorker.com/fact/content/?040216fa_fact (accessed December 16, 2004).

McDaniel, Charles. "Friedrich Hayek and Reinhold Niebuhr on the Moral Persistence of Liberal Society." *Journal of Interdisciplinary Studies* 16, no. 1–2 (2004).

Meyer, Frank S. "The Separation of Powers." In *Freedom and Virtue: The Conservative/Libertarian Debate*, edited by George W. Carey, 8–10. Wilmington, DE: Intercollegiate Studies Institute, 1998.

Miller, William Lee. "In Strange Company." *New Republic* 186 (April 21, 1982): 27–30.

Moorhead, James H. "Social Reform and the Divided Conscience of Antebellum Protestantism." *Church History* 48 (December 1979): 416–30.

Naylor, Thomas H. "Averting Self-Destruction: A Twenty-first Century Appraisal of Distributism." In *Distributist Perspectives*, vol. 1, *Essays on the Economics of Justice and Charity*. Norfolk, VA: IHS Press, 2004.

NBC News. *Meet the Press*. October 10, 2004. www.msnbc.com/id/6200928.

Neff, Jack. "Economy Watch: Executive Glut; Marketing Execs Set Adrift by Dot-Com Decline Fight for Fewer Jobs." *Advertising Age* 72 (April 9, 2001). Available online from WilsonSearchPlus, accession number: BBPI01029482.

Noll, Mark A. "Common Sense Traditions and American Evangelical Thought." *American Quarterly* 37 (Summer 1985): 216–38.

Podhoretz, Norman. "Neoconservatism: A Eulogy." *Commentary* 101 (March 1996): 19–27.

Public Broadcasting System. "Organ Farm." Documentary transcript. Available from the Public Broadcasting System website at www.pbs.org/wgbh/pages/frontline/shows/organfarm/etc/script1.html.

Rose, Charlie. "Interview with William Rehnquist." *The Charlie Rose Show*. Public Broadcasting System, February 16, 2001.

Rosen, Corey. Excerpt from introduction to *Corporate Governance in ESOP Companies* [publication information not given], 2002. Available from the National Center for Employee Ownership website at www.nceo.org/pubs/corpgov.html.

Runyon, Theodore. "Introduction: Wesley and the Theologies of Liberation." In *Sanctification & Liberation: Liberation Theologies in Light of the Wesleyan Tradition*, edited by Theodore Runyon, 9–48. Nashville: Abingdon Press, 1981.

Saltmarsh, John A. "Edward Bellamy's Religious Radicalism: *Looking Backward* as a Bible for Industrial America." *Journal of Interdisciplinary Studies* 2 (1990): 125–35.

Sclove, Richard. "Town Meetings on Technology." *Technology Review* 99 (July 1996): 24–31. Available from WilsonSearchPlus, accession number: BRDG96067088.

Shearmur, Jeremy. "The Austrian Connection: Hayek's Liberalism and the Thought of Carl Menger." In *Austrian Economics: Historical and Philosophical Background*, edited by Wolfgang Grassl and Barry Smith, 210–24. New York: New York University Press, 1986.

Sider, Ronald J. "Should We Give Up on Government?" *Christianity Today* 42 (March 2, 1998): 53–54.

Smith, Gary Scott. "The Men and Religion Forward Movement of 1911–12: New Perspectives on Evangelical Social Concern and the Relationship between Christianity and Progressivism." In *Modern American Protestantism and Its World*, vol. 6, *Protestantism and Social Christianity*, edited by Martin E. Marty, 166–93. Munich: K. G. Saur, 1992.

———. "The Spirit of Capitalism Revisited: Calvinists in the Industrial Revolution." *Journal of Presbyterian History* 59 (Winter 1981): 481–97.

Smith, Lawrence C. "Introduction." In *Distributist Perspectives*, vol. 1, *Essays on the Economics of Justice and Charity*. Norfolk, VA: IHS Press, 2004.

Stackhouse, Max, and Dennis McCann. "Max Stackhouse and Dennis McCann Reply." *Christian Century* 108 (January 23, 1991): 83–85.

Szasz, Ferenc M. "The Progressive Clergy and the Kingdom of God." *Mid-America* 55 (January 1973).

Vershoor, Curtis C. "Were Enron's Ethical Missteps a Major Cause of Its Downfall?" *Strategic Finance* 83 (February 2002): 22–24.

Wallis, Joe L. "Church Ministry and the Free Rider Problem: Religious Liberty and Disestablishment." *The American Journal of Economics and Sociology* 50 (April 1991): 183–96.

Weigel, George. "John Paul II and the Crisis of Humanism." *First Things* 98 (December 1999).

Welch, David R., and David C. Leege. "Dual Reference Groups and Political Orientations: An Examination of Evangelically Oriented Catholics." *American Journal of Political Science* 35 (February 1991): 28–56.

Wogaman, J. Phillip. "Theological Perspectives on Economics." In *Morality of the Market: Religious and Economic Perspectives*, edited by Walter Block, Geoffrey Brennan, and Kenneth Elzinga, 35–59. Vancouver, BC: Fraser Institute, 1985.

Zieba, Maciej. "From Leo XIII's *Rerum Novarum* to John Paul II's *Centesimus Annus*." *Journal of Markets and Morality* 5 (Spring 2002).

INDEX

Acquaviva, S. S., 72, 128, 129
Alighieri, Dante, 75
Aquinas, Thomas, 32, 75, 85
Austrian liberalism, 8, 14, 16, 72, 73–75, 76, 84, 87, 89, 183, 198, 233, 266

Bandow, Doug, 168
Baptiste, Jean, 167
Barnard, Christian, 126
Barnes, Roswell, 193
Bayer, Richard, 76
Becker, Gary, 160–61
Bell, Bernard Iddings, 41
Bell, Daniel, 14, 22
Bellah, Robert, 80
Belloc, Hilaire, 19, 230, 232, 270
Bentham, Jeremy, 195
Benne, Robert, 53
Bennett, John C., 56, 193
Bimeler, Joseph, 39
Bliss, W. D. P., 41
Bloom, Harold, 37, 157, 172
Bonino, Jose Miguez, 35
Bork, Robert, 168, 169, 170
Boyle, Nicholas, 91–93, 304, 309
Brinkman, June, 119
Brinkman, Richard, 119
Brodie, Fawn, 39
Brown, Charles C., 189
Bush, George W., 7, 8, 125, 170
Bushnell, Horace, 42

Canovan, Margaret, 242
Capitalism, 7, 9, 14, 15, 33, 45, 48, 54, 59, 60–62, 78, 92, 93, 107, 143, 145, 152, 156, 165, 171, 185, 187, 190, 194, 216, 234, 238, 252, 259, 272, 275, 278, 283, 295, 309, 310; industrial, 19, 191; victory of, 15, 61, 261
capitalist, 17, 34, 45, 53, 73, 84, 95, 121, 132, 152, 186, 205, 216, 231, 234, 237, 284, 292
Carnegie, Andrew, 42, 43
Carr, Edward Ellis, 40
Catholic social thought, 20, 57, 74, 76, 84, 85, 86, 89, 90, 262, 276
Catholic Worker Movement, 19
Cheney, Dick, 8
Chesterton, G. K., 17, 19–21, 260, 266, 271, 273, 283, 293, 302, 308; distributism, 173, 229–55
Christian Marxism, 9, 31, 45, 55
Christian personalism, 20–21, 76, 77, 263, 270, 307, 309
Christian progressivism, 48–53, 55, 60
Christian realism, 18, 185, 188, 194, 197, 198, 199, 203, 204, 212, 218, 219, 265, 303, 307, 309
Christian reconstructionism, 10, 16, 31, 52, 55, 59, 60, 303
Christian socialism, 18, 32, 40, 41, 42, 43, 44, 55, 60, 183, 185, 192, 193, 197, 204, 266

333

ABOUT THE AUTHOR

Charles McDaniel serves as visiting assistant professor in the J. M. Dawson Institute of Church-State Studies at Baylor University and is the book review editor for the *Journal of Church and State*. He returned to academics after a seventeen-year career in business to study the relationship of religion and law in American culture and the development of American Christian social thought, with particular emphasis on the philosophy of Christian realism as developed in the writings of Reinhold Niebuhr. He has authored numerous articles for academic journals, exploring issues as diverse as faith-based prison ministries and Islamic social thought.